Fusion

Integrated Reading and Writing | Book 1

KEMPER / MEYER / VAN RYS / SEBRANEK   Second Edition

Dave Kemper

Verne Meyer
Dordt College

John Van Rys
Redeemer University College

Pat Sebranek

CENGAGE
Learning·

Australia · Brazil · Mexico · Singapore · United Kingdom · United States

CENGAGE
Learning®

Fusion: Integrated Reading and Writing,
Book 1, Second Edition
Dave Kemper, Verne Meyer,
John Van Rys, and Pat Sebranek

Vice President, General Manager,
Developmental Studies: Liz Covello

Product Manager: Andrew Rawson

Senior Content Developer:
Liza Neustaetter

Associate Content Developer:
Kathryn Jorawsky

Senior Marketing Manager: Necco
McKinley

Senior Content Project Manager:
Rosemary Winfield

Senior Art Director: Linda May

Manufacturing Planner: Betsy Donaghey

IP Analyst: Ann Hoffman

IP Project Manager: Farah Fard

Compositor: Sebranek, Inc.

Production & Managing Editor: Tim Kemper
(Sebranek, Inc.)

Designer: Mark Lalumondier
(Sebranek, Inc.)

Cover Image: Leigh Prather, 2014 / Used
under license from Shutterstock.com

For product information and technology assistance, contact us at
Cengage Learning Customer & Sales Support, 1-800-354-9706.

For permission to use material from this text or product,
submit all requests online at **www.cengage.com/permissions.**
Further permissions questions can be emailed to
permissionrequest@cengage.com.

Library of Congress Control Number: 2014959333

ISBN-13: 978-1-305-10373-3

Cengage Learning
20 Channel Center Street
Boston, MA 02210
USA

Cengage Learning is a leading provider of customized learning solutions
with office locations around the globe, including Singapore, the United
Kingdom, Australia, Mexico, Brazil, and Japan. Locate your local office at
www.cengage.com/global.

Cengage Learning products are represented in Canada by Nelson
Education, Ltd.

For your course and learning solutions, visit **www.cengage.com**.

Purchase any of our products at your local college store or at our preferred online store **www.cengagebrain.com**.

Printed in the United States of America
Print number: 01   Print year: 2015

Fusion 1 Brief Contents

Chapter 3 Using Reading and Writing Strategies 43

Diego Cervo, 2014 / Used under license from Shutterstock.com

Chapter 4 Improving Vocabulary 61

Valeri Potapova, 2014 / Used under license from Shutterstock.com

Chapter 7 Organization 147

bopav, 2014 / Used under license from Shutterstock.com

lightpoet, 2014 / Used under license from Shutterstock.com

wavebreakmedia, 2014 / Used under license from Shutterstock.com

Part 3: Types of Reading and Writing 215

Chapter 10 Reading and Writing Narrative Texts 217

Fotovika, 2014 / Used under license from Shutterstock.com

Chapter **11** Reading and Writing Expository Texts **241**

Matej Kastelic, 2014 / Used under license from Shutterstock.com

Chapter 12 Reading and Writing Arguments 265

Monkey Business Images, 2014 / Used under license from Shutterstock.com

Part 4: Introduction to Research 289

Part 5: Sentence Workshops 311

wellphoto, 2014 / Used under license from Shutterstock.com

Part 6: Word Workshops 379

gary718, 2014 / Used under license from Shutterstock.com

paul prescott, 2014 / Used under license from Shutterstock.com

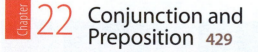

Part 7: Punctuation and Mechanics Workshops 439

Doug Lemke, 2014 / Used under license from Shutterstock.com

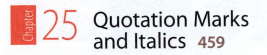

Pressmaster, 2014 / Used under license from Shutterstock.com

Camilo Torres, 2014 / Used under license from Shutterstock.com

Ron and Joe, 2014 / Used under license from Shutterstock.com

Part 8: Readings for Writers 477

Chapter 27 Anthology 479

Elena Elisseeva, 2014 / Used under license from Shutterstock.com

Preface

Fusion reflects the way instructors want to teach the integrated developmental reading and writing course. We know because we asked.

Informed by instructors from across the country, *Fusion: Integrated Reading and Writing, Book 1*, connects the reading and writing processes so that students learn to use the processes hand in hand. High-interest readings encourage students to participate in discussions and think critically. Students can then generate thoughtful writing that combines what they have learned with their own thinking about a topic. Strategies for analyzing readings and producing writing prepare students for their future college courses.

> *Fusion* combines an integrated approach to teaching both curriculums, focusing on the integration of reading and writing. The strength of the text is the integrated approach throughout the text, educating students on how and why teaching the curriculum in an integrated approach helps them be successful in all other course work. The authors of the textbook are longtime educators in the field of developmental reading and writing, and their expertise is evident throughout the content. This approach allows other educators to create a rich, pedagogically sound curriculum for their own students."
>
> Ulanda Forbess, North Lake College

> *Fusion* does not allow students or instructors to separate reading and/from writing. It shows the relationship between the two and helps students understand how one impacts the other. For an undertaking that was quite intimidating (teaching reading and writing together), this text has certainly helped lessen the load and demonstrates how such a blended approach is possible."
>
> Jenny Beaver, Rowan-Cabarrus Community College

> With feedback from students, I have taken the best ways I teach writing and the best ways I teach reading and integrated them together to create a completely new course that focuses on skill proficiency and critical thinking. *Fusion* helps me to accomplish this by reinforcing concepts I teach in the classroom and providing students with ample opportunities to study examples of content and apply these newly learned skills in their reading/writing assignments."
>
> Kina Lara, San Jacinto College South

> *Fusion* is as much a process for teaching reading and writing as it is a textbook. It shows students the clear connection between reading and writing while also demonstrating that the critical thinking, reading, and writing skills they learn are transferable to other academic areas. Its logical organization is what makes the process of teaching reading and writing a bit easier."
>
> Kim Davis, Oakland Community College

Presenting a More Integrated Approach to Reading and Writing

Fusion's Table of Contents has been restructured based on feedback from instructors across the country to better model the close relationship between reading and writing.

- **Parallel reading and writing strategies are introduced in Chapter 1: "The Reading-Writing Connection."** Students are introduced to the five shared features of reading and writing assignments. Similarly, students learn how to apply the traits of writing to their critical reading and writing.

- **NEW Chapter 2: "Understanding the Reading and Writing Processes" sets the stage for the integrated reading and writing in *Fusion*.** This chapter describes the steps in the interconnected reading and writing processes, providing detailed walk-throughs with models to help students understand both processes.

- **NEW Chapter 3: "Using Reading and Writing Strategies" provides common strategies to become a more effective reader and writer.** These strategies include identifying parts of a textbook, annotating, note taking, outlining, summarizing, and more.

- **NEW Part 2: "Reading and Writing Paragraphs" brings new emphasis to the integration of reading and writing.** Chapters 6 through 8 introduce students to important traits common to reading and writing—ideas, organization, and voice—and offer strategies for reading for these traits and for applying them in writing.

- **NEW Chapter 9: "Reading and Writing Essays" transitions students from reading and writing paragraphs to reading and writing essays,** beginning with a side-by-side comparison of the two forms.

Providing Skills Needed for Future Course Work

When students complete their work in *Fusion*, they will have acquired the reading and writing competencies needed for future course work.

- **NEW Chapter 4: "Improving Vocabulary" explains how building a strong vocabulary will help students succeed in school and beyond.** By covering a number of vocabulary-building strategies, this chapter provides students with the tools they need to learn, remember, and use new words. Vocabulary prompts throughout the book encourage students to practice using these strategies.

- **NEW Part 3: "Types of Reading and Writing" focuses on the kinds of reading and writing assignments students are likely to encounter in their future college courses.** Students are given strategies for reading and writing narratives, expository texts, and arguments. Relevant grammar instruction is provided within the context of the students' own writing. Additional grammar instruction and practice appears in the Workshops in Parts 5 through 7.

- **NEW Part 4: "Introduction to Research" includes the basics of conducting research.** It covers why research is included in writing; finding, evaluating, and citing sources; and the dangers of plagiarism.

Integrating Key Reading and Writing Course Objectives

Common Course Objectives	Where This Is Covered in *Fusion*
■ Use reading and writing strategies to draw conclusions and clearly articulate an analysis.	See the Enrichment feature at the end of chapters in Part 3: "Types of Reading and Writing" and in Part 8: "Readings for Writers." All provide prompts for thinking and writing critically.
■ Critically read and respond to a variety of texts, demonstrating the ability to draw inferences and analyze information.	See Chapter 5: "Critical Thinking and Viewing." Students learn to consider basic thinking patterns, ask critical questions, and use analysis and evaluation strategies.
■ Understand and use appropriate vocabulary in conjunction with clear and logical development of ideas to demonstrate reading comprehension.	See Chapter 3: "Using Reading and Writing Strategies" for detailed instruction for writing summaries; Chapter 4: "Improving Vocabulary"; and Part 2: "Reading and Writing Paragraphs," where students learn how to apply important traits to their reading and writing. Vocabulary practice is also reinforced with every reading.
■ Select and apply the appropriate rhetorical strategies in both reading and writing.	See Part 3: "Types of Reading and Writing," where students learn how to apply strategies to read and write narratives, explanatory texts, and arguments.
■ Identify audience and purpose, employ effective brainstorming strategies, gather relevant information, and integrate the ideas and words of other writers.	See Chapters 1 and 8, where identifying audience and purpose are discussed. In Part 4: "Introduction to Research" students learn how to find, evaluate, and incorporate sources of information into their writing.
■ Utilize revision strategies to ensure college-level work.	Part 3: "Types of Reading and Writing" features revising and editing instruction in context for narrative, expository, and argumentative writing. Part 5: "Sentence Workshops," Part 6: "Word Workshops," and Part 7: "Punctuation and Mechanics Workshops" provide additional grammar practice.
■ Read a wide variety of reading selections.	Part 8: "Readings for Writers" features selections demonstrating a variety of topics, voices, and patterns of organization. Each reading is accompanied by pre- and post-reading questions that emphasize reading and writing strategies.

Fostering Engagement and Critical Thinking

Fusion provides a selection of readings designed to capture students' attention and inspire higher levels of thinking. Each reading is supported by new critical thinking prompts to help students shape their own thoughtful responses to the text. In addition, the selections enrich college-ready vocabulary skills and serve as models for the types of reading and writing expected of them in their college courses.

- **Many NEW readings in the Enrichment sections** cover topics such as the following:

  College Success: "Top 10 Ways to Balance Work and School" (page 15)

  General Interest: "7 Reasons Introverts Make Great Leaders" (page 97)

  History: "The Civil Rights Movement" (page 210)

- **NEW Part 8: "Readings for Writers" offers an anthology of readings that can be used to foster critical thinking, discussion, and writing opportunities.** The readings vary in length, demonstrate different patterns of organization, and offer unique perspectives on timely topics. High-interest topics include the following:

  Health: "Death on Demand Is Not Death with Dignity" (page 483)

  Politics: "YouTube, Jon Stewart, and Stephen Colbert: Changing Politics for the Better?" (page 486)

  Technology: "Should We Live Life, or Capture It?" (page 501)

- **NEW Chapter 5: "Critical Thinking and Viewing" outlines the skills needed to become critical readers and writers.** This chapter introduces students to Bloom's Taxonomy and provides students with strategies and examples of how they can apply the different levels of thinking to both their reading and writing.

- **NEW Summarizing and critical thinking prompts:** Chapter 3 addresses the importance of summarizing reading material, and summarizing prompts have been included after the Enrichment readings so that students can practice this skill often. Also included are critical thinking prompts to challenge students to formulate their own thoughts about the readings.

> " I love this textbook! And so do the students. It works as a confidence builder and resource all in one. A great refresher for the returning student who has been out of academia for a number of years as well as a tutorial and reference for ELLs. Plus there are interesting readings that demonstrate the principles being studied and practiced. I wish we had more time to spend with the textbook (class is seven weeks)."
>
> Marcia Hines-Colvin, Saint Mary's University of Minnesota

Promoting Skills Development and Tracking Learning Outcomes

The integrated reading and writing course is often a new environment for instructors, and *Fusion* provides the perfect resource and guide for such a course.

■ **NEW** **MindTap is a fully online, highly personalized learning experience built upon *Fusion: Integrated Reading and Writing, Book 1*.** MindTap combines student learning tools—an interactive ebook, instructive animations, additional readings, video instruction, pre-built flashcards, practice activities, and assessments—into a singular Learning Path that guides students through their course. Instructors personalize the experience by customizing authoritative Cengage Learning content and learning tools with their own content in the Learning Path via apps that integrate into the MindTap framework. Engaging assignments powered by **Aplia™** reinforce key concepts and provide students with the practice they need to build fundamental reading, writing, and grammar skills.

- **Teaches and promotes study skills in students**—highlighting and note taking—a skill often needing more attention in this course than time usually allows
- **Addresses students' busy lives**—students can listen to chapters via the ReadSpeaker app while on the go, and watch course videos as they have time
- **Allows students to prepare ahead of time** so that class time can be spent working together on reading and writing strategies

> **"** Having the forward notice of what will be addressed in the next class is most beneficial to students. Students have that time to preview, complete a reading quiz, and come into the next class ready to `flesh' it out with other students and the instructor."
>
> Sarah Bruton, Fayetteville Technical Community College

■ **Aplia™ for *Fusion*.** Through diagnostic tests, succinct instruction, and engaging assignments, Aplia™ for *Fusion: Integrated Reading and Writing* reinforces key concepts and provides students with the practice they need to build fundamental reading, writing, and grammar skills:

- Diagnostic tests provide an overall picture of a class's performance, allowing instructors to instantly see where students are succeeding and where they need additional help.
- Assignments include immediate and constructive feedback, reinforcing key concepts and motivating students to improve their reading and writing skills.
- Grades are automatically recorded in the Aplia™ grade book, keeping students accountable while minimizing time spent grading.

- **The Individualized Study Path (ISP).** An ISP course generates a personalized list of assignments for each student that is tailored to his or her specific strengths and weaknesses. ISP assignments are randomized, auto-graded problems that correspond to skills and concepts for a specific topic. Students get as much help and practice as they require on topics where they are weak. Conversely, if there are topics they understand well, no remediation is necessary and no additional assignments will be present.

- **Instructor Manual and Test Bank.** The Instructor Manual and Test Bank is located on the Instructor Companion Site in a convenient printable format. This supplement features a wealth of resources for course enrichment, including
    - test bank material: chapter quizzes, a midterm exam, and a final exam;
    - detailed sample syllabi, including syllabi mapped to North Carolina, Texas, and Virginia state objectives;
    - a variety of writing prompts to be used in class or as homework assignments;
    - a success story about how Aplia™ and *Fusion* can be used together in the classroom; and
    - a guide to teaching ESL learners using *Fusion*.

- **Cognero®.** Cengage Learning testing powered by Cognero® is a flexible, online system that allows you to author, edit, and manage test-bank content from multiple Cengage Learning solutions, including the quizzes and exams available on *Fusion*'s Instructor Companion Site. Multiple test versions can be created in an instant, and tests can be delivered from your LMS or your classroom.

- **Instructor Companion Site.** Access the Instructor Manual and Test Bank plus PowerPoint slides organized around topics covered in the book, including a high-level chapter overview as well as an opening and closing activity.

- **Write Experience 2.0.** Students need to learn how to write well in order to communicate effectively and think critically. Cengage Learning's Write Experience provides students with additional writing practice without adding to your workload. Utilizing artificial intelligence to score student writing instantly and accurately, it also provides students with detailed revision goals and feedback on their writing to help them improve. Write Experience is powered by e-Write IntelliMetric Within—the gold standard for automated scoring of writing—used to score the Graduate Management Admissions Test (GMAT) analytical writing assessment. Visit www.cengage.com/writeexperience to learn more.

- **Course Redesign for Developmental Education.** Course Redesign is one of the latest trends impacting the landscape of higher education and developmental studies. Cengage Learning's trained consultants, instructional designers, subject matter experts, and educational researchers offer a variety of services to guide you through the process of redesigning your curriculum. Combining that with a wealth of powerful digital and print offerings allows us to personalize solutions to your state or institution's needs. Contact your Learning Consultant to learn more about these services or visit www.cengage.com/services.

Customizing *Fusion* to Tailor Your Course Materials

As the integrated reading and writing course continues to evolve, Cengage Learning can address your unique course needs. It's possible to align your course materials with custom solutions that deliver the content you want in your preferred style and format. Maximize learner engagement by

- adding, rearranging, and/or removing content.
- combining content from multiple sources.
- integrating supplements.
- simplifying access to digital resources.

Cengage Learning offers a variety of products, both online and in print, to expand the reading selections to be used with *Fusion*. For more information about these options, consult your Cengage Learning sales representative.

- **CourseReader.** CourseReader leverages Cengage Learning's Gale databases, including its authoritative reference content and full-text magazine and newspaper articles. The product offers instructors thousands of articles and historical documents, including both primary and secondary sources specific to their discipline, all in one location. Instructors select a series of materials from these databases for their courses, which are then compiled into an online collection for their students to access.

- **Compose.** Drawing from a vast library of educational materials including readings, cases, and labs, a custom reader is just a few clicks away with the intuitive search engine and a Custom Service and Sales team who specializes in the development of effective customized learning solutions. After selecting or organizing course materials, instructors can immediately review and then publish a printed custom reading collection.

- **National Geographic Learning Readers.** *Environment: Our Impact on the Earth* and *Diversity of America* are part of a groundbreaking new National Geographic Learning series that brings learning to life by featuring compelling images, media, and text from National Geographic. Pre- and post-reading pedagogy developed especially for developmental reading and writing students accompanies each article to reinforce reading skills and comprehension. The National Geographic Learning Reading Series connects current topics with reading and writing skills and can be used in conjunction with any standard texts or online material available for your courses.

> ❝ *Fusion* is a customizable package that reaches well beyond the minimum standards of the state, emphasizing the very objectives our content instructors complain about regarding students' ability to critically analyze. With the focus on 'summary' and 'critical thinking,' I believe our students will be much better prepared to meet the challenges that content teachers are assigning."
> Brian Longacre, Asheville-Buncombe Technical Community College

What's New in *Fusion: Integrated Reading and Writing, Book 1*?

Global Revisions

- The Table of Contents has been restructured to better model the reciprocal relationship between reading and writing, based on feedback from instructors who are teaching integrated reading and writing courses.
- Throughout the text, assignments are focused on paragraph-level practice to ensure students are building strong foundational reading and writing skills. In the end-of-chapter Enrichment activities, students have the opportunity to challenge themselves and strengthen their skill sets with essay-level practice.
- Summary skills are introduced in Chapter 3 and reinforced in the summarizing activities added to the end-of-chapter Enrichment readings.
- Exercises have been expanded and revised to emphasize critical thinking and put critical reading and writing skills to work.

Chapter Revisions

Part I: "Reading and Writing for Success"

Chapter 1: "The Reading-Writing Connection"

- **NEW** "Reading and Writing to Learn" lays the foundation for the integration of reading and writing skills.
- **NEW** "Establishing the Proper Attitude" emphasizes bringing a positive attitude to the classroom.
- **NEW** Enrichment reading, "Top 10 Ways to Balance Work and School"

Chapter 2: "Understanding the Reading and Writing Processes"

- **NEW CHAPTER** describes the steps in the interconnected reading and writing processes, providing detailed step-by-step walk-throughs with models to help students understand and apply both processes.
- **NEW** reading, "Dance of the Chinese Dragon," demonstrates annotating.
- **NEW** Enrichment reading, "High Jumping into Immortality"

Chapter 3: "Using Reading and Writing Strategies"

- **NEW CHAPTER** provides common strategies to become a more effective reader and writer, including identifying parts of a textbook, annotating a text, taking effective notes, using an outline, using a table diagram, and writing a summary.

Chapter 4: "Improving Vocabulary"

- **NEW CHAPTER** emphasizes the importance of vocabulary building and covers a number of vocabulary-building strategies, including keeping a vocabulary notebook, using a dictionary, using context clues, and understanding word parts.

Chapter 5: "Critical Thinking and Viewing"

- **NEW CHAPTER** introduces students to Bloom's Taxonomy and provides students with strategies and examples of how they can apply the different levels of thinking to both their reading and writing.
- **NEW** Enrichment reading, "7 Reasons Introverts Make Great Leaders"

NEW Part 2: "Reading and Writing Paragraphs"

- **Chapter 6: "Ideas"** builds the skills necessary for writing effective paragraphs: identifying and developing topics, reading for and developing main ideas in writing, and reading for and writing with strong supporting details. It also includes a new Enrichment reading, "Sleepless on Campus."
- **Chapter 7: "Organization"** highlights the three-part structure and emphasizes the importance of organized, clear writing. The basic patterns of organization are also covered.
- **Chapter 8: "Voice"** addresses reading for voice and utilizing voice most effectively in writing. Types of voice are covered as well as effective word choice and sentence style.
- **Chapter 9: "Reading and Writing Essays"** transitions students from reading and writing paragraphs to reading and writing essays, beginning with a side-by-side comparison of the two forms. It also includes a new Enrichment reading, "The Civil Rights Movement."

NEW Part 3: "Types of Reading and Writing"

- **Chapter 10: "Reading and Writing Narrative Texts"** introduces students to a variety of narrative forms and provides strategies for reading and responding to narrative texts as well as strategies for planning, writing, and revising a narrative text.
- **Chapter 11: "Reading and Writing Expository Texts"** explains the types of expository texts and provides strategies for reading and responding to an expository text as well as for planning, writing, revising, and editing an expository text. The chapter also contains a new reading, "Swimming in Limbo: Captive belugas are snared in ongoing controversy."
- **Chapter 12: "Reading and Writing Arguments"** describes common types of argumentation and provides strategies for reading and responding to an argument as well as planning, writing, revising, and editing an argument.

NEW Part 4: "Introduction to Research"

- **Chapter 13: "Conducting Research"** includes the basics of conducting research. It covers why research is included in writing; finding, evaluating, and citing sources; taking effective notes; summarizing, paraphrasing, and quoting; and the dangers of plagiarism.

Part 5: "Sentence Workshops," Part 6: "Word Workshops," and Part 7: "Punctuation and Mechanics Workshops"

- **REVISED** and expanded exercises provide additional practice.

NEW Part 8: "Readings for Writers"

- **Chapter 27: "Anthology"** offers additional readings that can be used to foster critical thinking, discussion, and various writing opportunities. It includes selections covering a wide variety of topics, modes, and patterns of organization. Readings are drawn from magazines, textbooks, newspapers, presidential remarks, and other sources so that students have the opportunity to engage with multiple sources. Each reading is accompanied by pre- and post-reading questions designed to utilize reading strategies and prompt students to think critically about their reading.

> **"** I am excited that summarizing activities have been worked into more areas of the textbook. I especially like that summarizing and critical thinking activities accompany all readings. I like that the Part 5 and Part 7 sections have been revised and expanded. I also like the new Part 8, which includes more reading selections and has pre-and post-reading questions. . . . Overall, I'm excited to see all of the changes."
>
> Tiffany Daniel, Oconee Fall Line Technical College

Acknowledgements

Second Edition

A special thanks to the *Fusion* Advisory Board for all the feedback they provided related to how they teach their integrated reading and writing courses and how *Fusion* can support their students.

Jenny Beaver, Rowan-Cabarrus Community College
Sarah Bruton, Fayetteville Technical Community College
Tiffany Daniel, Oconee Fall Line Technical College
Kim Davis, Oakland Community College
Ulanda Forbess, North Lake College

Marcia Hines-Colvin, Saint Mary's University of Minnesota
Kimberly Koledoye, Houston Community College
Kina Lara, San Jacinto College South
Brian Longacre, Asheville-Buncombe Technical Community College

Special thanks also to the many reviewers who have helped to shape *Fusion* into the text you have before you:

Sandra Blystone, University of Texas at El Paso; Wendy Crader, Northeast Lakeview College; Kathleen Cuyler, Coastal Bend College; Leona Fisher, Chaffey College; Marsi Franceschini, Central Piedmont Community College; Kris Giere, Ivy Tech Community College of Indiana; Scarlett Hill, Brookhaven College; Alice Kimara, Baltimore County Community College; Karen LaPanna, Collin College; Glenda Lowery, Rappahannock Community College; Irma Luna, San Antonio College; Gail Malone, South Plains College; Beth McCall, Gaston College; Annette Mewborn, Tidewater Community College; Marti Miles-Rosenfield, Collin College; Lana Myers, Lone Star College–Montgomery; Sonya Prince, San Jacinto College; Nancy Risch, Caldwell Community College and Technical Institute; Jennifer Riske, Northeast Lakeview College; Linda Robinett, Oklahoma City Community College; Robert Sandhaas, San Jacinto College South; Vanessa Sekinger, Germanna Community College; Tanya Stanley, San Jacinto College Central; Ra Shaunda Sterling, San Jacinto College; Claudia Swicegood, Rowan-Cabarrus Community College; Kelly Terzaken, Coastal Carolina Community College; Tondalaya VanLear, Dabney S. Lancaster Community College; Shari Waldrop, Navarro College; Charles Warnberg, Brookhaven College; Tina Willhoite, San Jacinto College

Previous Editions

Brenda Ashcraft, Virginia Western Community College; Teena Boone, Rowan-Cabarrus Community College; Mike Coulehan, El Paso Commuity College; Kris DeAngelis, Central Piedmont Community College; Meribeth Fields, Central Florida Community College; Cynthia Gomez, Hodges University; Eric Hibbison, J. Sargeant Reynolds Community College; Marcia Hines, Saint Mary's University of Minnesota; Alice Kimara, Baltimore City Community College; Kimberly Koledoye, Houston Community College; Kina Lara, San Jacinto College South; Alice Leonhardt, Blue Ridge Community College; Glenda Lowery, Rappahannock Community College; Breanna Lutterbie, Germanna Community College; Gail Malone, South Plains College; Deborah Maness, Wake Technical Community College; Abigail Montgomery, Blue Ridge Community College; Miriam Moore, Lord Fairfax Community College; Lana Myers, Lone Star College–Montgomery; Elizabeth Powell, Forsyth Technical Community College; Tony Procell, El Paso Community College; Robert Sandhaas, San Jacinto College South Campus; Melissa Shafner, Mitchell College; Deborah Spradlin, Tyler Jr. College; Claudia Swicegood, Rowan-Cabarrus Community College; Gene Voss, Houston Community College; Shari Waldrop, Navarro College; Dawn White, Davidson County Community College; Lori Witkowich, College of Central Florida; Wes Anthony, Cleveland Community College; Joe Antinarella, Tidewater Community College; Stacey Ariel, Santa Rosa Junior College; Margaret Bartelt, Owens Community College; Jon Bell, Pima Community College; Christina Blount, Lewis and Clark Community College; Mary Boudreaux, San Jacinto College; Kimberly Bovee, Tidewater Community College; Janice Brantley, University of Arkansas at Pine Bluff; Robyn Browder, Davenport University; Doris Bryant, Thomas Nelson Community College; Jennifer Call, Cape Fear Community College; Jana Carter, Montana State University Great Falls; Roberta Cohen, Union County College; Annette Dammer, Fayetteville Technical Community College; Melissa DuBrowa, Berkeley College; Arlene Edmundson, United Tribes Technical College; Mary Etter, Davenport University; Shannon Fernandes, Yakima Valley Community College; JoAnn Foriest, Prairie State College; Marty Frailey, Pima Community College; Johnanna Grimes, Tennessee State University; David Harper, Chesapeake College; Gina Henderson, Tallahassee Community College; Eric Hibbison, J. Sargeant Reynolds Community College; Donna Hill, College of the Ouachitas; Brent Kendrick, Lord Fairfax Community College; Shayna Kessel, Los Angeles City College; Sara Kuhn, Chattanooga State Community College; Glenda Lowery, Rappahannock Community College; Deborah Maness, Wake Technical Community College; Katherine McEwen, Cape Fear Community College; Carolyn Miller, Chattanooga State Community College; Miriam Moore, Lord Fairfax Community College; Ann Moser, Virginia Western Community College; Ray Orkwis, Northern Virginia Community College; Jay Peterson, Atlantic Cape Community College; Laura Powell, Danville Community College; Pam Price, Greenville Technical College; Carole Quine, Baltimore City Community College; Janet Rico Everett, Southern Arkansas University Tech; David Robinson, College of Southern Maryland; Mary S. Leonard, Wytheville Community College; Brenda Sickles, Tidewater Community College; Virginia Smith, Carteret Community College; Suba Subbarao, Oakland Community College; Claudia Swicegood, Rowan-Cabarrus Community College; Jennifer Taylor Feller, Northern Virginia Community College–Woodbridge; Nicole Tong, Northern Virginia Community College; Patricia Tymon, Virginia Highlands Community College; Kathy Tyndall, Wake Technical Community College; Julie Voss, Front Range Community College; Michelle Zollars, Patrick Henry Community College

Reading and Writing for Success

Part 1: Reading and Writing for Success

Chapter

1

> "Indeed, learning to write may be part of learning to read. For all I know, writing comes out of a devotion to reading."
>
> —Eudora Welty

The Reading-Writing Connection

The word *literate* has two levels of meaning. On one level it simply means "to be able to read and write." On another level it means "to be educated." You're in school to become educated so that you can enter the workforce with a degree and training. But to achieve this goal, you may need to improve your ability to read and write.

This chapter explores the special connection between reading and writing as learning tools. It also provides strategies that will help you identify the main parts of reading and writing assignments, such as subject, purpose, and audience; and analyze assignments for key traits, such as ideas, organization, and voice. The remaining chapters in Part 1 address other important aspects of academic reading, writing, and thinking.

Learning Outcomes

LO1 Read and write to learn.

LO2 Understand reading and writing assignments.

LO3 Use the traits for reading and writing.

What do you think?

According to the Welty quote, "learning to write may be part of learning to read." What do you think she means?

> "Tell me and I forget, teach me and I may remember,
> involve me and I learn."
>
> —Benjamin Franklin

L01 Reading and Writing to Learn

Reading assignments introduce you to many new ideas and concepts, and you can't possibly process all of them without some help. Writing can offer that help. The physical act of recording one word after another helps you focus on new ideas in your reading so that you can better understand and remember them. A writing activity as basic as listing can help you identify important ideas while you read, whereas something a bit more complex like writing a summary can help you better understand concepts afterward. In this way, reading and writing work together to help you learn.

Establishing the Proper Attitude

You've likely heard how certain athletes and performers work incredibly hard at their craft, putting in countless hours of practice and training. They watch their diet, keep physically and mentally fit, and avoid distractions. If they have a poor game or performance, they promise to improve. If they perform well, they resolve to do even better next time. What keeps them going is having the proper attitude—the will to do their best, to achieve a particular goal.

Having the proper attitude is just as important for you as a student. Some students simply put in their time, attending classes and completing assignments without any clear intention; other students take their studying very seriously, wanting to learn and do their best. Be sure you are one of the latter. To ensure that you approach your reading and writing with purpose, follow this advice:

- Approach each reading assignment as an opportunity to learn.
- Use writing-to-learn activities such as note taking and summarizing to help you understand your reading.
- With each writing assignment, explore and develop your thoughts about the subjects you are studying.
- Engage in class discussions about your reading and writing.
- Ask for help whenever you have questions about your work.
- Set high standards for yourself.

Practice ▷ Write freely for five minutes, exploring your strengths and weaknesses as a student. What are you really good at? In what areas do you want to improve?

Keeping a Class Notebook

Keeping a class notebook will help you make writing an important part of your learning routine. The writing that you do in a class notebook is personal and designed to help you learn. It isn't meant for evaluation. Use the following writing-to-learn strategies:

Writing-to-Learn Strategies

- **Note Taking** As you read or listen in class, take notes to help you keep track of the ideas that you are learning.

  > "In Africa, AIDS Has a Woman's Face"
  > by Kofi A. Annan
  >
  > – women backbone of African society
  > – development strategies must involve women
  > – partnerships needed between African women and their husbands

- **Listing** After reading or listening in class, you can freely list ideas as a quick review or progress check.

  > - Strong families lead to strong communities and strong countries.
  > - AIDS and famine are linked.
  > - Because of AIDS, farming skills that traditionally were passed on by women are being lost.
  > - When women die, the families collapse.

- **Status Check** Explore your thoughts during your reading or other class work. This writing helps you check your understanding of the material as it unfolds.

  > After the first part of the reading, I now understand the title "AIDS Has a Woman's Face," because 59 percent of people in Africa infected with HIV are women. Women are the backbone of African society, so when they are infected with HIV, family and community life suffer.

- **5 W's and H Questions** To review material, ask and answer *who? what? where? when? why?* and *how?* questions about it.

  > *Who* is involved in the subject of the reading?
  > *What* is said about the subject?
  > *Where* does it take place?
  > *When* did it start?
  > *Why* has something to do with the subject occurred?
  > *How* is it to be dealt with?

■ **Summarizing** Upon completion of your work, explain in your own words the main points in the reading.

> Famine and AIDS are threatening the agricultural societies in rural Africa. Women, the main unifying focus in African societies, make up 59 percent of individuals infected by the HIV virus. With so many woman suffering from AIDS, families and farming are suffering. These conditions have significantly contributed to famine and starvation. Immediate relief and long-term education are needed to deal with the problem.

■ **Forming Personal Responses** Explore your thoughts about new ideas to clarify your thinking about them.

> I'm kind of shocked by this article. Everybody is talking about Ebola in Africa, but people have forgotten that AIDS is an ongoing epidemic as well. The essay also makes me mad. Here in the States, AIDS has become treatable, and the spread is contained. Why is it still out of control in Africa? It's just like Ebola that way. Thousands of Liberians die of it, but Americans don't care until one of us gets sick. We should be doing more to help with both epidemics.

Practice ▶ List three things that you have learned so far about the reading-writing connection.

Including New Vocabulary

Proactive means "acting in advance" or "acting before." Reserving part of your notebook for new words is proactive because you are taking control of your vocabulary building. This strategy will prove especially helpful in challenging courses, when you are introduced to many new words. Write down definitions from your instructor, textbook, or dictionary. These examples show the kinds of information you might include for words in your notebook.

medieval (meˊde-eˊv l)
- medi (half, middle) + ev (age, from Latin aevum) + al (relating to)
- of or relating to the Middle Ages (commonly dated from A.D. 476 to 1453)
- The Canterbury Tales and Piers Plowman are famous pieces of medieval English literature.

Pronunciation
Word parts
Definition
Used in a sentence

metamorphosis (mĕt-ə-môrˊ-fə-sĭs)
- meta (change) + morph (form) + osis (process)
- a transformation, a clear change in appearance or character
- During its life cycle, an insect may undergo a metamorphosis or dramatic physical change.

Practice ▶ Create vocabulary entries for the four words listed here. Include the pronunciation, helpful word parts, a definition, and the word used in a sentence. For help, refer to a dictionary and Appendix C, which provides a glossary of common word parts.

- intercede
- supernova
- anthropology
- numerical

L02 Understanding Reading and Writing Assignments

At the start of any reading or writing assignment, you should identify exactly what is expected of you. The main parts of an assignment include *subject*, *purpose*, *audience*, *type*, and *role*. These two assignments will be considered for a discussion of each part.

Sample Reading Assignment: Read "How Unequal Is American Society?" in your government textbook. In this selection, the authors explore income inequality within the United States. Be prepared to discuss the distribution of wealth in this country.

Sample Writing Assignment: Share a personal experience in which race or bias played a significant role. Your writing should answer the 5 W's and H about the experience.

Subject

The **subject** or topic is the person, idea, event, or object being discussed. The subject for the reading assignment—income inequality within the U.S.—is clearly identified. Otherwise, you could identify the subject by skimming the title and first few paragraphs of the selection. The subject of the writing assignment—a personal experience involving race or bias—is clearly identified as well. If the subject of the writing is not clear to you, consult with your instructor before you get started.

Purpose

The **purpose** refers to the specific reason for reading or writing. The reason for most academic reading and writing assignments is *to inform*, *to persuade*, or *to share*. The purpose for reading assignments in textbooks, such as the one under discussion, is to inform. The same is true for most reports and articles in other informational sources, such as nonfiction books, magazines, or newspapers. If an author is expressing a personal opinion in an essay, column, or editorial, the primary purpose is to persuade. The main reason for personal narratives (true stories) is to share experiences with readers.

Often, a key word will help you determine the purpose for a writing assignment. The sample assignment asks students to share a personal experience, so that is the purpose. If another assignment asks students to explain, compare, define, or discuss something, the purpose is essentially to inform. If you are asked to argue for or against something, you are writing to persuade.

Audience

The **audience** is the intended reader for selections you read or write. In a reading assignment, such as the one from a government textbook, students are the intended audience. Instructors may also assign readings from other sources in which professionals and more well-informed readers are the intended audience. When this happens, be prepared to spend extra time on your reading because the text may be more challenging than textbook chapters.

The writing assignment in question asks students to share a personal experience, so the class and the instructor are the likely intended audiences. If another assignment asks students to summarize a chapter, the intended audience is probably just the instructor. An assignment such as the following one specifies a particular audience: *In a letter to the editor of a local paper, express how income inequality impacts your city.*

Understanding the intended audience helps you decide how to express your ideas in your own writing. When sharing a personal experience, you would use a somewhat informal, conversational style to form a personal connection with the reader. A more formal style would be fitting when writing a summary or a letter to the editor in which you are interested in communicating information.

Type

Type refers to the form of a reading selection or a piece of writing to be completed. The main type of academic reading will be textbook chapters, as with the assignment in question. Textbook chapters are well organized and contain headings, subheadings, labels, glossaries, graphics, and summaries to help you follow the information. Essays and articles from other sources may not be so easy to follow because they are not designed specifically for educational purposes.

Common academic writing assignments include paragraphs, summaries, essays, and narratives. It's important to understand the main features of each type of writing before beginning an assignment. In the example assignment, you would want to know the main features of narrative writing because you are asked to share a personal experience.

Role

Role applies only to writers and refers to the position that the writer assumes. For textbook reading assignments, the authors assume the role of experts. In the same way, authors of essays and articles in respected journals and magazines will be well informed about their subjects. Writers in some extreme publications and Web sites may try to sound knowledgeable but do not possess the training or expertise to be true experts.

Naturally, you assume the role of a student when you develop academic writing assignments. To do your best work, approach your writing as a process requiring multiple drafts before it is ready to share. The same approach applies to any important writing that you develop in the workplace or community.

Using the **STRAP** Strategy

The first letters of the parts of assignments can be arranged to spell **STRAP**. Knowing this will help you remember the five parts. Using the **STRAP** strategy, here are the main parts for the sample reading assignment from the government textbook.

Subject:	Income inequality within the U.S.
Type:	Government textbook selection
Role:	Textbook authors
Audience:	College-level students
Purpose:	To inform readers about the distribution of wealth

Here are the five parts of the sample writing assignment.

Subject: Personal experience involving race or bias
Type: Narrative (true story)
Role: Student in the class
Audience: Peers and instructor
Purpose: To share an experience

Practice Identify the main parts of these sample reading and writing assignments by answering the **STRAP** questions for each of them.

Sample Reading Assignment: Read "Economics" on pages 200-207 in your textbook. In this selection, the authors define *economics* and explain factors that affect economic systems.

Subject: What specific topic does the reading address?

_____

Type: What form (*paragraph, article, textbook selection*) does the reading take?

_____

Role: What position (*expert, observer, student*) does the writer assume?

_____

Audience: Who is the intended audience (*students, general readers, experts*)?

_____

Purpose: What is the reason for the text (*to define, to inform, to persuade, to share*)?

_____

Sample Writing Assignment: Write a paragraph explaining how to use a social network. Your writing is intended for older adults who have little experience with social media.

Subject: What specific topic does the writing assignment address?

_____

Type: What form (*paragraph, essay, blog post*) should my writing take?

_____

Role: What position (*guide, student, observer*) should I assume?

_____

Audience: Who is the intended audience (*students, older adults, experts*)?

_____

Purpose: What is the reason for the text (*to persuade, to share, to explain*)?

_____

L03 Using the Traits for Reading and Writing

The traits name the key elements or features of written language. The traits include *ideas, organization, voice, word choice, sentence fluency,* and *conventions.* Using these traits will help you know what to look for in reading assignments and develop your own paragraphs and essays for writing assignments.

Ideas
All writing is built around ideas. Your goal as a reader is to follow and understand the idea in a text, and your goal as a writer is to develop strong ideas in your paragraphs and essays. All of the other traits assist in communicating the ideas.

When reading, identify these ideas . . .	When writing, develop . . .
■ the topic,	■ a main idea or focus about the topic,
■ the main idea or focus, and	■ your thoughts about the topic, and
■ the details supporting the main idea.	■ effective supporting details.

Organization
Ideas and organization work in close association because ideas need structure to be understood. The information in your reading assignments—textbook chapters, essays, articles, and reports—will be sensibly organized so that you can follow the ideas. Your responsibility as a writer is to organize your own ideas so that they can be clearly understood.

When reading, identify . . .	When writing, develop . . .
■ the beginning, middle, and ending parts and	■ an effective beginning, middle, and ending and
■ the way details are organized to support the main idea.	■ an appropriate arrangement of details that support the main idea.

Voice
A reading selection has voice, meaning that it speaks to the reader in a particular way. To analyze voice, you can ask special forms of the **STRAP** questions:

- **S**ubject: What tone does the writer use about the subject (*serious, sarcastic . . .*)?
- **T**ype: How skillful is the writer with the type of writing (*masterful, hesitant . . .*)?
- **R**ole: What is the writer's personality (*cheerful, calculating, knowledgeable . . .*)?
- **A**udience: How formal is the writer with the reader (*formal, informal . . .*)?
- **P**urpose: What purpose does the voice show (*informing, persuading . . .*)?

When reading, identify . . .	When writing, use . . .
■ the voice as either formal or informal and	■ a voice appropriate for the assignment and
■ whether or not the voice holds your interest.	■ a confident and enthusiastic approach to your topic.

Word Choice
The words help carry the meaning and create voice in a reading. Textbook chapters and journal articles use many content-specific words in their explanations. Narratives and other autobiographical pieces contain more familiar words. The words in your own writing should be fitting for the assignment. All writing should use **precise nouns**, **active verbs**, and **engaging modifiers**.

- **Precise nouns** such as *Ferrari* are more specific than imprecise nouns propped up with modifiers, such as *fast sports car*.
- **Active verbs** tell what the subject is doing: "Anton *pitched* the ball." Passive verbs tell what is happening to the subject: "The ball *was pitched* by Anton."
- **Engaging modifiers** describe words in vivid language. Writing "*Pale corn* stalks chattered *restlessly in the wind*" is more descriptive than "Stalks chattered."

When reading, identify . . .	When writing, use . . .
■ the types of words used (content-specific or casual) and ■ the quality, clarity, and interest of the words.	■ words that are specific, clear, and fitting for the assignment and ■ words that demonstrate your understanding of the topic.

Sentence Fluency
Sentences also help carry the meaning in a text. Sentences in informational texts are generally more complex and detailed than sentences in narrative texts. In either case, sentences must clearly communicate ideas. Be sure that your own sentences are clear as well. Different sentence lengths have different uses:

- **Medium-length sentences** express one or two ideas, showing simple relationships. These sentences work best for most writing.
- **Long sentences** express three or more ideas, showing complex relationships. These sentences work well for technical or formal writing, but they can be hard to read.
- **Short sentences** express one quick thought and can punctuate ideas from longer sentences. Too many short sentences in a row become choppy.

When reading, consider . . .	When writing, use . . .
■ the effectiveness, clarity, and flow of the sentences.	■ sentences that accurately present ideas and are easy to read.

Conventions
The conventions are the rules for grammar, usage, and mechanics that produce clear and correct texts. You can expect that the texts you read follow the conventions, and it is your responsibility to produce clear, accurate writing in your own work.

When reading, consider . . .	When writing, develop . . .
■ the accuracy and clarity of the writing.	■ paragraphs and essays that follow the conventions of the language.

Practice To get a feel for using the traits for reading assignments, answer these questions about your reading of this chapter of *Fusion*.

Questions to Answer for Reading

Ideas: What is the topic of the chapter?
What details stand out? Name two.

Organization: How does the reading begin?
What is included in the middle part?
How does it end?

Voice: Do the writers sound formal or informal?
Do they seem interested and knowledgeable? Why or why not?

Word Choice: What words in the chapter are new to you?
How would you define these words?

Sentence Fluency: Are the sentences long, medium, short—or a mixture?
Are they easy to read?

Conventions: Does the reading use correct punctuation and spelling?

Practice To get a feel for using the traits of effective writing, answer these questions for this sample assignment:

■ **Sample Writing Assignment:** Write a paragraph explaining an idea for a new business. In your writing, try to answer the 5 W's and H (*who? what? when? where? why? and how?*) about the business idea.

Questions to Answer for Writing

Ideas: What topic will you write about?
What details about the topic will you include?

Organization: How will you begin your paragraph (*your topic sentence*)?
How will you organize the details in the paragraph?
How will you end your paragraph?

Voice: How will you try to sound in your writing (*formal, informal*)?

Word Choice: What special terms will you use to describe your business?

Sentence Fluency: Do you plan to use long, medium, or short sentences or a combination?

Conventions: What rules do you struggle with most (*punctuation, spelling, capitalization, sentence formation*)?
Who could help you edit your paragraph?

☑ Review and Enrichment

Reviewing the Chapter

Read and Write to Learn

1. Why is it important to write about your academic reading?

   _____

2. Name two things you can do to ensure that you carry out your assignments with the proper attitude.

   _____

3. Which of the writing-to-learn strategies have you already used?

   _____

4. How can making a status check be helpful?

   _____

Understand Reading and Writing Assignments

5. What are the five main parts of reading and writing assignments?

   _____

6. What is an author's purpose if he or she is defending a position (claim, opinion)?

   _____

7. Who is the intended audience for textbooks?

   _____

8. What is the **STRAP** strategy?

   _____

Use the Traits for Reading and Writing

9. What is the main trait of the written language?

   _____

10. What is voice?

   _____

"If the road is easy, you're likely going the wrong way."

—Terry Goodkind

Reading for Enrichment

You will be reading "Top 10 Ways to Balance Work and School," a Web article providing tips for students who must balance school and work. The author of this article is speaking from firsthand experience.

About the Author

Felicia Gopaul is a certified financial planner. She is currently balancing her work life, family life, and school, and understands the challenges adult students face as they pursue their educational goals. Gopaul is the publisher of *College Funding Resource*, a Web site offering college planning articles, videos, and other resources. She is also co-author of *101 Great Ways to Enhance Your Career*.

Consider the Traits

As you read, consider the **ideas**. What is the topic of the selection, and what information supports the topic? Also notice the **organization**. How does the structure of the article help you follow the ideas? Finally, consider the author's **voice**. Does she sound truly interested in helping the reader, and does she sound knowledgeable about the topic?

Prereading

Traditionally, young people enrolled in college or technical school as full-time students. They may have worked a few hours on campus or in a local business, but nearly all of their attention was focused on academic and campus life. There are still many traditional students in higher education, but the number of nontraditional students has increased dramatically. Today, many more individuals are balancing full- or part-time work with school. Other people are returning to school for retraining after losing their jobs. And many stay-at-home parents are taking classes to jump-start their re-entry into the working world. All types of people are returning to school after time in the workforce or at home.

Describe your own situation: Are you a traditional or nontraditional student? If you are employed, how many hours per week to do you work? Are you a full-time or part-time student? Do you have family responsibilities? How do you plan to give the proper attention to all areas?

Africa Studio, 2014 / Used under license from Shutterstock.com

What do you think?

How can you apply Goodkind's quotation to education and to work?

Before you read, answer the **STRAP** questions to identify the main features of the selection.

Subject:	What is the subject or topic of the reading selection?
Type:	What form (*textbook chapter, narrative, article*) does the reading take?
Role:	What position (*traditional student, nontraditional student, participant, professor*) does the author assume?
Audience:	Who is the intended audience?
Purpose:	What is the reason for the selection (*to persuade, to inform, to entertain*)?

Reading and Rereading

As you read, make it your goal to (1) identify the topic, (2) confirm the purpose and audience, and (3) pay careful attention to the advice provided. Consider taking notes to help you keep track of the key details. Also, reread the selection as needed to make sure you understand everything.

The Reading Process

Prereading → Rereading
↑ ↓ ↑ ↓
Reading → Reflecting

Top 10 Ways to Balance Work and School

There was a time when college students could bus tables at the local diner or work at the college bookstore a few hours a week, and that would be enough for a little extra spending cash. Today, however, students are more likely to work something closer to a full-time schedule—leaving little time for frat parties, football games, and dormitory shenanigans.   1

In fact, a recent report from Public Agenda found that among students in four-year schools, 45 percent work more than 20 hours per week. For community college students, more than a quarter work greater than 35 hours weekly. Additionally, nearly one-quarter of college students have dependent children.   2

In some cases, the rigors of juggling work and school prove to be too much. Given the choice between income and education, and   3 faced with fewer dollars to go around in terms of student loans, many students leave college before attaining a degree, choosing the immediate reward of a paycheck over the expected reward of a higher-paying job upon graduation.

For these nontraditional students, it's **imperative** to strategize   4
how to balance work and school. Using the tips outlined next, you can do both, without either one suffering.

1. **Take assignments with you.** While I **advocate** keeping work   5
and school separate, I do think you can fit in schoolwork at other times during the day. For instance, if you're sitting at your daughter's soccer practice or folding laundry, use the time to study. By getting your schoolwork done a little at a time, you'll avoid cramming the night before your chemistry exam or pulling an all-nighter to write a paper.

2. **Manage stress.** Exercise, meditation, adequate sleep, and brief   6
periods of outdoor time are all ideal ways to keep stress under control. Make time for fun, too, such as outings with family and friends. Even a few minutes of downtime before bed, spent reading a book or listening to music, will help you avoid burnout. Avoid drinking too much caffeine or alcohol, as they are more likely to increase your stress levels and disrupt your sleep.

3. **Communicate with managers.** Your managers aren't mind   7
readers. Speak up and let them know that your job is important to you but that you also have school and family as priorities, and they'll likely be more flexible.

4. **Use one family calendar.** Particularly if you have a spouse and [8] children, it's critical that you communicate your schedule so everyone is on the same page. That way, if you have a final exam, you can plan dinner and nighttime responsibilities together accordingly. An online calendar program works well, so you can update it in real time. Likewise, keep an online or handwritten "to do" list to help you prioritize tasks and stay organized daily.

5. **Schedule your time.** Estimate the amount of time you think [9] it will take you to complete your assignments, then double it. That way, there will be no surprises—except pleasant ones if you have time left over when your schoolwork is done. Block off time on your calendar for your studies and other priorities such as your family, just as you block off time for work. Adhere to those hours just as strictly.

6. **Limit your hours.** Avoid making work a priority over school [10] and family. Ideally, limit your weekly work hours to 20 or fewer. Work weekends to help free up some time during the week for your studies.

7. **Be realistic.** Don't over-commit yourself, thinking you [11] can do it all. Get in the habit of saying "no" if you know that your schedule won't allow a lot of additional commitments, while occasionally allowing you to say "yes" when it's important.

8. **Share the load.** Ask for help when you need it. If you have a family, your loved ones will understand that you can't prepare dinner, get the kids to bed, clean the house, and get your assignments done—all after an eight-hour workday. Share the responsibilities to keep everyone happy. Don't be afraid to let certain things go, too, for another day.   *12*

9. **Define goals.** What do you hope to get out of your academic degree? Set a career goal, write it down, and display it. Cut out pictures of anything that your degree will help you to attain, such as a house or a vacation. Look at your goal and pictures often. Remember that work helps pay the bills in the short term, and school will help you create a stable career in the long term. One does not trump the other.   *13*

10. **Keep going to the end.** If you quit your job, you would stop earning money and immediately feel the effects. If you quit school but keep working, you might not be affected until years later, when you're still earning a mediocre income. Stick with school, knowing that your hectic schedule is only temporary.   *14*

Above all, remember that you have what it takes to succeed in all areas of your life. It's simply a matter of staying organized, making yourself and your family a priority, and keeping your eyes on the graduation prize.   *15*

Gopaul, Felicia, "Top 10 Ways to Balance Work and School." Originally appeared at www.collegefundingresoure.com. Reprinted by permission of the author.

---

shenanigans
mischief, silly activities

rigors
difficulties, challenges, struggles

imperative
very important, essential

advocate
speak in favor of, argue for

mediocre
not very good, only moderate

Reflecting

1. What is the **Subject** of this reading?

   _____

2. What **Type** of writing is it?

   _____

3. What **Role** does the author take?

   _____

4. Who is the intended **Audience**?

   _____

5. What is the **Purpose** of this reading?

   _____

6. What **ideas** in the article are most helpful to you?

   _____

7. How did the author **organize** the ideas in the article?

   _____

8. How would you describe the writer's **voice**?

   _____

Vocabulary

How would you define the following vocabulary words?

1. **strategize**
   (paragraph 4)

2. **priorities**
   (paragraph 7)

3. **trump**
   (paragraph 13)

Critical Thinking

■ How would you define your goals for your education? (See paragraph 13.) What pictures would you cut out to represent these goals?

■ What do you think the writer means when she writes that "you have what it takes to succeed in all areas of your life"? (See paragraph 15.)

Writing for Enrichment

The Writing Process

What follows are possible writing activities to complete in response to the reading.

Prewriting

Choose one of the following writing ideas or decide upon an idea of your own related to the reading.

1. Discuss your previous and current work experiences. How have these experiences influenced your decision to continue your education? Do you intend to study in a field related to your current job? Or do you have a different field in mind?

2. In an email, inform your work supervisor about your education goals, class schedule, and any potential conflicts between work and school.

3. Explain your previous experiences with balancing work and school.

4. Reflect on your lifestyle in terms of its suitability to work, school, and play.

5. Describe a personal experience in which you had to deal with more work than you thought you could handle.

When planning . . .
- Complete the **STRAP** strategy for your writing.
- List ideas that you could include to explain your subject.
- Decide how you will organize these ideas.
- Consider what voice you will use—strictly serious and factual or more personal.

When writing . . .
- Identify your subject in the beginning part.
- Explain the subject in the middle part in an organized way.
- End your writing with your final thoughts about the subject.

When revising and editing . . .
- Carefully review your writing. Make sure you have included enough information to explain your subject.
- Ask at least one classmate to review your writing as well.
- Make the necessary changes accordingly.
- Then check your revised writing for correctness. (See Appendix B for an editing checklist.)

Chapter

2

"Education is a continual process; it's like a bicycle. . . .
If you don't pedal, you don't go forward."

—George Weah

Understanding the Reading and Writing Processes

Casually reading a magazine or popular novel lets you skim and skip. Academic reading is far more serious, requiring careful attention to every part of the text. To ensure that you carefully read academic texts, you need to employ a step-by-step reading process.

You can also casually write text messages, tweets, and emails, but academic writing assignments require much more attention to detail. You need to follow the steps in the writing process.

The reading process involves prereading, reading, rereading, and reflecting. The writing process involves prewriting, writing, revising, editing, and publishing. You'll use these parallel processes back and forth as you read to learn and write about what you have learned.

Learning Outcomes

LO1 Learn about the reading process.
LO2 Use the reading process.
LO3 Use other reading processes.
LO4 Learn about the writing process.
LO5 Use the writing process.

What do you think?

In the quotation, Weah compares bicycling to gaining an education. How would you explain this comparison?

L01 Learning about the Reading Process

If you cook, you know how important it is to follow the steps in certain recipes. The more challenging the recipe, the more important it is to follow each step. For academic reading assignments, it's just as important that you follow a step-by-step process, because you don't want to miss any important information. **Figure 2.1** identifies the steps in the reading process.

Figure 2.1 Steps in the Reading Process

Process	Activities
Prereading	First become familiar with the text and establish a starting point for reading.
Reading	Read the text once to get a basic understanding of it. Use reading strategies—such as note taking, annotating, or questioning—to help you remember important details.
Rereading	Complete additional readings and analysis as needed until you have a clear understanding of the text.
Reflecting	Review your reading experience: *What have you learned? How has this reading changed or expanded what you know about the topic? What questions do you have about the material?*

Figure 2.2 shows how the reading process often works. The arrows show that you may move back and forth between the steps. For example, after beginning your actual reading, you may refer back to something in your prereading.

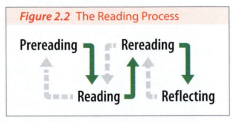

Figure 2.2 The Reading Process

Practice Explain the process you have used to complete reading assignments. In your explanation, consider how your own process compares with the process identified in **Figure 2.2**.

Planning Your Reading

Following the reading process can lead to effective academic reading, but only if you approach your reading in the proper way:

- **Find a quiet place to read.** Background music is okay if it helps you stay on task.
- **Gather your materials.** You'll need a notebook, a pen, and a highlighter or a laptop with Web access.
- **Divide the assignment into doable parts.** It's difficult to concentrate over extended periods of time. Instead, try to read for 15–30 minutes at a time, then rest for a brief period.

L02 Using the Reading Process

This reading assignment and text will be used to demonstrate the steps in the reading process. Review the assignment; then continue with "Prereading."

Sample reading assignment: Read "Dance of the Chinese Dragon," an essay describing a dance that highlights the Chinese New Year celebration. Be prepared to discuss the importance of the dragon in traditional Chinese society and what you learned about the dance.

Prereading

The following activities show how you could prepare to read "Dance of the Chinese Dragon."

- **Preview the selection:** Note the title, read the first paragraph, skim the first sentences of a few other paragraphs, and learn something about the author.

- **Answer the STRAP questions:** Here are answers for "Dance of the Chinese Dragon."

Subject:	What specific topic does the reading address?	*Chinese Dragon Dance*
Type:	What form does the reading take?	*essay*
Role:	What position does the writer assume?	*cultural writer*
Audience:	Who is the intended audience?	*general readers*
Purpose:	What is the goal of the reading?	*to inform*

- **Establish a starting point for reading.** Once you have answered the **STRAP** questions, write down your first thoughts about the topic. Consider what you already know about it and what you expect to learn. Here are one reader's first thoughts.

> I must have seen a photo of the dragon in the dance, because I can picture in my mind a huge dragon's head attached to a long, brightly colored tube of fabric. Other than that, I don't know anything about the Chinese Dragon Dance. I would hope that the essay explains why it is performed and how the dragon dances.

- **Write down questions.** Forming a set of questions helps you focus on the text *before* you read and gives questions to answer *as* you read. Base your questions on information that you learned while previewing the selection (*title, first paragraph, first sentences of other paragraphs*). For example, previewing the title "Dance of the Chinese Dragon" could prompt you to ask the following question:

> What is the Dance of the Chinese Dragon?

You will see additional prereading questions in the margins of the reading.

Reading

Reading an academic text requires your careful attention; your goal is to form a clear understanding of its contents. Below, you will see a text that one student read and annotated (marked up with questions, notes, and vocabulary words).

Practice Read "Dance of the Chinese Dragon," noting the annotations.

About the Author

Rob King has written numerous novels, many articles for magazines and Web sites, and a variety of instructional texts.

Dance of the Chinese Dragon

What is the Dance of the Chinese Dragon?

For nearly 2,000 years, dragons have danced in Chinese New Year celebrations. The Han Dynasty began the tradition of dragon dances to celebrate the time of planting. The powerful, **twining** dragon represents the forces of rain and weather that determine the fertility of the crops.

1

Why does it have so many different animal parts?

Perhaps because the dragon represents so many forces in nature, it takes its form from many different animals. It has stag horns, rabbit eyes, and bull ears. Its long, **sinewy** body is covered in fish scales, and its arms are tipped in tiger claws. The dragon can thus walk, swim, and fly, commanding land, sea, and weather.

2

In the dance, a block-long puppet depicts the courageous, **auspicious** creature. The dragon's **ornate** head can be green, gold, or red. Green represents a fertile crop, gold represents wealth, and red represents celebration and luck. More elaborate heads have spinning eyes or jaws that breathe smoke. The silver scales that shimmer across the dragon's body symbolize joy. Beneath these scales, bamboo hoops hold up each body section, and poles lift the hoops high in the air.

3

Why do dancers need martial arts training?

The puppet is brought to life by a team of dancers trained in different martial arts. Some dancers operate the head mask,

4

which bobs and weaves, its grinning jaws opening and closing as the dragon makes its way down the street. Other dancers snake in a long line behind them, using the poles to **animate** the twisting body of the beast. Sometimes two dozen dancers operate the body, for the longer the body of the dragon, the greater the luck it brings.

Why do people throw firecrackers at the dancers' feet?

Because of the weight, length, and complexity of the dragon puppet, the dancers must have great strength, endurance, and training. They use teamwork to **synchronize** the dragon's movement to drum beats and cymbal crashes. Dancers step lively to avoid the firecrackers that celebrants throw at their feet. These fireworks rouse the dragon from its winter slumber and drive away evil spirits. All together, the lead dancer and the team make the dragon coil, jump, twist, and writhe on its way down the street.

5

What is the Double Dragon Dance? What is the Nine Dragon Dance?

At some truly important celebrations, two dragons meet. This Double Dragon Dance features two gigantic puppets, driven by two large teams in a **sinuous** display. And if two dragons bring double the fortune, nine dragons bring all the more. The Nine Dragon Dance is called Kawlung and involves multiple groups of dancers in an elaborately **choreographed** interaction.

6

Why go to such lengths? The ancient Chinese sought to ensure the fertility of crops and prosperity of the people. Modern Chinese continue this tradition, but they also love the celebration as an expression of pageantry, mystery, artistry, and wonder.

7

Norman Chan, 2014 / Used under license from Shutterstock.com

twining
twisting, turning like twine

sinewy
muscular

auspicious
successful or fortunate

ornate
richly decorated

animate
bring to life

synchronize
move together in time

sinuous
snakelike, twisting

choreographed
arranged for dance

Reading (Continued)

When you read an academic text, use activities like these to ensure that you engage with the material in a thoughtful way. Here, you'll see the steps one student followed while reading "Dance of the Chinese Dragon."

- **Annotate the text.** Use highlighting or underlining. Also, write notes and questions in the margins. As you read, try to answer the questions.

  What is the Dance of the Chinese Dragon?

  The Chinese Dragon Dance is an ancient Chinese New Year ritual that is meant to ensure a successful planting season.

- **Take notes.** Record the main idea and supporting details to help you understand the text and how it is organized. List brief phrases rather than complete sentences, using your own words as much as possible.

  Dance of the Chinese Dragon

  – part of Chinese New Year, celebrating start of planting

  – dragon sacred and represents rain and weather

  – combo. of many animals such as the horns of a stag, the ears of a bull

  – dancers bring a colorful, block-long dragon puppet to life

  – dancers are martial artists; need strength and endurance

  – Double Dragon Dance has two dragons; Nine Dragon Dance has nine

- **Add new vocabulary in your notebook.** For each unfamiliar word, check a glossary or dictionary to find the type of information noted in the examples. To test your understanding, use the term in a sentence. You can do this during or after your reading.

  auspicious (aus-pi´-cious)

  – successful or fortunate

  – A dragon possesses auspicious powers including wisdom and good fortune.

  synchronize (seen -kro´-nize)

  – move together in time

  – The dancers must synchronize their steps to the sound of a drum and cymbals.

Rereading

Reread the text, or parts of it, as needed to make sure that you follow all of the information. When you reread, carry out these types of activities.

- **Add to your annotations and notes.** As you reread, add important facts and details that you may have missed during your first reading. Also revise any notes that you may have recorded incorrectly.

- **Review your notes.** Are you clear about the topic and the information that explains or supports it? Are the ideas easy to follow?

- **Confirm the author's purpose and audience.** Does your reading verify or support the purpose and intended audience that you identified during prereading?

- **Consider the author's voice, or writing style.** Does the writer seem knowledgeable about the topic and interested in it? And does the writing keep your interest?

Reflecting

The reflecting step helps you think about your reading after you have completed it. When reflecting, complete the following types of activities:

- **Write a summary of the reading.** Start with the main point. Then add key supporting details. Summarizing helps you test your understanding. Here is a sample summary.

  > The Chinese Dragon Dance is an ancient Chinese New Year ritual meant to ensure a successful planting season. The dragon represents rain and weather, and it combines parts of other animals, like stag horns, rabbit eyes, bull ears, and tiger claws, A block-long puppet has different colors to represent fertility, wealth, celebration, and luck. Dozens of dancers trained in different martial arts bring the puppet to life. They dance and weave down the street while onlookers throw fire crackers at their feet to wake the dragon from its winter sleep. The dance is a tradition to ensure prosperity but also is a celebration of artistry and wonder.

- **Identify questions you still have about the topic.** During your reflecting, new questions about the reading might come to mind. Write them down, and as time permits, seek out answers. Here is an additional question.

  > What does the music from the drums and cymbals sound like?

- **Research your additional questions.** Extend your learning beyond the original text by seeking answers to your questions. If you want to know what the music sounds like, for example, you could go online to search for videos of the Chinese Dragon Dance. This would allow you to hear and see the spectacle for yourself. When you take extra steps like these, your learning grows all the deeper.

L03   Using Other Reading Processes

Two other reading processes—KWL and SQ3R—are variations on the prereading, reading, rereading, and reflecting process.

KWL

KWL stands for what I *know*, what I *want to know*, and what I *learned*. Identifying what you know (K) and want to know (W) occurs during prereading. Identifying what you learned (L) occurs after your reading, rereading, and reflecting. See **Figure 2.3**.

1. Write the topic of your reading at the top of your paper. Then divide the paper into three columns and label them **K**, **W**, and **L**.
2. In the **K** column, identify what you already know.
3. In the **W** column, identify the questions you want answered.
4. In the **L** column, note what you have learned.

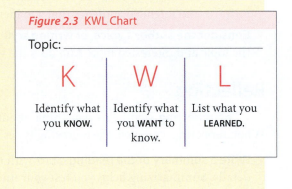

Figure 2.3   KWL Chart

Topic: _____

K	W	L
Identify what you **KNOW**.	Identify what you **WANT** to know.	List what you **LEARNED**.

SQ3R

SQ3R is a thorough reading process, very similar to prereading, reading, rereading, and reflecting. The letters SQ3R stand for *survey*, *question*, *read*, *recite*, and *review*.

Survey: When you survey, you skim the title, headings, graphics, and first and last paragraphs to get a general idea about the text.

Question: During this step, you ask questions that you hope the text will answer about the topic.

Read: While you read, you take careful notes and reread challenging parts.

Recite: At the end of each page, section, or chapter, you should state out loud what you have learned. (This could involve answering the 5 W's and H—*who? what? when? where? why?* and *how?*) Reread as necessary.

Review: After reading, you study your notes, answer questions about the reading, and summarize the text.

L04   Learning about the Writing Process

When you read a text, you annotate it, write notes about it, and summarize it. These activities are called "writing to learn." More formal types of writing need to follow the writing process, which runs parallel to the reading process. Always use the writing process when you are writing to share learning and when you are writing certain personal forms.

Reason	Forms	Purpose
Writing to share learning	Summaries, informational essays	To show your understanding of subjects you are studying
Personal writing	Personal essays, blog postings, short stories, plays	To share your personal thoughts, feelings, and creativity with others

If you try to complete a formal assignment in one general step, you (and your instructors) will be disappointed in the results. On the other hand, if you use the writing process, you'll give your writing the proper attention, one step at a time, and give yourself the opportunity to produce your best efforts. **Figure 2.4** identifies the steps in the writing process.

Figure 2.4 Steps in the Writing Process

Process	Activities
Prewriting	Start the process by (1) previewing the assignment, (2) selecting a topic, (3) gathering information about it, and (4) focusing your ideas for writing.
Writing	Then write your first draft, using your prewriting as a guide. Writing a first draft allows you to connect your thoughts about a topic.
Revising	Review your first draft, and have at least one classmate review it as well. Change any parts that need to be clearer, and add missing information.
Editing	Edit your writing by checking for smoothness, grammar, usage, punctuation, capitalization, and spelling.
Publishing	During the final step, prepare your writing to share with your instructor, your peers, or another audience.

Figure 2.5 shows how the writing process often works. The arrows show that you may move back and forth between the steps. For example, after writing your first draft, you may decide to collect more details about your topic, which is actually a prewriting activity.

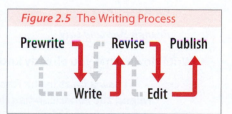

Figure 2.5 The Writing Process

L05   Using the Writing Process

Reading naturally leads to writing. When you read, you take in information; and when you write, you provide information. For example, after reading "Dance of the Chinese Dragon," you might write about a special event or celebration that you have experienced.

Sample writing assignment: Write a paragraph in which you describe a special feature or event within an important celebration, just as the Chinese Dragon Dance is a special feature within the Chinese New Year celebration. Be prepared to share your writing in class.

Prewriting

Prewriting is the first step in the writing process. In many ways, it is also the most important step because it involves all of the planning that comes before writing a first draft. Effective planning makes the actual writing easier and more effective. To prepare for this assignment, you should complete the following activities.

- **Answer the STRAP questions about the assignment.** Just as these questions can help you understand a reading assignment, they can also help you understand a writing assignment. If you can't answer all of the questions, ask your instructor for help.

Subject:	What specific topic does the writing assignment address?	*a special occurrence within an important celebration*
Type:	What form should my writing take?	*paragraph*
Role:	What position should I assume?	*student/observer*
Audience:	Who is the intended audience?	*classmates and instructor*
Purpose:	What is the goal of my writing?	*to inform (describe)*

- **Select a topic.** Choose a topic that meets the requirements of the assignment and that truly interests you. Here is one writer's brainstorming list of celebrations and special features of those events. He starred the special part he wanted to write about.

celebration	special part
city Xmas festivities	*lighting of Michigan Blvd.*
July 4th parade	*the Iwo Jima float**
WI State Fair	*savoring the famous cream puffs*
French Bastille Day	*roving minstrels*

- **Write down what you already know.** Think about why you selected the topic.

> I saw a float in the Racine 4th of July parade. It honors U.S. Marines who raised the American flag during the battle of Iwo Jima in World War II. Young vets recreated the event. Bronze paint made them look like a statue.

- **Conduct research.** Your reading skills are critical for this step. Read, annotate, take notes, and summarize what you learn. These reading notes will help you decide what details you will want to write about. Also, consider firsthand forms of research, like attending an event or visiting a museum exhibit. Take notes about these experiences, too. One student used the 5 W's and H strategy to organize his thinking:

  > What I found out about the
  > Iwo Jima float:
  > Who: Joe Rosenthal took a photo that captured the raising of the flag.
  > Felix de Weldon later created a memorial statue based on Rosenthal's
  > photo.
  > What: Shows five marines and a navy hospital corpsman raising the flag
  > Where: Mount Surbachi on Iwo Jima, a Pacific island held by the Japanese
  > When: On 5th day of battle, in Feb. of 1945
  > Why: To show that the marines had taken the mountain
  > How: Scaling the mountain (545 ft. high)

- **Establish a focus.** Identify a special part or feeling about the topic that you want to emphasize in your writing. Here is a possible focus for a paragraph about the Iwo Jima float.

Topic	Focus
Iwo Jima float	based on a famous U.S. war photograph and statue

- **Plan your writing based on your focus.** Decide what information to include and in what order you will present the ideas. The writer of the sample essay decided to focus on *who, what, where,* and *when* in the first part of the essay, and *how* and *why* in the second part. Here is how the information about Iwo Jima could be presented.

  > – the famous photo captures five marines and one navy corpsman raising a flag
  >   – on the 5th day of the battle of Iwo Jima during WWII
  >   – placed the flag on Mount Surbachi on Iwo Jima, a Pacific island
  >   – the flag showed that the Marines held the island after terrible fighting
  >
  > – the vets take the exact positions of the men on the photo
  >   – they are bronzed from head to foot and look like a statue
  >   – remain perfectly still during the parade
  >   – the parade honors our country's founding
  >   – the float honors the many people who have served to defend the nation

Julia Ivantsova, 2014 / Used under license from Shutterstock.com

Writing

Writing the first draft is the next step in the writing process. It is your first attempt to put your planning into writing. Here is a basic guide to writing a first draft.

- **Refer to your prewriting.** Using your planning as a basic writing guide, but also be open to new ideas that come to mind.

- **Form a meaningful whole.** A complete piece of writing contains an opening, a middle, and a closing. In the case of a paragraph that means a topic sentence, the sentences in the middle or body, and a closing sentence.

- **Allow yourself to explore.** Just because the topic sentence comes first doesn't mean you have to write it first. Some writers start by exploring the details and work their way back to the topic sentence. Do what works for you.

Remember, it's a draft. This is your first attempt at developing a writing idea. You will have plenty of opportunities to improve upon it later in the process. Here is the first draft paragraph describing the Iwo Jima float. It forms a meaningful whole, starting with a topic sentence that states the topic and focus. But the paragraph also needs more information in parts and contains some errors.

The Iwo Jima float in Racine's 4th of July parade is based on one of the most famous US war photographs every taken. The picture was taken by Joe Rosenthal. It shows five marines and one navy corpman raising a flag during a battle. They were on Mount Surbachi during the battle Iwo Jima. Area vets from more recent wars volunteer to participate. They take the exact positions of the men in the photo. What makes the float so impressive is that the men look like a statue that you would see in a city. They stay still in that position for the entire parade which covers about two miles. When the float passes, spectators clap out of respect for the event and the participants. The spectators no that the float stands for something special. It seems to be a perfect float for a Fourth of July parade

iko, 2014 / Used under license from Shutterstock.com

Revising

Revising is the third step in the process. During this step, you make changes in your first draft so it more effectively explains or describes your topic. Here is a basic guide to revising.

- **Review the STRAP questions.** Make sure that the **S**ubject, **T**ype, **R**ole, **A**udience, and **P**urpose of your writing match the assignment. The sample addresses a feature of a celebration (**S**ubject) in a paragraph (**T**ype) from the point of view of an observer (**R**ole) for other students (**A**udience), in order to describe the event (**P**urpose).

- **Review your draft.** Read it silently, and then reread it out loud to get an overall impression of your work.

- **Know four basic revising strategies: add, rewrite, cut, and reorder.** You can **add** information if important details are missing. You can **rewrite** ideas that might not be as clear as they should be. You can **cut** information that doesn't relate to your topic, and you can **reorder** information that seems out of order.

Here are the revisions the writer of the Iwo Jima paragraph made after carefully reviewing the first draft. Mainly, he adds information to make the paragraph clearer and combines some parts so they read more smoothly. He also replaces some general words or phrases, such as *is based on,* with more specific ones, like *commemorates.*

The Iwo Jima float in Racine's 4th of July parade~~is based on~~ **commemorates** one of the most famous US war photographs every taken. The picture ~~was taken~~ **was shot during World War II** by Joe Rosenthal, **who won the Pulitzer prize for the photograph.** It shows five marines and one navy corpman raising a flag during a battle. ~~They were~~ on Mount Surbachi during the battle of Iwo Jima. Area ~~vets~~ **veterans** from more recent wars volunteer to ~~participate~~ **portray the event.** They take the exact positions of the men in the **photograph with one soldier holding the pole and the other raising the flag.** ~~photo~~ What makes the float so impressive is that the men look like a statue that you would see in a city **park because they are completely covered in bronze.** They stay still in their positions for the entire parade which covers about two miles. When the float passes, spectators clap out of respect for the events and the participants, **and maybe for all war veterans, men and women.** The spectators no that the float stands for something special, **especially during** ~~It seems to be a perfect float for~~ a Fourth of July parade

Peer Revising

After you revise your work, ask a trusted classmate, friend, or family member to read your writing. This person can provide a reader's perspective, helping you see issues that you might otherwise miss. Have the person annotate your draft with questions and comments just like you did when you read someone else's writing. Then review the annotations and decide which revision strategies you will use to improve your paragraph.

Editing

Editing is the fourth step in the process, when you check your revised writing for grammar, punctuation, usage, and spelling. Editing becomes important after you have made all of the necessary changes and improvements to the ideas in your first draft. Here is a basic guide to editing.

- **Start with a clean copy.** Do your editing on a clean copy of your revised writing; otherwise, things become too confusing.

- **Use an editing checklist.** An editing checklist serves as a guide to help you know what to look for. See Appendix B for an example.

- **For spelling, first use the spell checker on your computer.** Be aware that a spell checker will not catch every error. You should read your writing from the last word to the first. Reading the words from the last to the first will help you truly focus on each word.

- **Enlist help.** Ask a trusted classmate, a writing tutor, or even your instructor to check your writing for errors as well. It's a challenge to catch everything by yourself.

Here is the edited copy of the Iwo Jima paragraph. Punctuation, capitalization, usage, and spelling errors are corrected.

The Iwo Jima float in Racine's Fourth of July parade commemorates one of the most famous U.S. war photographs ever taken. The picture was shot during World War II by Joe Rosenthal, who won the Pulitzer prize for the photograph. It shows five marines and one navy corpsman raising a flag on Mount Surbachi during the battle of Iwo Jima. Area veterans from more recent wars volunteer to portray the event. They assume the exact positions of the men on the photograph, with one soldier holding the pole in place and the others raising the flag. What makes the float so impressive is that the men look like a statue that you would see in a city park because they are completely covered in bronze. They stay perfectly still in their positions for the entire parade, which covers about two miles. When the float passes, spectators clap out of respect for the events, the participants, and maybe for all war veterans, men and women. The spectators know that the float stands for something special, especially during a Fourth of July parade.

Publishing

Publishing is the final step in the writing process. During this step, you prepare a final draft to submit to your instructor and/or to share with your classmates. Here is a basic guide to publishing.

- **Prepare a final copy.** Incorporate all of your editing changes.

- **Add a title.** If you haven't already added a title to your paragraph, do so now. Think of a title that sums up your paragraph in a way that grabs the reader's interest. (See example.)

- **Follow formatting requirements.** Format your final copy according to the requirements established by your instructor.

- **Proofread this copy.** Check your writing one last time for errors before submitting it.

Here is the final copy of the Iwo Jima paragraph, presenting a clean copy that incorporates the editing changes.

Captured in Bronze

The Iwo Jima float in Racine's Fourth of July parade commemorates one of the most famous U.S. war photographs ever taken. The picture was shot during World War II by Joe Rosenthal, who won the Pulitzer Prize for the photograph. It shows five marines and one navy corpsman raising a flag on Mount Surbachi during the Battle of Iwo Jima. Area veterans from more recent wars volunteer to portray the event. They assume the exact positions of the men on the photograph, with one soldier holding the pole in place and the others raising the flag. What makes the float so impressive is that the men look like a statue you would see in a city park because they are completely covered in bronze. The veterans stay perfectly still in their positions for the entire parade, which covers about two miles. When the float passes, spectators clap out of respect for the event, the participants, and maybe for all war veterans, men and women. The spectators know that the float stands for something special, especially during a Fourth of July parade.

☑ Review and Enrichment

Reviewing the Chapter

Learn about the Reading Process

1. What are the four steps in the reading process?

   _____

2. Why does **Figure 2.2** show arrows moving toward and away from each step in the reading process?

   _____

Use the Reading Process

3. What are two activities to complete during the prereading step?

   _____

4. What are two activities to complete during the reading step?

   _____

5. What are two activities to complete during the reflecting step?

   _____

Learn about the Writing Process

6. Why is it important to use the writing process for your academic writing?

   _____

7. What are the five steps in the writing process?

   _____

Use the Writing Process

8. What are three activities to complete during the prewriting step?

   _____

9. What is the purpose of the revising step?

   _____

10. What should you check for during the editing step?

    _____

"Talent is a wonderful thing, but it won't carry a quitter."
—Stephen King

Reading for Enrichment

You will be reading a selection from *Carlisle vs. Army*, a book about a forgotten but important football game pitting Native American athletes against the cadets of West Point. This selection describes the discovery of Jim Thorpe, a Native American who, many say, was the world's greatest athlete of the twentieth century.

About the Author

Lars Anderson, a graduate of the Columbia University Graduate School of Journalism, is a staff writer for *Sports Illustrated*. He covers motor sports and college football for the magazine. Anderson has authored four other books in addition to *Carlisle vs. Army*.

Prereading

We are fascinated with individuals who display special talents. Many of us praise the exploits of star athletes. Just as many of us applaud the talents of renowned musicians and performers. We also admire people with extraordinary talents in industry and medicine as well as individuals who display great leadership skills or uncommon bravery. In the space provided here, list four people, each with a different type of talent, who truly impress you.

Reading to Learn

As you read this selection, use the reading strategies you have studied in this chapter: **annotating, note taking,** and **defining vocabulary**. Which strategy helps you focus most? Which strategy is the most challenging for you? Why? How could you make the strategy easier to use? Explore and fine-tune your own reading process.

1. _____

2. _____

3. _____

4. _____

What do you think?

In the quotation, what do you think King is saying about talent? Do you agree with him? Explain.

Before you read, answer the **STRAP** questions to identify the main parts of the selection.

Subject:	What is the subject or topic of the reading selection?
Type:	What form (textbook chapter, narrative, article) does the reading take?
Role:	What position (instructor, professional writer, participant) does the author assume?
Audience:	Who is the intended audience (students, general readers, professionals)?
Purpose:	What is the reason for the selection (to inform, to persuade, to entertain)?

Then list two or three questions that you would like answered in the reading.

Reading and Rereading

As you read, make it your goal to confirm the purpose and audience of the text. Also pay careful attention to the information that explains the topic. Take notes as you read. Reread the selection as needed to make sure that you understand everything.

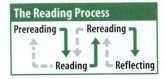

The Reading Process

Prereading — Rereading

Reading — Reflecting

High Jumping into Immortality

Jim Thorpe sauntered across the grassy upper practice field   *1*
at **Carlisle**, once again feeling good about the direction his life was
heading. He'd served his brief sentence for running away from the
farm in New Jersey and had been let out of the guardhouse. Time
also helped him move on from the loss of his father, who had passed
away three years earlier. Now, in late April of 1907, Thorpe was
about to play in an intramural football game with some of the other
students. A great secret was about to be exposed.

Thorpe was eighteen years old. He stood five feet, eleven inches   *2*
and weighed 160 pounds. The many months he'd spent away from
campus on his extended "outing" had made him more eager than
ever to play sports again, especially football. In his first days at
Carlisle before his father died, Thorpe had been a member of the
tailor shop football team. Each of the shop schools—the Tailors, the
Printers, the Harness Makers, the Blacksmiths—organized a football

squad, and they played one another in an intramural league most afternoons at four. If a player showed potential in those games, he might get asked to try out for the varsity.

Thorpe strolled through the spring sunshine on his way to one of these games. It was scheduled to be played on the lower practice field, but before Thorpe reached his destination he spotted several varsity track members performing the high jump on the upper practice field. He stopped to watch the boys. After the high jumpers cleared one height, they raised the bar higher. A few minutes passed, a few more jumps were made, and the bar was set at five feet, nine inches. The high jumpers tried repeatedly to **surmount** the bar, lifting themselves as high as they possibly could into the air, but they simply couldn't clear it.   **3**

Thorpe was **intrigued**. Before he left for his outing, Thorpe had become so quiet and introverted that he never would have approached boys he didn't know. But that time away from school had changed his personality. When he returned to Carlisle, Thorpe was no longer afraid to be the center of attention. He was now a young man who was gaining confidence by the day, and he felt there wasn't anything he couldn't do on the athletic fields.   **4**

Thorpe approached the group of high jumpers and asked them a question: Could he give it a try? The boys tried to muzzle their laughter, but failed. Thorpe—dressed in overalls and a heavy cotton shirt, and wearing a pair of sneakers that he had found earlier in the day in the gymnasium—looked like he should be out working the crops in the field, not attempting a leap over a bar on the track field. But the high jumpers, believing they were about to see a comedy routine unfold, told Thorpe to go for it, to give it his best shot.   **5**

Thorpe stepped back from the bar. Standing about fifteen yards away, without so much as stretching one muscle, he took off, blasting toward the mark. But just as he was about to take flight, he stopped abruptly. Thorpe was taking a practice run, just as he had seen the   **6** other boys do. He again stepped back from the bar. This time he accelerated even faster. The bar was twenty feet away, then fifteen, then five. When he reached the mark, Thorpe lifted off, leaping into the cool April air, twisting his body and arching his back. He sailed over the bar with ease, landing softly in a sandpit. Thorpe stood up, dusted himself off, and laughed as he rejoined his friends who were walking to the lower field for their football game. All the high jumpers were stunned. . . .

One student who saw Thorpe's giant leap in overalls, Harry 7
Archenbald, walked into [Coach Pop] Warner's office the next day to tell him what he had witnessed. Warner, who had never talked one-on-one with Thorpe before, immediately sent for him. An hour later Thorpe was standing in front of Warner's desk.

"Do you know what you have done?" Warner asked. 8

"Nothing bad, I hope" Thorpe replied. 9

Warner explained that, if the story of his jump was true, then 10
Thorpe had just broken the school record in practice. Warner walked around his desk and put his arm around Thorpe's shoulder, telling him that he'd get him a track uniform that afternoon because he was now on the track team, which Warner coached along with the football team. At this moment, here in Warner's office, their lives became **irrevocably** linked, this thirty-six-year-old man and this eighteen-year-old boy, the athletic equivalent of **Socrates** and **Plato**.

Carlisle
an industrial boarding school for Native Americans located in Carlisle, Pennsylvania

surmount
to get atop or over something; overcome

intrigued
to show interest or curiosity

irrevocably
forever; not to be altered

Socrates and Plato
ancient Greek philosophers, considered the best thinkers of time; Plato was a student of Socrates

Reflecting

1. The focus of this selection is identified at the end of the first paragraph—"a great secret about Jim Thorpe was about to be exposed." What is the secret?

   _____

2. What are three interesting details that you learned from the reading?

   _____

   _____

   _____

3. What information is provided in the closing paragraph?

   _____

   _____

   _____

Forming Personal Responses

- Write a paragraph exploring your personal thoughts about the reading. Answer these types of questions: *Did you enjoy the selection? Why or why not? Was the text easy for you to follow? What part did you like the best? Did the text answer your prereading questions? What questions do you still have about the topic?*

Vocabulary

Define each of the following words and use each one in a sentence.

1. **sauntered** (paragraph 1)   3. **introverted** (paragraph 4)

2. **intramural** (paragraph 1)   4. **abruptly** (paragraph 6)

Critical Thinking

- It is often said that some individuals have "god-given talent." What does this phrase mean to you? How does Thorpe's story illustrate it?

- Would someone like Jim Thorpe have gone unnoticed until he was 18 in modern America? Why or why not?

- What about Native American life in the early twentieth century is revealed in this selection?

Writing for Enrichment

The Writing Process

What follows are possible writing activities to complete in response to the reading.

Prewriting

Choose one of the follow writing ideas or decide upon an idea of your own related to the reading.

1. Share an experience about one of the individuals you listed earlier that illustrates something about his or her talent. This idea may require some research.

2. Report on the rest of Jim Thorpe's life after learning more about him.

3. Describe a personal experience that reveals one of your own talents.

4. Benjamin Franklin once said, "Hide not your talents; they were made for use." Form a personal response to this quotation in terms of your approach to your talents. Do you hide them or use them? Why?

5. Explain the term "talent." Consider dictionary definitions, synonyms and antonyms, famous quotations about talent, common examples, uncommon examples, and what the term means to you.

When planning . . .
- Complete the **STRAP** strategy for your writing.
- Research your topic as needed.
- List ideas that you could use to explain or describe your topic.
- Decide on a focus—a special point about your topic—that you want to emphasize.
- Organize your ideas in the most logical way.

When writing . . .
- Identify your topic and focus in the beginning part.
- Explain or describe your topic in the middle part.
- End your writing with some final thoughts about your topic.

When revising and editing . . .
- Review your writing. Make sure you have included enough information to explain your topic and that your ideas are clearly stated.
- Ask at least one other person to review your first draft.
- Make the necessary changes in your writing.
- Then check your revised writing for correctness. (See Appendix B for an editing checklist.)

Chapter

3

"Meaning doesn't reside ready-made in the text or in the reader; it happens during the transaction between reader and text."

—Robert Coover

Using Reading and Writing Strategies

Becoming an effective reader is a key to doing well in school and in the workplace. You're not alone, however, if your reading skills may not be as strong as they should be. Academic texts can be especially challenging because they contain so many new ideas and concepts. Fortunately, there are a number of strategies that you can employ to help you improve your reading skills and learn from challenging texts.

The reading strategies that help you the most include some form of writing. For example, you can take notes *while* you read to help you identify important ideas. You can also summarize the text *after* you read to help you better understand and remember ideas. This chapter provides guidelines for using a number of reading-writing strategies, including note taking and summarizing.

Learning Outcomes

LO1 Understand the structure of textbooks.
LO2 Annotate a text.
LO3 Take effective notes.
LO4 Use an outline.
LO5 Use a table diagram.
LO6 Write a summary.

What do you think?

According to the quote, when does meaning happen when reading? How does the quote relate to the chapter introduction?

L01 Understanding the Structure of Textbooks

In most of your college courses, you will be assigned a textbook, and your instructors will regularly assign readings from this text. Since reading textbooks plays such an important role in your coursework, you should be familiar with their structure.

Parts of a Textbook

- The **title page** is usually the first printed page in a book. It provides the full title of the book, the authors' names, the publisher's name, and the place of publication.

- The **copyright page** comes right after the title page. This page gives the year in which a copyright was issued, which is usually the same year the book was published. The copyright gives an author or publisher the legal right to the production, publication, and use of the text.

- The **table of contents** shows the major divisions (units, parts, chapters, and topics) in the textbook. It contains page numbers to locate the different divisions. Many textbooks precede the full table of contents with a brief table of contents used as a quick guide to the text.

- A **preface, foreword,** and/or **introduction** often follows the table of contents and introduces the reader to the book.

- The **body** is the main part of the book, containing the actual text.

- Following the body, an **appendix** is sometimes included. This section gives extra information, often in the form of charts, tables, letters, or copies of official documents.

- If included, the **glossary** follows the appendix and serves as the dictionary portion of the book. It is an alphabetical listing of key terms, with an explanation or definition for each one.

- Some textbooks then provide a **reference** section identifying the books or articles the author used during the development of the text.

- The **index** at the end of a textbook lists alphabetically the important topics, terms, and names appearing in the book and the page location for each one.

Practice Locate the different parts of one of your textbooks. Does the textbook contain all of the parts listed on this page? Are other parts included?

From Schmidt/Shelley/Bardes/Ford, *American Government and Politics Today*, 2013–2014 Edition, 16E. © 2014 Cengage

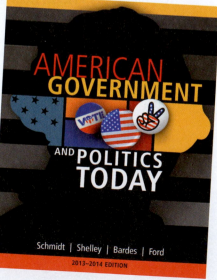

Parts of a Textbook Chapter

As you approach each textbook reading assignment, be aware that most chapters share common features. These features are designed to help you carry out your reading, so it's important that you know what they are and that you use them.

Key features in a chapter from *American Government and Politics Today* are identified and explained. Each one is an important part of the text.

- The **chapter title** identifies the topic of the chapter.
- **Learning outcomes** identify the different things that you can expect to learn from that chapter.
- Many chapters provide **special opening text** to prompt you to think about the chapter.
- **Key terms** are often highlighted and defined.
- **Main headings** are the largest headings and announce each main part of the topic to be discussed.
- **Subheadings** are smaller headings and help direct the reading of each main part. There can be different levels of subheadings. As they get more detailed, they are reduced in size.
- **Graphics** provide visual representations of important facts and figures.
- **Photographs** and **captions** enhance the discussion in the main text.
- **Side notes** can have a variety of uses depending on the textbook. They can define key terms, identify learning outcomes, or provide interesting facts or ideas, among other things.
- **Summaries** at the ends of chapters review the main ideas and details covered in the reading.
- **Resources** to additional reading or viewing may also be provided at the end of a chapter.

From Schmidt/Shelley/Bardes/Ford, *American Government and Politics Today*, 2013–2014 Edition, 16E. © 2014 Cengage Learning.

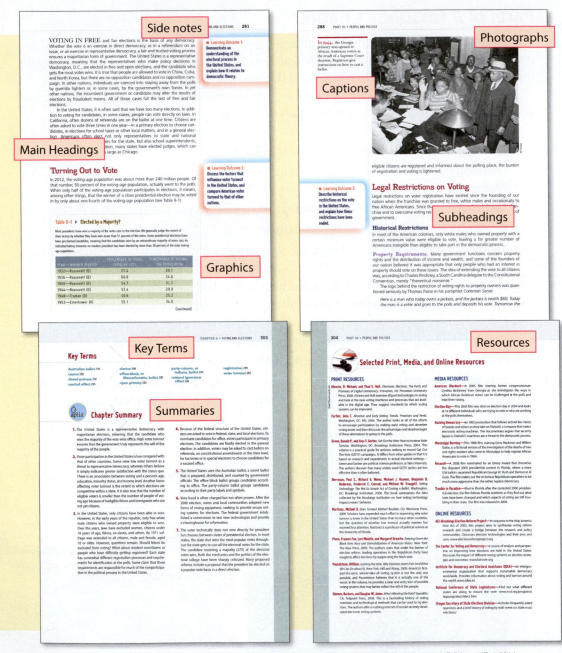

Side notes

Photographs

Captions

Main Headings

Subheadings

Graphics

Key Terms

Resources

Summaries

From Schmidt/Shelley/Bardes/Ford, *American Government and Politics Today*, 2013-2014 Edition, 16E. © 2014 Cengage Learning.

Practice ▸ Locate the different parts of a chapter in the textbook you used in the previous activity. Does the chapter contain all of these parts? Are other parts included?

L02 Annotating a Text

To annotate means "to add comments or make notes in a reading selection while you are reading." Annotating is an effective way to interact with the selection, which is important when it comes to understanding the ideas and details. Here are the types of annotations that you can make:

- Ask questions in the margins.
- Underline or highlight important ideas.
- Comment on the ideas in the margins.
- Circle unfamiliar terms and define them in the margins.
- Connect different parts.

NOTE: Annotate reading material only if you own the text or if you are reading a photocopy.

Here is an example of one reader's annotations from a passage in *American Government and Politics Today*.

What were the restrictions and grievances?

Money was power then, just like now

accustomed to: used to

Why was it called the Stamp Act?

boycotted: stopped buying or using

British Restrictions and Colonial Grievances

The conflict between Britain and the American colonies, which ultimately led to the Revolutionary War, began in the 1760s when the British government decided to raise revenues by imposing taxes on the American colonies. Policy advisers to Britain's young King George III, who ascended to the throne in 1760, decided that it was only logical to require the American colonists to help pay the costs for their defense during the French and Indian War (1756-1763). The colonists, who had grown accustomed to a large degree of self-government and independence from the British Crown, viewed the matter differently.

1

In 1764, the British Parliament passed the Sugar Act. Many colonists were unwilling to pay the tax imposed by the act. Further legislation was to come. In 1765, Parliament passed the Stamp Act, providing internal taxation—or, as the colonists' Stamp Act Congress, assembled in 1765, called it, "taxation without representation." The colonists boycotted the purchase of English commodities in return. The success

2

---

of the boycott (the Stamp Act was repealed a year later) generated a feeling of unity within the colonies.

The British, however, continued to try to raise revenues in the colonies. When Parliament passed ==taxes on glass, lead, paint, and other items== in 1767, the colonists again boycotted British goods. The colonists' fury over taxation climaxed in ==the Boston Tea Party==, when colonists dressed as Mohawk Indians dumped close to 350 chests of British tea into Boston Harbor.

Now I know why this happened.

3

From Schmidt et al. *American Government and Politics Today*, 16E. © Cengage Learning

restrictions
acts of limiting or controlling

grievances
reasons for complaining or being unhappy

Practice Carefully read this second passage from the same chapter. Then, if you own this book, annotate the text according to these directions:

- Write down at least two questions.
- Underline or highlight two ideas and comment on them in the margins.
- Circle two unfamiliar terms and define them in the margins.
- If you don't own this book, write your questions, make your comments, and define your terms on your own paper.

The Colonial Response

New York, Pennsylvania, and Rhode Island proposed the convening of a colonial congress. The Massachusetts House of Representatives requested that all colonies hold conventions to select delegates to be sent to Philadelphia for such a congress.

1

The First Continental Congress

The First Continental Congress was held at Carpenter's Hall on September 5, 1774. It was a gathering of delegates

2

from 12 of the 13 colonies (delegates from Georgia did not attend until 1775). At that meeting, there was little talk of independence. The Congress passed a resolution requesting that the colonies send a petition to King George III expressing their grievances. Resolutions were also passed requiring the colonies to raise their own troops and boycott British trade. The British government condemned the Congress's actions, treating them as open acts of rebellion.

The delegates to the First Continental Congress declared that in every county and city, a committee was to be formed whose mission was to spy on the conduct of friends and neighbors and to report to the press any violators of the trade ban. The formation of these committees was an act of cooperation among the colonies, which represented a step toward the creation of a national government.

3

The Second Continental Congress

By the time the Second Continental Congress met in May 1775 (this time all of the colonies were represented), fighting had already broken out between the British and the colonists. One of the main actions of the Second Continental Congress was to establish an army, naming George Washington as commander in chief. The participants in the Congress still attempted to reach a peaceful settlement with the British Parliament. One declaration of the Congress stated that "we have not raised armies with ambitious designs of separating from Great Britain, and establishing independent states." But by the beginning of 1776, military encounters had become increasingly frequent.

4

From Schmidt et al. *American Government and Politics Today*, 16E. © Cengage Learning

krcil, 2014 / Used under license from Shutterstock.com

LO3 Taking Effective Notes

Taking notes is an effective writing-to-learn strategy. Notes change information you are reading about to information that you are working with. Effective notes will serve you well when you are studying for exams or gathering information for writing projects.

Note-Taking Tips

- Use your own words as much as possible.
- List important ideas and details rather than complicated sentences.
- Use abbreviations and symbols to save time (*U.S.* for *United States*, *&* for *and*, *#* for *number*).
- Label and date your notes so you can easily refer to them later on.
- In texts, pay special attention to **boldfaced words**, *italicized words*, and graphics.

Using Two-Column Notes

To make your notes more active, use a two-column system called the Cornell Method. One column (two-thirds of the page) is for your main notes, and the other column (one-third of the page) is for questions and key terms. Fill in this column after you're done with your main notes. Save space at the bottom of the page to summarize or review the notes after class. Here is part of one reader's notes for "British Restrictions and Colonial Grievances."

> Insight To review your notes, cover the main notes and answer the questions in the left column.

"British Restrictions and Colonial Grievances," p. 33   March 30

Questions and key terms

Main notes

imposed—created

- Brit taxes beginning 1760
- first tax: imposed by advisors for King George III
- cols to help pay for Fr. & Indian War (1756-1763)
- second tax (Sugar Act) 1764

What exactly is the Stamp Act?

- third tax (Stamp Act) allowing internal taxation, 1775
- cols: "taxation without representation"
- in response, cols boycotted Brit products

Why did the British continue with the taxes?

- Stamp Act repealed
- more taxes: taxes (duties) on glass, lead, etc., 1776

Practice ▶ Take notes on "The Colonial Response," using the two-column note system.

L04 Using an Outline

Outlining information helps you reinforce your learning and see how ideas fit together. You can outline readings using one of two approaches:

- A **topic outline** expresses ideas in words and phrases.
- A **sentence outline** expresses ideas in complete sentences.

Topic Outline

Here is the start of a topic outline for "British Restrictions and Colonial Grievances." The entries are stated in brief phrases. Create a topic outline when you need to take quick notes.

I. British taxes
   A. 1760s war tax
      1. Imposed by King George's advisors
      2. Taxed colonists for French & Indian War costs (1756-1763)
   B. Sugar Act (1764)
      1. Taxed purchases of sugar
      2. Prompted displeasure

Sentence Outline

Here is the start of a sentence outline for the same information. The entries are stated in complete sentences. Create a sentence outline when you need to think more critically about the material.

I. The British taxed the colonies.
   A. In early 1760s, King George's advisors established a war tax.
      1. The tax made the colonies share the costs for the French & Indian War (1756-1763).
      2. The colonists disagreed with the tax.
   B. In 1764, the British imposed the Sugar Act.
      1. The act taxed sugar.
      2. Many colonist opposed the tax.

Practice Outline the key ideas in paragraph 2 of "The Colonial Response," using either a topic or sentence outline. In either case, you will have only one main point. Here is a starting main point for either type of outline:

Topic Outline: I. First Continental Congress

Sentence Outline: I. The colonies sent delegates to a congress in Philadelphia to discuss their grievances against the British.

LO5 Using a Table Diagram

Your outline does not have to take the form of a list. Some people prefer using a graphic organizer instead. A table diagram helps you identify and arrange the main idea and supporting details of readings.

At the top of a table diagram, you identify the main idea or focus. Beneath the top row, you list the important supporting details.

Figure 3.1 is a table diagram including the main idea and key supporting points in "British Restrictions and Colonial Grievances."

Figure 3.1 Table Diagram

The colonies displayed their displeasure about British taxes.			
The colonists disapproved of the war tax in the 1760s.	They also disapproved of the 1764 Sugar Act, which imposed a tax on sugar.	In response to the 1765 Stamp Act, the colonists boycotted British products.	The 1767 tax on other products prompted another boycott.

Practice In a table diagram, identify and arrange the key information in "The Colonial Response."

Thesis or main idea			
supporting point	supporting point	supporting point	supporting point

LO6 Writing a Summary

Writing a summary will tell you how well you understand a reading assignment. When summarizing, you explain the main points of a text using your own words. Generally, a summary should be about one-third as long as the original. These tips provide additional help:

- Start by stating the main idea of the reading.
- Follow with the key supporting facts and details.
- Arrange your ideas in a logical order.
- Tie everything together in a closing sentence.

This paragraph summarizes "British Restrictions and Colonial Grievances."

The opening states the main idea.

The middle provides supporting details.

The closing restates the main idea.

"British Restrictions and Colonial Grievances" identifies unpopular taxes the British placed on the colonies. In the 1760s the British created a war tax requiring the colonies to help pay for the costs of the French and Indian War. In 1764, they created the Sugar Act that taxed the colonies on sugar and in 1765 the Stamp Act that permitted internal taxation. A boycott of British products led to a repeal of the Stamp Act. Then in 1767, the British created a tax on other products such as lead and glass, and the colonists again boycotted British products and held the Boston Tea Party. With each British tax, the colonies expressed their disapproval.

Pete Spiro, 2014 / Used under license from Shutterstock.com

NOTE: Paraphrasing is similar to summarizing. When you paraphrase, you rewrite an idea, detail, or passage from a text in your own words at roughly the same level of detail as what existed in the text. Summaries explore a reading text as a whole, focusing on main ideas only; paraphrases explore a reading text detail-by-detail, restating individual ideas, details, or whole passages point-by-point.

Planning Your Summary

Most of your prewriting and planning will occur when you read and react to the text. During your planning . . .

- Annotate and take notes as needed.
- Name the thesis or main idea of the text.
- Identify the key points that support the thesis. Remember that in academic texts, each middle paragraph often addresses one key supporting point. This point is usually stated in the topic sentence.

Drafting Your Summary

Remember that you are writing a paragraph, starting with a topic sentence and following with supporting ideas. As you write your first draft . . .

- Use your own words as much as possible.
- Start with a topic sentence, naming the title, author, and topic of the text.
- Continue with the key points that explain the thesis. Focus on big ideas rather than specific details.
- Arrange your ideas in the most logical order.
- Add a closing sentence if one seems necessary.

Revising and Editing Your Summary

Remember that your summary should address the essential information from the original text. As you review your first draft . . .

- Determine if it identifies the main idea of the text.
- Decide if you've limited yourself to key supporting details.
- Check if your summary reads smoothly and logically.
- Determine if you've used your own words, except for key ideas. For example, you may find it necessary to include a few exact ideas or specialized words from the original text. When this type of information is taken directly from the text, enclose it within quotation marks.

  Exact idea: The author describes himself as "soaring with a lightness I'd never known before" after the ceremony.

  Specialized word: One teacher recognized as a master teacher serves as a "standard-bearer" for all great teachers.

- Check your summary for proper usage and grammar.
- Fix any spelling, capitalization, and punctuation errors.

Practice ▶ Write a summary paragraph of "The Colonial Response." Use these tips as a guide.

☑ Review and Enrichment

Reviewing the Chapter

Understand the Structure of Textbooks

1. What information does the table of contents provide?

2. What does the index list?

3. Within individual chapters, what are the differences between main headings and subheadings?

Annotate a Text and Take Effective Notes

4. What does it mean to annotate a text?

5. What are two-column notes?

Use an Outline and a Table Diagram

6. What does outlining help you do?

7. What is the difference between topic outlines and sentence outlines?

8. How do you arrange information on a table diagram?

Write a Summary

9. What is a summary?

10. How long is a typical summary?

"Something will have gone out of us as people
if we ever let the remaining wilderness be destroyed."

—Wallace Stegner

Reading for Enrichment

You will be reading a selection from an environmental textbook entitled *Living in the Environment* that discusses the protection of wilderness areas in the United States. Use the reading process and reading strategies to help you carry out your reading.

About the Authors

G. Tyler Miller, Jr., has a PhD from the University of Virginia and has written 59 textbooks on environmental science. Before devoting his time to writing, he taught for 20 years and created one of this nation's first environmental programs. **Scott E. Spoolman** is a textbook writer and editor and has worked with Miller since 2003. He holds a master's degree in science journalism from the University of Minnesota and is the author of many articles on science, engineering, business, and politics.

Prereading

Wilderness is defined as "an area essentially undisturbed by human activity." You may or may not have had any experiences in the wildness as it is defined here. But you have had experiences in the outdoors or in nature, even if they have been nothing more than enjoying a neighborhood park or stumbling upon some form of wildlife. List four of your most memorable experiences in the wilderness and/ or in the outdoors and nature.

Reading to Learn

As you read this selection, use one or more of the reading-to-learn strategies you have studied in this chapter: **annotating, note taking, outlining, and/or creating a table diagram**. Which strategy or strategies will you use? Why do you plan to approach the text that way?

_____

_____

_____

_____

What do you think?

In the quote, author Wallace Stegner says that something will be lost if we destroy the remaining wilderness areas. What is it that we might be losing? Explain.

Before you read, answer the **STRAP** questions to identify the main features of the reading selection.

Subject: What specific topic does the reading address?
Type: What form (*article, narrative, textbook selection*) does the reading take?
Role: What position (*observer, participant, professional*) do the writers assume?
Audience: Who is the intended audience?
Purpose: What is the general goal of the reading (*to inform, to persuade, to entertain*)?

Then list two or three questions that you would like answered in the reading.

Reading and Rereading

As you read, make it your goal to (1) identify the topic and focus, (2) pay careful attention to information that explains the topic, and (3) confirm the purpose and audience. Annotate the text, take notes, make an outline, and/or create a table diagram. Also, reread different parts as needed to help you understand the text.

Controversy over Wilderness Protection in the United States

In the United States, **conservationists** have been trying to save   *1*
wild areas from development since 1900. Overall, they have fought a losing battle. Not until 1964 did Congress pass the Wilderness Act. It allowed the government to protect undeveloped tracts of public land from development as part of the National Wilderness Preservation System. Such lands get the highest level of protection from human activities such as logging, mining, and motor vehicle use.

The area of protected wilderness in the United States increased   *2*
tenfold between 1979 and 2010. Even so, only about 4.7 percent of the U.S. land is protected as wilderness—almost three-fourths of it in Alaska. Only about 2 percent of the land area of the lower 48 states is protected, most of it in the West.

However, in 2009 the U.S. government granted wilderness   *3*
protection to over 800,000 hectares (2 million acres) of public land in
nine of the lower 48 states. It was the largest expansion of wilderness
lands in 15 years. The new law also increased the total length of wild
and scenic rivers (treated as wilderness areas) by 50 percent—the
largest such increase ever.

One problem is that only four of the 413 wilderness areas in   *4*
the lower 48 states are large enough to sustain all of the species they
contain. Some species, such as wolves, need large areas in which to
roam as packs, to find prey, and to mate and rear young. Also, the
system includes only 81 of the country's 233 distinct **ecosystems**.
Most wilderness areas in the lower 48 states are threatened habitat
islands in a sea of development.

Scattered blocks of public lands with a total area roughly equal   *5*
to that of the U.S. state of Montana could qualify for **designation** as
wilderness. About 60 percent of such land is in the national forest.
But for decades, the politically powerful oil, gas, mining, and timber
industries have sought entry to these areas—owned jointly by all
citizens of the United States—in hopes of locating and removing
valuable resources. Under the law, as soon as such an area is accessed
in this way, it automatically becomes disqualified for wilderness
protection.

From Miller, *Living in the Environment*, 17E. © 2012 Cengage Learning

---

conservationists
people who work to preserve
natural spaces and resources

ecosystem
complex web of living things in a
local environment

designation
official identification or
classification

Reflecting

1. As you annotated, took notes, outlined, and/or created a table diagram of this text, what did you identify as the main idea or focus?

   _____

   _____

2. List two details that support the main idea or focus.

   _____

   _____

3. What idea in the last paragraph seems most important to you?

   _____

   _____

4. Do you agree with the writer that more should be done to conserve wild spaces? Why or why not?

   _____

   _____

Summarizing

Write a summary paragraph of "Controversy over Wilderness Protection in the United States." Remember to use your own words as much as possible in your summary, and focus on the important ideas.

Vocabulary

Define each of the following words and use each one in a sentence.

1. **expansion**
   (paragraph 3)

2. **sustain**
   (paragraph 4)

3. **habitat**
   (paragraph 4)

Critical Thinking

- How important are wilderness areas to you? Has this reading influenced your thinking about their importance? Explain.
- How should the need for development be balanced with the need for preservation of wilderness areas?

Writing for Enrichment

What follows are possible writing activities to complete in response to the reading.

The Writing Process

Prewrite → Revise → Publish
Write → Edit

Prewriting

Choose one of the following writing ideas or decide upon an idea of your own related to the reading.

1. In a personal blog, share one of the experiences that you identified in the prereading activity. Include plenty of sights and sounds in your writing.

2. Report on a wilderness area in your state or section of the country. This will require some research.

3. Argue for or against the value of wilderness areas in the United States. Base your arguments on your own beliefs and on what others have to say about the topic.

4. Respond to this idea stated by naturalist John Muir: "There is a love of wild nature in everybody." Consider questions like these to form your response: Why would everyone have this love? Do you feel it? If you're not sure, how could you find out?

5. Explain how the wild encroaches on human development and/or how human development encroaches on the wild.

When planning . . .
- Complete the **STRAP** strategy for your writing.
- Research your topic as needed.
- List ideas that you could use to explain or describe your topic.
- Decide on a focus—a special point about your topic—that you want to emphasize.
- Organize your ideas in the most logical way.

When writing . . .
- Identify your topic and focus in the beginning part.
- Explain or describe your topic in the middle part.
- End your writing with some final thoughts about your topic.

When revising and editing . . .
- Review your writing. Make sure you have included enough information to explain your topic. Check that your ideas are clearly stated.
- Ask at least one other person to review your first draft.
- Make the necessary changes in your writing.
- Then check your revised writing for correctness. (See Appendix B for an editing checklist.)

Chapter **4**

"Colors fade, temples crumble, empires fall, but wise words endure."
—Edward Thorndike

Improving Vocabulary

You actually have four vocabularies, one each for reading, listening, speaking, and writing (listed here from largest to smallest). This ranking means that you recognize more words than you are able to use. It also means that you build your vocabulary most significantly through your reading. As you increase your reading, then, you naturally increase your opportunities to learn new words. And as your reading vocabulary grows, so do your other vocabularies, including your writing vocabulary. They just grow at different rates.

Simply reading new words, however, is almost never enough when it comes to truly understanding and remembering them. For that to happen, you need to use vocabulary-building strategies, including the ones covered in this chapter. Using these strategies is especially important when you are reading textbooks because they are full of challenging new words.

Learning Outcomes

LO1 Build your vocabulary.
LO2 Study new words.
LO3 Use a dictionary.
LO4 Use context clues.
LO5 Understand word parts.

What do you think?

In the quotation, what is meant by "wise words"? And what does it mean that they "endure"?

L01 Building Your Vocabulary

Building your vocabulary is one of the most important things that you can do to improve your ability to learn and succeed in school and in the workplace. Following these guidelines will help you learn new words.

- **Become a regular reader.** Read for your classes, read for self-improvement, and read for pleasure. As you expand your reading, you increase your opportunities to learn new words.

- **Keep a vocabulary notebook for your academic reading.** As you read, create vocabulary entries for any unfamiliar words you encounter. For each word, identify its part of speech and definition. Then try using the word in a sentence. **Figure 4.1** shows two sample vocabulary entries.

Figure 4.1 Sample Vocabulary Notebook

anthropology   *noun* ◀ Part of speech
- the scientific study of man ◀ Definition
- One aspect of anthropology is studying the origins of human beings.
▲
In a sentence

postscript   *noun* ◀ Part of speech
- a message added to a letter after ◀ Definition
  the writer's signature or information
  added to a book's main text
- The official added a postscript to her letter
  just before she sent it. ◀ In a sentence

Slavoljub Pantelic, 2014 / Used under license from Shutterstock.com

- **Learn new words on your own.** Be alert to new words that you read and hear outside of school. Some people make it a point to learn one new word a day. When you take an active interest in the language, you will naturally build your vocabulary.

- **Understand how words come into our language.** You can deepen your understanding of words by learning where they came from and how they became part of the English language. For example, many challenging words originate from words or word parts from other languages. The word *metropolis*, which means a "chief or major city," comes from the Greek *meter* meaning "mother" and *polis* meaning "city." Other new words are created from new technology (*pixel* and *hard drive*). Some words are even named after people. The word *pasteurization*, for example, is the process of heating beverages or foods to kill disease-causing microorganisms. This word is named after Louis Pasteur, the man who invented the process.

- **Know how to unlock the meaning of new words.** The strategies in this chapter provide different ways to learn the meaning of new words. If one of the strategies doesn't work for you, try another one.

LO2 Studying New Words

The first step in studying vocabulary is keeping a vocabulary notebook. The second step involves using the words that you've listed in your notebook in a real-world context. Keep your notebook at hand when you respond personally to your coursework and when you carry out writing assignments. Then you can incorporate some of the new words into your writing. Also have your notebook open during class and be ready to use these words in class discussions.

You can also quiz yourself on the words in your notebook by listing them on note cards or a blank sheet of paper. Try to define each word and use it in a sentence. Then check your notebook to see how well you've done. If you make these quizzes a regular part of your learning routine, you'll learn the new words.

If you have trouble remembering some words, it may help to illustrate them in some way. For example, to illustrate the word *contentment*, which means "satisfied or happy with things," you could draw a smiley face next to the word. It also may help you to group new words to help you remember them. For example, if one set of new words in your sociology class relates to traditional family customs, make a list of those words under that heading and then study them. **Figure 4.2** shows another example of each of these strategies.

Figure 4.2 Other Vocabulary Notebook Strategies

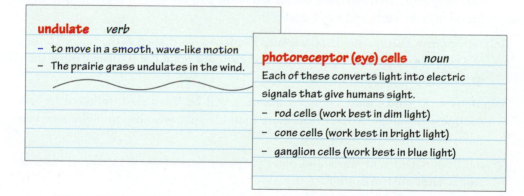

Practice List three new words that you have read or heard during class or in a previous class. Then follow the "Studying New Words" guidelines to learn these new words.

1. _____

2. _____

3. _____

LO3 Using a Dictionary

The dictionary is the primary reference tool for vocabulary building. You can use print or electronic dictionaries. Both versions contain essentially the same types of information. However, electronic dictionaries may include an audio feature so you can hear how a word is pronounced and hyperlinks to a wide range of additional information about the word. Here are some of the typical types of information that you can find in a dictionary. Also see **Figure 4.3**.

Spelling ▪ Words are arranged alphabetically in a dictionary according to their spelling.

Capitalization ▪ A dictionary tells you whether or not a word should always be capitalized.

Pronunciation and Syllabication ▪ A dictionary indicates how to pronounce a word by dividing it into phonetic characters or syllables. Most dictionaries will include a pronunciation key, which explains how each character or syllable is pronounced.

Parts of Speech ▪ A dictionary tells you if a word is used as a noun, verb, or another part of speech. An italicized abbreviation of the parts of speech is given, such as *n.* for noun, *v.* for verb, and *adj.* for adjective.

Related Forms ▪ Dictionaries list the related forms of a word, such as the various tenses of a verb (*grow, grew, grown*) or the plural form of a noun if it is formed other than by adding an *s* (*pl* children—for child).

Meanings ▪ A word's most common meaning will be listed first, followed by less common meanings. Always read more than the first meaning to make sure you really understand the word.

Special Uses ▪ Different labels and notes provide information about special uses of words. Here are two examples.
- **Usage notes** give special background information about the use of a word.
- **Status labels** indicate limitations on the usage or style of words (*slang, vulgar, figurative, informal*).

Synonyms ▪ Most dictionaries list synonyms (words having nearly identical meanings as the main entry). This information will appear after a label such as ***Syns***.

Etymology ▪ Dictionaries trace the etymologies, or origins, of many words. This information appears in brackets [ ]. Check the dictionary's list of abbreviations to identify the languages of origins of words. For example, *Lat.* or *L.* stands for Latin.

Illustrations and Photographs ▪ For words that are difficult to define, a picture or drawing might be provided. Photos of notable people and objects may also appear.

Figure 4.3 Sample Dictionary Page

Guide Word (Indicates the first word on a page) ——

Special use ——

Photograph ——
Synonym ——

Meaning ——

Capitalization ——

Related form ——

Part of speech ——

Pronunciation and Syllabication ——

divine   258

di·vine /dɪˈvaɪn/ *adj.* **1** heavenly, related to a godly force: *Do you believe in a divine power that controls all life?* **2** *fig.* excellent, wonderful: *We attended a divine party last night.* *-adv.* **divinely**.
—*v.* [I;T] **-vined, -vining, -vines** to guess, know by intuition: *The wise man divined the truth.*
—*n.frml.* a Christian minister or priest

divine right *n.* [U] the belief that a king's right to rule came from God: *The Bourbon kings ruled France by divine right.*

div·ing /ˈdaɪvɪŋ/ *n.* [U] various (under)water sports: *My friend has gone scuba diving in the Caribbean Sea.*

diving board *n.* a flat, flexible board used for the fun or sport of springing into water: *Swimmers run onto the diving board and jump into the pool.*

diving suit *n.* a tough, flexible covering with equipment for breathing used for work and exploration: *The deep-sea diver put on his diving suit.*

di·vin·ing rod /dɪˈvaɪnɪŋ/ *n.* a forked stick used to find underground water: *Some people have special talent for finding water with a divining rod.*

di·vin·i·ty /dɪˈvɪnɪti/ *n.* **-ties 1** a god **2 the Divinity**: God: *Many people pray to the Divinity.*
—*adj.* related to religion: *She is a divinity student.*

di·vis·i·ble /dɪˈvɪzəbəl/ *adj.* capable of being divided: *All even numbers, such as four and eight, are divisible by two.*

di·vi·sion /dɪˈvɪʒən/ *n.* **1** [C] a separation, breaking up (into parts, shares, etc.): *We need to agree on a fair division of labor.* **2** [C] a unit within a larger organization: *The marketing division is the largest unit in this company.* **3** [U] the mathematical operation of dividing one number by another: *An example of division is "4 divided by 2 equals 2."* **4** a large military unit: *an army division of 30,000 men* **5** a separation, esp. through disagreement: *There is a division in the union membership over accepting the new contract.*

> **THESAURUS** **division 1** a split, allotment, apportionment **2** a part, section, group.

di·vi·sive /dɪˈvaɪsɪv/ *adj.* causing disagreement and division between people: *He spreads false information and is a divisive force among the workers.*

di·vi·sor /dɪˈvaɪzər/ *n.* a number by which another one is divided: *In 4 divided by 2, the number 2 is the divisor and 4 is the dividend.*

di·vorce /dɪˈvɔrs/ *n.* [C;U] a legal ending of a marriage: *She sued her husband for divorce.*
—*v.* **-vorced, -vorcing, -vorces 1** [I;T] to end a marriage by law: *He divorced his wife.* **2** [T] to separate: *She believes in divorcing her personal life from her work life.*

> **THESAURUS** **divorce** *n.* a break-up, split-up, parting of the ways | separation, annulment.
> —*v.* **1** to break up, split, call it quits *infrml.* | annul **2** to detach.

di·vor·cé /dɪˌvɔrˈseɪ, -ˈsi/ *n.* a divorced man: *He became a divorcé last year.*

di·vor·cée /dɪˌvɔrˈseɪ, -ˈsi/ *n.* a divorced woman: *She is a divorcée now.*

di·vulge /dɪˈvʌlʤ/ *v.* **-vulged, -vulging, -vulges** to tell (s.t. that was secret), (*syn.*) to disclose: *He divulged his feelings to his closest friend.*

div·vy up /ˈdɪviˈʌp/ *v.* [T] **-vied, -vying, -vies** *infrml.* to divide into shares: *The partners divvied up the profits from the sale.*

Dix·ie /ˈdɪksi/ *n.infrml.* the southern part of the USA, esp. the Confederate States: *I want to leave New York and go home to Dixie.*

Dix·ie·land jazz /ˈdɪksiˌlænd/ *n.* [U] a type of jazz with a fast beat: *Dixieland jazz is played all over the country.*

diz·zi·ness /ˈdɪzinɪs/ *n.* [U] lightheadedness, a feeling of losing consciousness and balance: *Her high fever caused dizziness and she fell.*

diz·zy /ˈdɪzi/ *adj.* **-zier, -ziest 1** lightheaded, faint: *He felt dizzy from the heat (turning in circles, looking down from the top of the building).* **2** *infrml.fig.* foolish, silly: *She changes her mind constantly; she's just a dizzy person.*

diz·zy·ing /ˈdɪziɪŋ/ *adj.* highly exciting: *I went on a roller coaster ride and it was a dizzying experience.*

DJ /ˈdiˌʤeɪ/ *n. See:* disk jockey.

DNA /ˌdiɛnˈeɪ/ *n.* [U] & *abbr. of* **1** deoxyribonucleic acid; molecules carrying the genetic information in living cells that defines the person, plant, or animal type **2** a person's or organization's inner nature or essence: *Music was in Mozart's DNA. He loved composing and playing.*

do (1) /du/ *aux. verb* (**do, does, did** or their negatives **don't, doesn't, didn't**) **1** (used to form simple present or past tense questions): *Do they speak English?*||*Where did he go?*||*Don't you like this music?* **2** (used so as not to repeat words): *He likes jazz and I do too.*||*She works in Miami and so does her brother.*||*I didn't call her and he didn't either.* **3** (used for emphasis, to give another verb more force): *He really does need a haircut.* ||*But I did tell you the truth!*

Practice Answer these questions based on information provided in **Figure 4.4**.

1. What is the first part of speech indicated for the word *lackluster*?

   _____

2. What is the second definition of *ladder*? What status label is provided for the second definition?

   _____

3. What different forms of the word *ladle* are provided?

   _____

4. What are two antonyms for the word *lack* when the word is used as a noun?

   _____

5. How is *lactate* spelled when it is used as a noun?

   _____

6. What synonym is listed for the word *laden*?

   _____

7. What is the plural form of the word *lady*?

   _____

8. What is the definition of *lacy*? What part of speech is listed for the word?

   _____

9. What sentence is provided using the word *lacquer*?

   _____

Figure 4.4 Sample Dictionary Page

lackadaisical

—*v.* [T] **1** to be without (s.t. needed): *The villagers lacked food and medicine during the war.* **2** to have too little of (s.t. desirable): *He lacks care in his work; it's never well-done.* **3** *phrasal v. insep. frml.* **to lack for s.t.:** to have a need for s.t.: *His parents are very wealthy; they lack for nothing.*

> **THESAURUS** **lack** *n.* **1** a (complete) absence of s.t. **2** a scarcity, deficiency, dearth *frml. Ants.* sufficiency, abundance. —*v.* **1 and 2** to need, require. *Ant.* to have.

lack·a·dai·si·cal /ˌlækəˈdeɪzɪkəl/ *adj.* lacking interest, careless: *A lackadaisical attitude toward her studies brought low grades.*

lack·lust·er /ˈlækˌlʌstər/ *adj.* ordinary, dull: *The performance of the symphony was not good, it was lackluster.*

lac·quer /ˈlækər/ *n.* [C;U] a liquid that hardens into a shine: *That beautiful tray was painted with black lacquer.*

la·crosse /ləˈkrɔs/ *n.* [U] a ball game played on a field by two ten-player teams using sticks with nets for catching and throwing the ball: *Lacrosse is a very fast and often rough sport.*

lac·tate /ˈlækˌteɪt/ *v.frml.* [I] **-tated, -tating, -tates** to produce milk: *Female mammals lactate and nurse their young.* -*n.* [U] **lactation** /ˌlækˈteɪʃən/.

lac·y /ˈleɪsi/ *adj.* **-ier, -iest** looking like or made of lace: *She likes to wear beautiful lacy dresses.*

lad /læd/ *n.infrml.old usage* a boy or young man: *He was just a lad when he went to sea as a cabin boy.*

lad·der /ˈlædər/ *n.* **1** a piece of equipment used for climbing: *A carpenter climbed a ladder to fix the roof.* **2** *fig.* a series of upward steps: *She climbed the ladder of success at her company.*

lad·en /ˈleɪdn/ *adj.frml.* full of, (*syn.*) burdened with: *The truck is laden with goods for market.*

la·dies' man /ˈleɪdiz/ *n.* a man who likes women, esp. one liked by women: *He is a real ladies' man who loves to be with women.*

ladies' room *n.* a toilet facility for women: *She asked the waiter where to find the ladies' room. See:* bathroom, **USAGE NOTE.**

> **THESAURUS** **ladies' room** (women's) rest room, (public) bathroom.

la·dle /ˈleɪdl/ *n.v.* [T] **-dled, -dling, -dles** a type of large spoon: *I used a <n.> ladle to pour soup from the pan into my dish.*

la·dy /ˈleɪdi/ *n.* **-dies 1** (polite word for) a woman, esp. of good social standing: *"Ladies and gentlemen, may I have your attention, please."* **2** a title for women of British nobility: *Lady Walpole visited the Queen.*

From Rideout, Newbury House Dictionary, 4E. Copyright 2004 Heinle/Cengage Learning

L04 Using Context Clues

Your college textbooks will contain many words that will be unfamiliar to you. Some of these words will be highlighted and defined for you right on the page or elsewhere within the textbook. But that still leaves many other new words. If you simply skip over these words, you will miss important information in the reading. And if you refer to a dictionary for each one, your reading will become a slow, burdensome process.

What you can do is figure out the meaning of a new word in *context*—or by using the words and ideas surrounding it to figure out the word's meaning. In come cases, the clues can be very easy to identify. For example, in the following passage, the word *pasture* is defined right in the same sentence. (The definition is underlined.)

> Cattle, sheep, and goats graze on about 42 percent of the world's grassland. The 2005 Millennium Ecosystem Assessment estimated that this could increase to 70 percent by 2050. Livestock also graze in *pastures*, which are managed grasslands or fenced meadows usually planted with domesticated grasses.

Other times, you may need to study a text more closely for context clues. In the next example, an antonym in one sentence (underlined) helps you understand the word *monopolize* in a previous sentence. An antonym is a word that means the opposite of another word.

> Most people don't consistently try to *monopolize* conversations. If they did, there wouldn't be much talk in the world. In fact, turn-taking is one of the basic norms that govern conversations; people literally take turns talking to make conversation possible.

You can find antonyms by searching for opposite ideas within a reading. In the example, the writer states that "most people don't consistently try to monopolize conversations." Instead, "*turn-taking* is one of the basic norms that governs conversations." These clues suggest that *monopolize* and *turn-taking* have opposite meanings. And since the passage defines *turn-taking* as to "take turns," *monopolize* must mean "to do something entirely by yourself." The surrounding details support that definition.

Types of Context Clues

There are many types of context clues, as you will see in these examples:

Cause-Effect Relationships

Some passages analyze the cause and effect of something: One event (a cause) makes another event (an effect) happen. When the analysis contains a new word, the cause-effect relationship might help you understand it.

> Asking people to buckle up didn't work well, so the state made seat-belt use *mandatory*.

Definitions in the Text

Textbooks often define or explain new words within the same sentence to ensure that the reader understands it.

> Dr. Williams is an *anthropologist*, a person who scientifically studies the physical, social, and cultural origins of humans.

Comparisons and Contrasts

Informational texts commonly compare and contrast people, places, events, and ideas. When such a text contains a new word, the comparisons or contrasts might help you understand it.

> Laurie Jordon lives in New York, so she is used to a fast-paced lifestyle; Lynn Dery lives in the country, so she is used to a more *serene* lifestyle.

Words in a Series

Three or more words, phrases, or ideas may appear in a series in a sentence. If one of the items is unfamiliar to you, study the familiar items to help you identify the new word.

> Spaghetti, lasagna, and *ziti* all have their own special shape.

Synonyms

Sentences in informational texts often include synonyms (words with the same meaning) to help readers understand new or challenging words.

> Hector's essay contains too many *banal*, overused phrases.

Antonyms

Sentences in informational texts may also provide antonyms (words with the opposite meanings) to help explain unfamiliar words.

> Mrs. Wolfe appeared so energetic at first, but looked *haggard* after three hours of hard work.

The Tone of the Text

The overall feeling or atmosphere created in a passage may help you understand the meaning of an unfamiliar word.

> The street was filled with *bellicose* protestors who pushed and shoved their way through the crowd. The scene was no longer peaceful and calm, as the marchers promised it would be.

Practice Use context clues to define or explain the italicized word in each passage. Also indicate the type of context clue that helped you understand the word.

1.   In 2001 the Federal Bureau of Investigation recorded 9,730 *hate crimes,* or criminal incidents motivated by a person's race, religion, or ethnicity. Each incident may involve multiple offenses, such as assault and property damage.

From Brym/Lie, *Sociology, 2E.* © 2007 Cengage Learning.

Definition: _____

Type of context clue: _____

2.   To prevent future frostbite incidents, the administration intends to convert several of the existing sidewalks to protected walkways so that students can go from any building on campus to any other building without being exposed to *inclement* weather.   From Parks et al., *A Mathematical View of Our World, 1E* © 2007 Cengage Learning.

Definition: _____

Type of context clue: _____

3.   The president is the *ultimate* decision maker in military matters and, as such, has the final authority to launch a nuclear strike using missiles or bombs. Everywhere the president goes, so too goes the "Football"—a briefcase filled with all the codes necessary to order a nuclear attack.

From Schmidt et al., *American Government and Politics Today, 2013-2014 Edition, 16E.* © 2014 Cengage Learning.

Definition: _____

Type of context clue: _____

4.   The Blackfoot River flows among beautiful mountain ranges in the west-central part of the U.S. state of Montana. This large *watershed* is home to more than 600 species of plants, 21 species of waterfowl, bald eagles, peregrine falcons, grizzly bears, and rare species of trout. Some species, such as the Howell's gumweed and the bull trout, are threatened with extinction. In other words, this watershed is a precious jewel of biodiversity.

From Miller, *Living in the Environment, 17E.* © 2012 Cengage Learning.

Definition: _____

Type of context clue: _____

Practice Record two sentences or brief passages from one of your textbooks that each contain an unfamiliar word. Use context clues to help you define or explain the words.

L05 Understanding Word Parts

By studying the structure of a new word, it is possible to understand its meaning. Structurally, words start with a *root* or *base word*; they may also contain a *prefix* that comes before the root or base word and/or a *suffix* that comes after it.

- **Base words** like *moral* can stand alone. Base words are sometimes called roots.
- **Roots** like *liber* (as in liberate) or *rupt* (as in interrupt) are the starting point for larger words.
- **Prefixes** like *a* (as in amoral) or *inter* (as in interrupt) come before base words and roots to form new words.
- **Suffixes** like *ate* (as in liberate) or *ion* (as in interruption) come after base words and roots to form new words.

Each word part means something. For example, the base word *moral* means "considered right or good." The prefix *a* means "not or without," so the word *amoral* means "without morals." In the same way, the root *liber* means "free," and the suffix *ate* means "cause or make." So the word *liberate* means "to cause or make free." See Appendix C for a list of common prefixes, suffixes, and roots. A definition and example word are provide for each word part listed. Dictionaries also include the meanings of word parts.

Practice Define each of the following word parts and provide an example word including the part. Refer to Appendix C and a dictionary to complete this activity.

Prefixes:
- ante _____
- ex _____
- mal _____
- trans _____

Suffixes:
- dom _____
- ion _____
- oid _____
- ward _____

Roots:
- aud _____
- chron _____
- mega _____
- vict _____

The following examples show how multiple word parts can be combined to form words.

Transportation combines . . .

- the prefix *trans* meaning "across" or "beyond,"
- the root *port* meaning "carry," and
- the suffix *tion* meaning "act of."

} So, *transportation* means "the act of carrying across or beyond."

Biographic combines . . .

- the root *bio* meaning "life,"
- the root *graph* meaning "write," and
- the suffix *ic* meaning "nature of" or "relating to."

} So, *biographic* means "relating to writing about real life."

Micrometer combines . . .

- the root *micro* meaning "small" and
- the root *meter* meaning "measure."

} So, *micrometer* means "a device for measuring small distances."

Rearmament combines . . .

- the prefix *re* meaning "again,"
- the base word *arm* meaning "equip or supply with weapons," and
- the suffix *ment* basically meaning "act of."

} So, *rearmament* means "the act of arming again."

Practice Explain the word parts that combine to form these words. Then define the complete word.

- nominate (*nomin + ate*)
- hemisphere (*hemi + sphere*)
- senile (*sen + ile*)
- translucent (*trans + luc + ent*)

The following passage uses the word *multiculturalism*. You may already know the meaning of this word. If not, studying its parts can help you unlock its meaning.

> In contrast, for the past several decades, advocates of *multiculturalism* have argued that school and college curricula should present a more balanced picture of American history, culture, and society—one that better reflects the country's ethnic and racial diversity today (Nash, Crabtree, and Dunn, 129).
>
> From BRYM/LIE, *Sociology*, 2E. © 2007 Cengage Learning

Analysis of the word *multiculturalism*:

- **Word parts:** *Multi* is a prefix meaning "many." *Culture* is a root or base word meaning "the way a group conducts life." The suffixes *al* and *ism* basically mean "of or relating to."

■ **Definition/explanation of the word:** *Multiculturalism* logically means "of or relating to many cultures" or "of or relating to the many ways that groups conduct their lives."

After you define a word using word parts, you can reread the passage it appears in to determine if the definition makes sense. Does the definition of *multiculturalism* established in the word-part analysis make sense in the context of the previous passage?

Practice Study the italicized word in each of the following passages. Break it into recognizable word parts, explain what each part means, and then define the word. Use the example above as a guide.

1. The United States should limit carbon emissions and lessen its dependence on fossil fuels. To *counteract* its dependence on fossil fuels, the U.S. must invest in wind farms for its energy needs. A wind farm is made up of a group of large wind turbines, which convert wind into electric energy. . . .

Analysis of the word **counteract**:

Word parts: _____

Definition/explanation of the word: _____

2. Not all Greeks were able to find the truth they needed in philosophy. Probably the large majority of people were not exposed to the complex reasoning of the philosophers, so they turned instead to religion. Like most of the other peoples we have discussed, the Greeks were *polytheistic*. . . .

From Adler/Pouwels, *World Civilizations*, 6E. © 2012 Cengage Learning

Analysis of the word **polytheistic**:

Word parts: _____

Definition/explanation of the word: _____

Special Challenge As you learn more word parts, you reading vocabulary will expand. For example, if you know that the root *hydro* means "water," then it is easier to understand words such as *hydroelectric, hydroplane, hydrometer,* and *hydrospace.* Choose one of the roots that follow. Then list as many words as you can think of that contain that root. Repeat the activity a second time with another one of the roots.

  ■ *auto* meaning "self"   ■ *ped, pod* meaning "foot"

  ■ *leg* meaning "law"   ■ *port* meaning "carry"

☑ Review and Enrichment

Reviewing the Chapter

Build Your Vocabulary and Study New Words

1. Why does reading more help improve your vocabulary?

   _____

2. How can you use a vocabulary notebook to build your vocabulary?

   _____

Use a Dictionary

3. Why is a dictionary an important resource when it comes to vocabulary building?

   _____

4. What is the etymology of a word?

   _____

Use Context Clues

5. What are context clues?

   _____

6. What are two types of context clues?

   _____

Use Word Parts

7. What are the three main word parts?

   _____

8. Where can you look up the meaning of an unfamiliar word part?

   _____

9. What is the definition of *penta*? Of *vic*?

   _____

"We all worry about the population explosion,
but we don't worry about it at the right time."

—Art Hoppe

Reading for Enrichment

The reading selection "The Population of the Earth," which comes from a history textbook called *World Civilizations*, discusses the increasing population around the world. Use the reading process and reading strategies to help you carry out your reading.

About the Authors

Philip J. Adler taught courses in world history for nearly 30 years. He has published widely in the historical journals of this country and German-speaking Europe. **Randall L. Pouwels** has published widely. His book *Horn and Crescent: Cultural Change and Traditional Islam on the East African Coast, 800-1900* has become a standard work on African history. He taught for many years at LaTrobe University in Melbourne, Australia, and at UCLA.

Prereading

At some point in your education, you have likely discussed the growth of the world's population. It is one of those topics, like global warming, that is important to discuss frequently. What other topics also require frequent discussion because they are so important nationally or globally? Name three or four of them here.

Consider the Elements

As you read, pay careful attention first to the **ideas**—the topic and the details that explain it. (You may need to read this essay two or three times to follow all the information.) Also consider the **organization** of the essay: Is the information arranged in a logical way to make it easy to follow?

_____

_____

_____

_____

_____

What do you think?

In the quote, Hoppe says that we don't worry about the population explosion at the right time. What does he mean by that?

Before you read, answer the **STRAP** questions to identify the main features of the reading selection.

Subject: What specific topic does the reading address?

Type: What form (*narrative, editorial, textbook selection*) does the reading take?

Role: What position (*observers, participants, educational authors*) do the writers assume?

Audience: Who is the intended audience?

Purpose: What is the general goal of the reading (*to entertain, to inform, to persuade*)?

Also, write down any other questions that you would like answered by the reading.

Reading and Rereading

As you read, make it your goal to (1) identify the focus or main idea made about the topic and (2) pay careful attention to the details that develop the topic. Annotate the text and/or take notes to help you remember important details. Also, use the different vocabulary strategies to help you understand new words. Reread as needed to make sure that you understand the selection.

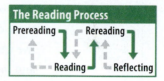

The Population of the Earth

A book appeared in the 1970s with the **arresting** title *The Population Bomb*. Written by a respected biologist, Paul Ehrlich, at an American university, it warned that a time was rapidly approaching when the earth would face massive, prolonged famine. The rate of population growth in the less-developed countries, it said, threatened to overwhelm the earth's capacity to grow food. **1**

Professor Ehrlich's **prognosis** of early famine proved erroneous. **2** The Green Revolution, plus a series of good crop years around the globe, actually increased the ratio of available food to mouths, but many believe that Ehrlich's basic argument is still valid: Inevitably, starvation will come. They point to the examples of the African Sahel (a semi-arid area of western and north-central Africa), Bangladesh since independence, and many of the Andean populations in South America to assert that the number of consumers is exceeding the available resources. It is just a matter of time, they argue, until the well fed will be using lethal weapons to hold off the starving hordes.

Other observers, however, argue that Ehrlich and similar doomsayers are not taking the so-called **demographic** transition into account. This transition occurs when parents stop viewing many children as a familial and economic necessity and instead produce a smaller number of better-cared-for children. Historically, this has occurred when a society becomes industrialized and urbanized. Children then become less economically necessary to the family, and a lower mortality rate means that most will live to maturity. Hence, parents no longer need to have many children to ensure that some will survive to care for them in their old age. Because the three continents where the large majority of nonindustrial peoples live (Africa, Asia, and South America) are rapidly developing urban and industrialized societies, it was hoped that birthrates would drop substantially within a generation, but this has not happened.

In Latin America, parts of Asia, and much of Africa, birthrates have remained at levels that are double or triple Western rates. The "gap" between the present-day medical and technological capacities to preserve and prolong life and the cultural demands to have children early and frequently so that some will survive into adulthood has not closed as swiftly as was hoped. Efforts to lower the birthrate by artificial means have worked in some places (China, for instance) but failed in most others.

Yet, some means of controlling the hugely increasing demands of the world's population on every type of natural resource (including privacy, quietude, and undisturbed **contemplation**) must be found soon, presumably.

The human inhabitants of Spaceship Earth are increasing in **geometric** fashion. The earth's first half-billion inhabitants took perhaps 50,000 years to appear, and the second half-billion appeared over 500 years (1300-1800), but nearly 2 billion people out of the 2009 total of 6.64 billion came aboard in a period of eighteen years! Most of this proportion lives in the less-developed countries, where the rate of natural increase—births over deaths without counting migration—is two to four times the industrial world.

From Adler/Pouwels, *World Civilizations*, 6E. © 2012 Cengage Learning

arresting
eye-catching

prognosis
stating an ending in advance

demographic
relating to the study of changes that occur in large groups

contemplation
careful thinking

geometric
increasing according to the principles of geometry

Reflecting

1. The topic of the reading is population growth. What is the focus or main idea developed about this topic? Is it that population growth is under control, or is it that population growth is still increasing in dangerous ways?

2. What details support the focus or main idea? Give two examples.

3. What do the statistics (numbers) in the ending paragraph tell you?

Summarizing

Write a summary paragraph of "The Population of the Earth." Focus on the most important information, and use your own words as much as possible.

Vocabulary

Use a dictionary to define these words.

1. **erroneous** (paragraph 2)
2. **capacities** (paragraph 4)

Use word parts to define these words.

1. **familial** (paragraph 3)

Use context clues to define these words.

1. **hordes** (paragraph 2)
2. **doomsayers** (paragraph 3)

2. **quietude** (paragraph 5)

Critical Thinking

- What are other factors that might affect population growth?
- To what degree will population growth be important in future political decisions?

Writing for Enrichment

What follows are possible writing activities to complete in response to the reading.

The Writing Process

Prewrite → Revise → Publish → Write → Edit

Prewriting

Choose one of the following writing ideas or come up with your own idea related to the reading.

1. In a personal blog, explore your thoughts about the topic. Use these questions to help you get started: How do you feel about population growth? Have population issues affected you in any way? Will it affect you in the future? What, if anything, should be done about it?

2. Explain how the size of families has changed over the years in the United States. This will require research.

3. Report on a country or area that is facing famine. This will require research.

4. Explain how China has dealt with runaway population growth. This may require research.

5. Explore your thoughts about one of the topics you listed in the prereading activity.

When planning . . .
- Complete the **STRAP** strategy for your writing.
- Gather plenty of details about your topic.
- Establish a main idea (thesis) to serve as a focus for your writing.
- Arrange your notes accordingly for writing.

When writing . . .
- Develop effective beginning, middle, and ending parts in your writing.
- Present your main idea in the beginning part.
- Support and explain the main idea in the middle part.
- Close your essay with final thoughts about your topic.

When revising and editing . . .
- Carefully review your first draft. Make sure that you have included enough details to explain your topic.
- Ask at least one peer to review your writing as well.
- Improve the content as needed.
- Edit your revised writing for smoothness and correctness.

Chapter

5

> "Read not to contradict or confute; nor to believe and take for granted; nor to find talk and discourse; but to weigh and consider."
>
> —Francis Bacon

Critical Thinking and Viewing

When painting a portrait, the artist will narrow in on a subject's face. Each detail is essential, so the artist will move section by section, observing the colors, shapes, shadows, lines, and textures that make the face unique.

Like a painter, you can narrow your focus to discover new meaning from what you read, write, and view. This type of deep, focused thinking is called critical thinking.

In this chapter, you'll progress through different levels of thinking to deepen your understanding of a text or visual. Then you'll ask and answer critical questions to further your understanding. Finally, you'll learn how to analyze and use visuals.

Learning Outcomes

L01 Apply different levels of thinking.
L02 Ask critical questions.
L03 Analyze visuals critically.

What do you think?

What point is Francis Bacon trying to make in his quotation? How can you "weigh and consider" a text or visual?

L01 Applying Different Levels of Thinking

Not all thinking is equal. Some types require a deeper level of thought and concentration than others. For instance, analyzing the biological impact of an invasive species takes a deeper level of thought than remembering the items you need to pick up at a convenience store.

Educational psychologist Benjamin Bloom highlighted this idea in his taxonomy of thinking. Bloom's taxonomy classifies thinking into six skills: *remembering, understanding, applying, analyzing, evaluating,* and *creating.* **Table 5.1** shows the progression of thinking skills, moving from surface thinking to deep thinking.

Table 5.1 Bloom's Revised Taxonomy of Thinking Skills

Surface Thinking		
	Remembering	means recalling basic information.
	Understanding	means explaining what the information means and why it is important.
	Applying	means using the information in a new purpose or context.
	Analyzing	means breaking down and studying the parts.
	Evaluating	means judging the strengths and weaknesses.
Deep Thinking	**Creating**	means shaping ideas to make something new.

Critical thinking focuses on the deep-thinking skills at the bottom of the list, particularly analyzing and evaluating. But before you can progress to those deepest levels of thought, you need to progress through the skills before them.

This concept is evident in academic reading and writing. Before you can understand what the information and concepts mean in a reading selection, you need to remember the basic details. Likewise, you need to understand a topic before you can apply your knowledge in writing. You'll be learning about strategies for mastering each level of thinking.

Practice What type of thinking do you do most often? What are some circumstances in which you would use one type of thinking over another? Be specific.

Ollyy, 2014 / Used under license from Shutterstock.com

Remembering

Remembering involves memory and recall. Though it is the most basic level of thinking, remembering is the foundation for deeper levels of thought. In reading, you need to remember main points, supporting details, and key terms. In writing, you need to recall basic information about the subject, audience, and purpose.

One of the best ways to remember key information is to write about it. You've already learned about effective writing-to-learn strategies, such as annotating. You can also create flashcards (note cards) of key information. For the best results, use both sides of the card. On one side write an important idea, term, or detail. On the other side, write additional information related to the idea. Then test your recall by reading one side and trying to remember what is on the other side. **Figure 5.1** shows sample flash cards.

Figure 5.1 Sample Flash Cards

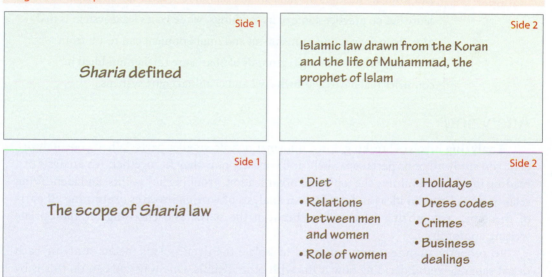

Side 1	Side 2
Sharia defined	Islamic law drawn from the Koran and the life of Muhammad, the prophet of Islam

Side 1	Side 2
The scope of *Sharia* law	• Diet • Holidays • Relations between men and women • Dress codes • Crimes • Role of women • Business dealings

Understanding

Understanding goes beyond basic recall. It involves knowing what a topic means and why it is important. When you explain or describe a subject, you show your understanding of a topic. In reading, understanding involves explaining what you've read, giving examples of key ideas, and knowing what information is most important. In writing, understanding involves drawing conclusions about a topic based on what you already know about it.

To make sure you understand a reading or writing topic, ask and answer the following critical questions.

- What is the topic?
- What is the most important idea about the topic?
- What are some examples of this idea?
- Why does the main idea about the topic matter?

Applying

Applying means putting information to use. In reading, applying involves identifying the main idea and crucial details, and showing your understanding. In writing, applying means formulating a main idea about the topic and outlining key details about it.

You can apply your understanding of a reading or a writing topic by using your own words to write a summary of the main idea and key supporting points.

Main idea
(underlined)

Muslims throughout the world practice Sharia law to varying degrees. *Sharia* refers to Islamic laws derived from the Islamic holy book and the life of Muhammad. The laws encompass both religious and lifestyle choices, such as dress code, business transactions, and the roles of men and women. Muslims in India are not bound to Islamic law in a legal sense but do practice some of its teachings, while Iran's legal system is tied directly to Sharia, and punishment and imprisonment can result from breaking its laws. The legal grounds of Sharia are further muddied in countries that have their own civil and criminal court systems.

Supporting
Points

Analyzing

Analyzing involves breaking down information into smaller parts. When you analyze a text, you study all of its parts separately and consider how they fit together. An analysis of a reading involves examining the topic and organization, grouping key points, and identifying relationships between ideas and details. An analysis of writing involves examining all parts of the topic, recognizing relationships between the parts, and choosing an appropriate writing approach.

To properly analyze a text, you need to isolate the details. This means studying each detail separately and deciding how it fits with other details. One way you can do this is by creating a graphic representation of the details. You've already learned about two ways to isolate details: an outline and a table diagram. **Figures 5.2–5.4** show three other graphics that you can use to analyze details.

Line Diagram

■ A line diagram helps you sort details into categories.

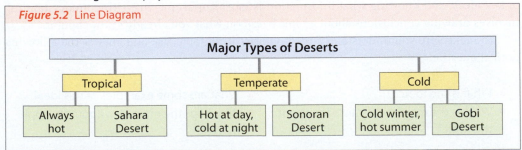

Figure 5.2 Line Diagram

Venn Diagram

- A Venn diagram helps you to compare and contrast two topics.

Figure 5.3 Venn Diagram

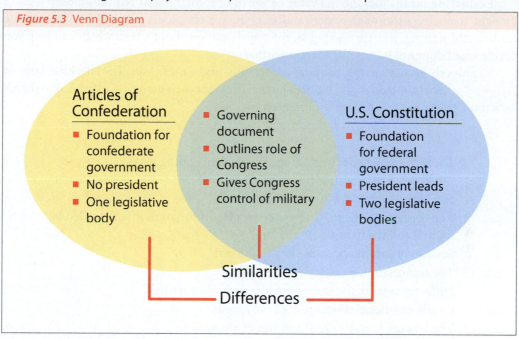

Cause-Effect Organizer

- A cause-effect organizer helps you trace the causes and effects of a topic.

Figure 5.4 Cause-Effect Organizer

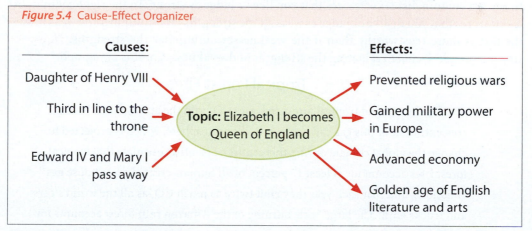

Evaluating

Evaluating means judging the value or worth of something. It requires a deep level of thought, including a thorough understanding of the subject and its parts. When you evaluate reading and writing, you are making an informed opinion about a text, which can help you decide whether or not it is useful or trustworthy.

To properly evaluate a text, consider its strengths and weaknesses. The checklist items in **Figure 5.5** will help you do so. If you can't answer "yes" for each item, you may need to search for a more trustworthy source of information.

Figure 5.5 Evaluation Checklist

_____ 1. The writing includes beginning, middle, and ending parts.

_____ 2. The writing is published by a scholarly source (academic journal, textbook) or a trustworthy news organization.

_____ 3. The coverage of the topic seems complete; information that is needed to understand the topic is not missing.

_____ 4. Sources of information are cited in the text.

_____ 5. The information is accurate and up to date.

_____ 6. Different sides of the topic are addressed in the writing.

_____ 7. Overly emotional language does not appear.

_____ 8. The writing is easy to read and free of errors.

_____ 9. The design looks clean and professional.

Another way to evaluate information is to create a T-chart of strengths and weaknesses. In the left column, list text features that you like or judge as strong. In the right column, list text features that you dislike or judge as weak. If the strengths far outnumber the weaknesses, the text is more trustworthy than if the weaknesses outnumber the strengths. **Figure 5.6** shows a sample T-chart evaluating the strengths and weaknesses of this paragraph.

Tropical Forest Fires

The burning of tropical forests releases CO_2 into the atmosphere. Rising concentration of this gas can help warm the atmosphere, which is projected to change the global climate during this century. Scientists estimate that tropical forest fires account for at least 17 percent of all human-created greenhouse gas emissions, and that each year they emit twice as much CO_2 as all the world's cars and trucks emit. The large-scale burning of the Amazon rain forest accounts for 75 percent of all Brazil's greenhouse gas emissions, making Brazil the world's fourth largest emitter of such gases, according to the National Inventory of Greenhouse Gases. Even if these forests are replaced by savannah, far less CO_2 will be absorbed by photosynthesis, resulting in even more atmospheric warming.

Figure 5.6 T-Chart

Strengths	Weaknesses
■ Many interesting facts ■ Up-to-date information ■ Sources provided ■ Beginning, middle, and ending included ■ Many effects of burning tropical forests presented ■ Academic language used	■ Uncommon words like "emissions" and "savannah" not defined ■ Chemistry term CO_2 not defined ■ Cause of tropical forest fires not mentioned

Practice Read the following paragraph. Complete a T-chart to list its strengths and weaknesses. Use the evaluation checklist to help you evaluate the content.

> The deadliest recorded outbreak of Ebola happened in the second half of 2014. More than 5,000 cases and 2,600 deaths occurred in 2014. In comparison, the second worst outbreak occurred in 1976, with 602 cases and 431 deaths. These numbers demonstrate the deadly nature of the virus. The mortality rate is 60 percent for infected patients, and there is no known cure or vaccine to prevent it.

Strengths	Weaknesses

Creating

Creating requires the deepest level of thinking. When you create something, you produce something of your own. In the context of academic writing, creating means developing writing with strong ideas that other people can read, understand, and learn from. To do your best work, apply all of the other thinking skills to your topic. Additionally, consider the parts of the **STRAP** strategy.

- **Subject:** Your topic
- **Type:** Form of writing
- **Role:** Your personal position or authority on the topic
- **Audience:** Your readers
- **Purpose:** Reason for writing

L02   Asking Critical Questions

Asking questions helps you think critically about your reading and writing. Like different modes of thinking, not all questions are equal. Some questions seek simple facts and short answers. Other questions expand your thinking, seeking deep possibilities and connections. The questioning strategies that follow will help you deepen your thinking while reading and writing.

Asking the 5W's and H Questions

The 5W's and H questions—*who? what? where? when? why?* and *how?*—are sometimes called journalistic questions because their answers provide the basic information needed to report any news story. Likewise, applying the questions to your reading texts can help you grasp essential information and gather details for a writing topic.

One of the best ways to utilize the 5W's and H is during prereading. As you preview a text, search for features such as titles, headings, bolded words, or author information. Then create 5W's and H questions for each feature. Record your questions and seek answers to them as you read. Review how one student turned textual features into prereading question.

Heading: Nonverbal Communication

- *What* is nonverbal communication?
- *What* impact does it have?
- *Who* uses nonverbal communication?
- *Where* and *when* does it work best?
- *Why* would someone communicate nonverbally?
- *How* does nonverbal communication work?

Subheading: Hand gestures

- *What* are examples of hand gestures?
- *What* types of information do hand gestures communicate?
- *When* do hand gestures work best?
- *How* do hand gestures help someone communicate nonverbally?
- *How* effective are hand gestures?
- *Why* are they used for communication?

Authors: Gary Ferraro and Susan Andreatta

- *Who* are Gary Ferraro and Susan Andreatta?
- *What* makes them qualified to speak on this subject?
- *What* is their education and professional background?
- *Why* are they trustworthy?

Practice ▶ Turn the following title into a series of journalistic questions: **"New Hope in the War on Terror."**

Asking Socratic Questions

Socrates was an ancient Greek philosopher who taught by asking open-ended questions that required his students to think deeply. While the 5W's and H questions mostly seek basic information, Socratic questions invite brainstorming and discussion. There are six types of Socratic questions that you can apply to your reading and writing.

1. **Clarifying questions** ask you to explain what something means.

   During reading ask . . .
   - How do I explain the ideas covered in the text?
   - What are some examples of . . . ?

   During writing ask . . .
   - What exactly am I trying to say about . . . ?
   - What are some more examples of . . . ?

2. **Assumption questions** ask you to question things that you assume are true.

   During reading ask . . .
   - Is the author assuming something is true when it is really not?
   - What if I assumed the opposite was true?

   During writing ask . . .
   - What assumptions am I making about the topic or my audience?
   - Am I taking something for granted when I say . . . ?

3. **Reasoning questions** ask you to question the logic and reasoning.

   During reading ask . . .
   - What evidence shows that this idea is true?
   - Are the reasons or evidence convincing?
   - How might this idea be refuted?

   During writing ask . . .
   - How do I prove my point? What evidence will strengthen my point?
   - What might someone say to disprove my point?

4. **Perspective questions** ask you to consider other points of view.

   During reading ask . . .
   - How would someone different from me see this topic?
   - How is the topic alike or different from . . . ?

   During writing ask . . .
   - How might someone with a different background or life perspective view the topic?
   - How else could I look at this topic?

5. **Consequence questions** ask you to consider what might happen.

   During reading ask . . .
   - What could result from this idea?

   During writing ask . . .
   - How does the topic affect . . . ?

6. **Recursive questions** ask you to reconsider your original question or position.

   During reading ask . . .
   - What was the point of reading this?
   - Why would someone read this?

   During writing ask . . .
   - Why did I write this in the first place?
   - What else can I say about this?

LO3 Analyzing Visuals Critically

As the saying goes, "A picture is worth a thousand words." That's because our minds can process visual information at much faster rates than words. It should be no surprise then that most reading texts include visuals to help you understand the information. Visuals include photographs, diagrams, paintings, drawings, and other art work.

Rather than taking visuals at face value, you should view them critically. The critical-viewing process will help you "read" visuals carefully to learn the most from them.

1. **Scan the visual.** View it as a whole, noting the features that catch your eye. The place where your eyes are initially drawn is likely the focal point, or subject, of the visual.

2. **Analyze the visual.** Take a much closer look, dividing the visual into small sections and studying each section separately. Search for small clues that might hint at a larger meaning.

3. **Question the visual.** Ask 5 W's and H questions.
   - **Who** created it?
   - **What** does it show?
   - **Who** or what is the subject?
   - **Where** is the setting?
   - **When** was it created?
   - **What** time period does it depict?
   - **Why** was the visual created?
   - **Why** am I viewing it?
   - **How** does it make me feel?

4. **Associate the visual.** Connect the visual with its title, caption, or surrounding text. Then connect it to what you already know about the visual or your knowledge about the subject.

5. **Interpret the visual.** Consider what the visual means. Use what you learned in the first four steps to make your own conclusions. Most visuals are open to many different interpretations.

Practice Apply the critical viewing process to the photograph in **Figure 5.7**. Answer the analysis questions for each stage in the process.

Figure 5.7 Analyzing a Photograph

Figure 3.5 A member of the Japanese Search and Rescue team searches through the damage and debris on March 17, 2011, in Unosumai, Kamaishi, Iwate, Japan. A 9.0 earthquake hit Japan on March 11 and caused a tsunami that destroyed anything in its path. *(Master Sgt. Jeremy Lock, U.S. Air Force)*

1. **Scan the visual.** What immediately draws your attention?

2. **Analyze the visual.** What did you learn by studying the visual section by section?

3. **Question the visual.** Ask and answer the 5 W's and H questions.

   Who is the subject?
   What?
   Where?
   When?
   Why?
   How?

4. **Associate the visual.** What personal associations do you make with the photo?

5. **Interpret the visual.** What conclusions can you make from the photo?

Understanding Symbols

Symbols are special types of visuals. They appear almost everywhere—on clothes and products, in streets and parks, and on television and the Internet. Each one may hold significant meaning. Some give directions and commands. Others represent cultures and beliefs or sell products and ideas.

To critically analyze a symbol, you need to study its surface meaning and make associations with it. You can discover surface meaning by scanning the symbol and analyzing its individual parts. You can make associations by asking and answering the following questions.

Figure 5.8 Apple Inc. Logo

Permission conveyed through Wikimedia Commons.

- How does the symbol make me feel?
- What do I already know about the symbol?
- What ideas do I associate with it?
- How might somebody with a different background, culture, or age from mine view it differently?

Practice ▸ Answer the questions about the symbol in **Figure 5.8**.

- What meaning does the symbol's physical features reveal?

_____

_____

- What do you already know about the symbol?

_____

_____

- What ideas do you associate with it?

_____

_____

- How might somebody whose background, culture, or age differs from yours view the symbol?

_____

_____

Reading Graphics

Graphics feature visual representations of numbers and data. Graphics are a common feature in many of your academic textbooks. They also accompany stories in newspapers, magazines, Web sites, and other media. Knowing how to read graphics and use them effectively is an essential aspect of academic reading and writing.

To understand and evaluate a graphic, you need to closely examine its parts.

- **Scan the graphic.** Consider it as a whole to get an overall idea about its message. Note its type (bar graph, pie graph, diagram, line graph), topic, labels, features, and level of complexity.

- **Study the specific parts.** Start with the main heading or title. Next, note any additional labels or guides (such as the horizontal and vertical guides on a bar graph). Then focus on the actual information displayed in the graphic.

- **Question the graphic.** Does it address an important topic? What is its purpose (to make a comparison, to show a change)? What is the source of the information? Is the graphic out of date or biased in any way?

- **Reflect on its effectiveness.** Explain in your own words the main message of the graphic. Then consider its effectiveness, how it relates to the surrounding text, and how it matches up to your previous knowledge of the topic.

Scan the pie graph in **Figure 5.9**. Then read the discussion to learn how all of the parts work together.

- **Scan and study:** This pie chart represents the division of the United States' energy use in 2013. The heading identifies the topic. The pie as a whole represents all of the U.S.'s energy use. Each slice represents a percentage of energy used in comparison to the whole. The color indicates the type of energy used, and the key shows what energy type each color represents.

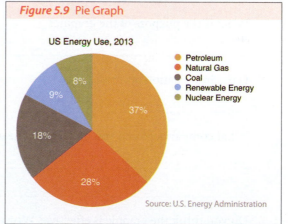

Figure 5.9 Pie Graph

US Energy Use, 2013

- Petroleum
- Natural Gas
- Coal
- Renewable Energy
- Nuclear Energy

37%
28%
18%
9%
8%

Source: U.S. Energy Administration

- **Question:** The graphic addresses a relevant topic—energy sources and their usage. Its purpose is to show the percentage of U.S. energy use per source. The information comes from the U.S. Energy Administration. It is not completely up-to-date since it ends in 2013.

- **Reflect:** By studying the graphic, you can learn that the United States most often uses petroleum. Natural gas and coal are the next two most common energies used.

Practice Read the graphic in **Figure 5.10** and answer the analysis questions about it.

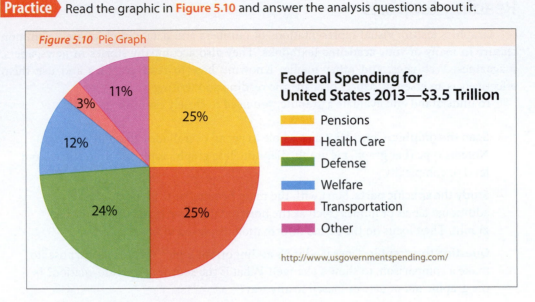

Figure 5.10 Pie Graph

Federal Spending for United States 2013—$3.5 Trillion

- Pensions
- Health Care
- Defense
- Welfare
- Transportation
- Other

http://www.usgovernmentspending.com/

1. What is the topic of **Figure 5.10**?

_____

2. What information do the pie slices represent?

_____

3. What is the purpose of the graphic?

_____

4. Is the information up-to-date?

_____

5. What comparisons can you make from the graphic?

_____

_____

6. Do you think the graphic is effective? Why or why not?

_____

_____

Using Graphics in Writing

Graphics can add value to your academic writing, especially if the topic focuses on numbers or data. Use one of many free software programs to create the graphic of your choice. Four of the most common graphics are line graphs, pie graphs, bar graphs, and diagrams.

Line graphs   Use line graphs when you want to show changes in amounts over time. A line graph starts with an L-shaped grid. Usually the time is represented on the horizontal line (x axis) and the amount on the vertical line (y axis). The middle line tracks data points where the quantity and time intersect. Line graphs are especially effective for displaying trends. (See **Figure 5.11**.)

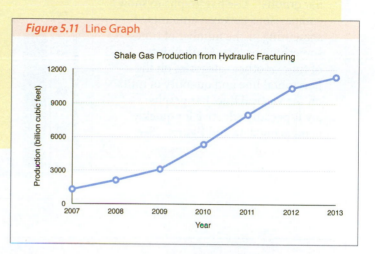

Figure 5.11 Line Graph

Pie graphs   Use pie graphs to show the parts that together make up a whole. Pie graphs should include a manageable number of sections, or slices. Each slice represents a value in comparison to the whole. Pie graphs are especially effective for showing the relative size of one value compared to others. (See **Figure 5.12**.)

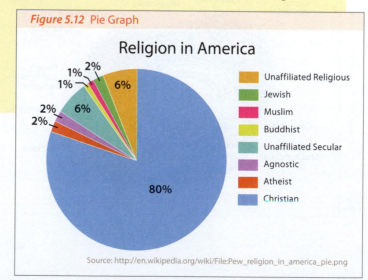

Figure 5.12 Pie Graph

Source: http://en.wikipedia.org/wiki/File:Pew_religion_in_america_pie.png

hywards, 2014 / Used under license from Shutterstock.com

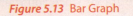

Bar graphs   Use bar graphs to show comparisons between amounts of something or the number of times something occurs. Mark points of time or other categories on the horizontal line and quantity of units on the vertical line. Bar graphs are especially effective for quickly comparing data and figures. (See **Figure 5.13**.)

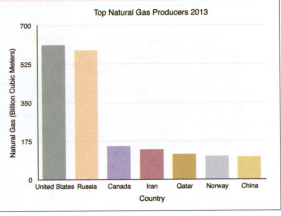

Figure 5.13 Bar Graph

Top Natural Gas Producers 2013

Natural Gas (Billion Cubic Meters)

700
525
350
175
0

United States Russia Canada Iran Qatar Norway China

Country

Designua, 2014 / Used under license from Shutterstock.com

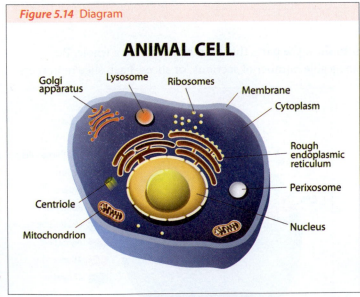

Figure 5.14 Diagram

ANIMAL CELL

Golgi apparatus
Lysosome
Ribosomes
Membrane
Cytoplasm
Rough endoplasmic reticulum
Perixosome
Nucleus
Centriole
Mitochondrion

Diagrams   Use diagrams to show how something is constructed, how its parts relate to one another, or how it works. Make certain to label each part in the diagram. (See **Figure 5.14**.)

☑ Review and Enrichment

Reviewing the Chapter

Apply Different Levels of Thinking

1. According to Benjamin Bloom, what are the six different thinking skills? Rank them in order from surface-level thinking to deep-level thinking.

   _____

2. What are two questions you should be able to answer to show your understanding of a reading or writing task?

   _____

3. What is the difference between *analyzing* and *evaluating* a text?

   _____

4. Name at least two characteristics that you should check for when evaluating a reading or writing text.

   _____

Ask Critical Questions

5. What questioning strategy can you apply to learn the basic information from a reading text?

   _____

6. What are Socratic questions? How are they different from the 5W's and H?

   _____

7. What are assumption questions? What is one example of an assumption question?

   _____

Analyze Visuals Critically

8. What five steps can you follow to critically view an image or photograph?

   _____

9. If you wanted to display a trend or show how something changes through time, what type of graphic might you use?

   _____

10. If you wanted to show the parts of something, what type of graphic might you use?

    _____

"The important thing is to not stop questioning."

—Albert Einstein

Reading for Enrichment

The following reading selection is from *Inc.* online, a magazine focusing on business and technology start-up companies. Be sure to follow the steps in the reading process to help you gain a full understanding of the text.

About the Author

Jessica Stillman is a freelance writer, blogger, and *Inc.* columnist based in London. Stillman's writing focuses on careers, specifically future job markets and generational differences. Her work has been published in a number of business publications such as *Forbes*, *Slate*, and *Business Insider*. She also serves an editor for *Women 2.0*, a technology community aimed at supporting women in the technology careers.

Prereading

1. What do the title, the first paragraph, and the first lines of other paragraphs tell you about the topic?

   _____

2. What do you already know about the topic? What do you want to know about it?

   _____

3. What makes the author qualified to write about this topic?

   _____

4. Turn the title into a series of journalist questions that you can answer when you read.

   _____

   _____

   _____

What do you think?

Reread Albert Einstein's quotation. How can questioning help you think more deeply about what you read and write? What types of questions should you ask of readings?

Reading and Rereading

As you read, make it your goal to analyze and evaluate the text. Consider annotating the text and/or taking notes to help you keep track of the information during your reading.

Also think carefully about your own personality. Do you share any of the traits mentioned in this article? What role does personality serve in leadership? What characteristics do you normally associate with great leaders?

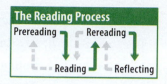

7 Reasons Introverts Make Great Leaders

There's a **paradox** at the heart of how we think about leaders. Ask someone to picture a stereotypical leader and most people will think of someone confident, **brash**, and outgoing—the classic extrovert. But ask a person to think of real-life business visionaries and many of the people they're likely to name, from Bill Gates to Warren Buffet, are textbook examples of introverts.   1

What we expect leaders to be like and the qualities that actually make a leader great are often at odds, in other words. We're **seduced** by **charisma** and overlook the lower-key charms of the quieter folks among us.   2

Which can be a huge mistake. Not only have some studies shown the bottom-line benefits that introverted leaders can provide under the right conditions . . . but expert after expert insists that more introverted personality types come equipped with significant leadership advantages. Here are seven: 3

1. They're better listeners.

"Introverts typically appear to be better listeners," says Karl Moore, a management professor at McGill University. "They wait for others to express their ideas before they jump in with theirs; they don't need to be at the center of every conversation."   4

2. They're better prepared.

Introverts don't wing it, according to Jennifer Kahnweiler, author of the books *The Introverted Leader: Building on Your Quiet Strength* and *Quiet Influence: The Introvert's Guide to Making a Difference*. A PsychCentral post explaining her ideas quotes Kahnweiler: "They spend time thinking through their goals and preparing for questions, which gives them an edge." **5**

3. They go deep.

Kahnweiler further explained the advantages of introverted leaders in a post for *Forbes*, including their propensity to dive deeply into a subject. "Introverted leaders seek depth over breadth," she writes. "They like to dig deep, delving into issues and ideas before moving on to new ones. They are drawn to meaningful conversations, not **superficial** chitchat, and they know how to ask great questions and really listen to the answers." Among other benefits, this in-depth study means "executives can learn what's actually happening in the far reaches of their organizations and engage and retain their top talent." **6**

4. They don't mind solitude . . .

. . . and being alone is essential for reflection, focus, and the formation of deeply considered opinions. "As clinical psychologist Laurie Helgoe states in *Introvert Power: Why Your Inner Life Is Your Hidden Strength*, introverts have an 'internal power—the power to birth fully formed ideas, insights, and solutions,'" explains author Bruna Martinuzzi on American Express OPEN Forum. Quiet time is essential to bring these breakthrough ideas into the world. **7**

"One of the greatest advantages introverts have is their ability to stay focused, where others around them might be distracted," Martinuzzi writes. "They're generally not afraid of solitude, because they know it's fruitful. It gives them opportunities for self-reflection, thinking, theorizing, observing, planning, or imagining. . . . It improves our ability to think."

VasilkovS, 2014 / Used under license from Shutterstock.com

Figure 5.15 Extroverts and Introverts

5. They keep their cool.

To illustrate this point, Martinuzzi quotes Beth Buelow, author of *Insight: Reflections on the Gifts of Being an Introvert*: "My energy tends to be a calming presence, which means I don't take up too much space in a room or conversation. And I don't need to take up a lot of space. I have a greater influence when I am intentional and deliberate in my speech and presence."   8

Martinuzzi and Buelow aren't the only ones noting the calming effect of having an introvert at the top. Kahnweiler agrees, arguing, "Introverted leaders are low key. In times of crisis, they project a reassuring, calm confidence—think President Obama—and they speak softly and slowly regardless of the heat of the conversation or circumstances."   9

6. They don't settle.

Introverts aren't known for their self-satisfaction, notes Rahul Sinha, who rounded up recent findings on introverted leaders for a LinkedIn post. This continual striving for improvement can be a huge benefit in business settings. Introverts, he writes, are "likely to be aware about areas where they need to improve. This type of focus and awareness is very important to the growth of a leader and   10 their team. This will to challenge oneself will motivate teams to do the same by evaluating themselves, their colleagues, and the team to improve."

7. They write more.

It's an old-fashioned skill that's easy to let **atrophy** in our tech-mad world, but strong writing skills usually lead to clear thinking and communication, according to Kahnweiler, so introverts' skill behind the keyboard offers them an advantage.   *11*

"Introverted leaders usually prefer writing to talking," she writes. "This comfort with the written word often helps them better articulate their positions and document their actions. It also helps them leverage online social networking tools such as Twitter, creating new opportunities to be out there with employees, customers, and other stakeholders."   *12*

What have been your experiences working for (or as) an introverted leader?   *13*

introvert
shy or quiet people

paradox
a statement or idea that seems like it should be false or contradictory but may in fact be true

brash
confident and aggressive, oftentimes in a harsh manner

seduced
persuaded

charisma
a charming, inviting, or outgoing personality

superficial
unimportant, surface-level

atrophy
lose or waste away

Summarizing

Write a summary of "7 Reasons Introverts Make Great Leaders." Remember that a summary presents the main points in a clear, concise form using your own words.

Reflecting

1. What is the topic of the reading? What important idea about the topic is the author trying to make?

2. What does **Figure 5.15** show, and how does it relate to the reading?

3. Did your understanding of the topic change after reading this? If so, how did it change?

4. Create a T-chart to list the strengths and weaknesses of the reading.

Vocabulary Practice

Create vocabulary entries for the following words. For each word, identify the pronunciation and helpful word parts, give a primary definition, and use the word in a sentence.

1. **extrovert** (paragraph 1)
2. **solitude** (heading 4)

Critical Thinking

- How could you break this reading into smaller parts to analyze the details?
- Based on your evaluation of the reading, what is your informed opinion of the text? Is it strong or weak? How can you tell?
- In what way did the reading call into question your own values or beliefs?
- How would an extrovert react to this reading? How would an introvert react?
- What information from this reading could help you improve your leadership skills?
- Is the author making any assumptions about leadership in this reading? What are they? How would the reading change if those assumptions were untrue?
- What would happen if all business leaders read this article and assumed the information was true? What changes might happen?

Writing for Enrichment

Prewriting

Choose one of the following writing ideas, or decide upon an idea of your own related to the reading.

1. Write a paragraph that describes three to five ways you would make a great leader.

2. Write a response to "7 Reasons Introverts Make Great Leaders" that makes a case for extroverts in leadership roles.

3. Choose a real-life leader who is described as an introvert. Research the leader. Explain how the leader exhibits some or all of the characteristics from the article.

4. Find an important symbol of leadership. Write a paragraph that describes your associations with this symbol.

5. What does leadership look like? Browse media images of people or events. Choose one photo or illustration that you believe shows leadership. Write an analysis of the image. Make sure to explain why you associate it with leadership.

When planning . . .

- Research your topic as needed to learn about it, taking thorough notes as you go along.
- Establish a thesis for your essay.
- Review your notes for key ideas to support your thesis.
- Decide on the details that you will use to develop these ideas.

When writing . . .

- Include a beginning, a middle, and an ending in your essay.
- Present your thesis in the beginning part.
- Support the thesis in the middle paragraphs.
- If possible, add a graphic to support your thesis.
- Close your essay with final thoughts about your thesis.

When revising and editing . . .

- Carefully review your first draft.
- Ask at least one peer to review your writing as well.
- Improve the content as needed.
- Then edit your revised writing for style and correctness.

PART 2:

Reading and Writing Paragraphs

Part 2: Reading and Writing Paragraphs

Chones, 2014 / Used under license from Shutterstock.com

Chones, 2014 / Used under license from Shutterstock.com

Chapter

6

"Bring ideas in and entertain them royally, for one of them may be king."

—Mark Van Doren

Ideas

You read to learn about the ideas expressed by other people, and you write to share your own ideas or thoughts. All of what you learn and know is based on ideas. Other elements of writing, such as organization and word choice, are important for one reason—to help make ideas clear and easy to follow.

In this chapter, you will learn about paragraphs, which are distinct groups of sentences used to develop ideas. Then you will learn about identifying different types of ideas in your reading, including topics, main ideas, and supporting details. You will also learn about developing topic sentences, using supporting details, and creating closing sentences for your own paragraphs.

Learning Outcomes

L01 Understand paragraphs.
L02 Read for topics.
L03 Select a topic for writing.
L04 Read for main ideas.
L05 Establish a main idea for writing.
L06 Read for supporting details.
L07 Choose supporting details in writing.
L08 Close a paragraph.

What do you think?

In the quote, Van Doren says he entertains ideas royally when he's writing. Why does he treat ideas in a special way?

L01 Understanding Paragraphs

A paragraph is a group of sentences that work together to develop and support an idea about a particular topic (person, place, object, or idea). It usually begins with a **topic sentence** that identifies the topic and focus of the writing. Sentences in the **body** or middle part of a paragraph explain or support the topic. A **closing sentence** completes a paragraph by making a final statement about the topic. **Figure 6.1** shows the three parts of a paragraph.

Figure 6.1 Parts of a Paragraph

Topic sentence:	Names the topic and focus
Body sentences:	Explain or support the topic
Closing sentence:	Makes a final statement about the topic

Each sentence in a paragraph should relate to the topic so that the paragraph forms one unified unit of thought. As you read this paragraph, you will see that the three main parts are labeled. The paragraph is unified because all of the ideas are related to a specific topic.

Communicating by Braille

Topic sentence

Braille is a system of communication used by the blind. It was developed by Louis Braille, a blind French student, in 1824. The code consists of an alphabet using combinations of small raised dots. The dots are imprinted on paper and can be felt, and thus read, by running *Body sentences* the fingers across the page. The basic unit of the code is called a "cell," which is two dots wide and three dots high. Each letter is formed by different combinations of these dots. Numbers, punctuation marks, and even a system for writing music are also expressed by using different arrangements. These small dots, which may seem insignificant to the *Closing sentence* sighted, have opened up the entire world of books and reading for the blind.

Occasionally, the topic sentence appears at the end of a paragraph, in the form of a summary statement. This is the case in the following paragraph about community service.

Serving to Learn

Body sentences

Community service teaches basic job skills such as being on time and completing tasks. Volunteer Anna Hernandez said, "The residence expected me to be there at 3:00 when the board games started." Community service also helps students appreciate the problems facing Burlington. Scott Thompson, part of a clean-up crew, never realized how thoughtless people can be until he started cleaning up after them. As he stated, "Some people really trash the parks." Most importantly, community service teaches the value of giving back. According to Ms. Sandra Williams, the community service advisor, "Working in the community shows students that a lot of people need help."

Summary statement

Essentially then, community service gives students a taste of real life at just the right time.

Types of Paragraphs

- A **narrative paragraph** shares an experience. A strong narrative paragraph answers *who? what? when? where?* and *why?* about the experience. In this paragraph from the autobiography *Gifted Hands*, Dr. Ben Carson shares a hurtful experience from his adolescence.

Topic sentence

A second, more shocking episode of racial prejudice occurred when I was in eighth grade.

Body sentences

At the end of each school year the principal and teachers handed out certificates to the one student who had the highest academic achievement in seventh, eighth, and ninth grades respectively. I won the certificate in the seventh grade, and that same year Curtis won for the ninth grade. By the end of eighth grade, people had pretty much come to accept the fact that I was a smart kid. I won the certificate again the following year. At the all-school assembly one of the teachers presented my certificate. After handing it to me, she remained up in front of the entire student body and looked out across the auditorium. "I have a few words I want to say right now," she began, her voice unusually high. Then, to my embarrassment, she bawled out the White kids because they had allowed me to be number one. "You're not trying hard enough," she told them.

Closing sentence

While she never quite said it in words, she let them know that a Black person shouldn't be number one in a class where everyone else was White.   Excerpted from *Gifted Hands* by Dr. Benjamin Carson. Copyright 1990 by Review and Herald (R) Publishing Association.

■ A **descriptive paragraph** presents a clear picture of a person, a place, a thing, or an idea. The descriptive details in this paragraph help the reader visualize or see the topic.

Topic sentence

The **Don Quixote** figure in my room is certainly odd looking. It is a small plaster statue of an old man in battered armor sitting on a broken-down horse. The helmet on Quixote's head is dented, and its visor is bent. In the opening, a face appears with squinting eyes, a wide wedge of a nose, and a wild mustache and beard. His breastplate and shield are so worn that whatever marks or emblems they once held have been lost. The statue contains many visible cracks where it has been glued back together after being knocked over. A bit of electrician's tape keeps Quixote's bent lance attached to the rest of the statue. Despite these repairs, he still stares ahead

Body sentences

Closing sentence

with a look of hope. And even though the object now looks pretty bad, it will stay on display for a while longer.

Don Quixote (ke-ho'-te)
the hero in a Spanish novel of the same name; a fumbling knight battling life's injustices but failing

■ An **expository paragraph** explains, discusses, compares, defines, classifies, or illustrates. In this paragraph from an environmental textbook, the writers discuss the history and current status of the Colorado River as a water resource.

Topic sentence

The Colorado River, the major river of the **arid** southwestern United States, flows 2,300 kilometers (1,400 miles) through seven states to the Gulf of California. Most of its water comes from snowmelt in the Rocky Mountains. During the past 50 years, this once free-flowing river has been tamed by a gigantic plumbing system consisting of 14 major dams and **reservoirs**, and canals that supply water to farmers, ranchers, industries, and cities. This system provides water and electricity from hydroelectric plants at the major dams for roughly 30 million people—about one of every ten people in the United States. The river's water is used to produce about 15% of the nation's crops and livestock. It also supplies water to some of the nation's driest and hottest cities. Take away this tamed river and Las Vegas, Nevada, would be mostly **uninhabitable** desert area; San Diego and Los Angeles, California, could not support their present populations.

Body sentences

Closing sentence

From *Living in the Environment*, 17E. © 2012 Cengage Learning.

---

arid
very dry

reservoirs
areas where water is collected

uninhabitable
not capable of being lived in

■ An **argument paragraph** supports an opinion or claim with strong details. In this paragraph, the writer supports her opinion that text messaging while driving should be banned nationwide. (The sources of information are indicated within the parentheses.)

Topic sentence | Text messaging while driving should be banned in all states. Car crashes rank among the leading causes of death in the United States, but many people blame alcohol and ignore the dangers of texting while driving. Studies by the National Highway Traffic Safety Administration show that text messaging while driving is about six times more likely to result in an accident than drunk driving (Pennsylvania Truck Accident Lawyers). And according to the Human Factors and **Ergonomics** Society, mobile devices contribute to 2,600 deaths and 330,000 injuries per year ("The Use of Cell Phones"). Some critics say teenage drivers are the problem, but 20 percent of adults in a recent **AAA** study admitted to regularly sending text messages while driving ("Text Messaging"). At least 34 states and the District of Columbia have banned texting while driving. Let's ban text messaging in all the states.

Body sentences

Closing sentence

---

ergonomics
the science of the design of things to make them safe and easy to use

AAA
American Automobile Association

Practice ▶ Label the three main parts of this paragraph. Then identify the type of paragraph.

Defying Gravity

Unlike race cars or trains, roller coasters do not rely on powerful engines for speed. Instead, roller coasters let gravity do much of the work. (Gravity is the force that constantly pulls objects of mass toward the ground.) When a roller-coaster track slopes down, the passenger cars accelerate forward because gravity pulls the front car downward. When the track tilts up, the cars decelerate because gravity pulls the back car downward. But gravity is not the only factor in maintaining speed. Another factor is momentum. On most roller coasters, the first drop is the tallest and steepest. Coasters are designed this way to create enough momentum to carry them forward through the rest of the track. Momentum is especially needed to make it up hills and through loops as gravity pulls the cars in the opposite direction. This tug-of-war between gravity and momentum makes for exciting rides.

■ Circle the type of paragraph: *narrative*   *expository*   *argument*

> "Understanding a paragraph is like solving a problem in mathematics. It consists of selecting the right elements of the situation and putting them together in the right relations."
>
> —Edward Thorndike

LO2 Reading for Topics

A paragraph, an essay, and any other reading selection centers around a **topic**. A topic may be a specific person (*Pope Francis*), a place (*the White House*), an object (*a vinyl record*), or an idea (*opportunity*). Identifying the topic is the important first step when carrying out a reading assignment. The topic is often stated in the title or first sentence in a paragraph or in the title or first paragraph in an essay.

Steps to Follow

 1 For paragraphs, read the title and first sentence. If you're still not sure, check the closing sentence, too.

 2 For essays, read the title, any additional headings, and the first paragraph. If you're still not sure, read the first sentences of the first few paragraphs.

Topic Stated in the Title and First Sentence

The Black Death

The **Black Death** of the mid- and late fourteenth century is the most massive epidemic on record and by far the most **lethal** in the history of Europe, Asia, and parts of Africa. What was it, and why did it deal such a blow to Old World populations? Until recently, scholars thought that it was a form of bubonic plague common in the Asian **steppes** but previously unknown to Europeans. Most believed that fleas living on rats spread the plague *Bacillus*, and the rats were then (as now) found everywhere humans lived. However, this theory has come under attack. Some now think that the Black Death was a form of **anthrax** or even an Ebola-like fever.   From Adler/Pouwels, *World Civilizations*, 6E. © 2012 Cengage Learning

Elnur, 2014 / Used under license from Shutterstock.com

---

lethal
deadly

steppes
a large, flat area of grassland

anthrax
a deadly disease of livestock, transmitted to humans

Topic Stated in the First Sentence of a Paragraph

In the Right Direction

The National Football League (NFL) has **new safety measures** in place to deal with head injuries. First of all, the league has improved its baseline testing for players who suffer head injuries during a game. Before being allowed to re-enter a game, an injured player must pass a six- to eight-minute test that measures memory, balance, and concentration. The NFL is also limiting full-time contact practices so players have less time to bang their heads. In addition, the league is imposing stricter fines and penalties for illegal helmet-to-helmet hits during a game. It will be interesting to see what additional safety measures will come in the future.

Topic Stated at the End of the First Paragraph in an Essay

On the Streets

On a chilly February afternoon, an old man stands on a city sidewalk and leans against the fence. In his hands a sign reads: "Will work for food. Please help!" Imagine, for a moment, the life this man leads. He probably spends his days alone on the street begging for handouts and his nights searching for shelter from the cold. He has no job, no friends, and nowhere to turn. Some Americans would like to believe that cases like this are rare. However, the National Coalition for the Homeless estimates that as many as three million people in this country share this man's condition. To understand this problem, it's important to understand the factors than contribute to **homelessness**.

According to Pastor Martin Walker, the director of the Gospel Missions Shelter in Sioux City, Iowa, most homeless are unemployed males, and from 40 to 50 percent have alcohol- or drug-related problems. Walker is quick to note, however, that the image of the "typical" homeless person is changing. . . .

People are on the streets despite the billions of dollars that are spent on them. Some blame the national housing shortage, arguing that the 2 percent vacancy is not great enough to fill the country's need for shelter. . . .

Practice ▸ Identify the topic in each of the following texts by circling the correct choice. Then write where the topic is first stated.

1.   The Growth of Franchising

Franchising, which began in the United States around the time of the Civil War, was used originally by large firms such as the Singer Sewing Company to distribute their products. Franchising has been increasing steadily in popularity since the early 1900s, primarily for filling stations and car dealerships; however, this retailing strategy has experienced enormous growth since the mid-1970s. The franchise **proliferation** generally has paralleled the expansion of the fast-food industry. Three of *Entrepreneur* magazine's top-rated franchises for 2010 were in this category.

---

franchising
business relationship in which one party has a license to sell the product of another party

proliferation
great growth

a. the first franchise

b. the history of franchising

c. the growth of franchising

---

2.   The sheriff is a very important figure in American law enforcement. Almost every one of the more than 3,000 counties in the United States (except those in Alaska) has a sheriff. In every state except Rhode Island and Hawaii, sheriffs are elected by members of the community for two- or four-year terms and are paid a salary set by the state legislature or county board. As elected officials who do not necessarily need a background in law enforcement, modern sheriffs resemble their counterparts from the political era of policing in many ways. Simply stated, the sheriff is also a politician.

From GAINES/MILLER, Cengage Advantage Books: *Criminal Justice in Action*, 6E. © 2011 Cengage Learning

a. American law enforcement

b. sheriffs in law enforcement

c. politicians

3.

Improving Our Society

Former First Ladies Eleanor Roosevelt and Barbara Bush shared a concern for social change. Eleanor, wife of Democratic President Franklin Roosevelt, lectured about youth unemployment and supported the National Youth Administration, a program that found jobs for young people. Barbara, wife of Republican President George H. Bush, helped young people by starting reading programs for children throughout the United States and establishing the Barbara Bush Foundation for Family Literacy. In addition, Eleanor promoted racial equality and chaired the commission that drafted the Universal Declaration of Human Rights. For her part, Barbara promoted better health care, raised money for cancer research, and helped the homeless. Both women used their positions to improve our society.

a. Eleanor Roosevelt

b. Eleanor Roosevelt and Barbara Bush

c. Barbara Bush

4.

Movies

Today the center of the movie industry is movie production. Independent companies produce most of the movies that are distributed by the major studios and exhibited at your local theater. Although these production companies work independently, and each company is organized differently, jobs in movie production fall mainly into six categories.

Every movie begins with a story idea, and these ideas come from screenwriters. Screenwriters work independently, marketing their story ideas through agents, who promote their clients' scripts to the studios and to independent producers. . . .

Producers are the people who help gather the funding to create a movie project. . . .

a. jobs in movie production

b. popularity of movies

c. movie producers

L03 Selecting a Topic for Writing

Just as a chef needs ingredients to cook a meal, a writer needs good ideas to develop a piece of writing, starting with the topic. When you begin a writing assignment, try to select a topic that attracts you. Otherwise, you will have a hard time developing your writing. Your choices may be limited for some of your assignments. Even so, do your best to select an interesting topic.

"There are few experiences quite so satisfactory as getting a good idea. You're pleased with it and feel good."

—Lancelot Law Whyte

Choosing a Topic

Most writing assignments identify a general subject area, and you must find a specific writing idea related to this subject. A topic for a paragraph, of course, should be more limited than a topic for an essay or report. For example, a topic such as *hunger* would be too broad for a paragraph, whereas *the need for more food banks* would be more suitable. **Figure 6.2** shows how the selecting process should work, moving from a general subject area to a specific topic.

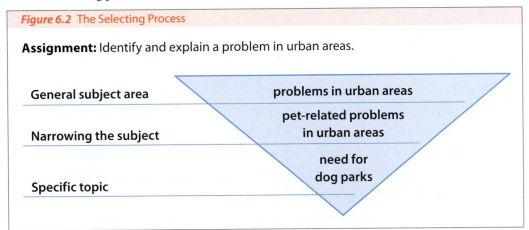

Figure 6.2 The Selecting Process

Assignment: Identify and explain a problem in urban areas.

General subject area — problems in urban areas

Narrowing the subject — pet-related problems in urban areas

Specific topic — need for dog parks

Practice ▸ Identify a specific topic for the following assignment. (Use **Figure 6.2** as a guide.)

Assignment: Argue for a solution to a problem in your community.

1. General subject area
2. Narrow the subject
3. Specific topic

Searching Strategies

If you can't think of a good topic, review your class notes, your textbook, and the Web for ideas. You may also want to try one of these searching strategies.

- **Listing:** Freely list ideas as you think about your writing assignment. Keep going as long as you can. Then review your list for possible topics.
- **Clustering:** Begin a cluster (or web) with the general subject area or an important word related to the assignment. Circle it and then cluster related words around it. As you continue, you will come up with possible writing ideas. See **Figure 6.3**.

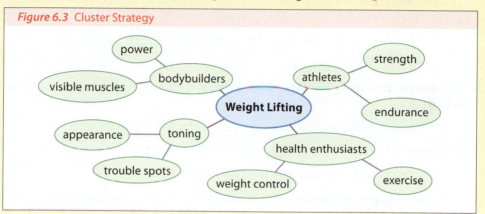

Figure 6.3 Cluster Strategy

- **Freewriting:** Discover possible topics by writing nonstop for five minutes about your assignment.

  - Begin with an idea related to the assignment. (*"I work at a fitness center and see a lot of weight lifters. . . ."*)
  - Don't stop to judge, edit, or correct your writing. You are just searching for possible writing ideas.
  - Stick with one idea as long as you can. Then go on to something else.
  - Afterward, underline any words or phrases that could serve as possible writing ideas.

Practice Use freewriting to identify possible writing topics related to one of the following general subject areas:

exercise   careers

popular music   technology

L04 Reading for Main Ideas

Almost everything you read—be it a paragraph, an essay, or a textbook chapter—develops a **main idea**. This idea is usually stated in the topic sentence in a paragraph and in a thesis statement in longer texts. There are times, however, when the main idea comes later, perhaps in a closing sentence or ending part of a text. You may also read a few texts in which the main idea is implied rather than stated directly. The main idea tells you what the reading is about.

- In a **narrative text**, the main idea often tells you how a writer feels about his or her topic, which will be an experience or event.

  > My final moments on stage during the musical *Grease* are ones I'll never forget.

- In an **expository text**, the main idea may tell you what part of the topic the writer will focus on.

  > Medical reports about the Ebola virus strike fear into many people.

  Or it may indicate a pattern of organization (*process, comparison*, etc.).

  > The prevention of flood damage is a four-step process.

- In an **argument text**, the main idea identifies the claim or opinion that the writer will argue for.

  > If United States senators had term limits, they would better serve the American people.

The following steps will help you identify the main idea in a longer text such as an essay or a textbook chapter.

1 Skim the title and any headings in the reading selection.

2 Then read the opening paragraph or few paragraphs.

3 In the opening, look for a sentence that seems to direct the reading. Often, this sentence appears at the end of the first or second paragraph.

4 Then, as you continue to read, see if this statement makes sense as the main idea. Each new paragraph should explain or support it.

5 If your thinking changes, identify what you now consider to be the main idea.

Topic Sentences and Thesis Statements

A topic sentence identifies the main idea of a paragraph, and a thesis statement identifies the main idea of a longer work. A topic sentence or thesis statement usually has two parts: (1) a specific topic and (2) a special feature, part, or feeling about the topic.

> Captain Chesley Sullenberger (*topic*) performed an emergency landing in the Hudson River (*feature*).
>
> ---
>
> A nationwide investment in wind power (*topic*) will reduce our need for fossil fuel (*feeling*).

The following paragraph from a psychology textbook explains common techniques for disciplining children. Read the paragraph and the explanation that follows.

Discipline

Parents typically discipline children in one of three ways. Power **assertion** refers to physical punishment or a show of force, such as taking away toys or privileges. As an alternative, some parents withhold affection by refusing to speak to a child, threatening to leave, or otherwise acting as if the child is temporarily unlovable. Management techniques combine praise, recognition, approval, rules, reasoning, and the like to encourage **desirable** behavior. Each of these approaches can control a child's behavior, but their side effects differ considerably.

From Coon/Mitterer, *Psychology: A Journey*, 4E, © 2011 Cengage Learning.

---

assertion
the act of forcefully exercising authority

desirable
positive, pleasing

Explanation: The topic sentence identifies the topic (*disciplining children*) and an important feature about it (*carried out in one of three ways*). The sentences in the body identify the three ways to discipline children.

The following paragraph from a health textbook discusses the value of forgiving. Study the paragraph and then read the explanation that follows.

The Three Most Difficult Words

While "I forgive you" may be three of the most difficult words to say, they are also three of the most powerful. The word *forgive* comes from the Greek for "letting go," and that's what happens when you forgive: You let go of all the anger and pain that have been demanding your time and wasting your energy. To some people, forgiveness seems a sign of weakness or **submission**. People may feel more in control, more powerful, when they're filled with anger, but forgiving **instills** a much greater sense of power. . . . When you forgive, you *reclaim* the power to choose. It doesn't matter whether someone deserves to be forgiven; you deserve to be free. However, forgiveness isn't easy. It's not a one-time thing but a process that takes a lot of time and work.   From Hales, *An Invitation to Health*, 7E, © 2012 Cengage Learning.

---

submission
yielding to authority or superior force

instills
provides, fills [something] with

Explanation: The topic sentence identifies the topic (*saying "I forgive you"*) and a feeling about it (*is difficult but powerful*). The sentences in the body explain the topic sentence.

This opening in a section from a sociology textbook discusses clothing as a status symbol. The brief opening paragraph and the first sentence of the next three paragraphs are included. Read the selection and the explanation that follows.

Status and Style

Often rich people engage in **conspicuous** displays of **consumption**, waste, and leisure not because they are necessary, useful, or pleasurable but simply to impress their peers and inferiors. This is evident if we consider how clothing acts as a sort of language that signals one's status to others (Lurie, 1981).

For thousands of years, certain clothing styles have indicated rank. In ancient Egypt, only people in high positions were allowed to wear sandals. . . .

European laws governing the dress styles of different groups fell into disuse after about 1700. That is because a new method of control emerged as Europe became wealthier. . . .

Today we have different ways of using clothes to signal status. Designer labels loudly proclaim the dollar value of garments. . . .

From Brym/Lie, *Sociology: Your Compass for a New World*, 2E, © 2007 Cengage Learning.

---

conspicuous
easy to notice

consumption
the act or process of buying

Explanation: In this selection, multiple paragraphs are needed to explore the main idea. Therefore, the main idea is located in a thesis statement, which appears at the end of the first paragraph. The thesis statement identifies the topic (*clothing*) and special feature about it (*acts as a language that signals status*). The first sentences in the next three paragraphs show that the thesis statement will be developed.

Practice Identify the topic sentence or thesis statement in the next three reading selections. Then name (1) the topic and (2) the special feature, part, or feeling about it.

1. What Is Social Media?

Social media is not an easy concept to define. The word *social* has to do with human interaction, and the word *media* means "systems of communication." Together, these words seem easy enough to understand as "human systems of communication." But *social media* most often refers to electronic communications, which include text messages, selfies, and maybe short videos for friends. People also use social media as a form of self-expression. A person who is having a bad day can mention it online, and friends can help him or her deal with it. In fact, Lee Rainie of the Pew Research Center says, "Social media is a rich environment for learning and sharing of important material." So the best definition of *social media* may be "a diverse, digital form of conversation."

Topic sentence: _____

Two parts: _____

_____

2. Understanding the Arrow of Time

The arrow of time always flies forward, never backward, but why? For a long while, the standard answer was **entropy**. Entropy states that within a closed system, matter and energy tend to go from states of order to states of disorder. Think of an abandoned home. After a few years, it begins to decay and revert to dust. You can't turn time back to get the home you once had. But on a large scale, the universe has gone from a very disordered state to a very ordered one. A universe of pure energy at the **Big Bang** is much less ordered than our current universe with stars, planets, and galaxies. Gravity has created complexity that can't be reversed. So, on a small scale like a house, entropy may keep time going forward, but on a universal scale, time may be driven by creation of order.

entropy
moving toward disorder

Big Bang
the birth of the universe

Topic sentence: _____

Two parts: _____

_____

3.   Diverse Eating

Whatever your cultural heritage, you have probably sampled Chinese, Mexican, Indian, Italian, and Japanese foods. If you belong to any of these ethnic groups, you may eat these **cuisines** regularly. Each type of ethnic cooking has its own nutritional benefits and potential drawbacks.

Mediterranean Diet

Several years ago **epidemiologists** noticed something unexpected in the residents of regions along the Mediterranean Sea: a lower incidence of deaths from heart disease. . . .

Ethnic Cuisines

The cuisine served in Mexico features rice, corn, and beans, which are low in fat and high in nutrition. However, the dishes Americans think of as Mexican are far less healthful. . . .

African American cuisine traces some of its roots to food preferences from west Africa (for example, peanuts, okra, and black-eyed peas). . . .

The mainland Chinese diet, which is plant-based, high in carbohydrates, and low in fats and animal protein, is considered one of the most healthful in the world. . . .

Many Indian dishes highlight healthful ingredients such as vegetables and legumes (beans and peas). However, many also use ghee (a form of butter) or coconut oil; both are rich in saturated fats. . . .

From Hales, *An Invitation to Health*, 7E, © 2012 Cengage Learning.

Subbotina Anna, 2014 / Used under license from Shutterstock.com

---

cuisines
manners or styles of preparing food

epidemiologists
medical professionals who study the causes and control of diseases

Thesis statement: _____

Two parts: _____

_____

Implied Main Ideas

There are times when the main idea is implied or not directly stated. You will know this is the case if no particular sentence directs or controls the writing. When this happens, follow these steps:

1   Identify the topic.

2   Pay close attention to each set of details.

3   Write down the important idea that covers all of the details.

4   Read the text again to make sure that this idea covers the details.

5   Revise your statement of the important idea as needed.

This paragraph is about families, but the main idea about this topic is not stated. Read the paragraph and then see below how the implied main idea is identified.

> Early on, many Americans lived on family farms clustered around small towns and villages. These farm families consisted of parents, children, and grandparents all living under one roof. As industry grew, people began to move from family farms to cities to work in factories and offices. With this move, the "nuclear family"—composed of a father, a mother, and children—was born. When the children of these families reached working age, they moved out to start their own nuclear families. Today, in the Information Age, the nature of work is changing again, and so are the families. Many adult children are living at home with their parents, just as in the past.

Topic: _work and family life_

Key details: _farm life meant big families, industry meant nuclear families, Information Age means bigger families again_

Idea that covers the details: _Work has changed the makeup of families._

Implied main idea: _In our history, the way people work has affected the family unit._

Practice Read the following paragraphs. Then identify the implied idea by filling in the chart that follows.

1.   Some parts of the brain produce thoughts, some parts process thoughts, and some parts store thoughts. Some parts of the brain produce the thinking that we are best known for: **reflecting**. Other parts coordinate reflexes as well as automatic functions of the body. The parts most important for survival, the brain stem and **medulla**, are housed deep inside masses of brain tissue. At any given time, the brain may be working on several levels, including **conscious** thinking, memory, physical motion, and imagination. Sometimes the parts work together, and sometimes they are in conflict.

reflecting	**medulla**	**conscious**
thinking seriously	lowest part of brain	awake and able to understand

Topic: _____

Key details: _____

Idea that covers the details: _____

Implied main idea: _____

2.   In the United States, Mara Salvatrucha (MS-13) has about 10,000 members. The FBI has set up a task force to deal with this gang. U.S. immigration officials routinely deport members back to their home countries in Central America. One of these countries, El Salvador, has responded to the influx of violent gang members with strict anti-gang legislation. These laws make it easier for police to detain suspects who show certain characteristics, such as having gang tattoos or hanging out in known gang areas. Still, several years ago, MS-13 members fired on two crowded buses in San Salvador, killing 17 people and outraging many people. Under a new law, just belonging to a gang is punishable by four to six years in prison, even if no other criminal activity is proved.   From Gaines/Miller, *Criminal Justice in Action*, 6E, ©2011 Cengage Learning

Topic: _____

Key details: _____

Idea that covers the details: _____

Implied main idea: _____

L05 Establishing a Main Idea for Writing

To write about a topic, you need to gather plenty of information. Some of this information will come from your own thoughts about the topic. Other ideas will come from reading and learning about the topic.

Brainstorming Ideas

These brainstorming ideas will help you identify what you already know about a topic.

- **Five W's of Writing:** Answer the five W's (*who? what? when? where?* and *why?*) to identify basic information about your topic. Add *how?* to the list for more coverage.
- **Listing:** List your first thoughts about your topic as well as questions about it. Record ideas nonstop for as long as you can.
- **Clustering:** Begin the cluster with your topic. Cluster related ideas around it. See **Figure 6.4**.

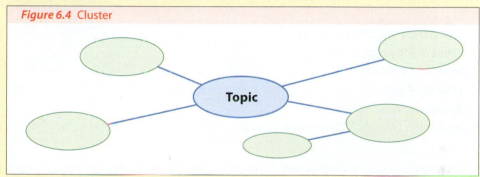

Figure 6.4 Cluster

Topic

- **Focused Freewriting:** Write freely about your specific topic for at least five minutes to see what thoughts and feelings you can uncover. Keep writing for as long as you can.
- **Dialoguing:** Discuss your specific topic in a creative dialogue between you and another person of your choice.

Practice Using one of these strategies, collect your thoughts about a topic you've already identified or one of the topics listed here.

- a person you admire
- a memorable experience
- something needed in your community, school, or workplace

> "To write about people you have to know people, to write about bloodhounds you have to know bloodhounds, to write about the Loch Ness monster you have to find out about it."
>
> —James Thurber

For most writing assignments, your own thoughts will not be enough. You will need to collect additional information by reading, by observing, and by discussing your topic with other people.

Questioning

Questions can guide your search for additional information about a topic. For example, you can answer the 5 W and H questions about the particular event or experience that you are writing about. See **Figure 6.5**.

Figure 6.5 The 5 W and H Questions

- **When** did the event take place?
- **What** exactly happened?
- **Who** was involved?
- **Why** did it occur?
- **Where** did it take place?
- **How** did it turn out? (Were there any problems?)

You can also explore a topic from different viewpoints by answering questions that help you see and think about it in different ways. See **Figure 6.6**.

Figure 6.6 Differing Viewpoint Questions

- What parts does my topic have? (*Break it down.*)
- What do I see, hear, or feel when I think about my topic? (*Describe it.*)
- What is it similar to and different from? (*Compare it.*)
- What value does it have? (*Evaluate it.*)
- How useful is it? (*Apply or use it.*)

Practice Discover more about your topic from the previous activity by using one of these questioning strategies to answer at least three questions.

Choosing a Focus

You must identify a focus for your writing so you know what information to include and in what order. Suppose you are writing about land preservation. There are many things that you could say about this topic, perhaps too many, so you would need to select a specific focus for your writing. For example, you could address the national park system, and your opinion about the economic impact of the system could serve as the focus for your writing.

- **Topic:** *land preservation*
- **Focus:** *economic impact of the national park system*

Without a clear focus, a piece of writing will go in all directions and confuse the reader. For example, trying to describe everything about your current job may be too much for one piece of writing. Focusing on what you like best and/or worst about the job would be much more manageable.

Practice Rate the quality of each focus below by circling the proper star. To make your rating, decide if the focus is clear, reasonable, and worth writing about it. Explain your choices.

1. **Topic:** Sports drinks | **Focus:** The best choice for long workouts

   weak ★ ★ ★ ★ ★ strong _____

   _____

2. **Topic:** Google | **Focus:** Headquartered in Mountain View, California

   weak ★ ★ ★ ★ ★ strong _____

   _____

3. **Topic:** Recreational fishing | **Focus:** My favorite hobby

   weak ★ ★ ★ ★ ★ strong _____

   _____

4. **Topic:** Food trucks | **Focus:** Steps to start your own food truck business

   weak ★ ★ ★ ★ ★ strong _____

   _____

Practice Review the information that you have collected so far about a topic. Then identify a focus that could be the main idea of a paragraph.

   Topic: _____

   Focus: _____

Forming a Topic Sentence

A topic sentence is the controlling idea in a paragraph. The following formula can be used to write a topic sentence. (This same formula can be used to write a thesis statement, which is the controlling idea in a longer work.)

A specific topic		**a special feeling, feature, or part about it**		**a strong topic sentence**
Electronic textbooks	**+**	benefit students with disabilities	**=**	Electronic textbooks benefit students with disabilities.

Practice Write a focus and topic sentence for each of the following writing assignments.

1. **Writing Assignment:** Explain how to perform a particular task
   Specific Topic: Using chopsticks

   Focus: _____

   Topic Sentence: _____

2. **Writing Assignment:** Reflect on a social issue
   Specific Topic: Minimum wage

   Focus: _____

   Topic Sentence: _____

3. **Writing Assignment:** Describe a specific style of clothing
   Specific Topic: (Your Choice)

   Focus: _____

   Topic Sentence: _____

Practice Write a topic sentence that states the focus or main idea about your topic from the previous activities. Use the formula (a specific topic + a special feature, part, or feeling) to help you form this sentence.

Specific Topic: _____

Focus: _____

Topic Sentence: _____

_____

"The greatest gift we can give to others is a good example."

—Thomas Morrell

L06 Reading for Supporting Details

The focus or main idea usually appears near the beginning of a reading selection, and it directs the rest of the text. The supporting details explain or develop the main idea, and they are located in the body or main part of the text. The effectiveness of a text depends on the quality of the supporting details. To gain a complete understanding of a reading assignment, you need to identify and understand the supporting information.

Recognizing Types of Details

The following types of supporting details are commonly used in informational reading selections. The examples come from an article about the Crazy Horse Memorial in South Dakota. A reading selection may combine any of these types of details.

- **Facts and statistics** provide data to support a main idea.

  The head of Crazy Horse will be 87 feet high, which is 20 feet higher than any of the heads of the presidents at Mount Rushmore.

- **Explanations** give information to clarify a main idea.

  There is no verifiable photograph of Crazy Horse. What will be captured in the carving is the spirit of this man.

- **Examples** relate specific instances or occurrences to illustrate the main idea.

  Crazy Horse was that last leader to surrender to the U.S. military, and he did so because the people who followed him were suffering so much. *(This example shows that Crazy Horse tried to stay true to the Lakota ways of life as long as he could.)*

- **Definitions** explain unfamiliar or complex terms.

  The Crazy Horse Memorial will also act as a repository, or museum, of Native American arts and crafts.

- **Descriptions** or **observations** show how something or someone appears.

  Crazy Horse will be seen leaning over his horse's head, pointing his left hand toward his sacred lands.

■ **Reasons** answer the question "Why?"

> Crazy Horse is being memorialized because he was known as a courageous fighter, a humble man, a giver and provider, and someone true to the Lakota way of life.

■ **Quotations** share the specific thoughts of people knowledgeable about the main idea.

> "The development of this memorial is not without controversy. For example, descendants of Crazy Horse feel that the family wasn't properly consulted at the outset of the project," stated local historian Marcie Smith.

■ **Reflections** offer the writer's personal thoughts and feelings.

> Because of Crazy Horse's private nature, one can only assume that he would have had little interest in such a memorial.

■ **Analysis** shows the writer's critical thinking about the topic.

> The memorial seems like a good idea, a way to honor a great man. Unfortunately, it is also a reminder of the difficult history of Native Americans.

Practice ▸ Identify the type or types of supporting details that are underlined. The first one is done for you.

1. By the 1800s, there were believed to be between 3,000 and 5,000 wolves living in the state (Wydeven). Around the same time, many European settlers arrived in the area.

   fact/statistic

2. When I was in first grade, our circus field trip was one huge disappointment. First of all, I couldn't see much of anything because we were sitting in one of the last rows. I could barely make out tiny figures scurrying around the three rings.

3. Rent control is a main factor in determining the number of homeless people a city will have. For example, the number of homeless in high-rent Santa Monica, California, is so great that the city has been called "The Homeless Capital of the West Coast."

4. Since Asian carp present so many dangers, it is clear that the shipping canal must be closed so the species does not enter Lake Michigan. The cost of the closure is estimated at $3.2 billion and could take six years, but it provides a permanent solution.

_____

5. Webster's defines "eclectic" (i-klek´-tik) as selecting elements from different sources or systems. *Eclectic* suggests variety. But what a great way to say variety. Variety sounds so plain, so Brand X. But *eclectic* is rich with imagination.

_____

6. She placed my hand under the spout, and spelled into the other the word "water." The living word awakened my soul, gave it light, hope, joy, set it free. There were barriers still, but they were barriers that could, in time, be swept away.

—Helen Keller

_____

Details in Context

The types of details used by writers depends on the nature of the reading selection. **Figure 6.7** shows the types of details often used for three common types of readings.

Figure 6.7 Using Details

Writing Assignments	Types of Details
Narrative texts	explanations, descriptions, reasons, reflections
Expository texts	facts and statistics, explanations, examples, analysis
Argumentation texts	facts and statistics, explanations, examples, reasons, quotations, analysis

The number of details writers include vary as well. At times, an author may concentrate on one main type of detail. For example, in a narrative, an author may find it sufficient to simply describe an experience because the descriptive details speak for themselves. In expository or argumentation texts, an author may find it necessary to include three or four different types of details to effectively support the main idea.

Some types of details naturally work together. For instance, an explanation often needs examples, facts and statistics often require analysis, and a quotation can often use an explanation. These passages show how details can work together. (The main idea is underlined in each one.)

A banyan tree is not the largest tree in the world, but it is certainly the most complicated. A banyan tree's life begins when birds drop the banyan seeds onto branches of host trees. The seeds soon sprout, sending long rope-like shoots from the branches downward to root in the soil. These shoots gradually thicken into hundreds of trunks or exposed roots, and they can eventually cover the host tree. The largest banyan tree is found in India. In the United States, the largest tree, located in the state of Hawaii, covers two-thirds of an acre. Thomas Edison planted the first banyan tree on the main land; it now covers 400 feet.

Explanation

Examples

Men and women are very different in the way they speak, behave, solve problems, and even remember. Many scientists say the differences are all in our heads, or more precisely in the way men's and women's brains are designed. A century ago, the discovery that female brains were about 10 percent smaller than male brains was cited as proof that women could never be as smart as men—contributing to their status as second-class citizens. We now know that size isn't everything when it comes to brainpower. Our I.Q.s are the same. In fact, the highest recorded I.Q. belongs to a woman.   From "The Brain Game" via ABC News

Reason

Facts

Examples

Marshall McLuhan understood long ago that technology would dramatically alter the way we look at and understand the world. What he saw really alarmed him. He stated, "The world has become a computer, an electronic brain. And as our senses have gone outside of us, **Big Brother** goes inside. Unless we are aware of this, we move into a phase of panic terrors." If we are to believe McLuhan then, our choices are either to understand and control our technology or to live in fear of it. . . .

Quotation

Explanation

Big Brother
a concept from George Orwell's novel *1984*; represents oppressive total control

Practice ▸ Read the following passages. Then circle the types of details used to support the main idea. Each passage contains at least two types of details working together.

1.   Throughout history, men have tried to understand whale suicides or **strandings**. Even Aristotle, the ancient Greek philosopher, considered them and eventually said, "They happen without any apparent reason." But modern biologists are not so sure. They feel that the strandings can't be **random** acts, but probably occur for a number of reasons. To make this point, they compare beached whales to crashed planes. One theory will never explain all events.

---

strandings
situations in which whales beach themselves

random
without a pattern

a. quotation   **b.** explanation   **c.** description   **d.** statistic

2.   **Sects** form by breaking away from churches as a result of disagreement about church **doctrine**. Sometimes sect members choose to separate themselves geographically, as the Amish do in their small farming communities in Pennsylvania, Ohio, and Indiana. However, even in urban settings, strictly enforced rules concerning dress, diet, prayer, and intimate contact with outsiders can separate sect members from the larger society. Hasidic Jews in New York and other large American cities prove that the isolation strategy works. Sects are less integrated into society and less **bureaucratized** than churches.   From Brym/Lie, *Sociology: Your Compass for a New World,* 2E, © 2007 Cengage Learning.

---

sects
groups forming within a larger group

doctrine
belief held sacred by a group

bureaucratized
controlled by officials

a. definition   **b.** quotation   **c.** examples   **d.** descriptions

3.   The crime statistics of the 1990s are startling. Even with the upswing at the beginning of the decade, from 1990 to 2000 the homicide rate dropped 39 percent, the robbery rate 44 percent, the burglary rate 41 percent, and the auto theft rate 37 percent. By most measures, this decline was the longest and deepest of the twentieth century. In retrospect, the 1990s seem to have encompassed a "golden era" for the leading indicators of low crime rates.   From Gaines/Miller, *Criminal Justice in Action,* 6E, ©2011 Cengage Learning

a. definition   **b.** statistics   **c.** examples   **d.** analysis

Evaluating the Support

Your academic reading assignments include textbook chapters, articles, and essays from reliable sources. Your instructors assign these texts because they trust the details in them. For the most part, the authors are experts in their fields, and their writing has been carefully reviewed by other experts to make sure that the details are accurate and trustworthy.

Reliable Support

Shirley Biagi is the author of the bestselling textbook *Media/Impact*. In addition to being a published author, she is a professor of communications and has served as the editor of a national media history periodical. As you read this paragraph from *Media/Impact*, you can trust that her supporting details are accurate and important.

> Advertisers flocked to major Internet sites when they first were established. They expected quick returns, as consumer use of the Internet skyrocketed. Advertisers primarily used banner advertising, which meant their advertising messages scrolled across a Web site or appeared in a box on the site. Internet sites also tried pop-up advertisements, which meant an ad popped up either behind a Web site screen when someone left the site or on top of the Web site home page when someone first visited. Advertisers quickly learned, however, that no matter how they packaged the message, advertising on an Internet site didn't necessarily bring increased sales for their products. What advertisers call the **click-through rate** is less than 1 percent. This is a very disappointing return, especially because Web site advertising can be expensive.   From Biagi. *Media Impact,* 10E © 2011 Cengage Learning.

---

click-through rate
the rate at which people who see an ad on an Internet site click it to learn more

Unreliable Support

What if Biagi had not been trained in communications? You wouldn't (or shouldn't) feel as confident in her information about Internet advertising. Likewise, you wouldn't feel as confident in her information about Internet advertising if she used vague details or didn't sound professional:

> Many advertisers have tried the Internet, and they thought they would make a killing. They tried things like banner ads, but nothing seemed to work. They even tried something called click-throughs to get more information, but people didn't bother to click. A lot of money has been spent with little to show for it.

Always consider whether you can trust the ideas in your readings. For example, the details on some Web sites are questionable, especially sites that promote a cause or product. Also, you should be wary of some fringe magazines or texts that are out of date.

You can trust the details in your reading if it meets the following standards:

1. The source is a textbook, an essay in a respected journal or magazine, or a Web site with a reliable domain such as *.edu*, *.org*, or *.gov*.
2. The author is identified and writing in his or her field of training.
3. The topic is covered fairly and with proper detail. When necessary, sources of information are cited, sometimes in parentheses like this (Marshall, 1997).

Read this paragraph that shares a story about coming to America. Then read the evaluation of the supporting details.

Frances Opeka

Frances Opeka's journey to the United States was a painful experience. Frances was a young woman in Yugoslavia when the Russians invaded her country. In May of 1945, her grandfather's brother knocked on her family's window at night and said, "If you're coming with us, we're leaving in a half an hour." So Frances, her sister, who was seven months pregnant, and her sister's three children left. They did not have time to say good-bye to anyone, including their own parents. They just left. Their first stop was a camp in Austria, and then they went to Italy where they lived for five difficult years in a refugee camp. At times, they slept on the cold ground. At night, Frances would often go without her coat because she wanted her pregnant sister to keep warm. For food, they received bread and soup. To get a potato was a treat. Germs spread easily, so they all went through times of sickness. Frances's sister had her child in the refugee camp. After that, the Opekas were the first family from the camp allowed to come to America.

1. What is the main idea of the paragraph? Frances Opeka's journey to the United States was a painful experience.

2. What details support it? They had to leave their home in the night. They fled to Austria and then to Italy. Sleeping conditions were bad, food was scarce, and sickness was common.

3. Do the details seem reliable and trustworthy? Explain. Yes, the paragraph uses a variety of vivid details, each of which focuses on the main idea.

4. What questions do you still have about the main idea? How did they get to Austria and Italy? Why was her family chosen first to come here?

Practice This paragraph from a cultural anthropology textbook discusses financial inequality experienced by women. Read the paragraph and then evaluate the supporting details by answering the questions.

Women throughout the world continue to carry a heavy burden of financial inequality. Although they make up half of the world's population, women do two-thirds of the work, earn one-tenth of the world's income, and own less than 1 percent of the world's property. While there have been some political and economic advances, women in many parts of the world are falling further behind their male counterparts. Moreover, gender inequality does not necessarily depend on how wealthy a country is. Vicki Bakhshi (1999) noted more than a decade ago that some developing countries have done much better at narrowing the gender gap than have some wealthy, industrialized nations. For example, Costa Rica was making considerably better progress than Italy or France, while Poland was ahead of Japan. Globally, women still have a long way to go to achieve financial equality.   From Ferraro/Andreatta, *Cultural Anthropology*, 9E.© 2012 Cengage Learning.

1. What is the main idea of the paragraph?

_____

2. What details support it?

_____

_____

_____

3. Do the details seem reliable and trustworthy? Explain.

_____

_____

4. What questions do you still have about the main idea?

_____

_____

L07 Choosing Supporting Details in Writing

Planning a writing assignment involves selecting a topic, gathering details about it, and choosing a focus or main idea for your writing. At this point, you are ready to decide how to use the details you have collected. Let's say a student is planning a paragraph about the growing mobile food industry, and she decides to focus on the four main types of mobile food carriers.

- **Topic:** mobile food industry
- **Focus:** four main types of food carriers
- **Topic Sentence:** Potential mobile-food owners (*topic*) can choose among four main types of food carriers (*focus*).

Here are her notes about this topic. The side notes (**in red type**) show her thoughts as she reviews her notes.

Notes About the Mobile Food Industry

Entrepreneur **Web site**
"Food Truck 101: How to Start a Mobile Food Business" by Entrepreneur Press and Rich Mintzer 7/25/2011

- a $1 billion industry
- low overhead and portable
- need a business plan and start-up money
- includes food kiosks, food carts, and food trucks

I will arrange the types by mobility.

food kiosk (a booth or stand)
- often located in mall or stadium
- not very mobile
- two-person operation
- low overhead
- need licensing agreement to operate
- some businesses franchise kiosks (Ben & Jerry's)

food cart
- best known
- traditionally sold hot dogs and ice cream
- pulled by vehicle or pushed by hand
- food prepared in advance
- choices expanding
- some people own several carts

Stuart Monk, 2014 / Used under license from Shutterstock.com

food truck

- more sophisticated
- able to store, cook, and serve
- work well at corporate parks and places with limited food choices
- now gourmet food trucks operated by young chefs
- some restaurants have food trucks
- some do catering business

***Forbes.com* Web site**
"The Cost of Starting a Food Truck" 9/27/12

I will give the range of investment needed.

- more than 15,000 individuals serving street food
- street cart—up to $3,000 for cart, $500 for food, $1,000 for permits
- food truck—reasonable range $70,000-$80,000 plus fuel, upkeep, permits, equipment, rentals, fuel, supplies, and advertising
- popularity means it is getting more expensive
- many hidden expenses
- labor intensive—10-hour days

***Entrepreneur* Web site**
"Beyond the Food Truck" Entrepreneur Press 9/26/11

- 3 million food trucks in the U.S.
- 5 million food carts
- options for mobile food business countless

concession trailers

- found at fairs, sporting events, and special events
- anywhere where the trailer can be unhitched for awhile
- allow for cooking
- room for two or three people

gourmet trucks

A gourmet truck is a type of food truck.

- have specialty foods
- chefs involved
- high-end equipment

After reviewing these notes, the student arranges the following types of mobile vehicles in order of mobility (from least mobile to most mobile).

1. Food carts
2. Food kiosks
3. Food trailers
4. Food trucks

Next, she identifies the details that she will use to describe the differences between each type of vehicle.

1. Food carts
- most common
- food prepped beforehand
- pushed or towed in place
- least expensive (average $3,000- $5,000)

2. Food kiosks
- indoors (rent space in stadiums or malls)
- not very mobile
- two-person business
- may be sold as a franchise

3. Food trailers
- at fairs, sporting and special events
- towed in place
- allows for cooking
- room for three people

4. Food trucks
- very mobile
- able to store, cook, serve
- maybe the most innovative
- expensive (average $70,000-$80,000)

Practice ▸ Collect details from three sources that address the topic sentence you wrote in this chapter. Take notes as you go along. Then decide on two to four key points that support your topic sentence. Finally, list details that you could use to develop each one.

L08 Closing a Paragraph

You learned that a closing sentence makes a final statement about a topic. It may help to think of the topic and closing sentences of a paragraph as bookends that hold all of the supporting details in place. In the paragraph that follows, the closing sentence serves as an effective bookend by explaining the ideas presented in the topic sentence.

Topic sentence

In 1960, Jane Goodall set out on a research expedition that would transform human understanding of chimpanzees. She arrived at Gombe Stream National Park in Tanzania and began to track and observe chimpanzees in the wild. Previous researchers had studied the animals in zoos or laboratories, so they had little understanding of primate behavior outside captivity. Previous researchers also had avoided personal connection with the creatures. Goodall's approach was quite different. She followed the chimpanzees through the forest and gave them names. When eventually they approached her, she connected with them. The trust that Goodall established with the animals allowed her to witness chimp behavior in the wild like no one ever before.

Body sentences

Closing sentence

Practice Complete the following paragraph by writing a closing sentence for it.

In ancient times, the diets of ordinary people were usually plain and unvaried. The commoners of Mesopotamia and Egypt lived on such staples as bread and beer. Most Greeks and Romans ate coarse bread, olives, and goat cheese, while vendors roamed city streets selling roasted meats, fried fish, and sweets. A special preparation of maize provided the people of ancient Mexico with the tortilla, the foundation of their diet. The diet of India's ancient culture consisted of a wide variety of vegetable and dairy products and a complex mixture of seasonings known by Westerners today as a curry.

From Chon/Maier, *Welcome to Hospitality*, 3E. © 2010 Cengage Learning

Closing Sentence: _____

_____

Practice Write a paragraph for the topic that you have been working with in this chapter. Be sure to include a topic sentence, body or supporting sentences, and a closing sentence.

☑ Review and Enrichment

Reviewing the Chapter

Understand Paragraphs

1. What are the three parts of a paragraph?

2. What are the four types of paragraphs?

Read and Write for Topics

3. Where are topics usually first stated in paragraphs and essays?

4. What is freewriting?

Read and Write for Main Ideas

5. How is a main idea different from a topic?

6. What two parts are included in a topic sentence?

Read and Write for Supporting Details

7. What are two types of supporting details?

8. What should you look for to judge the reliability of supporting details?

9. Why is it important to include plenty of details in your writing?

"I'm a morning person, really alert."

—Alice Temperley

Reading for Enrichment

You will be reading a selection from the college textbook *An Invitation to Health*. The selection examines the typical sleeping habits of college students. Be sure to follow the steps in the reading process to help you gain a full understanding of the text.

About the Author

Dianne Hales is an nationally known freelance journalist, an author of more than a dozen books, and a recipient of numerous writing awards.

Prereading

Experts who study the relationship between health and learning often focus on the sleeping habits of students. Educational psychologists and physicians contend that good sleeping habits help students succeed in the classroom. As a result, you should evaluate your own sleeping routine. In order to do so, answer these questions:

Consider the Elements

As you read, first identify the **topic** and **main idea** of the selection. Then pay careful attention to the details that support the main idea. Also consider the different types of **details** used and in what combinations.

■ How many hours of sleep do you typically get?

_____

■ Do you follow a regular sleeping routine? Explain.

_____

■ Do you consider yourself a light or heavy sleeper?

_____

■ How alert are you during the day?

_____

■ What is one thing that you need to change about your sleeping habits?

_____

What do you think?

In the quotation, Alice Temperley says she is a morning person. What does that mean? And is it good to be a morning person? Explain.

Before you read, answer these questions:

1. What do the title, the opening two paragraphs, and any headings tell you about the selection?

   _____

2. What are your first thoughts about the author's purpose and audience?

   _____

3. What questions would you like answered in your reading?

   _____

Reading and Rereading

As you read, make it your goal to (1) identify the topic and main idea, (2) pay careful attention to the supporting details provided, and (3) answer the questions you listed during prereading. Annotate the text and/or take notes to help you keep track of important information during your reading.

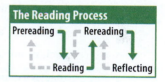

Reread as needed to make sure you understand the ideas in the text. Also think about the value of the topic and the quality of the information included.

Sleepless on Campus

You stay up late cramming for a final. You drive through the night to visit a friend at another campus. You get up for an early class during the week but stay in bed until noon on weekends. And you wonder: "Why am I so tired?" You're not getting enough sleep.   *1*

You're hardly alone. According to a recent report by the Centers for Disease Control and Prevention, only one-third of Americans say they get enough sleep. An estimated 50 to 70 million American adults suffer from sleep and wakefulness **disorders**. Women are more likely than men to report not getting enough sleep. African Americans reported getting less sleep compared with all other   *2* ethnic groups. Only 8 percent of adolescents get the nine hours of sleep recommended for their age group; more than two-thirds get less than seven hours.

Inadequate sleep has been *3* linked to a host of problems, including mental distress, depression, anxiety, obesity, hypertension, diabetes, high cholesterol, and risky behaviors such as smoking, physical inactivity, and heavy drinking. Drowsy drivers are responsible for almost 20 percent of all serious car crash injuries.

Sleep problems start young. *4* Nearly one-half of adolescents sleep less than eight hours on school nights; more than half report feeling sleepy during the day. College students are **notorious** for staying up late to study and socialize during the week and sleeping in on weekends.

In a national survey, three- *5* quarters of undergraduates reported occasional sleep

Your Strategies for Change
How to Sleep Better

- Keep regular hours for going to bed and getting up in the morning. Stay as close as possible to this schedule on weekends as well as weekdays.
- Develop a sleep ritual—such as stretching, meditation, yoga, prayer, or reading a not-too-thrilling novel—to ease the transition from wakefulness to sleep.
- Don't drink coffee late in the day. The effects of caffeine can linger for up to eight hours. And don't smoke. Nicotine is an even more powerful stimulant—and sleep **saboteur**—than caffeine.
- Don't rely on alcohol to get to sleep. Alcohol disrupts normal sleep stages, so you won't sleep as deeply or as restfully as you normally would.
- Although experts generally advise against daytime napping for people who have problems sleeping at night, a recent study of college students found that a 30-minute "power nap" lowers stress and refreshes energy with no disruption in nighttime sleep.

MR.LIGHTMAN, 2014 / Used under license from Shutterstock.com

problems while 12 percent experienced poor sleep quality. The most common complaints are general morning tiredness and insomnia. Risky behaviors linked with poor sleep include fighting, suicidal thoughts, smoking, and alcohol use.

On average, college students go to bed 1 to 2 hours later and sleep 1 to 1.6 hours less than students of a generation ago. When compared to exhaustion levels reported by workers in various occupations, college students score extremely high. 6

Sleep affects academic performance. In a recent study of undergraduates, the students reporting the poorest sleep quality had lower grades than those who slept better. 7

Fortunately, college students can learn to sleep better. In an experiment with introductory psychology students—mostly freshmen—those who learned basic deep sleep skills significantly improved their overall sleep quality compared with students who did not receive such training. 8

How Much Sleep Do You Need?

Over the last century, we have cut our average nightly sleep time by 20 percent. More than half of us try to get by with less than seven hours of shut-eye a night. College students are no exception, with an average sleep time slightly less than seven hours, with little difference between men and women. 9

No formula can say how long a good night's sleep should be. Normal sleep times range from five to ten hours; the average is seven and a half. About one or two people in a hundred can get by with just five hours; another small minority needs twice that amount. Each of us seems to have an innate sleep appetite that is as much a part of our genetic programming as hair color and skin tone. 10

To figure out your sleep needs, keep your wake-up time the *11* same every morning and vary your bedtime. Are you groggy after six hours of shut-eye? Does an extra hour give you more stamina? What about an extra two hours? Since too much sleep can make you feel sluggish, don't assume that more is always better. Listen to your body's signals, and adjust your sleep schedule to suit them.

Are you better off pulling an all-nighter before a big test or *12* closing the books and getting a good night's sleep? According to researchers, that depends on the nature of the exam. If it's a test of facts—Civil War battles, for instance—cramming all night works. However, if you will have to write analytical essays in which you compare, contrast, and make connections, you need to sleep to make the most of your reasoning abilities.

From Hales, *An Invitation to Health*, 7E. © 2012 Cengage Learning.

disorders
disturbances to regular or normal function

notorious
negatively known

saboteur
a person who makes a mess of things on purpose

Summarizing

Write a summary of "Sleepless on Campus." Remember that a summary presents the key points in a clear form using your own words.

Reflecting

1. What is the main idea of the selection?

   _____

2. What is the primary type of detail used in paragraph 2—*definitions, quotations,* or *statistics*? (Circle the correct one.)

3. What process is explained in paragraph 11?

   _____

   _____

4. How would you characterize the quality of the details in this selection? Do they seem reliable?

   _____

5. What conclusion can you draw from this selection?

   _____

   _____

Vocabulary

Create vocabulary entries for these words. For each word, identify the pronunciation and helpful word parts. Also give a primary definition of the word and use it in a sentence.

1. **hypertension**
   (paragraph 3)

2. **insomnia**
   (paragraph 5)

3. **ritual**
   ("Your Strategies for Change" sidebar)

Critical Thinking

- How does lifestyle affect sleep?
- What role does technology play in our sleeping habits?
- Why is sleep an issue with college-aged students?

Writing for Enrichment

Choose one of the following writing ideas, or decide upon an idea of your own related to the reading. Be sure to follow the steps in the writing process to develop your work.

1. Write a personal blog in which you describe your typical sleeping routine. Refer to your answers in the opening prereading activity for ideas for your writing.

2. Compare your sleeping habits with another student or a family member. How are your sleeping habits similar and how are they different?

3. Explain how your sleep habits affect your academic performance.

4. Report on the use of sleeping pills by college students. This will require some research.

5. Explain how sleeping habits have changed from early generations until now. This will require some research.

When prewriting and planning . . .

- Research your topic as needed, taking thorough notes as you go along.
- Establish a topic sentence for your paragraph.
- Review your notes for key ideas to support your paragraph.
- Decide on the details that you will use to develop these ideas.

When writing . . .

- Include a beginning, middle, and ending in your paragraph.
- Present your main idea in the topic sentence.
- Support the main idea in the body sentences.
- Close your paragraph with final thoughts about your main idea.

When revising and editing. . .

- Carefully review your first draft, making sure that you develop each key point with sufficient details.
- Ask at least one peer to review your writing as well.
- Improve the content as needed.
- Then edit your revised writing for style and correctness. See Appendix B for an editing checklist.

Chapter

7

"Organizing is a journey, not a destination."
—Source unknown

Organization

Organization gives ideas structure and makes them understandable. Most narratives organize details according to time (*what happened first, second, third, . . .*). An explanation might organize details by comparing and contrasting them or showing their causes and effects. A persuasive essay presents supporting details in a convincing order. Simply put, well-organized texts make ideas clear and compelling.

In this chapter, you will learn about the patterns of organization commonly used in informational reading selections. You will also learn about the different transitions or linking words often used with each pattern. Then you will examine how to make the best choices when it comes to choosing the right pattern of organization and transitions for your own writing.

Learning Outcomes

LO1 Read for common patterns of organization and transitions.

LO2 Organize details for writing.

What do you think?

How is organizing a journey?

L01 Reading for Common Patterns of Organization and Transitions

Informational texts usually follow one main pattern of organization. These patterns include *chronological, spatial (descriptive), cause-effect, comparison-contrast, examples,* and *logical.* Sometimes, portions of longer texts will follow secondary patterns as well. For example, a text that compares and contrasts two people may also include a few descriptive passages that are organized spatially. Knowing how these patterns work will help you follow the ideas in your reading assignments.

In addition, it's important to know that there are **transitions**, special linking words and phrases, used with each pattern. Transitions connect ideas and/or show relationships between them, and they are used within paragraphs and from one paragraph to the next.

Linking ideas within a paragraph:

Loggers can use more sustainable practices in tropical forests. For example, they can use sustainable selective cutting and strip cutting to harvest tropical trees for lumber instead of clear-cutting the forests. Loggers can also be more careful when cutting individual trees. . . .

Connecting paragraphs:

Ecologists and forest fire experts have proposed several strategies for reducing fire-related harm to forests and to people who use the forests.

One approach is to set small, contained surface fires to remove flammable small trees and underbrush in the highest-risk forest areas. These burns require careful planning and monitoring to keep them from getting out of control. Local officials in populated parts of fire-prone California use herds of goats to eat away underbrush.

A second strategy is to allow some forest on public lands to burn. This burn removes flammable underbrush and smaller trees, as long as the fires do not threaten human structures and life. . . .

A third approach is to protect houses and other buildings in fire-prone areas by thinning a zone of about 60 meters around them. These structures must not use highly flammable construction materials such as wood shingles. . . .

A final approach is to thin forest areas that are vulnerable to fire by clearing away small fire-prone trees and underbrush under careful environmental controls. Many forest fire scientists warn that such thinning operations should not remove economically valuable medium-sized and large trees. . . .

From *Living in the Environment*, 17E. © 2012 Cengage Learning.

Chronological Order

Narratives recall experiences, so they usually follow chronological (time) order. Expository texts that discuss a process or explain how to do something follow chronological order as well. Certain transitional words or phrases connect ideas using chronological order. **Table 7.1** shows some of these transitions.

Table 7.1 Common Chronological Transitions			
first	later	soon	now
second	today	in the future	in the past
third	eventually	earlier	finally
next	at some point	later	then
before	after	tomorrow	soon

This narrative paragraph shares an interesting historical story. The underlined transitions show that chronological order is used. (The specific dates also show that time order is used.)

> Frances Anne Slocum was born in Rhode Island in March of 1773. The next year her family moved to Pennsylvania. She lived a happy childhood there until she was five. But on November 2, 1772, Delaware Indians raided her home. No one was hurt, but Frances was taken from the family and lost for 57 years. Then in 1835, a fur trader named Colonel Ewing stopped at the home of a widow of the Chief of the Miami Indians. Colonel Ewing became interested in her because her features and coloring were different. Eventually, Ewing learned she was born to white parents and her last name was Slocum. At some point, one of Frances Slocum's brothers read about his lost sister in a newspaper and reunited with her.

This expository paragraph explains a political process—how a bill becomes a law. Chronological transitions (underlined) help the reader follow the text.

> A bill becomes a law following a specific process. First of all, a senator or representative introduces a bill by sending it to a clerk of his or her house, who gives it a number and title and sends it to the proper committee. If the committee members decide the bill is worthwhile, they then debate the bill and eventually vote on it. A favorable vote sends the bill back to the floor to be dealt with by all the members. Next, the clerk reads the bill sentence by sentence to the house. This is known as the second reading. Members may debate the bill and offer amendments. What follows is the third reading by title only, and the bill is put to a vote. Then if the bill passes, it goes to the other house for debate and a vote. If the bill passes there and is signed by the president, it becomes a law.

Spatial Order

Some descriptions are organized spatially, meaning that they are organized according to location—near to far, top to bottom, or left to right. Transitional words and phrases like the ones in **Table 7.2** help organize descriptions spatially.

Table 7.2 Common Spatial Transitions	
above	beneath
back	down
onto	toward
next to	alongside
back and forth	in the distance
from	forward
through	around
behind	over
on the left	below
across	behind

This paragraph describes the unsanitary conditions experienced by the author Richard W. Sonnenfeldt and other German Jews living in England who were **interned** by the British during WWII, on the same ship, no less, that held captured Nazi soldiers. The spatial transitions (underlined) help describe their "living quarters."

The commander of the guards encouraged the **sadistic** treatment of prisoners. Of course, we knew none of this as we were herded to our hold below the water line. The space was bare except for long benches and tables and sleeping hammocks strung from the ceiling. Sixteen holes in boards, with seawater flowing beneath them in an open gutter, were the "head," or toilet facilities, for our contingent of 980 internees up forward. The shallow gutter often flooded from accumulations of human waste, which spilled onto the floor and then floated back and forth with the rolling of the boat. The **queues** to the head were never-ending and accidents happened.

From Richard Sonnenfeldt, *Witness to Nuremberg*. Arcade Publishing, New York, Copyright 2006

---

interned
confined or held during wartime

sadistic
violent, cruel

queues
lines

Cause-Effect Order

Cause-effect is one of the most common patterns of organization in academic texts. For example, a science textbook may discuss the causes and effects of an environmental condition. Or a business textbook may explore the causes and effects of a new buying trend. **Table 7.3** shows transitions often used in cause-effect writing.

Table 7.3 Common Cause-Effect Transitions			
Causes:	the reason is	since	the main cause is
	because	results from	in fact
Effects:	thus	as a result	instead
	then	therefore	the main effect

This paragraph explains the causes of the decline of interest in print newspapers and magazines and the effects this decline has on journalists. The underlined transitions show the causes and effects.

Students interested in journalism may want to consider another major. The reason is simple. Fewer and fewer people are buying newspapers. Instead, they are getting their news on the Internet. Fewer buyers of newspapers and magazines mean less income from sales. And since there are fewer readers, there are also fewer ad dollars, which is a major source of revenue. As a result, newspapers are going out of business or cutting back, and thus there are not enough jobs for experienced journalists, let alone recent college graduates. However, not all is lost. The Internet may offer new career choices, especially for people who understand and appreciate the power of electronic communications.

Compare-Contrast Order

Informational texts often compare and contrast topics—two people, two events, two objects, two cultures, or two ideas. Certain transitions like the ones listed in **Table 7.4** are used to show the similarities and differences between two topics.

Table 7.4 Common Comparison-Contrast Transitions			
Comparing:	both	similarly	just as
	likewise	in comparison	in the same way
Contrasting:	although	despite	but
	in contrast	while	on the other hand

This paragraph compares China's drive to control its population with India's efforts to do the same. The underlined transitions show that comparisons and contrasts are being made.

China and India have both been dealing with serious population growth issues. China's goal has been to sharply reduce population growth by promoting one-child families. Married couples pledging to have no more than one child receive a number of benefits, including better housing, more food, free heath care, and salary bonuses. Between 1972 and 2010, the country cut its birth rate in half. Likewise, India has provided family planning services, strongly encouraging smaller families. But their results can't come close to China's efforts. Indian women still have an average of 2.6 children. The Indian poor believe they need several children for work, and like the Chinese, they value male children. So despite similar family planning efforts, many more Indian families keep having children because of their traditional values.

From *Living in the Environment*, 17E. © 2012 Cengage Learning.

Using Examples

Writers often use examples to illustrate, explain, or justify ideas. **Table 7.5** lists the types of transitions used with examples. The paragraph that follows shows other transitions.

Table 7.5 Common Example Transitions			
also	one approach	in addition	for instance
for example	in another case	in other instances	moreover
first of all	in another example	another	often

This paragraph shows why young people are being called the "Elsewhere Generation." The underlined transitions signal a new example will be provided to support the main idea.

Some commentators call us the "Elsewhere Generation" because of our constant use of social media. Often we ignore people in the same room while electronically interacting with people in other locations. For example, two gamers sit in the same room and play online—not with each other but with people in other countries. Meanwhile, a group of friends gathers in a cafe, but instead of talking with each other, they text people who are miles away. On campus, students update their Facebook statuses during lectures, and in the park, two joggers run side by side but talk on headsets to other people. With our constant social multitasking, we maintain more friendships than previous generations, even if many of our friends are elsewhere.

Logical Order

Sometimes an informational text simply presents information in a sensible order, moving logically from one idea to the next. **Table 7.6** lists transitions used with this pattern.

Table 7.6 Common Logical Order Transitions

however	actually	besides	nevertheless
after all	moreover	for this reason	in other words

This paragraph from a hospitality textbook discusses the challenges facing professionals in the resort business. The underlined transitions help the reader move through the text.

Managers and crew members at resorts are in the full-time business of pleasing their guests. Doing that, however, isn't as glamorous as it might seem. According to Tom Norby, manager of community services for Sea Pines [a resort], "From the outside looking in, the resort business looks like a world of leisure. But if you're on the inside, you're working hard." For this reason, the hospitality professional in this specialized area will discover a challenging career, since it is the nature of resorts to respond to guest demands. Besides being interested in relaxation and pampering, resort customers are interested in exploring local attractions.   From Chon/Maier, *Welcome to Hospitality*, 3E. © 2010 Cengage Learning

Practice Carefully read each of the following paragraphs. Then circle the pattern of organization used in each. The underlined transitions and key words will help you make your choice.

1.   We have access to the creek through the property of some friends a short drive down the road. They're not home, and all is quiet as we park the car and I unbuckle Jane from her seat. We make our way around behind the house and down a footpath through the trees and into a patch of canary grass taller than my head. Forcing my way through the grass toward the gurgling sound of the creek, I find a spot where a log projects out over a sandbar and we step into the shallows. "Huh, huh, huh!" Jane says at the first cold shock of the water on her feet, but she acclimates quickly, stomping and splashing. The creek is barely ten feet wide, but the current is swift and the sand bar drops off darkly, so I grip her hand at all times.   From *Visiting Tom*, Michael Perry, Harper, an Imprint of HarperCollins Publishers, Copyright 2012

a. chronological   c. cause-effect   e. examples

b. spatial   d. comparison-contrast   f. logical

2.   Race is often the first thing people think of when they hear the word **diversity**. Actually, most of us are a blend of **ethnicities**, and how we see ourselves may be different from the way others see us. For example, people may assume that a Pacific Islander with light-brown skin, dark hair, and dark eyes is Hispanic. For that matter, a classmate you may assume is white may think of himself as black. Moreover, consider this: If you have a Chinese mother and a white father, you may not know which "race box" to check on standard forms. Should you choose Asian or Caucasian? Though people often focus on race, biologists tell us that there's more variation within a race than there is between races.

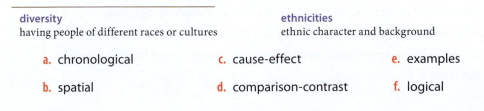

diversity
having people of different races or cultures

ethnicities
ethnic character and background

a. chronological   c. cause-effect   e. examples

b. spatial   d. comparison-contrast   f. logical

3.   The old man grumbled as he wiped his eyes with the back of his gnarled hand and watched the proceedings. <u>Then</u> he glanced at his wife standing a short distance away. She, too, was old, but he still saw her as a much younger woman. His thoughts went back. <u>First</u>, he recalled the black and white dishes on which she had so proudly served him home-cooked meals. <u>Next</u>, he thought about the chairs, tables, and other furnishings in their home. So many people and things came to mind. <u>Then</u> the auctioneer's voice brought him back to the present. He shifted in the seat of his old John Deere tractor that was being auctioned. The other machinery would be sold, too—piece by piece. A half-century of thoughts and feelings went with everything on display.

a. chronological   **c.** cause-effect   **e.** examples

b. spatial   **d.** comparison-contrast   **f.** logical

4.   Haiti, a country with 9.2 million people, was once a tropical paradise. Much of it was covered in forests. Now it is an ecological disaster. Largely <u>because</u> its trees were cut for fuel wood and to make charcoal, only about 2% of its land is now covered with trees. With the trees gone, a main <u>effect</u> is that soils have eroded away in many areas, <u>making</u> it much more difficult to grow crops. This unsustainable use of natural capital has <u>led to</u> a downward spiral of environmental **degradation**, poverty, disease, social injustice, crime, and violence. <u>As a result</u>, Haiti, is classified as one of the world's failing states, which are countries that may not survive this century. Haiti's plight was <u>made worse</u> by a major earthquake in 2010.   From *Living in the Environment*, 17E. © 2012 Cengage Learning.

Yuriy Boyko, 2014 / Used under license from Shutterstock.com

---

degradation
the process of ruining

a. chronological   **c.** cause-effect   **e.** examples

b. spatial   **d.** comparison-contrast   **f.** logical

Using a Graphic Organizer

Once you identify the pattern of organization, you may want to use a graphic organizer to help you keep track of the important details during your reading. You can make changes to any of these organizers to meet your needs for a particular text.

Chronological: Use a time line to identify the steps in a narrative or process. See **Figure 7.1**.

Figure 7.1 Time Line

Subject: _____
1 ┼ _____
2 ┼ _____
3 ┼ _____

Figure 7.2 Cause-Effect Organizer

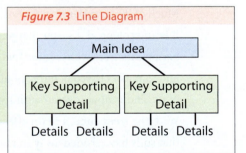

Cause-Effect: Use a cause-effect organizer to identify the key details following this pattern of organization. See **Figure 7.2**.

Logical: Use a line diagram to identify the main points and supporting details for some texts following the logical pattern of organization. See **Figure 7.3**.

Figure 7.3 Line Diagram

Main Idea

Key Supporting Detail   Key Supporting Detail

Details Details   Details Details

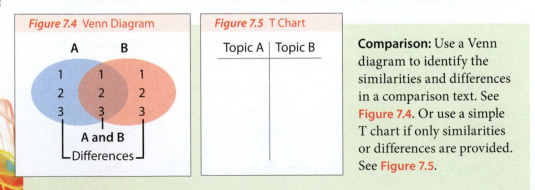

Comparison: Use a Venn diagram to identify the similarities and differences in a comparison text. See **Figure 7.4**. Or use a simple T chart if only similarities or differences are provided. See **Figure 7.5**.

LO2 Organizing Details for Writing

To write a strong paragraph, you need to gather effective details that support your topic. Once you do that, you must decide on the best pattern of organization for these details. Sometimes, the appropriate pattern is stated or suggested in the assignment itself. For example, suppose your instructor made the following assignment: *In a narrative paragraph, recall your most surprising work-related experience.* Since you are recalling an experience, you would use the chronological pattern of organization. Or suppose an instructor made this assignment: *Provide a clear description of a favorite space.* Since you are being asked to describe a space, you would most likely organize your details spatially, arranging them from near to far, right to left, or top to bottom.

Practice   Identify the pattern of organization suggested in each of these writing assignments.

1. Explain why two introductory drawing classes have been eliminated by the art department and the effect this move will have on the art program.

2. Discuss how the senators' views on gun control are similar and different.

3. Give three reasons why close friendships are important while attending college.

4. Develop a sensible argument stating why serving your country in the military or in some other capacity is a valuable experience.

Choosing an Appropriate Pattern

If a writing assignment does not suggest a pattern of organization, you can decide on one after you identify a main idea for your paragraph. Suppose you receive this assignment: *Discuss your favorite diner, drive-in, or dive.* No pattern is suggested. You decide to focus on the three best things about your favorite breakfast place. For that focus, the example pattern (*first of all, in addition, also*) would work well to organize supporting details.

Consider another assignment: *Recommend to your community's planning commission a practical use for some vacant acreage.* Again, no pattern is indicated. Suppose you want the land to become a dog park. You need to write a paragraph that explains why a dog park will benefit the community. For this focus, the cause-effect pattern (*the main reason why, the main effect will be*) would work well.

Steps to Identify a Pattern of Organization

 First, study the assignment. A pattern of organization might be built into it.

 If that isn't the case, study your main idea and supporting details.

 Decide on the best pattern of organization to use based on the information you have gathered.

 Arrange the supporting details accordingly.

Practice Identify a topic, main idea, and pattern of organization that you could use for each of these writing assignments. The first one is done for you.

1. **Writing Assignment:** Discuss the fashion or clothing style you feel most comfortable wearing.

   Topic: _Well-worn T-shirt and jeans_

   Main Idea: _Provide the casual feel that I love_

   Possible Pattern of Organization: _Logical—to explore my feelings about this_
   type of clothing

2. **Writing Assignment:** Explain why you want to pursue a particular career.

   Topic: _____

   Main Idea: _____

   Possible Pattern of Organization: _____

   _____

3. **Writing Assignment:** Examine an important feature of mass transportation.

   Topic: _____

   Main Idea: _____

   Possible Pattern of Organization: _____

   _____

"Work hard to master the tools. Simplify, prune, and strive for order."

—William Zinsser

Arranging the Details

Before you begin your actual writing, you may find it helpful to arrange your supporting details according to the pattern of organization you have chosen. Here are three ways to arrange the details.

- **Make a quick list** of key details arranged according to the pattern.
- **Create an outline**—an organized arrangement of key points and supporting details.
- **Fill in a graphic organizer** with supporting details.

Making a Quick List

A **quick list** (see **Figure 7.6**) works well for paragraphs and shorter essays or when you are responding to a writing prompt on an exam. For example, for a narrative paragraph, you can simply list the key details in the order that they happened. For a descriptive paragraph, you can list the details spatially—left to right, top to bottom, near to far. For an expository paragraph following the cause-effect pattern, you may decide to list the causes first and then the effects. Here is a quick list for a paragraph about comfortable fashion.

Figure 7.6 Quick List

Topic statement: A basic T-shirt and a well-worn pair of jeans (*topic*) make a comfortable fashion statement (*focus*).

1. Show individual style
2. Get softer as you wear them
3. Are all-American
4. Can dress them "up" or "down"

Practice Write a topic sentence and a quick list for a paragraph based on the information you gathered for one of the assignments in the previous activity.

Topic statement: _____

_____

1. _____

2. _____

3. _____

4. _____

Using an Outline

An **outline** is a more complete arrangement, showing more carefully how details fit together. You may outline the details for a paragraph, but it is more likely that you would use an outline for an essay or report. The ideas in a topic outline are stated in words and phrases; the ideas in a sentence outline are expressed in sentences. In a traditional outline, if you have a "I," you should have at least a "II." If you have an "A," you should have at least a "B."

You can also change or simplify an outline to meet your writing needs. **Figure 7.7** shows part of a simplified outline with key points stated in sentences and supporting details in phrases.

Figure 7.7 Simplified Outline

Thesis statement: Humpback whales are by far the most playful and amazing whale species.

1. Most observers note that humpbacks appear to enjoy attention.
   - lift bodies almost completely out of water (breaching)
   - slap huge flippers against the water
   - thrust their flukes (tail portion) straight out of water

2. Humpback whales "sing" better than other whales.
   - song lasts up to 30 minutes
   - head pointed toward ocean floor when singing
   - seem to engage in group singing

Practice Create a simplified outline for a paragraph about becoming a leader. A topic sentence and two main supporting details are provided. Arrange these details in the best order and make up one or two ideas to explain each one.

Topic statement: To become an effective leader, a person must develop two main traits.

Main supporting details: Leaders must earn the respect of others. They must display good work habits.

1. _____

   - _____

   - _____

2. _____

   - _____

   - _____

Using a Graphic Organizer

You can also use a **graphic organizer** to arrange your supporting details. For example, a line diagram works well to organize details for a writing assignment that gives examples or reasons or identifies types or methods. **Figure 7.8** shows a line diagram.

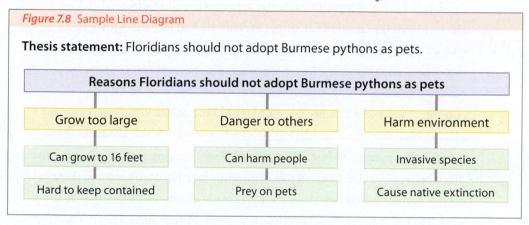

Figure 7.8 Sample Line Diagram

Thesis statement: Floridians should not adopt Burmese pythons as pets.

Reasons Floridians should not adopt Burmese pythons as pets		
Grow too large	Danger to others	Harm environment
Can grow to 16 feet	Can harm people	Invasive species
Hard to keep contained	Prey on pets	Cause native extinction

Other types of graphic organizers include time lines, Venn diagrams, and cause-effect organizers. Use a time line for details organized chronologically and a Venn diagram or T Chart when you are comparing and contrasting details.

Practice ▸ Use a line diagram to arrange the details for a paragraph starting with this topic sentence: *Close friendships in college are important for three reasons.* Provide one or two specific details under each reason.

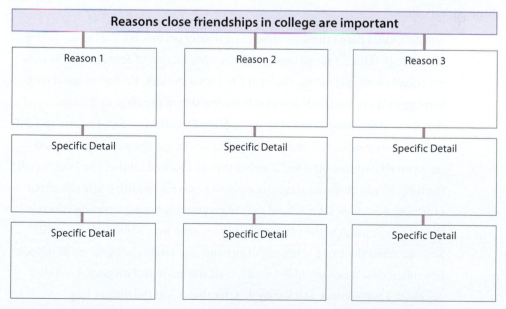

Reasons close friendships in college are important		
Reason 1	Reason 2	Reason 3
Specific Detail	Specific Detail	Specific Detail
Specific Detail	Specific Detail	Specific Detail

Using Transitions

Use transitions to help you create clear and organized pieces of writing. This student paragraph lacks transitions, so it does not read as smoothly and clearly as it could.

I didn't think of myself as a theater person. That all changed. My friend Devon played the Ghost of Christmas Present. He had to stand with Scrooge on a set of stairs that rolled from one side of the stage to the other. They needed someone to push the stairs. Devon was 6 feet 4 inches and 260 pounds. They needed somebody strong. Guess who got the job? They dressed me in an elf costume. I was 6 feet 2 inches myself. I looked kind of like Will Ferrell from *Elf*. I hadn't been on stage since playing a carrot in a 4th grade skit about nutrition. Somehow I'd managed to land an even more embarrassing costume. Devon wasn't much better off in a huge green robe with white fake fur. Scrooge stood there in a white nightshirt and cap. Dramatic lights made us look less ridiculous. It all started to feel magical. I couldn't believe it. I was onstage and loving it. I had the theater bug.

Remember that there are specific transitions associated with each pattern of organization (*chronological, spatial, cause-effect, compare-contrast, examples,* and *logical*). You can use transitions related to just the pattern of organization that you have chosen, or you can use a variety of transitions to show different kinds of connections. Here is the same paragraph with mostly chronological transitions added (underlined). These words improve the clarity of the paragraph.

As a kid, I didn't think of myself as a theater person, but during my senior year of high school, that all changed. In our production of *Scrooge: The Musical,* my friend Devon played the Ghost of Christmas Present. He had to stand with Scrooge on a set of stairs that rolled from one side of the stage to the other, and they needed someone to push the stairs. Since Devon was 6 feet 4 inches and 260 pounds, they needed somebody strong. Guess who got the job? They dressed me in an elf costume. At 6 feet 2 inches myself, I looked kind of like Will Ferrell from *Elf.* I hadn't been on stage since playing a carrot in a 4th grade skit about nutrition. Somehow I'd managed to land an even more embarrassing costume. Devon wasn't much better off in a huge green robe with white fake fur, while Scrooge stood there in a white nightshirt and cap. Dramatic lights made us look less ridiculous. When we added music, it all started to feel magical. I couldn't believe it. I was onstage and loving it. After that, I had the theater bug.

Practice Identify transitions to complete each of these student texts.

1. Expository paragraph following the example pattern

Capital punishment should be abolished for three reasons. _____ , common sense tells us that two wrongs don't make a right. To kill someone convicted of murder contradicts the reasoning behind the law that taking another person's life is wrong. The state is committing the violent act it is condemning. _____ , the death penalty is not an effective deterrent. Numerous studies show that murder is usually the result of deep problems and that most murderers do not consider the penalty before committing the act. _____ , death is final and cannot be altered. Errors in deciding guilt and innocence will always be present. So there is too great a risk that innocent people will be put to death. For these reasons, capital punishment should be replaced with another punishment.

2. Expository paragraph following the cause-effect pattern

Email has the power to create great mayhem. _____ a confusing message goes out to 30 people, the writer can expect a flurry of confused responses. _____ an angry message goes out, angry responses return. And people aren't the only ones creating havoc. Corporations send email blasts that _____ inboxes to overflow. Harmful programs called "bots" post scam emails _____ get people's passwords and steal their identities. _____ such scams arrive, email services try to shunt them to the "Junk" folder. But _____ , some important messages also get trashed and discovered too late by the recipient. Email can cause such harm _____ it is such a powerful form of communication. _____ we know the potential for harm, we ought to take more care before clicking "Send."

3. Narrative following the chronological pattern

_____ the East languished under last January's "Polar Vortex," we residents of the desert Southwest stayed warm and dry. To see snow, my friends and I took a trip from Tucson to Mount Lemmon, which had a snowpack.

_____ we drove up the winding mountain road, the temperature plunged.

_____ our ears felt plugged, we yawned to let them "pop." _____ we passed the snow line. We continued driving up to our favorite sledding spot, called Bear Hollow.

"Sledding" is a bit of an exaggeration. Few people in Tucson have sleds, so we brought substitutes: garbage can lids, cafeteria trays, and inner tubes.

_____ we tried the lids and the trays, we didn't get very far. The inner tubes were another story. _____ I flew down the hill so fast that I hit a plastic snow fence and went over it, into a drainage ditch. _____ some muddy scrambling, I hauled myself and my tube back over the fence and ran up the slope for another turn. _____ everyone else started calling "dibs" on the inner tubes.

_____ the sun started to set, and we knew it was time to pack up our "sleds" and head home. _____ we got back to town, it was completely dark, and the thermometer read 32 degrees—just cold enough for snow. We went to bed, hoping that we might have a rare Tucson snow the next morning.

_____ we woke up, the thermometer said 70, and the day got warmer. We even went swimming. That's life in Oro Valley!

☑ Review and Enrichment

Reviewing the Chapter

Read for Common Patterns of Organization and Transitions

1. When is the chronological pattern of organization used?

   _____

2. What are some common chronological transitions? Name three.

   _____   _____   _____

3. When is the spatial pattern of organization used?

   _____

4. What are some common spatial transitions? Name three.

   _____   _____   _____

5. When is the logical pattern of organization used?

   _____

6. What are some common logical transitions? Name three.

   _____   _____   _____

Organize Details for Writing

7. Why is it important to review the assignment when deciding on a pattern of organization to use in your writing?

   _____

8. What else will help you decide on a pattern of organization?

   _____

9. What are three ways to arrange details for writing?

   _____

10. Why is it important to use transitions in your writing?

   _____

"When I was a boy of 14, my father was so ignorant I
could hardly stand to have the old man around. But
when I got to be 21, I was astonished at how much the
old man had learned in seven years."

—Mark Twain

Reading for Enrichment

In the first part of this section, you will read and react to a personal narrative entitled "A Very Lucky Daughter." This narrative is the type of writing that is commonly found in magazines and memoirs or autobiographies. In the second part you will develop a piece of writing in response to your reading.

About the Author

Sharon Liao is a freelance writer and editor specializing in health, nutrition, and fitness. Her writing has appeared in many magazines. This essay appeared in *Reader's Digest* and the *Washingtonian* (a magazine) in 2001.

Prereading

Traveling can put people in difficult or embarrassing situations, especially when there are language barriers. That is what happens to the author in this narrative. You may have had a similar experience yourself. Write for three to five minutes about one of your own difficult or challenging traveling experiences.

Consider the Traits

As you read, pay careful attention to the **ideas**—especially the details that you learn about the author's parents. Also consider the **organization** of the ideas: Do the ideas follow a particular pattern of organization? Upon completing the reading, ask yourself why the writer organized details the way that she did.

_____

_____

_____

_____

_____

What do you think?

Consider the quotation by Mark Twain: Through the use of humor, what point is he really trying to make?

Before you read "A Very Lucky Daughter," answer these three questions.

1. What do the title and first five brief paragraphs tell you about the text?

   _____

2. Who might be the intended audience for this narrative?

   _____

3. What do you expect to learn in this essay?

   _____

Reading and Rereading

As you read, make it your goal to (1) follow the details in the author's story, (2) notice her use of dialogue and description, and (3) consider how the text is organized.

NOTE: Annotate the text and/or take notes as you read to help you follow the events.

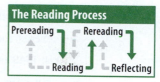

A Very Lucky Daughter

I should have been just another face in the hotel lobby in Zhangjiajie, a city in central China. But my words singled me out.   *1*

"Yun dou," I repeated to the clerk. Maybe he understood English: "Do you have a gym here?"   *2*

The clerk blinked, and then reached behind the counter and pulled out an iron.   *3*

I smiled blankly. My brain rooted through my limited Chinese vocabulary. Just then my dad strolled up, his eyebrows arched in amused triangles.   *4*

"She wants to know where the gym is," he supplied in rapid Mandarin Chinese, his native language. He turned to me and explained gently, "Yun dong is exercise, Sharon. Yun dou means iron."   *5*

I mumbled a sheepish apology to the laughing clerk and glanced at my dad. A look of recognition flashed through his eyes. We'd gone   *6* through this before. Only this time, the tables were turned.

When I was younger, I would try to imagine my parents growing up in China and Taiwan. But I could only **envision** them in the grainy black-and-white of their faded childhood pictures. Their childhood stories didn't match the people I knew. I couldn't picture my domestic mom, unsure of her halting English, studying international economics at a Taiwanese university. I laughed at the image of my stern father, an electrical engineer, chasing after chickens in his Chinese village. *7*

I related to my parents' pre-American lives as only a series of events, like facts from some history exam. My dad fled to Taiwan in 1949 as a 14-year-old, after the Communists won the civil war. His father fought for the losing side, the Nationalists. My mom's father, a Nationalist navy captain, also retreated to Taiwan. My mom, who was born in Taiwan, grew up thinking that her family would eventually return to China, after the Nationalists reclaimed their homeland. *8*

But that didn't happen. As young adults, my parents moved to the United States to lead better lives. They did not step onto Chinese soil for more than 50 years. Then their friends arranged a trip to China. And they asked me to join them on the six-city tour. *9*

My list of why-nots was jam-packed. And yet something inside—I could not explain what—urged me to go. *10*

When the plane jerked to a stop in Shanghai, our first destination, all of those reasons I decided to go **materialized** in the expression on my parents' faces. My mom folded and unfolded her hands impatiently in her lap. I was surprised and slightly scared to see my stoic dad's eyes glimmering with emotion. He slipped his hand, soft and spotted with age, in mine. *11*

"Last time I was here," he said, "my parents going from north to south, away from the Communists. So much bombing. A lot of *12* people starving." He leaned close. "You very lucky, Sharon."

That was my dad's line. When I would whine as a child, my ***13*** dad's response was **inevitable**: "Some people not as lucky as you."

But I never cared about being lucky. I just wanted to be like the ***14*** other American kids.

My parents, however, intended for me to become a model ***15*** Chinese American. Starting when I was six, they would drag me away from Saturday cartoons to Chinese church. I would squirm like a worm in my seat while a teacher recited Chinese vocabulary. I dutifully recited my *bo po mo fos*—the ABCs of speaking Mandarin. But in my head, I rearranged the chalk marks that made up the characters into pictures of houses and trees.

When I turned nine, I declared I wasn't going to Chinese school ***16*** anymore. "This stinks," I yelled. "None of my friends have to go to extra school. Why do I have to go?"

"Because you Chinese," my mom replied coolly. ***17***

"Then I don't want to be Chinese," I shouted back. "It's not fair. ***18*** I just want to be normal. Why can't you and Dad be like everybody else's parents? I wish I were somebody else's kid."

I waited for my mom to shout, but she just stared at me with ***19*** tired eyes. "If you don't want to go, don't have to," she said. . . .

My mom speaks English like I speak Chinese, slowly and ***20*** punctuated by *ums* and *ahs*. When someone speaks English too rapidly, my mom's eyes cloud with confusion. I instantly recognize her I-don't-get-it look, and I know it's time to explain something.

About a month before we left for China, I helped my mom ***21*** return a purchase to Wal-Mart.

The clerk rudely ignored my mom's slow English, speaking to ***22*** me instead.

Later my mom thanked me for my help. "Xie xie, Sharon," she ***23*** said, patting my shoulder. "I have a good American daughter."

"It's nothing, Mom," I said.   *24*

In the airport before we departed for China, my parents' friends   *25*
herded around me. "Your parents so proud of you," said one man.
"Always talking about you."

His words surprised me. I felt like I barely spoke with my   *26*
parents. Did they really know who I was? Then another question, the
one I always managed to skirt, surfaced in my conscience: Did I even
come close to understanding them . . . ?

Often during the tour, my own face resembled my mom's   *27*
I-don't-get-it look. At meals, my parents answered my constant
questions about each colorful bowl that would rotate on a lazy Susan.

My parents chuckled at the response when a waiter put a bowl of   *28*
soup on our table. While the other diners shouted with excitement,
I was horrified to see the remnants of a turtle floating in the clear
yellow broth.

My table cried in dismay when I let the soup circle past me.   *29*
"Strange," said one man, shaking his head. "Such good soup."

A few days after "the iron incident," as my run-in with the   *30*
hotel clerk became known in our tour group, my parents and I sat
on a bench overlooking monoliths. "Too bad I don't speak fluent
Chinese," I said. "I should have listened when you tried to teach me."

My dad looked at me with understanding. "It's okay," he said.   *31*
"You learning it now."

My mom smiled supportively. "Never too late," she said.   *32*

From Sharon Liao, "A Daughter's Journey." Reprinted by permission of the author.

---

envision
see

materialized
appeared, became real

inevitable
certain

monoliths
giant rocks and stones

Reflecting

1. What is the author's purpose—*to inform, to share, to persuade*? Circle one.

2. What specific details stand out to you? Name two.

   _____

3. How are paragraphs 13–18 organized—*chronologically* or *spatially*? Circle one.

4. What transitions indicate this pattern? Name two.

   _____

5. What is one other paragraph or set of paragraphs that uses transitions to indicate the same pattern?

   _____

Vocabulary

Use context clues to define the following words in "A Very Lucky Daughter."

1. **sheepish** (paragraph 6)

   clues: _____

   definition: _____

2. **stoic** (paragraph 11)

   clues: _____

   definition: _____

3. **remnants** (paragraph 28)

   clues: _____

   definition: _____

Critical Thinking

- What truth about the relationship between parents and their children is communicated in this narrative?
- What words would you use to describe the author's parents? Why?

Writing for Enrichment

The Writing Process
Prewrite → Revise → Publish
Write → Edit

What follows are possible writing activities to complete in response to the reading.

Prewriting

Choose one of the following writing ideas, or create your own idea.

1. **Blog (Journal) Writing:** For one day, pay careful attention to the conversations that you hear and participate in. Then write a blog or journal entry exploring your thoughts about these conversations.

2. **Paragraph Writing:** Describe an experience in which language led to misunderstanding, embarrassment, or worse.

3. Share interesting facts and details about someone in your family's past.

4. Explain the value of learning a second (or even a third) language.

5. Reveal something important about your relationship with your parents or grandparents through one or more personal experiences.

When planning . . .
- Use the **STRAP** strategy to identify the Subject, Type, Role, Audience, and Purpose of the assignment.
- Select a topic (experience) that means a lot to you.
- Gather your thoughts and ideas about the topic.
- Decide on an interesting or revealing main idea to develop.
- Arrange your details according to an appropriate pattern of organization.

When writing . . .
- Get all of your thoughts and ideas on paper.
- Don't worry about correctness at this point.
- Form a meaningful whole, with a beginning, middle, and ending.

When revising and editing . . .
- Let your first draft sit unread for a bit. Then reread it carefully.
- Check for clarity and completeness. (Have you left anything out? And have you clearly organized your ideas?)
- Ask a classmate to react to your first draft.
- Make the necessary improvements in the content of your writing.

lightpoet, 2014 / Used under license from Shutterstock.com

8

> "Knowing a topic well is the foundation of voice."
> —Vicki Spandel

Voice

When it comes to voice, we usually think of sound quality. We might say that a speaker's voice is easy to listen to or that a singer has a beautiful voice. But voice can also refer to the way an author expresses his or her ideas in print. For example, most informational writers such as authors of textbooks use a serious voice to present their ideas. On the other hand, writers in popular magazines or Web sites may use a more casual, friendly voice. The voice a writer uses depends on his or her purpose and intended audience.

In this chapter, you will learn how to recognize academic and personal voices in your reading assignments and how to use an appropriate voice in your own writing. You will also learn how authors choose certain types of words and sentences for their texts and how you can choose the best words and sentences for your own writing.

Learning Outcomes

L01 Read for voice.

L02 Write with voice.

L03 Read for word choice and sentences.

L04 Write with specific words and strong sentences.

What do you think?

According to the quotation, knowing a topic helps a writer express him- or herself with an effective voice. Why do you think this is the case?

"Voice is the aspect of writing closest to the writer."
—Dan Kirby

L01 Reading for Voice

An author's voice or tone can be thought of as his or her writing personality. The personality an author decides to project depends on the purpose of and audience for the writing. Some texts require a serious, straightforward voice; other texts are better served with a more personal, friendly voice. This section will help you understand how an author establishes an appropriate voice for a piece of writing.

Considering Purpose and Audience

You learned that **purpose** refers to the reason why a text was written. Authors write for a variety of purposes, including *to inform, to persuade,* and *to share.* You also learned that the **audience** is the intended reader for a text. The audience depends on the author's purpose and the form of writing.

Purpose

A textbook will be your main source of reading in most of your classes. Textbooks are written to inform you about the subjects you are studying, and the authors will use a serious, academic voice. Your instructors may also assign additional informational essays or articles related to your coursework.

Some of your assigned reading will express opinions about important topics such as climate change or the economy. The purpose of these texts is to persuade as well as to inform. The authors will present important facts and details in order to convince the reader to support or accept their opinions. Persuasive writing includes essays of argumentation, editorials, and personal columns.

If the readings come from a professional source such as a technical journal, the authors will use an academic, professional voice. If the texts come from newspapers or popular magazines, the authors will use a less academic voice.

You may also be assigned narrative texts in the form of personal essays and autobiographies, in which the authors write to share their thoughts about their lives. Authors almost always speak in a conversational or personal voice in narrative writing because they want to connect with the reader on a personal level.

---

purpose
the specific reason for reading or writing

audience
the intended reader

Audience

Students are the intended audience for textbooks. You should know that textbooks are written at different levels of difficulty. Freshmen textbooks introduce students to subjects of study, so they are written with a first-year audience in mind. Textbooks for more advanced students are more challenging because the intended audience is ready for more complex information.

Professionals may be the intended audience for other informational and persuasive pieces assigned by your instructors. If this is the case, you may find these additional readings more challenging than your textbooks. On the other hand, essays or articles from newspapers and popular magazines are intended for the general public, so these readings will likely be easier for you to understand.

Authors of personal essays and autobiographies may have a particular audience in mind (sports fans, foodies, techies) but may also try to appeal to a general audience. **Table 8.1** summarizes the voices authors use for different purposes and audiences.

Table 8.1 Purpose, Voice, and Audience

	Purpose	**Audience**	**Voice**
Textbooks	to inform	students	academic
Professional texts	to inform and/or persuade	professionals	academic
Texts from newspapers and magazines	to inform and/or persuade	general	less academic
Narratives and other personal writing	to share	varies	personal

Nowik Sylwia, 2014 / Used under license from Shutterstock.com

Practice ▸ Identify the purpose and audience for each reading selection that follows. For the purpose, choose among *to inform, to persuade,* or *to share.*

- A chapter in a biology textbook
- A music review in a popular magazine (A review reveals a personal opinion.)
- A newspaper article about a local business
- A personal narrative by a sports star
- A discussion of a personality disorder in a psychology journal
- A newspaper editorial
- A technical Web site explaining a system or process

Academic Voice

Authors of textbooks, professional journal articles, and white papers use an **academic voice**. An academic voice sounds serious, follows **formal English**, and sticks to the facts. This paragraph from a cultural anthropology textbook uses an academic voice. (Cultural anthropologists study the cultural development of people.) Notice that the text uses a serious tone, sticks to the facts, and refers to important research: "(Friedman 1999a)."

With industrial farming becoming more competitive, a small but growing number of farmers in North America are attempting to gain a competitive edge by using the very latest information technology. For example, some farmers equip their grain-harvesting combines with transmitters that allow a GPS satellite to track their exact position in their fields at any given time (Friedman 1999a). The sophisticated technology now available enables farmers to keep records on how much they harvest from each acre of land as well as the precise crop variety, water level, and fertilizer that will produce the highest possible yield for each parcel of land. This high-tech farm management is good for the environment because it uses fertilizer more economically, and it is good for the farmer because it increases the overall yield per unit of land.   From *Cultural Anthropology*, 9E. © 2012 Cengage Learning.

Personal Voice

Authors of personal narratives, personal essays, autobiographies, personal blogs, and many articles in popular magazines use a **personal voice**. A personal voice sounds somewhat relaxed and conversational, uses **informal English**, and includes the author's thoughts and feelings. The following description from an autobiography uses a personal voice.

One Capewell photograph is proudly displayed in our house. It's a black-and-white photograph of two people neatly attired in their best military uniforms, and it was taken during World War II in a small studio in Leicester, England. What makes this photograph so special to our family is the occasion that prompted it. It's my great-grandparents' wedding picture. They were both on leave for a day or two to get married. Their honeymoon had to wait until after the war. This photograph is one of the few keepsakes that we have left from their military experience and wedding day, and we take very special care of it.

---

academic voice
the voice used in textbooks and other professional materials

formal English
a serious style of writing used in academic texts

personal voice
the voice used in personal essays, autobiographies, and blogs

informal English
a relaxed style used in personal writing

Practice > Carefully read the following passages. Then identify whether the voice used in each one is academic or personal.

1. It has been more than two years since my telephone rang with the news that my younger brother Blake—just 22 years old—had been murdered. The young man who killed him was only 24. . . . As I wept for Blake, I felt wrenched backward into events and circumstances that seemed light years gone.

   Voice: _____

2. What Stella Liebeck's lawyers proved was that McDonald's was making its coffee 30 to 50 degrees hotter than other restaurants. In fact, the Shriner Burn Institute had already warned McDonald's not to serve coffee above 130 degrees. Yet the liquid that burned Liebeck was the usual temperature for McDonald's brew—about 190 degrees.

   Voice: _____

3. Several factors contributed to the tragedy in Walkerton, Ontario, including human error. First, according to *The Edmonton Journal*, a flaw in the water treatment system allowed the infested water to enter Walkerton's well (Blackwell, 2001). Even after the manure washed into Walkerton's well, the chlorine should have killed the bacteria.

   Voice: _____

4. On a cold August morning, the stars blanketed the night sky over the outskirts of Quito, Ecuador. I stood on the street corner, shaking underneath my wool sweater, waiting for a guide to show me around this massive market.

   Voice: _____

5. The major danger associated with texting is the distraction it causes to the driver. When a driver's eyes are concentrating on a phone instead of the road, he or she is more likely to get in an accident. Some critics say teenage drivers are the problem, but 20 percent of adults in a recent AAA study admitted regularly texting while driving.

   Voice: _____

L02 Writing with Voice

Your writing voice is the way that you express yourself on paper. To use the proper voice, you must think about the purpose and audience for the assignment.

Considering Purpose and Audience

- **Narrative Writing:** When an assignment directs you to write a narrative paragraph or a personal essay, your purpose is to share. And in most cases, your audience will be your instructor and classmates unless a more specific audience is named in the assignment. For narrative writing, you should use a personal voice because you will include your own thoughts and feelings.

- **Expository Writing:** When an assignment directs you to write an expository paragraph, summary, or report, your purpose is to inform. Your audience will again be your instructor and/or classmates unless a different audience is specified. For expository writing, you should use an academic voice, presenting facts and details to inform the reader about your topic.

- **Writing Arguments:** When an assignment asks you to write an argument or persuasive paragraph, your purpose is to persuade. Your audience will, again, be your instructor and classmates unless otherwise directed. When developing arguments, use an academic voice.

Personal voice: A personal voice should sound somewhat like a conversation with a classmate. Here are the common features of personal voice.

- **Uses the first-person point of view,** meaning that you share your thoughts and ideas using first-person pronouns—*I, me, my, we, us*:

    As I rode up the mountain trail, my thighs ached and my lungs burned, but I couldn't have been happier.

- **Expresses personal thoughts and feelings,** which means that personal voice is subjective:

    "It's good having you back, man," I responded. With that we hopped on our bikes and continued our adventure.

- **Uses easy-reading sentences** that sound like a conversation:

    Just then the fog disappeared, and we stopped for a breather. The evergreen trees seemed to stretch for miles.

- **Includes familiar words** to make the writing easy to read:

    Keith pedaled 50 feet in front of me. This adventure was his idea.

Academic voice: An academic voice should sound serious and somewhat formal. Here are the common features of academic voice.

- **Uses the third-person point of view**, meaning that you inform readers using third-person pronouns—*it, its, he, she, his, her, they, them*:

  On a chilly February afternoon, an old man sits sleeping on the sidewalk outside a New York Hotel. He probably spends his days alone on the street, begging for handouts, and his nights searching for shelter.

- **Focuses on facts and details**, rather than on personal thoughts or feelings, which means that the voice is objective:

  In New York City, unless the poor have access to rent-controlled apartments, they are forced to find housing at middle- to upper-income prices.

- **Contains longer, more complex sentences** that sound more formal and serious:

  According to William Tucker, a writer who has done extensive research on the homeless, the existence of rent control is the primary factor that determines the number of homeless a city will have.

- **Uses special words and phrases** to reveal knowledge of the topic:

  The experimental voucher program and the rent-control system are intended to provide shelter for low-income families.

- **Gives credit for sources of information** that you include in your writing:

  Families who rely on the voucher system pay less for rent than those who rent apartments on their own. Therefore, a family could raise its income by becoming homeless (Coulson 16).

- **Avoids contractions, slang and familiar sayings**, all of which are too informal:

  The voucher system makes sense if there is (not *there's*) enough housing, but at present there is (not *there's*) not enough.

Practice Write a paragraph about an animal. Use either a personal or academic voice depending on the purpose of your paragraph.

Developing a Writing Voice

Your individual writing voice, or special way of saying things, will develop through practice and experience. In other words, you won't write with "voice" just by learning about it. You must work on it. Here are a few things that you can do.

- **Practice writing.** Write nonstop for at least 10 minutes a day. Write about anything and everything. This practice will help you feel more comfortable with writing, which will help you write with a more confident voice.

- **Become a regular reader.** Read newspapers, magazines, blogs, books. As you read, you will learn about different ways of expressing yourself.

- **Watch for good models.** If you really like the sound of something you read, try to write a brief passage like it.

- **Know your topics.** If you know a lot about a topic, it's easier to sound interested and knowledgeable.

- **Know your purpose and assignment.** For informational paragraphs and essays, you will need to sound more formal and academic. For narratives and personal essays, you should sound more conversational and personal.

- **Be honest.** And keep things simple. This may be easier said than done. As editor Patricia T. O'Conner says, "Simplicity takes practice."

Practice ▷ Write nonstop for 5 to 10 minutes (time yourself) about any topic, but be sure not to stop. (If you draw a blank, write "I'm stuck" until some new ideas come to mind.) If you need help getting started, complete one of the open-ended sentences listed below, and then continue writing about the idea to see what you discover.

- I can't help but wonder . . .
- I hope . . .
- I wish . . .
- If only I . . .
- I have learned that . . .

- I'm beginning to wonder . . .
- I was surprised to find that . . .
- I want to promise myself to . . .
- I never thought I'd see the day when . . .

Afterward, count the number of words you have written. Continue this practice daily or every other day, and the number of words that you can write will increase dramatically. In the process, your individual writing voice will begin to develop.

"I love the taste of words. They have a taste and a weight and a color as well as a sound and shape."

—Philip Pullman

L03 Reading for Word Choice and Sentences

As part of your course work, you will read to be informed, to learn about important subjects. Your focus is, rightly so, on the main ideas, explanations, and examples in the text. As a result, you may not give much thought about the sentences an author writes or his or her choice of words. But knowing how a writer expresses his or her ideas can add to your understanding and appreciation of a reading selection.

Word Choice

The words used in a text help create the voice in the writing. A textbook or similar professional text will contain many specific words related to the subject of the writing, and these words will help create the academic voice in the text. On the other hand, the word choice in narratives and autobiographies will often be more general and recognizable, which helps create a personal voice in the writing.

Passage from an academic text with content-specific words (underlined)

Wind farms are a clean energy source. Unlike power plants, which emit dangerous pollutants, wind farms release no pollution into the air, meaning less smog, less acid rain, and fewer greenhouse emissions. The American Wind Energy Association reports that running a single wind turbine has the potential to displace 2,000 tons of carbon dioxide, or the equivalent of what one square mile of forest trees can do.

Passage from a personal essay with recognizable words

There was this old guy I used to know. His name was Jimmy, but I called him "Admiral" because he had been in some war. He was about five feet tall and smelled of cigar smoke mixed with coffee and other scents I didn't recognize. He had smoke-stained teeth that were crooked. His white hair always looked like it needed to be washed, and he wore the same wrinkled clothes. But he had beautiful blue eyes, the deepest blue I've ever seen.

Practice Carefully read each of the following passages. Then identify the word choice as *academic* or *personal*.

1. Frida Kahlo's path toward political and artistic fame was paved by pain. As a child, Kahlo was bedridden for nine months with polio. Then, at age 18, she was critically injured in an automobile accident.

   Word Choice: _____

2. Coach Brown didn't allow any goofing around in his gym class. Two guys learned this the hard way when they kept throwing the football when the rest of us stopped. Coach went after them with fire in his eyes.

   Word Choice: _____

3. When most Americans talk about mustard, they think of the bright yellow version that the rest of the world hardly recognizes. Actually, there are four basic types of mustard. A yellow mustard is made from finely ground mustard seeds, vinegar, and a bright yellow coloring called turmeric. Yellow mustard is mild and a common seasoning on grilled foods like hot dogs and hamburgers.

   Word Choice: _____

4. My wife and I love each other, but it's hard to imagine how we could be more different. Lupe is always meeting people for coffee, talking on the phone, or texting her friends. I'm much more private. I go to work at U.S. Steel and come right home. I don't need to see anybody else but Lupe.

   Word Choice: _____

5. It was in November that the Arab oil-producing nations cut off all oil shipments to the United States because it continued to support Israel in the Middle East war. The supply of gas was abruptly at a critical low. As a result, homeowners responded by voluntarily turning down their thermostats by an average of two degrees.

   Word Choice: _____

6. When I was six, my parents went to Europe for a month. As usual it was my mother's idea. I think even then I knew my father was not eager to leave.

   Word Choice: _____

"Any words that are not working
for you are working against you."

—Michael Kaplan

Diction Glossary

Diction refers to an author's choice of words. Common terms related
to diction are listed here.

- **Colloquialisms** are words or phrases used in
  informal texts. They help create a personal voice.
  You will not find colloquialisms in academic and
  professional texts.

  > We searched one building that was a real
  > rattrap. I could tell by the litter in the hallway that
  > it was used as a shooting gallery [a drug house].

- **Jargon** (technical diction) is a specialized language used by a
  specific group. Jargon is often associated with academic writing.

  > **Computer jargon:** *hypertext* (meaning "a system of web-like
  > links among pages on the Internet or within a program")
  > **Police jargon:** *code eight* (meaning "an officer needs immediate help")
  > **Medical jargon:** *agonal* (meaning "a major, negative change in
  > a patient's condition")
  > **Political jargon:** *left wing* (meaning a "liberal, progressive approach")

- **Idioms** are words used in special ways that may be different from their actual
  meaning. Idioms are used in personal writing, but are usually avoided in academic
  texts.

  > *blew my top* (meaning "to show great anger")
  > *dead of night* (meaning "in the middle of the night")
  > *pull your leg* (meaning "to tease you or tell a little lie as a joke")

- **Slang** is nonstandard language used by a particular group. It is used in fiction and
  in some personal writing for special effect, but it is not used in academic writing.

  > *emo* (meaning "to be depressed, moody, and emotional over extended
  > periods of time")
  > *iceman* (meaning "someone who maintains control of his emotions")

Sentences

Sentences come in all shapes and sizes. How an author shapes his or her sentences depends on the purpose for writing and the intended audience. Academic authors carefully compose their sentences so they clearly and completely communicate important facts and details. Authors of narrative pieces create sentences with a conversational tone. Sentences in personal writing are usually easier to read than sentences in academic writing.

Sentences in Academic Texts

The sentences in most textbooks are often long and complex, sometimes containing many ideas. This makes sense because textbooks must share information thoroughly and accurately. Here are some longer sentences from academic texts. In each one, the core concept is underlined. Notice all of the additional information added to each one.

- Public housing was built in Chicago because of the Great Migration, the name given to the movement of African Americans from the South to the North.

- Over time, the first musical instruments, which were stone and clay sound-producing objects, evolved into wind instruments including flutes and windpipes.

- While North American wealth grew out of the Industrial Revolution, today's capitalism is a system largely based on consumerism—an attitude that values the purchase of goods in the belief that it is necessary.

- In the past couple of decades, the status of the flight attendant (i.e., the position of the flight attendant in relation to others) has changed. In the era of shoe searches, deep-discount no-frill service, and packaged peanut snacks, little of the glamour remains.

Sentences in Personal Texts

The sentences in personal essays are usually simpler than the ones that you will find in academic texts. As such, they are easier to follow, and they move along more quickly. As a general rule, you will find more variety in the sentence length and structure. Notice how easy it is to read the following passages from personal essays.

- The smell of burnt oil was the first thing I would notice. On the right wall, Grandpa had pictures of the Smith Family. Some days, I would study all of the smiling faces in the pictures.

- I had locked myself in the walk-in freezer. I knew I would get out. Someone *had* to open the door. But when? All around me, I saw frozen shrimp, crab legs, and lobsters. I couldn't even eat any of it.

■ My Indian culture is important to me, but that doesn't mean that I don't value my independence. During this semester, I have had a chance to think about my life. And I realize that I am an Indian and an American.

Practice ▷ Carefully read the following sentences. Then identify each one as either academic or personal in style and structure.

1. The type of Latin American music known as urban popular music combines a dynamic sound with calls for social change.

   Sentence style: _____

2. It's laundry night for me, and the Laundromat is buzzing and thumping.

   Sentence style: _____

3. Waking up is hard. I'd rather dream about winning the lottery.

   Sentence style: _____

4. The Dutch fear of Islamic extremism has also increased, brought on in part by international attacks such as September 11, 2001, and later attacks in Madrid and London.

   Sentence style: _____

5. Indeed, maintaining the caste system in India depends largely on a system of arranged marriages.

   Sentence style: _____

6. I wonder why people bother to get married. Many marriages end early, and divorces can be ugly.

   Sentence style: _____

7. I remember the sound of music from the ice-cream truck on weekends.

   Sentence style: _____

L04 Writing with Specific Words and Strong Sentences

An important part of writing is using words and sentences that fit the assignment. For example, the words and sentences you use in informational writing will not be the same as the ones you use in personal writing.

Choosing Specific Nouns and Verbs

Generally speaking, specific words (*LeBron soars*) are better to use than general ones (*the basketball player jumps*). And fresh words (*a mind-warping movie*) are usually better than overused ones (*an unusual movie*).

It's especially important to use specific nouns and verbs because they carry the most meaning in your sentences. **Table 8.2** shows different examples of general versus specific nouns and verbs.

Table 8.2 General vs. Specific Words

General nouns:	personal computer		adventure		performer
Specific nouns:	iMac		bungee jumping		Jennifer Lopez

General verbs:	laugh	run	look		build
Specific verbs:	giggle	sprint	inspect		erect

Practice List examples of specific nouns and verbs that come to mind when you inspect the photograph below.

Specific Nouns	Specific Verbs

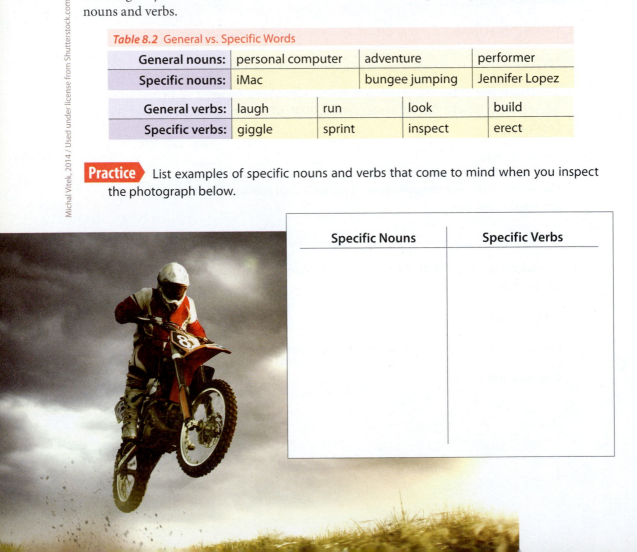

What to Watch for with Words

For each of your writing assignments, try to use words that clearly communicate your ideas. Also watch for the following:

- **Adjectives that are too general**, such as *big, neat, pretty, small, cute, fun, bad, nice, good, great,* and *funny.* Instead, use specific adjectives.

  General adjective: Josie makes a **good** pizza crust.
  Specific adjectives: Josie makes a **light, crispy** pizza crust.

- **Connecting too many adjectives.** A series of adjectives can be distracting.

  Too many adjectives: A **shocking** column of **dense, black** smoke shows the **specific** spot where the boiler exploded.
  Revised for clarity: A column of **black** smoke marked the spot where the boiler exploded.

- **The same word used again and again.** Repeating a word too many times can also be distracting.

  Repeated words: After breakfast, I watched **my grandfather. My grandfather** was working in his garden. With a steady hand, **my grandfather** planted a row of radishes.
  Revised to avoid repetition: After breakfast, I watched **my grandfather** working in his garden. With a steady hand, **he** planted a row of radishes.

- **Too many "be" verbs** (*is, are, was, were*). Instead, try to use specific action verbs.

  "Be" verb: Laura **is** a graceful swimmer.
  Specific action verb: Laura **swims** gracefully.

- **Words used incorrectly.** Words such as *your* and *you're* or *to, two,* and *too* are often misused.

  For next week, **you're** (not *your*) scheduled to work second shift.
  I worked **too** (not *to* or *two*) hard last night.

Practice ▶ Write a paragraph about an unforgettable teacher, boss, mentor, or coach. Afterward, check your writing for the word problems discussed on this page. For any problem you find, write a new sentence with improved word choice.

Writing Clear Sentences

To write strong, clear sentences, you must first understand the basics. By definition, a simple sentence expresses a complete thought and contains a subject and a verb. But not all sentences are "simple." There are compound sentences and complex sentences, as well as other types. **Table 8.3** provides a basic guide to sentences.

Table 8.3 A Basic Guide to Sentences

Correct Sentences

Simple sentence: My father operates a complicated machine. (*one compete idea*)

Compound sentence: I resemble my father in looks, but we have different personalities. (*two complete ideas*)

Complex sentence: Dad wears work pants and flannel shirts, while I favor T-shirts and jeans. (*one main idea and one subordinate, or lesser, idea*)

Sentence Errors

Fragment: Marisa at guard on the basketball team. (*no verb*)
Complete: Marisa starts at guard on the basketball team. (*verb added*)

Fragment: Lost his passport. (*no subject*)
Complete: Thomas lost his passport. (*subject added*)

Comma Splice: I love getting a tan, I may be damaging my skin. (*missing a connecting word or end punctuation*)
Corrected: I love getting a tan, but I may be damaging my skin. (*connecting word added*)

Run-on: Many species are considered endangered human interference is one of the main causes. (*no punctuation*)
Corrected: Many species are considered endangered. Human interference is one of the main causes. (*punctuation added*)

Practice Check your writing from the previous activity for sentence errors. Also put a star (*) next to any compound or complex sentences that you used.

Checking Sentences for Style

Knowledge of sentence basics is the first step when it comes to writing strong sentences. Checking your sentences for style is another consideration. Revise to remove these issues:

- **Short, choppy sentences:** Too many short sentences in a row will sound choppy. To correct this problem, combine some of the ideas.

  Choppy sentences: A tornado struck a small town. The residents had no warning. Many homes were destroyed. Four people lost their lives.

  Combined sentences: The residents had no warning when a tornado struck their town. Many homes were destroyed, and four people lost their lives.

- **Sentences with the same beginning.** This problem often creates repetitive sentences. To correct this problem, vary some of your sentence beginnings and lengths.

  Repetitive sentences: The rules for makeup work are unfair. The rules are sometimes strictly enforced. The rules don't allow for excuses. The rules don't care if we have other activities.

  Revised sentences: When it comes to makeup work, some instructors go strictly by the rules. They don't want to hear excuses. Our other activities don't matter.

- **Sentences with passive verbs.** With passive verbs, the subject receives the action of the verb. Sentences with passive verbs can be slow-moving and awkward. To fix this problem, change the passive verbs to active ones.

  Passive verb: The writing tutor is loved by English students.

  Active verb: English students love the writing tutor.

  Passive verbs: He is visited by students before and after school and is involved in some interesting discussions.

  Active verbs: Students visit him before and after school and share in some interesting discussions.

Practice ▸ Use this strategy to check the sentence style of your paragraph about an unforgettable person.

1. List the opening words in your sentences. Decide if you need to vary some sentence beginnings.

2. List the number of words in each sentence. Decide if you need to vary some sentence lengths.

3. List the main verbs used. Decide if you need to replace any passive verbs with active verbs.

☑ Review and Enrichment

Reviewing the Chapter

Read for Voice

1. What is the purpose of editorials and essays that express an opinion?

   _____

2. Who is the intended audience for newspaper articles?

   _____

3. Does a personal voice include the author's thoughts or feelings, or does it stick to the facts?

   _____

Write with Voice

4. Who is the intended audience for most of your writing assignments?

   _____

5. Why should you avoid contractions, slang, and familiar sayings in your academic writing?

   _____

Read for Word Choice and Sentences

6. What is jargon?

   _____

7. Why are sentences in academic texts usually longer than sentences in personal texts?

   _____

Write with Specific Words and Strong Sentences

8. If too many of your sentences contain "be" verbs (*is, are, was, were*), what can you do to correct this problem?

   _____

9. Why is it a problem if too many of your sentences begin in the same way?

   _____

"Life is a perpetual instruction in cause and effect."

—Ralph Waldo Emerson

Reading for Enrichment

The reading selection "The Pros and Cons of Gambling" comes from a textbook devoted to the hospitality business. Use the reading process to help you gain a full understanding of the text.

About the Authors

Kaye Chon, PhD, is the Chair Professor and Director of Hotel and Tourism Management at the Hong Kong Polytechnic University. He has published more than 200 articles on hospitality tourism issues. **Thomas A. Maier**, PhD, is an International Professor of Service Leadership and Innovation at the Rochester Institute of Technology in Dubai. He is also president of TAM—Global Services, Inc.

Prereading

This selection examines the creation of gambling as a big business in this country and the effects, both good and bad, this business has had on communities and individuals.

Gather your first thoughts about this topic in a cluster or web. To begin, write "gambling" in the middle of a piece of paper, then cluster ideas around it as they come to mind. Keep going until you run out of thoughts.

Consider the Traits

As you read this selection, focus first on the **ideas**—the topic, main idea, and supporting details. Also consider the **organization** of the text. What pattern of organization does it seem to follow? And finally, pay special attention to the **voice** projected in the writing. Do the authors use an academic or personal voice?

gambling

What do you think?

How would you explain the Emerson quotation on this page? (*Perpetual* means "lasting forever.")

Before you read, answer the **STRAP** questions to identify the main feature of the reading selection.

Subject: What specific topic does the reading address?

Type: What form does the reading take?

Role: What position does the writer assume?

Audience: Who is the intended audience?

Purpose: What is the goal of the reading?

Also, write questions you would like answered in your reading.

Reading and Rereading

Read the following selection from *Welcome to Hospitality: An Introduction* in which the authors examine the pros and cons of gambling.

As you read, make it your goal to (1) study the causes and effects of the topic, (2) identify the voice projected in the selection, and (3) decide if your questions have been answered. Consider annotating the text and/or taking notes as you read.

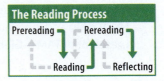

The Pros and Cons of Gambling

Because of the large amounts of money generated, gaming has **inherent** bonuses and risks. When politicians see the amount of money generated by the gaming industry, everyone wants a piece of the action. From a local perspective, it begins with the construction trade, since a construction company (or companies) will be selected to build the casino. Then, as the hiring begins, people move to the area for the jobs. They need to buy or rent homes, and then they need banks, grocery stores, drugstores, and other retailers to supply their day-to-day living needs. The expansion of the local population increases the need for public facilities like schools and hospitals, infrastructure development like roads, and other public projects. All of these people and businesses pay taxes both directly and indirectly. The government takes the taxes and prospers.   *1*

In addition, tourists coming to gamble need hotels, restaurants, shopping complexes, spas, and world-class entertainment venues. In fact, many casino visitors say they come for the food, shows, and other entertainment than come for the gaming alone. This creates   *2* jobs for the locals and generates many different tax bases for the government. To meet the needs of the visitors, the new tax revenues are used to improve and further expand local infrastructures that support the traffic. As the commercial base continues to expand, more new businesses open to support the growing number of tourists and locals. As a result, gaming is a very strong economic development tool. Casino development creates an upward spiral that increases jobs, adds more taxes from businesses and tourists, and decreases taxes for the townspeople. When residents see the projected economic impact, they are likely to agree that the positive aspects of gaming are impressive.

However, as with any growth in tourism, this expansion comes **3** with costs. The main problem is rooted in the business itself. Casinos generate millions of dollars a day in hard currency. For example, to convert the customers' paper money to chips and back again, the casinos have many areas called cages. They act as mini-banks. At any given moment, the average cage may hold five million dollars in cash. That figure does not even include all the money that is on the tables, in the slot machines, or in the **patrons'** possession at that moment.

Think about being around that kind of money! Does it make you **4** contemplate some different ideas? It does for everyone. This leads us to the negative aspects of the industry. It is perfectly normal to watch millions of dollars changing hands and think what it would be like to have some of it for your very own. Politicians, employees, customers, and local people are not exempt from this fantasy. This has sometimes led to bribery, graft, money laundering, and other illegal and/or criminal operations and has given gambling its negative image. In addition, because enormous amounts of money are located in one place, organized crime has always been **reputed** to be a part of the gambling industry. However, when respected businesspeople like Howard Hughes and Baron Hilton invested their money in casinos, gambling gained social acceptance. Although gambling's criminal background will always be part of the excitement of a casino, strict government regulation of casino employees and owners, as well as the formation of large business **conglomerates**, has helped to alter the reality.

There are two main problems for casino employees and players: **5** wanting the casino's money and spending too much of their own. Understanding both sides of these issues is important so that you, as an individual, can decide how you stand on each issue.

The first issue is that some people want the cash they see in the **6** casinos. If they cannot win it, they may want to steal it. This is one of the arguments that many anti-gaming **advocates** use to deter people from voting to allow gaming in their community. They speculate that crime will increase in the areas where casinos operate. Casino owners understand that the open display of cash is a temptation. The casinos do not want big winners to be robbed, because it is bad for business. People who do not feel secure are not going to come back. Therefore, security and **surveillance** are a major part of any casino operation. Good security deters people from thinking about theft.

The second issue is that people become obsessed with trying **7** to win the jackpot and stay at a casino too long. A select few will become problem gamblers. Problem gamblers tend to follow similar patterns. Usually, they win big early in their careers, and then they chase their losses. This means that if they lose, they double the bet to get money back. This is a bad strategy and rapidly increases gambling debts. However, less than 2 percent of gambling players are at risk of becoming addicted to gambling. Some researchers have stretched this statistic to 40 or 50 percent of the population.

The key point to remember is that there are many ways to define **8** "problem." Do you become a problem gambler when you spend $10 more than you budgeted, or when you steal to get money to gamble? Keep in mind that problem gamblers are a very small percentage of players overall. On the whole, over 98 percent of the people who come to a casino will not suffer any ill effects from the experience.

From Chon/Maier, Welcome to Hospitality, 3E. © 2010 Cengage Learning

---

inherent
basic part of something

patron
customer

reputed
believed to be

conglomerates
business organizations involved in many areas

advocates
people who support a cause

surveillance
the act of careful watching

Summarizing

Write a summary paragraph of "The Pros and Cons of Gambling." Remember to use your own words as much as possible.

Reflecting

1. What is the main idea of the text?

   _____

   _____

2. What is the purpose of the reading—*to inform, to share,* or *to persuade*? (Circle one.) And who is the intended audience?

   _____

   _____

3. What voice is used in the reading—*personal* or *academic*? (Circle one.)

4. What characteristics of the writing project this voice? Name two.

   _____

   _____

   _____

5. Study this sentence from the selection; then answer the questions that follow it.

   > As the commercial base continues to expand, more new businesses open to support the growing number of tourists and locals.

   Is this a *simple* or *complex* sentence? (Circle one.)

   Does it project a *personal* or *academic* voice? (Circle one.)

Vocabulary

Use context clues to define these words:

1. **infrastructure** (paragraph 1)
2. **graft** (paragraph 4)
3. **deter** (paragraph 6)

Critical Thinking

- Why is gambling so popular? And what does its popularity say about people?
- Does gambling "come with a cost"? Explain.

Writing for Enrichment

What follows are possible writing activities to complete in response to the reading.

The Writing Process
Prewrite → Revise → Publish
Write → Edit

Prewriting

Choose one of the following writing ideas or decide upon an idea of your own related to the reading.

1. In one or more personal blogs, examine you own experiences with gambling.
2. Explain a gambling-related topic that you recorded in your prereading cluster.
3. Report on some aspect of gambling that was mentioned in the reading selection. This will require some research.
4. Describe a gambling scene you have witnessed.
5. Explore the causes and effects of one of your "vices," such as a junk food addiction, excessive TV viewing, extravagant shopping, etc.

When planning . . .
- Complete the **STRAP** strategy for your writing.
- Gather plenty of details about your topic.
- Establish a main idea (thesis) to serve as a focus for your writing.
- Arrange your notes accordingly for writing.
- Consider the voice you want to project.

When writing . . .
- Develop effective beginning, middle, and ending parts in your writing.
- Present your main idea in the beginning part.
- Support and explain the main idea in the middle part.
- Close your writing with final thoughts about your topic.

When revising and editing . . .
- Carefully review your first draft. Make sure that you have included enough details to explain or support your main idea.
- Check for the appropriateness of your voice.
- Ask at least one peer to review your writing as well.
- Improve the content as needed.
- Make sure you have used effective words and sentences.
- Then edit your revised writing for smoothness and correctness.

Chapter 9

"Probably no subject is too hard if people take the trouble to think and write and read clearly."

—William Zinsser

Reading and Writing Essays

Many topics are too broad to cover in a single paragraph. In such cases, the essay becomes the ideal writing form. Essays allow you to elaborate on a topic, expanding ideas and providing many supporting details. Throughout your academic career, you'll be required to explain ideas and concepts in essays of varying lengths.

While essays generally require more thought than paragraphs, both have similar characteristics. Both paragraphs and essays have three main parts that function in similar ways. Likewise, all of the same qualities that go into creating an effective paragraph—ideas, organization, voice—matter just as much in essays.

This chapter will help you identify the main parts of professional essays and plan, research, and write an essay of your own.

Learning Outcomes

LO1 Understand essays.

LO2 Read and respond to essays (identify the main parts and outline the essay).

LO3 Plan an essay.

LO4 Write the first draft.

LO5 Revise the writing.

LO6 Edit the writing.

What do you think?

What experience do you have reading and writing essays? In what ways can essays clarify your thinking about difficult topics?

L01 Understanding Essays

Essays are vehicles for academic research and learning. Reading essays helps you broaden your knowledge by introducing you to new topics and expanding your thoughts about familiar topics. Writing essays allows you to explore topics more deeply and show your learning.

If you think of an essay as one big unit, your reading or writing task may feel overwhelming. Indeed, essays do require you to explore topics in greater depth and detail than paragraphs. However, essays can be broken down into manageable chunks just like paragraphs can.

Comparing Paragraphs and Essays

Both paragraphs and essays include three basic parts. **Figure 9.1** compares and contrasts the basic structure of each.

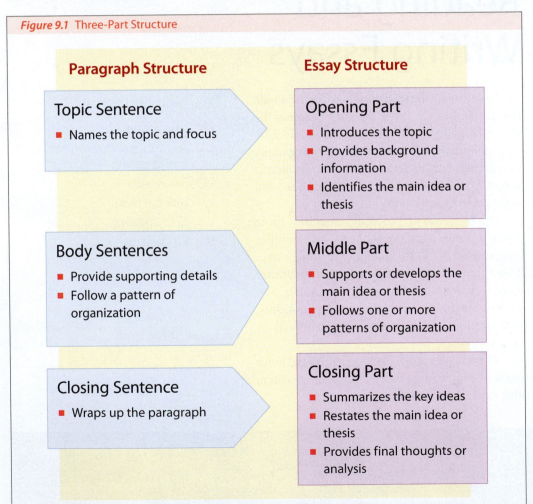

Figure 9.1 Three-Part Structure

Paragraph Structure

Topic Sentence
- Names the topic and focus

Body Sentences
- Provide supporting details
- Follow a pattern of organization

Closing Sentence
- Wraps up the paragraph

Essay Structure

Opening Part
- Introduces the topic
- Provides background information
- Identifies the main idea or thesis

Middle Part
- Supports or develops the main idea or thesis
- Follows one or more patterns of organization

Closing Part
- Summarizes the key ideas
- Restates the main idea or thesis
- Provides final thoughts or analysis

While paragraphs and essays bear similarities, note these important differences.

Paragraphs	Essays
■ Paragraphs are built from sentences.	■ Essays are built from paragraphs.
■ A paragraph opens with a topic sentence and ends with a closing sentence.	■ An essay begins with an opening paragraph and ends with a closing paragraph.
■ The topic sentence establishes the focus of the paragraph by identifying the topic and expressing a special idea or feeling about it.	■ The opening paragraph establishes the focus of the essay in a thesis statement.
■ Body sentences support the topic sentence through details.	■ Middle paragraphs support the thesis statement through main points (in topic sentences) and details.
■ The closing sentence brings the paragraph to a logical end.	■ The closing paragraph brings the essay to a logical end.

Types of Essays

There are three basic categories of essays: narrative, expository, and argument essays. Each type serves a different writing purpose.

■ **Narrative essays** re-create real or imagined events or experiences. They are structured according to time and are often written from a first-person point of view. The narrative essays in *Fusion* focus on real-life events.

■ **Expository essays** are sometimes referred to as informational writing because they are meant to inform readers about a certain topic. The writer's goal is to explain information accurately and logically. These essays may draw on information the writer already knows, but they often involve additional research. Expository essays are typically written in an academic voice with few personal pronouns.

■ **Argument essays** use reason and logic to try to convince readers of a certain position, belief, or conclusion. To do so, a writer must make a claim and defend it with evidence. The purpose of an argument is to change the reader's thinking, move the reader to action, or convince the reader of something's worth. Like expository essays, argument essays are written in an academic voice with few personal pronouns.

L02 Reading and Responding to Essays

To fully understand an essay, you need to identify its main parts.

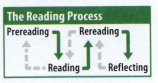

The Reading Process

Identifying the Main Parts

Essays have opening, middle, and closing parts. Here is what you should expect to find by reading each part.

The Opening Part

Start your reading by identifying the topic and thesis statement. Essay topics are usually identified in the title and/or the first paragraph. The first paragraph will often begin with background information about the topic and then lead to the thesis statement (main idea).

The thesis is the sentence that directs the rest of the essay. It includes the topic and a special feeling or idea about it. Sometimes an essay will include multiple paragraphs that lead up to the thesis statement, but the thesis almost always is located at the end of one of the first few paragraphs.

Fast Food Grows Up

The title and first few sentences identify the topic.

Value menus, kids' meals, drive-through windows—60 years ago, these fast-food terms were foreign to most people in the United States. Now they are recognized across the world. This is just one sign of the massive rise

Background information leads to a thesis statement (underlined).

of the fast-food business. <u>Fast food has grown into a multi-billion dollar industry that affects the United States' economy, family dynamics, and health.</u>

The Middle Part

Search the middle part for ideas that support the thesis statement. In some longer essays, headings will sometimes be used to signal new supporting ideas. But in general, key supporting points will be located in the topic sentences (first sentences) of the middle paragraphs.

Remember, a topic sentence controls the flow of a paragraph. So the details within each middle paragraph should support their corresponding topic sentence, which, in turn, should support the thesis statement. Common supporting details include the following:

- **Reasons** answer why something is true.
- **Facts and statistics** show how ideas connect to reality.
- **Examples** demonstrate an idea in action.
- **Explanations** discuss, clarify, interpret, or expound upon a key point.

Each new paragraph starts with a new supporting idea.

> Three factors contributed to the growth of fast food in the United States. More women joined the workforce in the 1960s and 1970s. Drive-in restaurants started national chains. An improved economy meant more time for leisure activities outside of the home.

> Today, the multibillion-dollar fast-food industry is a major contributor to the country's economy. Consumers spent $110 billion on fast food in 2000, compare to $6 billion in 1970. . . .

Note: Each supporting idea is supported with additional details.

The Closing Part

Look for the closing thought in the last paragraph. A closing thought restates, reinforces, or sums up the thesis statement. It may be located near the beginning of the closing paragraph or at its end. Some closing paragraphs include more than one closing thought.

The first sentence restates the thesis, and the last sentence provides the author's final analysis.

> Fast food has changed America's economy, culture, and health, and the industry will continue to do so in the future. However, fast-food businesses have shown they are willing to change to meet consumers' demands. One thing remains clear: Fast food is here to stay, even if it won't look exactly like it used to.

Outlining the Essay

You can keep track of the important information in essays by creating an outline of the main parts. **Figure 9.2** shows an outline for the sample essay on fast food. Start with the essay's thesis statement. Then find the topic sentence in each body paragraph. You can also record any key details as subpoints to each topic sentence. Finally, note the closing thought.

Figure 9.2 Simplified Outline

Thesis statement: Fast food has grown into a multi-billion dollar industry that affects the United States' economy, family dynamics, and health.

1. Three factors contributed to the growth of fast food in the United States.
   – Women joined the workforce.
   – Drive-in restaurants started national chains.
   – Americans had more leisure time outside the home.
2. The fast food industry is a major contributor to the country's economy.
3. Fast food has altered the way families eat and interact.
4. Fast food has contributed to bad health.

Closing thought: Fast food is here to stay, even if it won't look exactly like it used to.

Practice ▷ Read the following essay. Circle the thesis statement and underline the key supporting ideas in the middle paragraphs. Then create an outline of the essay.

Accomplishments of the Endangered Species Act

Critics of the Endangered Species Act (ESA) call it an expensive failure because only 46 species have been removed from the endangered list. Most biologists insist that it has not been a failure, for four reasons.   1

2

First, species are listed only when they face serious danger of extinction. Arguing that the act is a failure is similar to arguing that a poorly funded hospital emergency room set up to take only the most desperate cases, often with little hope for recovery, should be shut down because it has not saved enough patients.

Second, it takes decades for most species to become endangered or   3
threatened. Not surprisingly, it also takes decades to bring a species in critical condition back to the point where it can be removed from the critical list. . . .

Third, according to federal data, the conditions of more than half of the listed   4
species are stable or improving, and 99 percent of the protected species are still surviving. A hospital emergency room taking only the most desperate cases and then stabilizing or improving the conditions of more than half of those patients while keeping 99 percent alive would be considered an astounding success.

Fourth, the 2010 budget for protecting endangered species amounted to   5
an average expenditure of about 9 cents per U.S. citizen. To its supporters, it is amazing that the ESA, on such a small budget, has managed to stabilize or improve the conditions of more than half of the listed species. . . .

Most biologists and wildlife conservationists believe that the United States   6
also needs a new law that emphasizes protecting and sustaining biological diversity and ecosystem functioning rather than focusing mostly on saving individual species.

LO3   Planning an Essay

Essay writing is best approached as a process. It requires planning, research, drafting, revising, and editing. To write a strong essay, you need to give attention to each stage.

The planning stage includes identifying, focusing, and researching your topic. Sometimes instructors will assign you specific writing topics, but more commonly they will provide a general subject area that serves as a starting point for a topic. You must then narrow the focus to a specific topic that can be covered in an essay.

Choosing a Topic

When narrowing your focus, try to pick a topic that truly interests you and fulfills the requirements of the assignment. The topic needs to strike the right balance. It shouldn't be so broad that you cannot cover all of the important parts in an essay, nor should it be so specific that you could cover all of the important parts in one or two brief paragraphs. **Figure 9.3** shows how the selecting process should work from the general subject area to a specific topic.

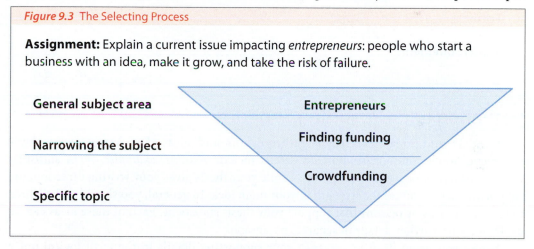

Figure 9.3 The Selecting Process

Assignment: Explain a current issue impacting *entrepreneurs*: people who start a business with an idea, make it grow, and take the risk of failure.

General subject area   Entrepreneurs

Narrowing the subject   **Finding funding**

                                   Crowdfunding

Specific topic

Practice ▶ Narrow these general subjects into specific topics: *renewable energy;* the *Iraq War*.

If you are having trouble selecting a specific topic, search the Internet for topics. You could also try one of these strategies to unlock ideas:

- **Clustering:** Write down your general or narrowed subject and circle it. Write down and connect all of the words that come to your mind related to the subject.
- **Freewriting:** Write down a particular thought about the assignment or subject. Then write for 5–10 minutes nonstop about whatever comes to mind about the subject.

Practice ▶ Choose an essay topic related to something you are currently studying. Or choose one of the specific topics you identified in the last activity. You will develop it in the following pages.

Forming a Thesis Statement

Once you have identified your topic, you should do some initial research using a variety of sources. Then form a thesis statement. Your thesis statement is the controlling idea for your essay; it identifies the unique part of the topic that your essay will explore. You can use the following formula to create a thesis statement.

A specific topic		a particular feature, part, or feeling		an effective thesis statement
Crowdfunding	**+**	a new way for entrepreneurs to fund business ideas	**=**	Crowdfunding offers a new avenue for entrepreneurs to fund projects.

Practice Use the formula that follows to create a thesis statement for your essay.

Topic: _____

Focus: _____

Thesis Statement: _____

_____

Gathering and Organizing Support

Conduct additional research to gather details and ideas that support your thesis statement. Some common supporting details include *reasons, examples, facts, statistics, definitions, reflections,* and *descriptions*. While your thesis gives your writing direction, the supporting details reveal the strength of your main idea. In general, you should gather three to five main ideas or reasons that support your thesis statement. Each of these ideas can be explained with further details in separate paragraphs.

Before you begin drafting, arrange your supporting details in the most logical order using a list or outline.

- A **list** works well for shorter essays or when your planning time is limited. Simply list the details in the order that they should appear.
- Use an **outline** for more thoughtful arrangement. Start with your thesis at the top. Then put your main supporting ideas one level below. In a new level under each supporting idea, write additional details that support that idea.

L04　Writing the First Draft

Follow your prewriting plan to help you write the first draft of your essay.

Practice　Read the sample essay, noting the opening, middle, and closing parts.

The New Funding Stream

Background information leads to a thesis statement.

In the past, very few funding options were available to entrepreneurs. 1
They could secure funding through venture capital, meaning they could
pitch ideas to investors, and it was up to the investors to decide whether
the idea was worth funding. Or they could seek money from friends and
family, an option with pitfalls of its own. Today, entrepreneurs are turning
to a new funding strategy. Crowdfunding is the newest avenue for funding
projects, and it's revolutionizing the way entrepreneurs do business.

The author defines the topic and explains how it works.

"Crowdfunding" is the practice of seeking small amounts of money 2
from a large number of people, typically via the Internet. Entrepreneurs
use a crowdfunding Web site to launch a campaign publicizing a business
product or idea. The campaign may include a short video or written
statement about the idea. Then the entrepreneurs create a target monetary
goal for the campaign and incentives for donating to the project.

The author introduces the first benefit with statistics and an example.

The most obvious benefit of crowdfunding is the chance to gain 3
funding to make new business ideas into a reality. By the end of 2014,
crowdfunding injected $65 billion into the economy and created up to
270,000 jobs. One successful example is Bluff Works, a business creating
wrinkle-free men's pants. Bluff Works raised more than $128,000 through
crowdfunding, far surpassing its original goal of $13,500. The money
helped pay for the materials and the production of pants.

More crowdfunding benefits are introduced in separate paragraphs.

Another benefit of crowdfunding is that the risk is minimal for both 4
entrepreneurs and donors. If the campaign doesn't meet its target goal,
donors get their money back. If it does, donors receive an incentive for their
contribution, and their money goes to help launch a product or idea.

A successful campaign shows entrepreneurs that there's a market for 5
what is being offered. Getting additional funding is easier when a core
group of people expresses interest in the business idea. Entrepreneurs may
also gain free feedback from donors about ways to expand business ideas.

The ending restates the thesis and gives a closing thought.

One report estimates 90 percent of the world's population has access 6
to crowdfunding platforms. That's an enormous market for entrepreneurs
and a great opportunity for getting a new business idea up and running.
Crowdfunding is perhaps the most democratic way to finance a startup.

Opening Strategies

The main objective of the opening paragraph is to lead up to the thesis statement. But before then, the paragraph should introduce the topic in an interesting way. Here are some strategies for introducing your topic.

- **Ask an important or challenging question.** This strategy will naturally lead the reader into the text because he or she will seek an answer to the question.

  > What did Roman gladiators use to replenish their sapped strength?

- **Share a brief, engaging story.** Readers are naturally attracted to interesting stories, even if they are very brief.

  > When U.S. Airways Flight 1549 struck a flock of birds, it became a flying brick.

- **Provide a surprising or little-known fact.** This strategy works well if readers are unfamiliar with the topic.

  > One study recently concluded that a near-starvation diet can increase longevity.

- **Create a scenario related to the topic.** This strategy gets the reader involved.

  > Imagine a street with no sidewalks, no crosswalks, no curbs, no lane markings— basically no distinctions among pedestrians, cyclists, and drivers.

- **Make a bold statement.**

  > Sometimes a seating assignment can be a death sentence.

Practice Introduce your essay topic in two different ways using the prescribed strategies.

Closing Strategies

The closing part offers important final impressions. More specifically, it helps the reader better understand and appreciate the importance of the topic and thesis. Consider using one or more of these strategies when writing your closing.

- **Remind the reader of the thesis.**

  > Crowdfunding is perhaps the most democratic way to fund a startup.

- **Reflect on the explanation or argument you presented in the essay.**

  > There is nothing like eye-to-eye contact or the sharing of an experience through the real act of engaging in a conversation with friends and family.

- **Offer a final idea.**

  > Candidates at all levels will be watching the influence of new media closely in the years to come.

Practice Close your essay using at least one of the prescribed strategies.

L05 Revising the Writing

Revising involves major improvements, especially in ideas, organization, and voice.

Using Transitions Between Paragraphs

In essays, a transition word or phrase often signals the relationship of one paragraph to the next. In this sentence, "Another benefit of crowdfunding is that the risk is minimal for both entrepreneurs and donors," the word *another* signals to the reader that a new benefit of crowdfunding is about to be discussed. **Table 9.1** shows common transitions that signal different relationships between ideas.

Table 9.1 Transitions

Words used to show location:

above	away from	beyond	into	over
across	behind	by	near	throughout
against	below	down	off	to the right
along	beneath	in back of	on top of	under
among	beside	in front of	onto	
around	between	inside	outside	

Words used to show time:

about	before	later	soon	until
after	during	meanwhile	then	when
afterward	finally	next	third	yesterday
as soon as	first	next week	today	
at	immediately	second	tomorrow	

Words used to compare things (show similarities):

also	in the same way	likewise	
as	like	similarly	

Words used to contrast things (show differences):

although	even though	on the other hand	still
but	however	otherwise	yet

Words used to emphasize a point:

again	for this reason	particularly	to repeat
even	in fact	to emphasize	truly

Words used to conclude or summarize:

all in all	finally	in summary	therefore
as a result	in conclusion	last	to sum up

Words used to add information:

additionally	also	as well	for example	likewise
again	and	besides	for instance	next
along with	another	finally	in addition	second

Words used to clarify:

for instance	in other words	put another way	that is

Practice ▶ Use the checklist in **Figure 9.4** to guide your revision. Keep revising until you can check off each item in the list.

Figure 9.4 Revising Checklist

Ideas

_____ **1.** Does my essay have an interesting topic that fulfills my purpose?

_____ **2.** Do I support my thesis statement with a variety of information?

_____ **3.** Do I thoroughly explore the focus?

Organization

_____ **4.** Does my essay have an opening, a middle, and a closing?

_____ **5.** Do I use transitions to signal new ideas?

Voice

_____ **6.** Does my writing voice show my interest in the topic?

L06 Editing the Writing

The main work of editing is correcting the revised draft for spelling, grammar, and usage. **Figure 9.5** shows an editing checklist you can use to edit your essay.

Figure 9.5 Editing Checklist

Words

_____ **1.** Have I used specific nouns and verbs?

_____ **2.** Have I used more action verbs than "be" verbs?

Sentences

_____ **3.** Have I used sentences with varying beginnings and of varying lengths?

_____ **4.** Have I avoided improper shifts in sentences?

_____ **5.** Have I avoided fragments and run-ons?

Conventions

_____ **6.** Do I use correct verb forms (*he saw,* not *he seen*)?

_____ **7.** Do my subjects and verbs agree (*she speaks,* not *she speak*)?

_____ **8.** Have I used the right words (*their, there, they're*)?

_____ **9.** Have I capitalized first words and proper nouns and adjectives?

_____ **10.** Have I carefully checked my spelling?

"Tell the readers a story! Because without a story, you are merely using words to prove you can string them together in logical sentences."

—Anne McCaffrey

☑ Review and Enrichment

You will be reading and responding to an essay from the textbook *American Government and Politics Today*. The essay explains two different approaches to protesting during the Civil Rights Movement.

About the Authors

Steffen W. Schmidt is a professor of political science at Iowa State University. **Mack C. Shelley, II,** is a professor of political science and statistics at Iowa State University. **Barbara A. Bardes** is a professor *emerita* of political science. **Lynne E. Ford** is a professor of political science at the College of Charleston.

Prereading

This reading focuses on the Civil Rights Movement, but more specifically the protest tactics used during this period. Before you read the selection, write freely for five or ten minutes about your prior knowledge of protesting in American culture. Here are some questions to help you get started: What makes protesting an appropriate topic for an American government textbook? What other periods of American history included significant moments of protest? Are protests still effective today?

Rena Schild, 2014 / Used under license from Shutterstock.com

What do you think?

Is it possible to write an essay as if you are telling the story of your topic to your reader? How might you do that?

Before you read, answer these questions:

1. What do the title, headings, and bolded items tell you about the topic?

_____

2. What might be the authors' intended purpose and audience?

_____

3. What questions do you want answered by this reading?

_____

Reading and Rereading

Read the following expository selection from *American Government and Politics Today*. During your reading, consider your prior knowledge of the Civil Rights Movement and protesting.

As you read, make it your goal to (1) identify the three main parts, (2) locate the thesis statement, and (3) note how the authors support the thesis statement. Annotate the text as needed as you read.

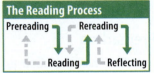

The Civil Rights Movement

In December 1955, a 43-year-old African American woman, **1** Rosa Parks, boarded a public bus in Montgomery, Alabama. When the bus became crowded and several white people stepped aboard, Parks was asked to move to the rear of the bus (the "colored" section). She refused, was arrested, and was fined $10, but that was not the end of the matter. For an entire year, African Americans boycotted the Montgomery bus line. The protest was headed by a 27-year-old Baptist minister, Dr. Martin Luther King, Jr. In 1956, a federal district court issued an **injunction** prohibiting the segregation of buses in Montgomery. The era of civil rights protests had begun.

King's Philosophy of Nonviolence

The following year, in 1957, King formed the Southern Christian **2** Leadership Conference (SCLC). King advocated nonviolent civil **disobedience** as a means to achieve racial justice. King's philosophy of civil disobedience was influenced, in part, by the life and teachings of Mahatma Gandhi (1869-1948). Gandhi had led resistance to the British colonial system in India from 1919 to 1947. He used tactics such as demonstrations and marches as well as nonviolent, public disobedience to unjust laws. King's followers successfully used these methods to gain wider public acceptance of their cause.

Nonviolent Demonstrations. For the next decade, African   3
Americans and sympathetic whites engaged in sit-ins, freedom rides, and freedom marches. . . . In the beginning, such demonstrations were often met with violence, and the contrasting image of nonviolent African Americans and violent, hostile whites created strong public support for the civil rights movement. In 1960, when African Americans in Greensboro, North Carolina, were refused service at a Woolworth's lunch counter, they organized a sit-in that was aided day after day by sympathetic whites and other African Americans. Enraged customers threw ketchup on the protesters. Some spat in their faces. The sit in movement continued to grow, however. Within six months of the first sit-in at the Greensboro Woolworth's, hundreds of lunch counters throughout the South were serving African Americans. . . .

Marches and Demonstrations. One of the most famous of the   4
violence-plagued protests occurred in Birmingham, Alabama, in 1963, when Police Commissioner Eugene "Bull" Connor unleashed police dogs and used electric cattle prods against the protesters. People throughout the country viewed the event on television with indignation and horror. King was thrown in jail. The media coverage of the Birmingham protest and the violent response by the city government played a key role in the process of ending Jim Crow laws in the United States. The ultimate result was the most important civil rights act in the nations's history, the Civil Rights Act of 1964.

In August 1963, African American leaders A. Philip Randolph   5
and Bayard Rustin organized a massive March on Washington for Jobs and Freedom. Before nearly a quarter-million white and African American spectators and millions watching on television, King told the world his dream: "I have a dream that my four little children will one day live in a nation where they will not be judged by the color of

their skin but by the content of their character."

Another Approach—Black Power

Not all African Americans agreed with King's philosophy
of nonviolence or with the idea that King's strong Christian
background should represent the core spirituality of African
Americans. Black Muslims and other African American separatists
advocated a more militant stance and argued that desegregation
should not result in cultural assimilation. During the 1950s and
1960s, when King was spearheading nonviolent protests and
demonstrations to achieve civil rights for African Americans, black
power leaders insisted that African Americans should "fight back"
instead of turning the other cheek. Some would argue that without
the fear generated by black militants, a "moderate" such as King
would not have garnered such widespread support from the white
American.

6

From Schmidt/Shelley/Bardes/Ford, *American Government and Politics Today*, 2013-2014 Edition, 16E. ©
2014 Cengage Learning.

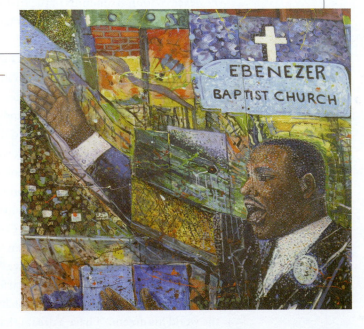

injunction
a written order

disobedience
refusal to obey something

sympathetic
showing agreement or understanding
with another person or issue

Jim Crow laws
laws that segregated (separated) black
people from white people

militant
aggressive and sometimes violent

cultural assimilation
the process of mixing different cultures

Summarizing

Write a summary of "The Civil Rights Movement." Remember that a summary presents the main points in a clear, concise form using your own words.

Reflecting

1. What opening strategy do the authors use?

   _____

2. What is the thesis statement of the essay?

   _____

3. What details in the middle part support the thesis statement?

   _____

4. What is the closing thought of the essay?

   _____

5. Does the essay include any transition words or phrases? Identify the ones you find.

   _____

6. What topics introduced in the essay could you develop or expand upon in a separate essay?

   _____

Vocabulary

Use context clues to explain or define the following words from the text.

1. **enraged**
   (paragraph 3)

2. **separatists**
   (paragraph 6)

Critical Thinking

- Would the Civil Rights Movement as a whole be a good topic for an essay? What are some reasons a college textbook is an appropriate medium for writing about such a subject?
- What type of protest style is more effective—violent or nonviolent? Provide reasons for your answer.
- What part of the essay would you revise or change, and why?

Writing for Enrichment

Choose one of the following writing ideas, or decide upon an idea of your own related to the reading.

1. Choose one of the specific protests or demonstrations mentioned in the essay. Develop the example into a topic for an essay. Do further research and write an essay about it.

2. Write an essay that explains another successful protest, demonstration, or movement in American history.

3. Write an essay about a time when you experienced or witnessed injustice.

4. Research and write an essay about a place or country that limits protests or other public free speech. Explain the impact of such laws.

When planning . . .

- Choose a topic that interests you and that meets the parameters of your assignment or writing purpose.
- Collect plenty of details about your topic.
- Create an initial thesis statement for your essay.
- Arrange the details in the most effective order.

When writing . . .

- Include an opening, a middle, and a closing in your essay. Each part has a specific role.
- Follow your planning notes, but feel free to include new ideas that pop into your mind as you write. Some of these new ideas may be your best ones.
- Use different types of supporting details for different effects. For example, use statistics to quantify an issue. Use definitions and examples to clarify an unfamiliar or complex concept.
- When relating an anecdote, include dialogue and personal thoughts to re-create the experience for your reader. Also use sight, sound, smell, taste, and touch.

When revising and editing . . .

- Check to see if your thesis statement is clear and well supported by the ideas and details in the middle paragraphs.
- Consider whether your middle paragraphs are in the best order. If necessary, rearrange them so that they lead the reader from one idea to the next in a sensible manner.
- Insert transitions between paragraphs or ideas as necessary to help carry the reader along.
- Edit your revised writing for style and correctness.

PART 3:

Types of Reading and Writing

Part 3: Types of Reading and Writing

Chapter

10

"We write to taste life twice, in the moment, and in retrospection."

—Anaïs Nin

Reading and Writing Narrative Texts

No one is sure when or why people started telling stories, but storytelling certainly predates reading and writing. Historians speculate that the first stories were told by clan leaders as a way to calm fears and gain respect. None of this was written down, since oral storytelling didn't find its way into written words until the time of the pharaohs, Homer, and the writers of the *Bible*.

In this chapter, you will read stories from other people's lives and share ones from your own. But unlike ancient clansmen, you won't embellish your actions. Instead, you will use essential storytelling techniques to share true events and experiences from your life.

Learning Outcomes

LO1 Understand narrative texts.

LO2 Read and respond to a narrative text (using a time line, asking the 5 W's and H, and recording sensory details).

LO3 Plan a personal narrative.

LO4 Write the first draft.

LO5 Revise the writing.

LO6 Edit the writing.

What do you think?

According Anaïs Nin, writing allows you "to taste life twice." What does this mean to you?

L01 Understanding Narrative Texts

To narrate is "to give an account of an event." Writers often narrate events from their own lives because these stories hold a special meaning. As author William Faulkner said, "The past is never dead; it's not even past." Our experiences continue to shape who we are and what we become long after they are over.

Writing narratives allows writers to retell events for readers and relive the experiences themselves. Narratives commonly focus on an event that has some heightened importance in a writer's life. The event may be painful or embarrassing. But sharing these experiences helps writers make sense of life, the world, and their place in it. As you encounter the narratives in this chapter, remember that the most memorable and inspiring stories are often the most authentic ones. Truth generates interest.

jiris, 2014 / Used under license from Shutterstock.com

Types of Narrative Texts

When you write a narrative text, you should choose a form that fits your purpose. Select from one of the forms of narrative texts listed here.

Personal Narrative A personal narrative re-creates a specific event or experience through vivid description and details. It shares what happened in an interesting way.

<table>
<tr>
<td>First-person perspective</td>
<td rowspan="4">As I rode up the mountain trail, my thighs ached and my lungs burned, but I couldn't be happier. Fifty feet in front of me pedaled my brother, Keith, fresh off his tour with the Marines. This mountain biking adventure was his idea. The green, forest-lined trail was rugged, with sharp turns and steep descents. At one point we hit a patch of fog, and I lost sight of Keith. It felt as if we were riding through clouds. The ghostly air was damp and smelled like rain. I slowed down and called for my brother, "Are you still up there?" "Would I be anywhere else?" he yelled back. When the fog disappeared, we stopped for a break on a ridge that overlooked a vast valley. A sea of pointy evergreens stretched for miles, ending near the peak of a distant mountain. While I snacked on a peanut-butter granola bar, Keith glanced over at me and said, "This is fun, isn't it?" I replied, "It's good having you back, man." With that, we hopped on our bikes and continued our adventure.</td>
</tr>
<tr>
<td>Specific descriptions and sensory details</td>
</tr>
<tr>
<td>Dialogue between characters</td>
</tr>
</table>

Personal Essay A personal essay is similar to a personal narrative in that it shares an event or experience. However, in a personal essay, the writer also reflects on the significance of the event or experience—why it was important, what lesson was learned, or how it relates to society as a whole. This type of analysis differentiates it from a personal narrative. The following paragraph is an excerpt from a personal essay about the experience of working on a cattle farm.

Reflection on the experience, revealing what is learned

> It's been three years since I worked on the cattle farm, and I feel an empty spot inside when I think of it. Never again will our entire family get together to do a job the way we did back then. It amazes me how quirky life is. There are so many experiences that we truly appreciate only once we move on. I'm sure my father felt this way when he left Grandpa's home, and I think my kids will feel the same way when they leave home, too.

Autobiography and Memoir An autobiography provides a detailed account of the writer's own life. In a sense, an autobiography is a collection of personal narratives and essays, because it covers key events in the writer's life. A memoir is like an autobiography, but it focuses on one specific aspect of the writer's life. The following excerpt comes from a memoir by Tim Russert, a popular television journalist, and his son, Luke Russert. The memoir focuses on Luke Russert's relationship with his father. In the passage, Russert retells an event that illustrated his father's personality and character.

Specific details arranged in time order

> When the bus pulled into the school parking lot to drop off dozens of my classmates and me, I heard loud laughs from my best buddies. My pal Paul Grayson screamed, "Luke, look at your dad!" . . . There was my dad with a jack-o'-lantern grin, waving an American flag and holding up a sign that read WELCOME HOME BOYS!

Dialogue, first-person pronouns, and a friendly voice

> Some might find it strange that the well-known host of *Meet the Press* was yelling and waving a flag like a maniac, but that was Dad. He was so excited to see me and his love was so strong that he didn't care that he might look silly greeting me as if I had just been deployed. At first I was a little annoyed at him because I thought his stunt was corny, but he rounded up my friends and shouted, "We're going to Burger King! After a week of rabbit food, supersize for everybody!" You just had to love him.

A personal reflection about the event

> But even then, I didn't fully appreciate his intense love till I left for college. It was hard on both of us because I knew I could no longer open his door, plop down in a chair and talk, but we adapted, thanks to cell phones. If my future kid ever reads this, we'll be on the unlimited texting plan because I'll be blowing up your phone!

Excerpted from *Big Russ & Me: Father & Son: Lessons on Life* by Tim Russert and Luke Russert.

L02 Reading and Responding to a Narrative Text

To gain the most from reading narratives, record the key details in a time line, ask and answer the 5 W's and H, and collect sensory details in a sensory chart.

Using a Time Line

When reading a narrative, it's important that you follow the key actions in the order they occur. Almost all narratives follow chronological order, meaning details are arranged in time order. A graphic organizer called a time line works well for tracking the key details. **Figure 10.1** shows an example of a time line.

If you are having trouble identifying the sequence of events, search for transition words and phrases that show time. Transitions signal that an event is beginning, continuing, or ending. The following list includes common transition words and phrases in narratives.

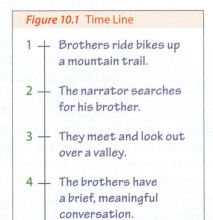

Figure 10.1 Time Line

1 — Brothers ride bikes up a mountain trail.

2 — The narrator searches for his brother.

3 — They meet and look out over a valley.

4 — The brothers have a brief, meaningful conversation.

after	during	lastly	second
after that	finally	later	soon after
as soon as	first	meanwhile	then
before	in the beginning	next	third
currently	in the past	now	yesterday

Answering the 5 W's and H

To understand a narrative, you need to identify the key actions. To do this, you can answer the 5 W's and H about the story (**Figure 10.2**). These questions will help you collect the most important details.

Figure 10.2 5 W's and H

Who was involved in the experience?

What happened?

When did it happen?

Where did it happen?

Why did it happen?

How did it happen?

Recording Sensory Details

After you record the key events and answer the 5 W's and H, focus on the quality and arrangement of details. Narrative writing should be rich with description, details, and dialogue. Ideally, reading a narrative should feel like you are participating in the event itself.

You can use a sensory chart to keep track of and analyze the details in a narrative. (*Sensory* means "related to the senses.") A narrative may not address all of the senses, but it should include a variety of them to make the story come to life. **Figure 10.3** shows a sensory chart for a personal narrative about two brothers mountain biking.

Figure 10.3 Sensory Chart

Sight	Sound	Smell	Taste	Touch
–forests of evergreens –dirt path –mountain ranges –thick fog	–"Are you still up there?" –birds chirping –crunching leaves	–fresh air –smell of rain	–peanut-butter granola bar	–bumpy trail –smooth metal handle bars

Practice Fill in the chart with any sensory details from the following paragraph.

This grime is infectious. The smell of old cigarettes and expired perfume is constricting my sore, scratchy throat and turning my stomach. I pop a breath mint into my mouth. I'm on an underground subway platform, changing trains in Toronto. The weight of my bulging backpack thrusts me forward with the rush-hour crowd. When the subway door opens, I hurry inside and look around frantically. A robotic voice chimes in: "Doors closing. Stay clear of the doors." I find a seat at the end of the car, next to a small, tired woman clutching a paper sack overflowing with groceries.

Sight	Sound	Smell	Taste	Touch

Reading and Reacting to a Professional Narrative

This professional narrative focuses on a tragic experience—the murder of the writer's brother. As you can imagine, the event had a major impact on the author. He describes it in great detail in the narrative.

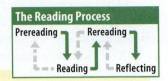

The Reading Process

Prereading → Rereading → Reading → Reflecting

About the Author

Brent Staples is an award-winning author and journalist. The oldest of nine siblings, Staples grew up in Chester, Pennsylvania, but moved several times due to financial difficulties before finishing junior high school. He later graduated from Widener University and started a career in journalism. He is currently an editorial writer for *The New York Times*. His book *Parallel Time: Growing Up in Black and White* won the Anisfield-Wolf Book Award for distinguished writing on racism and human diversity.

Before you read, answer these questions:

1. What does the "About the Author" feature suggest about the writer's perspective?

_____

2. What do the title, first paragraph, and first lines of other paragraphs tell you about the text?

_____

3. What might be the author's purpose in sharing this story?

_____

_____

As you read, (1) track the key details in a time line, (2) search for answers to the 5W's and H, and (3) identify what the author learns from the experience. Annotate the text and take notes as needed.

tobkatrina, 2014 / Used under license from Shutterstock.com

A Brother's Murder

It has been more than two years since my telephone rang with the news that my younger brother Blake—just 22 years old—had been murdered. The young man who killed him was only 24. Wearing a ski mask, he emerged from a car, fired six times at close range with a massive .44 Magnum, then fled. The two had once been inseparable friends. A senseless rivalry—beginning, I think, with an argument over a girlfriend—escalated from posturing, to threats, to violence, to murder. The way the two were living, death could have come to either of them from anywhere. In fact, the assailant had already survived multiple gunshot wounds from an accident much like the one in which my brother lost his life.

As I wept for Blake, I felt wrenched backward into events and circumstances that had seemed light-years gone. Though a decade apart, we both were raised in Chester, Pennsylvania, an angry, heavily black, heavily poor, industrial city southwest of Philadelphia. There, in the 1960s, I was introduced to mortality, not by the old and failing, but by beautiful young men who lay wrecked after sudden explosions of violence. The first I remember from my fourteenth year—Johnny, brash lover of fast cars, stabbed to death two doors from my house in a fight over a pool game. The next year, my teenage cousin, Wesley, whom I loved very much, was shot dead. The summers blur. Milton, an angry young neighbor, shot a crosstown rival, wounding him badly. William, another teenage neighbor, took a shotgun blast to the shoulder in some urban drama and displayed his bandages proudly. His brother, Leonard, severely beaten, lost an eye and donned a black patch. It went on.

As I fled the past, so Blake embraced it. On Christmas of 1983, I traveled from Chicago to a black section of Roanoke, Virginia, where he then lived. . . . One evening . . . standing in some Roanoke dive among drug dealers and grim, hair-trigger losers, I told him I feared for his life. He had affected the image of the tough he wanted to be. But behind the dark glasses and the swagger, I glimpsed the baby-faced toddler I'd once watched over. I nearly wept. I wanted desperately for him to live. The young think themselves immortal, and a dangerous light shone in his eyes as he spoke laughingly of making fools of the policemen who had raided his apartment looking for drugs. He cried out as I took his right hand. A line of stitches lay between the thumb and index finger. Kickback from a shotgun, he explained, nothing serious. Gunplay had become part of his life.

4   I lacked the language simply to say: Thousands have lived this for you and died. I fought the urge to lift him bodily and shake him. This place and the way you are living smells of death to me, I said. Take some time away, I said. Let's go downtown tomorrow and buy a plane ticket anywhere, take a bus trip, anything to get away and cool things off.

5   He took my alarm casually. We arranged to meet the following night—an appointment he would not keep. We embraced as though through glass. I drove away.

6   As I stood in my apartment in Chicago holding the receiver . . . I felt as though part of my soul had been cut away. I questioned myself then, and I still do.

7   Did I not reach back soon or **earnestly** enough for him? For weeks I awoke crying from a recurrent dream in which I chased him, urgently trying to get him to read a document I had, as though reading it would protect him from what had happened in his waking life.

8   His eyes shining like black diamonds, he smiled and danced just beyond my grasp. When I reached for him, I caught only the space where he had been.

posturing
bragging or threatening without taking action

assailant
the person who does the attacking

light-years
an extremely great distance

affected
adopted or pretended

earnestly
seriously or with deep feeling

Summarizing

Write a summary of "A Brother's Murder." Remember that a summary presents the main idea of a text in a clear, concise form using your own words.

Reflecting

1. Answer the 5 W's and H questions for the narrative.

   _____

   _____

2. Circle the types of details the author uses—*sensory details, statistics, personal thoughts and feelings.*

3. What stands out most in the narrative—the author's thoughts and feelings, the dialogue, and/or the sensory details? Explain.

   _____

4. How does the author open the narrative? How does he close it?

   _____

5. What does the author learn from this experience?

   _____

Vocabulary

Create vocabulary entries for these words. For each word, identify the pronunciation and helpful word parts, give a primary definition, and use the word in a sentence.

1. **inseparable** (paragraph 1)   3. **recurrent** (paragraph 7)
2. **immortal** (paragraph 3)

Critical Thinking

- Besides grief and sadness, what other emotions does Staples portray in the narrative? How does he portray these other emotions?
- What influence, if any, do you think being the oldest of nine brothers and sisters had on the author's reaction to his brother's murder?
- Do you think this narrative would have had the same impact if it were written by an outsider looking in on the situation?
- Author Rick Riordan says, "It takes strength and courage to admit the truth." How does this narrative reveal the author's strength and courage?

LO3 Planning a Personal Narrative

Your narrative paragraph should focus on a special moment in your life. Remember that special moments are different for different people. Not everyone has bumped into a famous person, won the lottery, or survived a tsunami. Everyday occurrences can hold great meaning, too.

The Writing Process

Prewrite   Revise   Publish

Write   Edit

If you are having trouble thinking of a topic, consider finishing one of the following sentence starters:

- A moment that thrilled me was when . . .
- A moment that surprised me was when . . .
- A moment that saddened me was when . . .
- A moment in which I learned a great lesson was when . . .

Once you pick a topic, think carefully about it, recording the actions and conversations related to it. List as many of the important details as you can. Be certain to record details that answer the 5 W's and H about the experience. If you are having trouble remembering the details, try freewriting or talking about the experience with someone.

Practice List four important memories from your own life. Consider experiences that covered a brief span of time, from a few minutes to a few hours. Then choose one of the experiences to write about, and list key actions and conversations related to the topic.

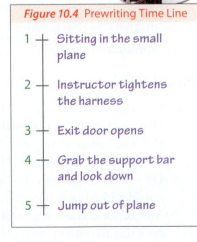

Paewlumfaek, 2014 / Used under license from Shutterstock.com

Creating a Time Line

After you have gathered the main actions of your story, organize the details chronologically (by time). This will also make your paragraph easier to read and understand.

The best way to gather the details of the narrative chronologically is to create a simple time line. The time line will serve mainly as a reference point for writing the narrative, so don't worry about adding all the specific details. **Figure 10.4** shows a prewriting time line of key events in the narrative "The Earth Below Us."

Practice Complete a time line to organize the key details of your narrative in chronological order.

Figure 10.4 Prewriting Time Line

1 — Sitting in the small plane

2 — Instructor tightens the harness

3 — Exit door opens

4 — Grab the support bar and look down

5 — Jump out of plane

Gathering Showing Details

The most realistic narrative paragraphs use a mix of telling and showing details. Telling details involve reporting what happened. Those are the details you gathered in your time line. Showing details recreate the experience for your reader. These details are far more interesting to read because they help readers feel like they're actually part of the story.

Sensory details help "show" the reader what happened by describing the experience in terms of sight, sound, smell, taste, and touch. You can use a sensory chart like the one in **Figure 10.5** to gather the sensory details for your narrative. Your paragraph may not address all of the senses, but adding a variety of sensory details can help you re-create the experience for readers.

Figure 10.5 Sensory Chart

Sight	Sound	Smell	Taste	Touch
clouds below	buzz of the engine	musty loading zone	grape bubble gum	blast of wind
square plots of farm land	conversation with Dale			ice-cold support bar
body dangling out of the plane				

Practice Create a sensory chart by describing your experience in terms of sight, sound, smell, taste, and touch. (Your experience might not have details in every category.)

Other showing details can help your narrative come alive: dialogue, personal reflections, and references to the setting.

- **Dialogue** shares conversations between people.

  "Dude, I'm telling you—I almost blacked out," he offered, only half-jokingly.

- **Personal reflections** reveal your thoughts and feelings at the time.

  I realized I had reached a point of no return.

- **References to the setting** (time and place of the action) help the reader visualize the experience.

  Some 9,000 feet off the ground, I peered down at the clouds below me. . . .

Practice Create dialogue for your narrative. Though it may be almost impossible to recall every last detail or conversation from a past experience, you can still capture the spirit of the time and place by creating realistic conversations.

LO4 Writing the First Draft

Follow your prewriting plan to help you write the first draft of your narrative. The paragraph that follows is a sample narrative to consider before you write.

Practice ▸ Read the personal narrative, noting how the writer created effective opening and closing parts. Also note how the writer uses the middle part to share a mix of telling and showing details.

The Earth Below Us

Topic Sentence
starts right in on the action.

Some 9,000 feet off the ground, I peered down at the clouds below me and realized I had reached a point of no return. I was about to jump out of a tiny, musty-smelling airplane. Earlier that day, when I asked my brother about his first time skydiving, he singled out this moment as his most frightening. "Dude, I'm telling you—I almost blacked out," he offered, only half-jokingly. Those words were embedded in my mind as my tandem partner, Dale, tightened the harness that held us together and guided us to the open exit door. With half of my body dangling outside the plane, I reached out and gripped the ice-cold support bar under the right wing. I had to tighten my grip to fight the wind, which pushed with the force of a charging linebacker. Below me I could see perfectly square plots of farmland in between breaks in the clouds, and I almost missed Dale's final instructions over the buzz of the Cessna's twin engines and the screech of the wind. "When you are ready, cross your arms over your chest, and we'll jump," he yelled.

Body Sentences
use a variety of details to recreate the experience.

Closing Sentence
ends with an exciting moment.

Surprisingly, I didn't black out. I was ready. So I crossed my arms, and we jumped.

Reflecting

1. What do you like best about this paragraph?
2. What are two of your favorite details?
3. How much time does the event cover?
4. Does the writer say just enough about the experience, too much, or too little?

Writing Tips

When you write a narrative paragraph, you are essentially sharing a story. As you begin drafting, think about your purpose for telling the story—to inform, entertain, amuse, surprise, or shock. Also consider these storytelling techniques to interest your readers.

- **To make your beginning special,** jump right into the action (rather than starting with a more traditional topic sentence).
- **To give your story impact,** include dialogue, but be selective. Make sure the conversation enhances or adds to the story.
- **To bring your writing to an effective end,** offer a final analysis of the experience. Reflect on what the experience meant to you or what lesson the experience revealed to you.

The Working Parts of a Paragraph

A paragraph consists of three main parts, each of which has a special function. **Figure 10.6** explains how each part should function in a narrative paragraph.

Figure 10.6 Parts of a Narrative Paragraph

Topic Sentence:	A topic sentence sets the stage for the paragraph. It should introduce the topic in an interesting way. Consider jumping right into the action with surprising dialogue or a dramatic detail about the experience.
Body Sentences:	The body sentences support the topic sentence. Include specific details to make each main point clear to the reader. Provide sensory details to bring the experience to life.
Closing Sentence:	A closing sentence (or two) captures the importance of the experience.

NOTE: Remember the transitional words used to show time order, such as *after, after that, as soon as, before, later, meanwhile, next, soon after, then,* and *to begin with.*

Practice ▷ Develop your first draft using these tips and your planning as a guide.

L05   Revising the Writing

Revising a first draft involves adding, deleting, rearranging, and reworking parts of the writing. Start revising by reading your draft two or three times. Then ask one of your peers to review your work using a response sheet. Search for and cut any unnecessary ideas.

Adding Specific Nouns, Verbs, and Modifiers

You can improve your paragraph by making nouns, verbs, and modifiers specific.

General Noun	Specific Noun
My **teacher**, Dale.	My **tandem partner**, Dale.

General Verb	Specific Verb
Dale **put on** the harness.	Dale **tightened** the harness.
I **looked** down at the clouds.	I **peered** down at the clouds.

Read aloud the first draft and then the revised version of the excerpt. Note how the specific words bring the writing to life.

half of   dangling   gripped the ice-cold
With my body, <s>on the</s> outside of the plane, I reached out and <s>held a</s> support bar under the
right   pushed with the force of a charging linebacker
wing. I had to tighten my grip to fight the wind, which <s>was blowing really hard.</s>

Practice   Improve your writing by replacing general nouns, verbs, and modifiers with more specific ones. Use a revising checklist like the one in **Figure 10.7** to check your ideas, organization, and voice. Continue working until you can check off each item in the list.

Figure 10.7 Revising Checklist

Ideas

_____ 1. Do I focus on one specific experience or memory?

_____ 2. Do my details answer the 5Ws and H about the experience?

_____ 3. Do I include sensory details and dialogue?

Organization

_____ 4. Does my paragraph have an opening, a middle, and a closing?

_____ 5. Is the story organized chronologically?

Voice

_____ 6. Is my interest in the story obvious to the reader?

L06 Editing the Writing

The main work of editing is correcting the revised first draft for spelling, grammar, and usage.

Using Direct and Indirect Quotations

Most narratives include dialogue to reveal the personalities of the people involved in the story. When you include conversations between people using their exact words, place quotation marks before and after the **direct quotation**. However, when you share what people say without using their exact words, do not use quotation marks before and after the **indirect quotation**. The word *that* often indicates dialogue that is being reported rather than quoted.

Direct Quotation

Sitting in my one-room apartment, I remember Mom saying, **"Don't go to the party with him."**

Indirect Quotation

I remember Mom saying **that I should not go to the party with him.**

NOTE: Direct quotations should sound like real conversation. Read direct quotations out loud to make sure they sound natural.

Practice Read the sentences. Indicate where quotation marks ("") should be placed before and after the speaker's exact words in direct quotations. If the sentence contains no direct quotations, write "C" for correct on the blank line following the sentence. The first example has been done for you.

1. "Christina, could you give me a ride to the airport?" I asked. _____

2. You are one lucky guy, said Reid. _____

3. The tour guide said that we should get our cameras out. _____

4. There's little chance I'll ever eat octopus, joked Hailey. _____

5. Before we left, I said, Don't forget your wallet and cell phone! _____

6. Kyle said if he goes to the movie tonight, he will miss the party. _____

7. Where did you get that dress? asked Brianna. _____

8. Derrick says that he thinks your sweater shrunk in the dryer. _____

Practice Read your narrative. Check the dialogue (with direct quotations) to make sure that it is properly marked with quotation marks. If you did not include any dialogue, consider adding some.

Punctuating Dialogue

As you edit your narrative paragraph, pay special attention to the punctuation marks used with quotation marks. Here are the rules to follow:

- **When a period or comma follows quoted words**, place the period or comma *before* the end quotation mark.

  "Never be afraid to ask for help," advised Mrs. Williams.

  "With the evidence we now have," Professor Howard said, "many scientists believe there could be life on Mars."

- **When a semicolon or colon follows quoted words**, place the semicolon or colon *after* the end quotation mark.

  You said, "Let's stay late"; however, you left the party early.

- **When quoted words are a question (or an exclamation),** place the question mark (or exclamation point) *before* the end quotation mark.

  "Bill, do you want to go the gym with me?" I asked.

- **When the question mark or exclamation point belongs with the whole sentence instead of the quoted words,** place the punctuation *after* the end quotation mark.

  Were you serious when you said, "I want to go home"?

- **Use just one piece of end punctuation.**

  Incorrect: I heard you ask, "Why?". **Correct:** I heard you ask, "Why?"

Practice Correct the punctuation of the dialogue in each sentence.

1. "Please hand your papers in by the end of the week", instructed Professor Hopkins.
2. Mark said, "See you soon;" however, he missed his flight.
3. "With everything that happened", my boss said, "it might be best to take Friday off."
4. "Don't be late"! exclaimed Lisa.
5. "Should we meet tomorrow"? asked Renee.
6. Did you really mean it when you said, "We are just looking?"
7. "Remember, you have a doctor's appointment on Thursday", my mom reminded me.
8. "Can you pass me the ketchup"? I asked.

Practice Review your narrative paragraph closely for the punctuation of any dialogue.

Practice Read the narrative, looking for errors in spelling, punctuation, capitalization, and usage. Then correct the model using correction marks. One correction has been done for you.

Creature of Habit?

People say I'm a creature of habit͵but that's not entirely true. For instance, I like try new foods. When I was in New hampshire, I ate raw oysters. People say they taste like the ocean Indeed, they are very salty. I do enjoy the thrill of a new food, oysters will not become a staple of my diet. Besides eating bizarre foods, I also enjoy going on weeknd adventures. Last saturday, my friends and I went camping outside the city. We didn't even set up tents, deciding to sleep under the stars. Unfortunately, the rising sun woke us up at about 6:00 a.m. I got only about for hours of sleep, so I tired and crabby for the rest of the day. I guess that's won way I am a creature of habit. I like my sleep. Another unusual activity I enjoy is Pilates. For some reason my friends think this makes me a wimp but I bet they couldn't make it threw one class. I would love to see them try

Correction Marks

℈	delete	⋏͵	add comma	word ⋀	add word
d̲	capitalize	? ⋀	add question mark	⊙	add period
⌀	lowercase	ᵛ,	insert an apostrophe	◯	spelling
⋀	insert			⊓	switch

Using an Editing Checklist

Use an editing checklist to edit the remainder of your paragraph for style and correctness.

Practice ▸ Prepare a clean copy of your revised narrative and use the checklist in **Figure 10.8** to look for errors. Continue working until you can check off each item in the list.

Figure 10.8 Editing Checklist

Words

____ **1.** Have I used specific nouns and verbs?

____ **2.** Have I used more action verbs than "be" verbs?

Sentences

____ **3.** Have I used sentences with varying beginnings and lengths?

____ **4.** Have I avoided improper shifts in sentences?

____ **5.** Have I avoided fragments and run-ons?

Conventions

____ **6.** Do I use correct verb forms (*he saw*, not *he seen*)?

____ **7.** Do my subjects and verbs agree (*she speaks*, not *she speak*)?

____ **8.** Have I used the right words (*their, there, they're*)?

____ **9.** Have I capitalized first words and proper nouns and adjectives?

____ **10.** Have I used commas after long introductory word groups and to separate items in a series?

____ **11.** Have I correctly punctuated any dialogue?

____ **12.** Have I carefully checked my spelling?

Adding a Title

Finish the narrative by adding an attention-getting title. Here are three simple strategies.

- **Use a phrase from the piece:**

    Creature of Habit?

- **Use a main idea** from the paragraph:

    A Brother's Murder

- **Paint a picture in the readers' minds:**

    The Earth Below Us

"The universe is made of stories, not of atoms."

—Muriel Rukeyser

☑ Review and Enrichment

You will be reading and responding to an excerpt from Helen Keller's autobiography, *The Story of My Life*. The excerpt tells of a life-changing moment and includes Keller's analysis of the event. Use the steps in the reading process to work through the text. After the reading activities, you'll find a number of writing ideas to help you create a narrative paragraph or essay of your own.

About the Author

Helen Keller lost her sight and hearing at the age of 18 months. With the help of her teacher, Anne Sullivan, Keller gained the ability to communicate and eventually earned a college degree in 1904. Keller later became a leading social activist and humanitarian, fighting for women's and labor rights. Her autobiography was turned into the 1977 television drama *The Miracle Worker*. In 1999, Gallup named Keller to its list of most widely admired men and women of the 20th century.

Prereading

Most of us take our ability to see and hear for granted. Consider the important function eyesight and hearing play in your daily communication. Now imagine losing your ability to see or hear. What adjustments would you have to make to communicate without the ability to hear? What adjustments would you have to make to communicate without the ability to see? Write freely about each scenario. In doing so, consider the adversity Keller, who was both deaf and blind, faced as she first learned the concept of language.

_____

_____

_____

What do you think?

Consider Muriel Rukeyser's quotation: What does it say about the importance of stories? Why do you think she feels this way?

Before you read, answer these questions:

1. What do the title, the opening two paragraphs, and the first lines of the other paragraphs tell you about the topic?

_____

2. What might be the author's intended purpose and audience?

_____

3. What questions do you want answered by this reading?

_____

Reading and Rereading

Read the following narrative excerpt from Helen Keller's *The Story of My Life*. In it, Keller shares an incredible, life-changing experience that reveals the significance of something that most of us take for granted: language.

As you read, make it your goal to (1) answer the 5 W's and H questions, (2) appreciate the specific details and dialogue, and (3) consider any questions that the story brings to mind. Annotate the text as needed.

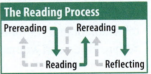

The Key to Language

We walked down the path to the well-house, attracted by the **fragrance** of the honeysuckle with which it was covered. Someone was drawing water, and my teacher placed my hand under the spout. As the cool stream gushed over one hand, she spelled into the other the word "water," first slowly, then rapidly. I stood still, my whole attention fixed upon the motions of her fingers. Suddenly I felt a misty consciousness, as of something forgotten—a thrill of returning thought; and somehow the mystery of language was revealed to me. I knew then that "w-a-t-e-r" meant the wonderful cool something that was flowing over my hand. That living word awakened my soul, gave it light, hope, joy, set it free. There were **barriers** still, it is true, but barriers that could, in time, be swept away.

I left the well-house eager to learn. Everything had a name, and each name gave birth to a new thought. As we returned to the house,

1

2

every object I touched seemed to **quiver** with life. That was because I saw everything with the strange, new sight that had come to me. On entering the door I remembered the doll I had broken. I felt my way to the hearth and picked up the pieces. I vainly tried to put them together. Then my eyes filled with tears; for I realized what I had done, and for the first time I felt **repentance** and sorrow.

I learned a great many new words that day. I do not remember what they all were; but I do know that mother, father, sister, teacher were among them—words that were to make the world blossom to me. It would have been difficult to find a happier child than I was as I lay in my crib at the close of that eventful day and lived over the joys it had brought me and, for the first time, longed for a new day to come. . . . 3

I had now the key to all language, and I was eager to learn to use it. Children who hear acquire language without any particular effort; the words that fall from others' lips they catch on the wing, as it were, delightedly, while the little deaf child must trap them by a slow and often painful process. But whatever the process, the result is wonderful. Gradually, from naming an object we advance step by step until we have **traversed** the vast distance between our first stammered syllable and the sweep of thought in a line of Shakespeare. 4

At first, when my teacher told me about a new thing, I asked very few questions. My ideas were **vague**, and my vocabulary was inadequate, but as my knowledge of things grew, and I learned more and more words, my field of inquiry broadened, and I would return again and again to the same subject, eager for further information. Sometimes a new word revived an image that some earlier experiences had engraved on my brain. 5

I remember the morning that I first asked the meaning of the word "love." This was before I knew many words. I had found a few early violets in the garden and brought them to my teacher. She tried to kiss me; but at that time I did not like to have anyone kiss me except my mother. Miss Sullivan put her arm gently around me and spelled into my hand "I love Helen." 6

"What is love?" I asked. 7

She drew me closer to her and said, "It is here," pointing to my *8*
heart, whose beats I was conscious of for the first time. Her words
puzzled me very much because I did not then understand anything
unless I touched it.

I smelt the violets in her hand and asked, half in words, half in *9*
signs, a question [that] means, "Is love the sweetness of flowers?"

"No," said my teacher. *10*

Again I thought. The warm sun was shining on us. *11*

"Is this not love?" I asked, pointing in the direction from *12*
which the heat came, "Is this not love?"

It seemed to me that there could be nothing more beautiful *13*
than the sun, whose warmth makes all things grow. But
Miss Sullivan shook her head, and I was greatly puzzled and
disappointed. I thought it strange that my teacher could not show
me "love."

A day or two afterward I was stringing beads of different *14*
sizes in **symmetrical** groups—two large beads, three small ones,
and so on. I had made many mistakes, and Miss Sullivan had
pointed them out again and again with gentle patience. Finally I
noticed a very obvious error in the sequence and, for an instant,
I concentrated my attention on the lesson and tried to think how
I should have arranged the beads. Miss Sullivan touched my
forehead and spelled with decided emphasis, "Think."

In a flash, I knew that the word was the name of the process *15*
that was going on in my head. This was my first conscious
perception of an abstract idea.

Helen Keller, *The Story of My Life*, copyright 1905 Doubleday. Used under permission of the public
domain.

fragrance
distinct smell

barriers
obstacles; hardships

quiver
shake or tremble

repentance
regret for something done

traversed
moved from one place to another

vague
unclear or not specific

symmetrical
equal patterns or proportions

Summarizing

Write a summary of "The Key to Language." Remember that a summary presents the main points in a clear, concise form using your own words.

Reflecting

1. Answer the 5 W's and H about the narrative.

2. What main idea is developed in the narrative? (Hint: Use what you learned by answering the 5W's and H to help you describe the main idea.)

3. What types of sensory details does Keller include?

4. What is unique about the dialogue in the narrative? Remember, Keller could neither see nor hear.

5. How has the text changed or expanded your understanding of the subject?

Vocabulary

Use context clues to explain or define the following words from the text.

1. **consciousness**
   (paragraph 1)

2. **vainly**
   (paragraph 2)

Critical Thinking

- What qualities of water made it possible for Keller to learn the word even though she couldn't see or hear?
- Why was a word such as "water" easier for Keller to learn than words such as "think" and "love"?
- The events described in the narrative happen before 1900. How would Keller's experience have been different if she had gone through it in modern times?
- What is "the key to language" that Keller describes in paragraph 4?

Writing for Enrichment

Choose one of the following writing ideas, or decide on an idea of your own related to the reading.

1. Respond to a photograph from your childhood. Be sure that your writing answers the 5 W's and H questions about the experience.

2. Have you ever had a learning experience that altered your perspective of the world? Describe the experience in a narrative paragraph or essay.

3. Share a story or moment when you gained a greater appreciation for a mentor, teacher, or instructor.

4. Using Keller's essay as a guide, write a personal narrative that describes how you overcame an obstacle.

5. Develop a narrative paragraph or essay about an important childhood experience.

When planning . . .

- Choose a specific personal experience to write about.
- Consider your purpose (to inform, to entertain, and so on), your audience (peers, family members, and so on), and the main point you would like to share.
- Collect plenty of details (sensory details, dialogue, personal thoughts).
- Review the narratives in this chapter to see how they are developed.

When writing . . .

- Include an opening, a middle, and a closing in your narrative. Each part has a specific role.
- Follow your planning notes, but feel free to include new ideas that pop into your mind as write. Some of these new ideas may be your best ones.
- Remember that sensory details include more than just sight. Also consider sound, smell, taste, and touch.
- Include dialogue and personal thoughts to re-create the experience for your reader.

When revising and editing . . .

- Determine if you've done too much telling and not enough showing.
- Also ask yourself if your story will interest and engage your reader. If it doesn't, determine what changes need to be made.
- Have at least one trusted peer react to your narrative. Ask for his or her honest reaction.
- Edit your revised writing for style and correctness.

Chapter

11

"Good writing is clear thinking made visible."

—Bill Wheeler

Reading and Writing Expository Texts

Expository writing explains information. As a result, most of the reading you do in college will be expository in nature. The more skilled you become at reading expository texts, the better you'll learn in every class. Writing expository texts can help you think about your learning and demonstrate your understanding and thoughts to instructors.

The first model in this chapter focuses on captive beluga whales. A later paragraph focuses on measures to reduce brain injuries in football. The final model addresses income inequality in the United States.

In each of these readings, you'll see how professional writers explain information in writing. Afterward, you'll get the chance to write your own expository texts.

Learning Outcomes

LO1 Understand expository texts.

LO2 Read and respond to an expository text (using a line diagram).

LO3 Plan expository writing.

LO4 Write the first draft.

LO5 Revise the writing.

LO6 Edit the writing.

What do you think?

What is the importance of information? How can it empower you?

L01 Understanding Expository Texts

Expository writing provides information, so it is common in magazines and textbooks. One professional model in this chapter comes from *Smithsonian* magazine, and the other comes from the textbook *American Government and Politics Today*. The authors use facts, statistics, anecdotes, examples, quotations, and other details to explain their topics.

Types of Expository Texts

When you write expository texts, you should choose a form that fits your purpose. Select from one of the forms of expository texts listed here.

Illustration An illustration explains or clarifies a main idea with specific reasons, facts, and details.

Main Idea
Facts and Details
Reasons

Beluga whales are curious, friendly, and intelligent denizens of the arctic seas. These white whales have large humps on their foreheads, making them almost as recognizable as their cold-water cousins, the horned narwhals. Belugas are among the smallest whales but are also among the most talkative, communicating with their pods using a variety of clicks, whistles, and hoots. They sometimes imitate other sounds, including human voices. Belugas feed on fish and crustaceans, and they in turn are food for killer whales, polar bears, and indigenous people of the North. Belugas are especially vulnerable when the northern seas freeze over, so they migrate south to avoid being trapped beneath the ice. During the Cold War, U.S. scientists trained belugas for underwater missions against the Soviets. Some say belugas are too curious and intelligent for their own good.

Classification A classification breaks a subject into categories, explaining each category and relating them to the larger whole.

Subject
Category 1
Category 2
Category 3
Category 4

When most Americans talk about mustard, they mean a type of bright-yellow goo that the rest of the world hardly recognizes. Actually, there are four basic types of mustard. Yellow mustard is the most common in America, made from finely ground mustard seeds, vinegar, and a bright yellow coloring called turmeric. For a spicier flavor, people enjoy brown mustard, which is made from coarse-ground mustard seeds. For an even stronger flavor, mustard lovers turn to the famous mustard called Dijon, named after the French city where it was first processed. Dijon mustard is finely ground and is usually mixed with wine instead of vinegar. Finally, there are many specialty mustards, including everything from honey to jalapeños. There's a mustard for just about everybody.

Definition A definition explores the meaning of a key word or concept. The writing may include synonyms, antonyms, etymology (history), examples, and comparisons.

Key Word [*Pandemic* is a medical term that strikes fear into people everywhere. But

Definition [what exactly is a pandemic, and where did this word come from? A pandemic is an "infectious disease covering a wide geographic area and affecting a large proportion of the population." Being "infectious" is a key feature: Influenza can

Example [be pandemic, but cancer cannot. Some people use *pandemic* interchangeably

Comparison [with *epidemic*. But an epidemic doesn't become pandemic until it covers an

Etymology (History) [extremely widespread area, such as a series of countries. *Pandemic* comes from the Greek *pandemos*: The Greek root *pan* means "every" or "all," and *demos* means

Examples ["common people." Thus, *pandemos* means "all the people." Two pandemics that are often cited are the Black Death during the Dark Ages and the flu pandemic in 1918 that killed from 40 to 50 million people. Current pandemics include H1N1 (an infectious flu virus), HIV, and Ebola. Here's a scary final thought: Globetrotting provides an easy way for pandemics to spread.

Process Most process texts give step-by-step instructions for completing a task. Other process texts focus instead on how something works, such as how a match makes fire.

Task [One of the most frustrating situations to deal with is a car with

Equipment [a dead battery. To jump-start a car battery, you will need a set of jumper cables and a second car with a fully charged

Step 1 [battery. First, line both cars up so the batteries are as close as they can be. Make sure both cars are

Step 2 [turned completely off. Next, familiarize yourself with the positive (+) and negative (–) terminals of

Step 3 [both car batteries. After you have done so, connect one end of the positive jumper cable (usually red or orange) to the positive terminal of the dead battery. Then connect the

Step 4 [other end of the positive cable to the positive terminal of the live

Step 5 [battery. Next, connect the negative cable (usually black) to the negative

Step 6 [terminal of the live battery. Finally, clamp the other end of the negative cable to a solid, unpainted metal part of the engine of the dead car. From there, stand back

Step 7 [and start the car that's providing the jump. Wait about five minutes, and then try

Step 8 [to start the car with the dead battery. If it starts, remove the cables in the reverse

Step 9 [order in which you put them on. Then you can hit the road.

Suchat Siriboot, 2014 / Used under license from Shutterstock.com

Cause-Effect A cause-effect text identifies the reasons that a certain event, condition, or set of circumstances occurred and explores what resulted from it. The text links causes to effects, exploring chains of events.

Cause	In January 2009, U.S. Airways Flight 1549 struck a flock of geese, causing the plane to lose power in both its engines. The situation forced pilot Chesley
Effect 1	"Sully" Sullenberger to perform an emergency landing on the Hudson River outside of New York City. Not only did he land safely, but all 150 passengers
Effect 2	survived without a single serious injury. The event had many meaningful effects. Massive media coverage of the landing made "Sully" a household name. Many
Effect 3	hailed him as an American hero. Meanwhile the passengers on the flight, though safe, suffered emotional trauma from the landing. Many refuse to step back
Effect 4	onto a plane. Maybe the greatest effect, however, was the impact on the airline industry. The emergency landing led to a greater awareness of the dangers of bird populations near airways. Government agencies have gone so far as to wipe out geese populations in the proximity of airports. In the end, a tragic collision and remarkable emergency landing may result in safer air travel for years to come.

Comparison-Contrast A comparison-contrast text explains how two or more subjects are alike and different. Some comparisons focus on similarities and others on differences. Some focus first on one subject and then the other, while others consider each subject point by point.

Subjects	People often say I look like a younger version of my father, but in most ways,
Appearance: Similarities/ Differences	we are very different. Our appearance is similar in that I have Dad's brown eyes and black hair. We even have similar smiles, according to my mom. But no one would say we look the same in the clothes we wear. Dad dresses old school in work pants and button-down shirts, always tucked in. For me, it's jeans and a Padres
Personalities: Similarities/ Differences	jersey, never tucked in. Our different dress shows our different personalities. Dad is quiet, shy, and hardworking, while I am very friendly and sometimes a little crazy. Neither of us, however, is interested in causing trouble. Most of our
Background: Differences	differences come from our different backgrounds. Dad was born in Mexico in a small town south of Monterrey. He moved to San Diego as a young man and has worked very long hours as a cook ever since. It has taken him a long time to feel comfortable in this country, while the United States is all I have ever known.
Summary	Dad's tough life has made him more careful and serious than I am, but if he had lived my life, he would be much more like me.

L02 Reading and Responding to an Expository Text

The main idea in an expository paragraph is generally located in the first sentence—the topic sentence. It expresses a point that the writer wants to make about the topic. Once you determine the main idea, look for details that support it. The facts, examples, quotations, and other details should be provided in the sentences that follow.

The number of supporting details in a paragraph depends on the main idea. One writer may share a single example or story in great detail to support the main idea. Another writer may use three, four, or five brief examples. It all depends on what the writer feels is the best way to develop her or his main idea.

Main Idea [Autism causes my son to struggle in understanding other people's minds. We

Anecdote [often play hide and seek, and his sisters find excellent hiding spots. But when my son goes to hide, he often simply goes to another room and sits on the floor. He struggles to know how to hide because he doesn't know what other people think.

Main Idea [Autism causes my son to struggle in understanding other people's minds.

Example [He does not hide well during hide and seek. He doesn't lie because he can't

Example [understand that he might manipulate what someone else knows. He has trouble

Example [predicting how someone will feel. My son finds other people perplexing.

Using a Line Diagram

To keep track of the key components in an expository text, consider using a line diagram (see **Figure 11.1**). Identify the main idea along the top of the diagram and the supporting points on the legs. If the text includes additional details about any of the supporting points, add legs to show the details.

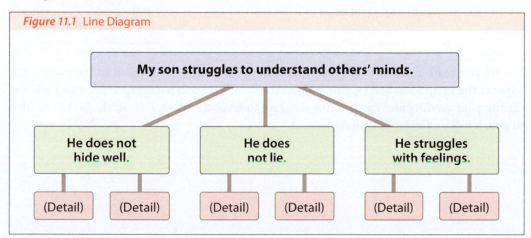

Figure 11.1 Line Diagram

My son struggles to understand others' minds.

He does not hide well. — He does not lie. — He struggles with feelings.

(Detail) (Detail) (Detail) (Detail) (Detail) (Detail)

Reading and Reacting to a Professional Exposition

The following reading focuses on captive beluga whales. These whales help educate the public about their species, but some would say that captivity is cruel for such intelligent and social creatures. Use the reading process to gain a full understanding of this professional text.

The Reading Process

Prereading ┐ ┌ Rereading

└ ↓ ↓ ↑ ↑ ↓

└ Reading ┘ └ Reflecting

About the Author

Jerry Adler has written for numerous publications, including *Smithsonian, The New Yorker, New York, Wired, Esquire,* and *The Huffington Post.* He spent 30 years as a writer and editor at *Newsweek,* producing more than 120 cover stories. He has written two books: *The Price of Terror: How the Families of the Victims of Pan Am 103 Brought Libya to Justice* and *High Rise: How 1,000 Men and Women Worked Around the Clock for 5 Years and Lost $200 Million Building a Skyscraper.* At the Web site for *Newsweek,* Adler composes satirical poems about politics and life.

Before you read, answer these questions:

1. What does the "About the Author" feature tell you about the writer's perspective?

   _____

2. What do the title, subtitle, and beginning paragraph tell you about the text?

   _____

3. What do you know about beluga whales and the amusement parks that keep them?

   _____

4. What questions do you hope to have answered by the reading?

   _____

As you read, make it your goal to (1) identify the main idea, (2) note the points that support the main idea, and (3) think about the details in each paragraph. Annotate the text during your reading and create a line diagram to trace the ideas. Reread the text as needed to gain a full understanding of its content.

Swimming in Limbo
Captive belugas are snared in ongoing controversy

Is it possible for any animal to be too smart for its own good? We don't mean the ones who invented atomic weapons; that's obvious. But the qualities that the Navy sought to harness in [their trained **beluga** whale] Noc—intelligence, curiosity and a willingness to cooperate with humans—make whales and dolphins sought-after attractions at marine parks. The price of intelligence thus includes the possibility of capture and a lifetime in what the aquarium industry refers to as "human care," otherwise known as "captivity."   1

The issue was raised recently by the documentary *Blackfish*, an account of a killer whale who fatally attacked his trainer at Sea World in Orlando. A federal appeals court recently denied Sea World's appeal of stricter regulations on human-whale interactions imposed after the death. Meanwhile, six public and private institutions led by the Georgia Aquarium are suing to overturn a ruling by the National Oceanic and Atmospheric Administration, denying their permit to import 18 belugas from Russia. The whales, captured several years ago in the North Pacific, languish in administrative **limbo** at a Russian facility near the Black Sea.   2

NOAA's decision was focused on belugas in the wild, a "near-threatened" species whose habitat is being degraded by climate change and pollution. The aquariums, the agency ruled, had failed to prove that capturing the animals did not adversely affect the wild population. Scott Higley, a vice president of the Georgia Aquarium, contends that the best way to preserve the species is to bring a few of them to a place like Atlanta, where scientists can study them. Belugas can be bred in captivity, but there are only 30 or so in U.S. aquariums and, Higley says, they need an infusion of fresh genes to stay healthy.   3

But this technical dispute is a **proxy** for deeper questions. Many of the 9,000 public comments to the agency—described by a   4

NOAA spokesperson as "overwhelmingly" opposed to the permit—addressed the impact of captivity on belugas' health and longevity. "They do very poorly in captivity," says Lori Marino, a neuroscientist at Emory University. "They are forced into a social grouping foreign to them and show abnormalities like repetitive behavior and **hyperaggression**. When they give birth, they don't know how to take care of their babies."

Belugas are **docile** enough to be fed and petted by visitors, an experience the Georgia Aquarium markets for $180 a ticket. "We foster important connections between animals and people," says Higley. "[Visitors] begin to think about how they can promote conservation."   5

"They have it pretty good," Higley says of the four whales at the Georgia Aquarium, citing "restaurant-quality" seafood, veterinary care, freedom from **predation**. He claims whales in human care live at least as long as those in the wild, which Marino disputes. Captivity is **unethical**, she believes, especially for intelligent creatures who live in family groups in open ocean. "They don't want to be fed," Marino says. "They want to hunt." Even if they lived longer in captivity, she says, it wouldn't change her mind. "We shouldn't be doing this to anyone."   6

Adler, Jerry, "Swimming in Limbo." Appeared in *Smithsonian* June 2014. Reprinted by permission of the author.

---

beluga
small white whale from the Arctic

limbo
place of suspension, awaiting fate

proxy
stand-in, substitute

hyperaggression
excessive anger

docile
gentle, obedient, easily taught

predations
being attacked by other animals

unethical
opposed to standards of conduct; immoral

Summarizing

Write a summary of "Swimming in Limbo." Remember that a summary presents the main idea of a text in a clear, concise form using your own words.

Reflecting

1. What is the purpose of this selection?
    to entertain   *to explain*   *to persuade*   *to evaluate*

    _____

2. What is the main idea of this text? (If you can't find a statement, infer one.)

    _____

3. Create a line diagram to show the main idea and the two sides of the situation.

4. This article originally appeared in *Smithsonian,* a monthly magazine produced by the Smithsonian Institution, which oversees a collection of museums in Washington, D.C. How does the author's voice reflect the context of the publication?

    _____

5. What detail do you find most interesting or valuable? Why?

    _____

Vocabulary

Create vocabulary entries for these words, giving definitions for each.

1. **marine parks** (paragraph 1)
2. **languish** (paragraph 2)
3. **longevity** (paragraph 4)
4. **abnormalities** (paragraph 4)

Critical Thinking

- The writer asks, "Is it possible for any animal to be too smart for its own good?" Do you think beluga whales are too smart for their own good? What evidence from the text could you use to support your idea?
- The writer uses a variety of interesting details: descriptions, explanations, anecdotes, court rulings, and quotations from experts. What details made the strongest impression as you read the text? Why were these details especially effective? Explain.
- What do you think of belugas in captivity? Do you agree with those who say that these whales "have it pretty good" or that we "shouldn't be doing this to anyone"? What does the word "anyone" reveal about how Lori Marino views belugas?

L03 Planning Expository Writing

You've just finished reading a wide variety of expository paragraphs as well as an expository article. Now it's time to take what you learned in your reading and apply it as you write your own expository paragraph.

The Writing Process

Prewrite → Write → Revise → Edit → Publish

To start, you need to find a subject that interests you. In order to narrow down all the possible subjects to one specific topic, let's focus our attention on some aspect of modern culture—a type of television show, a type of technology, a brand of clothing, a favorite type of music. Creating a topic list can help you think of any number of interesting topics.

Practice ▶ Create a topic list like the one that follows. List broad subjects across the top row. Under each subject, list at least one or two possible topics that interest you. (The topic list in **Figure 11.2** provides one example for you.) Then circle the topic that you want to write about in an expository paragraph.

Figure 11.2 Topic List

Favorite . . .

books	television shows	music	sports	cars
Insurgent	The Big Bang Theory	Beyonce	football	Mustang
Gone Girl	Sunday Night Football	Jay-Z	baseball	T-Bird
	Homeland	Lorde	basketball	Gran Torino
	CSI			

Deciding on a Focus

Once you choose a topic, decide on a feature of this topic that you could focus on in your paragraph. To write about a feature of football, a writer might explain changes that are being made because of head injuries.

Practice ▶ Decide on the feature or part of your topic that you will focus on in your paragraph.

Insight Finding a focus for your writing is a crucial part of prewriting. It gives you direction to move forward with your planning and writing. Make sure the topic is not so broad that it will not fit in a paragraph.

Too broad: ➡   **Well focused:**
Football   Measures taken to reduce brain injuries in football

Identifying Your Supporting Points

Once you have established a focus, you need to identify the points that will help support this focus. For example, the writer of the paragraph on brain injuries in football listed the following three supporting points.

Better in-game concussion testing

Limits on full-contact and off-season practice time

Stricter fines and penalties for illegal head hits

Practice List three points that you could use to support your focus.

_____

_____

_____

Gathering Your Details

After you think of supporting points, you may have to come up with additional details to clarify each point. For example, the writer of the paragraph about football safety would need to explain how players are tested during games for concussions.

Practice Identify details that are necessary to clarify any of your supporting points. You may have to do some research to complete this part.

Forming Your Topic Sentence

Your topic sentence should state your topic and identify your focus. The following formula can help you write your sentence.

Specific Topic		Thought or Feeling About It		Topic Sentence
Head injuries in the NFL	+	additional safety measures	=	Numerous head injuries in the NFL have led to additional safety measures.

Practice Write your topic sentence using the formula above as a guide. If necessary, write two or three versions, and then choose the best one.

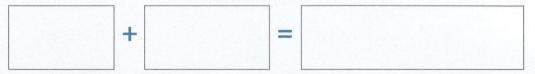

L04 Writing the First Draft

After you have completed your prewriting and planning, you are ready to write your paragraph. The following is a sample expository paragraph to consider before you write.

Practice Read the paragraph, noting the topic sentence, supporting points, details, and closing sentence.

Heading in the Right Direction

Topic Sentence — Numerous head injuries in the NFL have led to additional safety measures. New studies conclude that concussions can lead to long-term, crippling brain damage. **Supporting Point 1** — As a result, the league has beefed up its baseline testing for players who suffer head injuries during a game. **Detail** — Before gaining permission to re-enter the game, a player in question must now pass a six- to eight-minute test that measures things such as memory, balance, and concentration. **Supporting Point 2** — The NFL is also cutting back on practice time and off-season programs, as well as limiting full-contact practices in the pre-season and regular season. **Detail** — With less time to bang heads, fewer concussions should happen. **Supporting Point 3** — In addition, the league is enforcing stricter fines and penalties for illegal helmet-to-helmet hits—those hits where a player launches himself headfirst to strike an opposing player's helmet. **Supporting Point 4** — The measures listed above are just a few of the steps the NFL is taking to make the game safer. **Detail** — Still, the media, lawmakers, and former players say the league is failing to do enough to protect players. **Closing Sentence** — It will be interesting to see what additional safety measures will come in the future. The game may soon look much different than it does today.

Practice Reflect on the reading by answering the following questions:

1. What do you like best about the paragraph?

2. Do the supporting points help clarify the main idea?

3. What are your two favorite details?

4. How does the writer create a knowledgeable voice?

Writing Tips

When you write an expository paragraph, you are clarifying a main idea by providing supporting points and details. Consider the following techniques to give your reader a clear understanding of your main idea.

- Use at least three strong points to support your main idea.
- Arrange the supporting points in an order that makes the best sense. (Remember that supporting points in expository paragraphs may work in more than one order.)
- Clearly detail each supporting point so it is clear to the reader.
- Review the models you have read in this chapter for ideas for your own paragraph.

The Working Parts of a Paragraph

A paragraph consists of three main parts, each of which has a special function. **Figure 11.3** explains each part.

Figure 11.3 Parts of a Paragraph

Topic Sentence:	The topic sentence states the topic and the focus of the paragraph.
Body Sentences:	The body sentences provide examples and other details that explain the main idea, which was established in the topic sentence.
Closing Sentence:	The closing sentence sums up the main point or recasts it in a new or interesting way.

NOTE: Remember the transitional words used to add information: *additionally, along with, also, another, as well, finally, for example, for instance, in addition, next,* and *other.*

Practice Develop your first draft using the information on this page and your planning as a guide.

L05 Revising the Writing

Start revising by reading your draft two or three times. Then have one of your classmates read and react to your work. Look for opportunities to cut unnecessary ideas.

Cutting Unnecessary Ideas

Unnecessary ideas repeat what was already said or include unrelated or inaccurate information. They should be deleted.

Repeated Idea: The power of groups to ensure conformity is often a valuable asset. ~~It can be very useful.~~

Unrelated Idea: With their immersion in social media, millennials are being called the "Elsewhere Generation." ~~Young people don't understand the value of hard work.~~

Inaccurate Information: The NFL is enforcing stricter fines and penalties for illegal helmet-to-helmet hits. If a referee judges a tackle as a helmet-to-helmet, he can penalize the guilty player's team ~~five yards.~~ *(The penalty is 15 yards.)*

Read aloud the unrevised and then the revised version of the following passage. Notice that a repeated idea and an unrelated idea have been cut.

Hurricane Katrina led to the largest displacement of Americans since the Civil War. More than a half-million people sought shelter outside their homes ~~elsewhere.~~ The New Orleans area was hit hardest, with more than 90 percent of its residents evacuated. ~~New Orleans is known as "The Big Easy" because of its easy-going, laid-back attitude.~~

EVACUATION ROUTE

L06 Editing the Writing

When you are writing to explain, your sentences must be very clear. Three types of sentence errors can sabotage your ideas: fragments, comma splices, and run-ons.

Avoiding Fragments and Run-Ons

Fragments and run-ons are errors that can derail the clarity of writing. A fragment is a word group that lacks a subject, verb, or some other essential part, making the thought incomplete. A run-on sentence occurs when two or more independent clauses are joined without adequate punctuation or a connecting word. See the fragment and run-on examples that follow and note how each is corrected.

Fragment:	Forgot the present for his mother.
Corrected:	Raymond forgot the present for his mother.
Run-On Sentence:	Kate decided to wear shorts the weather was beautiful.
Corrected:	Kate decided to wear shorts because the weather was beautiful.

Practice ▶ On the short blank next to each example, identify the word group as a fragment (F), run-on (R), or complete sentence (C). Then rewrite the fragments and run-ons to make them correct, complete sentences.

1. Left the door open. _____

   Correction: _____

2. The water park was a blast the water was extremely cold. _____

   Correction: _____

3. While the dog was chasing his tail. _____

   Correction: _____

4. I was late for the movie because my car ran out of gas. _____

   Correction: _____

Practice ▶ Read your expository paragraph, making sure all of your sentences are complete and clear.

Avoiding Comma Splices

Another sentence error that can undermine your expository writing is a comma splice. Comma splices occur when two independent clauses are connected ("spliced") with only a comma. To correct the error, replace the comma with a period or a semicolon, or add a coordinating conjunction after the comma. Consider the examples that follow.

Comma Splice: People speak of sporting events in the same way they discuss war, that's not a fair comparison.

Corrected with a period: People speak of sporting events in the same way they discuss war. That's not a fair comparison.

Corrected with a semicolon: People speak of sporting events in the same way they discuss war; that's not a fair comparison.

Corrected with a coordinating conjunction: People speak of sporting events in the same way they discuss war, but that's not a fair comparison.

NOTE: If you connect two sentences using a coordinating conjunction (*and, but, or, nor, for, so,* and *yet*), you must include a comma before the conjunction.

Practice ▶ Rewrite these examples to correct the comma splices.

1. Shelly compared her haircut to a natural disaster, I thought it looked good.

   _____

2. My roommate won't stop talking, I don't understand why he says this stuff.

   _____

3. I hate it when the dryer fails to fully dry my clothes, I need to find more quarters.

   _____

4. I'm anxious for my test scores to arrive, my future depends on the outcome.

   _____

5. One test score isn't everything, there are more important things in life.

   _____

Practice ▶ Read your expository paragraph, checking for any comma splices. Correct any that you find.

Practice Correct the following paragraph, using the correction marks that follow. One correction has been done for you.

Forged by Pain

Frida Kahlo͗s path toward political and artistic fame was paved by pain. As a child, Kahlo were bedridden for nine months with polio. Then, at age 18, she was critically injured in an autobus acident. During the collision Kahlo was impaled by a handrail and suffer fractures in her spine and pelvis. it took months of painful rehab to walk again, and the pain and injuries lingered throughout her lifetime. But during the months of agonizing rehab, kahlo took up painting. It was during this period when Kahlo started working on her first of many famous self-portraits. The physical pain she epxerienced as a youth and the emotional pain from her unsteady marriage are reflected in her self-portraits many people belief that is what makes the paintings so powerful.

Correction Marks

ዔ delete	⋏, add comma	word ⋀ add word
ᵈ capitalize	? ⋀ add question mark	⊙ add period
ø lowercase	⌄, insert an apostrophe	⬭ spelling
⋀ insert		ᴨ switch

Using an Editing Checklist

Now it's time to correct your own paragraph.

Practice Create a clean copy of your revised paragraph and use the checklist in **Figure 11.4** to check for errors. Continue working until you can check off each item in the list.

Figure 11.4 Editing Checklist

Words

_____ 1. Have I used specific nouns and verbs?

_____ 2. Have I used more action verbs than "be" verbs?

_____ 3. Have I used signal words to help my reader follow the ideas?

Sentences

_____ 4. Have I used sentences with varying beginnings and lengths?

_____ 5. Have I avoided improper shifts in sentences?

_____ 6. Have I avoided fragments, run-ons, and comma splices?

Conventions

_____ 7. Do I use correct verb forms (*he saw*, not *he seen*)?

_____ 8. Do my subjects and verbs agree (*she speaks*, not *she speak*)?

_____ 9. Have I used the right words (*their, there, they're*)?

_____ 10. Have I capitalized first words and proper nouns and adjectives?

_____ 11. Have I used commas after long introductory word groups and to separate items in a series?

_____ 12. Have I correctly punctuated any dialogue?

_____ 13. Have I used apostrophes correctly in contractions and to show possession?

Adding a Title

Make sure to add an appropriate title for your essay. Here are three strategies to try.

- Highlight the main idea:

   Swimming in Limbo

- Think creatively:

   Heading in the Right Direction

- Make a dramatic pronouncement:

   Forged by Pain

> "Example is not the main thing in influencing others;
> it is the only thing."
> —Albert Schweitzer

☑ Review and Enrichment

You'll be reading and responding to an essay that comes from a textbook entitled *American Government and Politics Today*. The essay "How Unequal Is American Society?" examines wealth in the United States. Remember to use the reading process to help you gain a full understanding of the text. The reading activities are followed by a number of writing ideas to choose from to write an expository paragraph or essay of your own.

About the Authors

Steffen W. Schmidt is a professor of political science at Iowa State University. **Mack C. Shelley II** is a professor of political science and statistics at Iowa State University. **Barbara A. Bardes** is a professor *emerita* of political science at the University of Cincinnati. **Lynn E. Ford** is a professor of political science at the College of Charleston.

Prereading

The American Dream suggests that, through hard work and skill, a person can become economically independent and successful. This dream depends on an open society in which everyone has the same chance. Do you think the American Dream is a reality? Or do you think inequality in this country keeps many people from achieving economic success? Write freely for five minutes about economic equality and inequality.

Read to Learn

As you read this essay, identify the main idea, supporting points, and details. Consider using a table diagram to plot the ideas in this essay.

What do you think?

Albert Schweitzer's quotation refers to "example" as having great influence. How can examples be important?

Practice ▸ Before you read, answer these three questions:

1. What do the title and beginning paragraph tell you about the essay?

_____

2. What might be the authors' purpose?

_____

3. What do you expect to learn in this reading?

_____

Reading and Rereading

This essay explains how differences in wealth in the United States affect the larger society.

As you read, (1) identify the main idea, (2) locate each detail that supports the main idea, and (3) consider the value of this essay for yourself and other students.

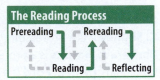

How Unequal Is American Society?

In the early days of the American nation, the distribution of wealth among the people was, of course, unequal. Relatively few large landholders owned large farms and plantations, and relatively few wealthy merchants owned ships and traded in goods. There were, of course, craftspeople, lawyers, and other professionals who were better off than the rest of the citizens. Most of the free people of the United States were farmers or craftspeople working in their own communities. They probably owned their land, tools, furnishings, and products, but nothing more. In the southern states, most of the free individuals owned no slaves or only a few. Only a very few wealthy individuals owned a large number of enslaved persons. Wealth, at the levels known today, was unheard of. As the United States developed economically, many individuals did well enough to form a strong middle class.   *1*

Many commentators and economists believe that the United States today is a much less equal society than it was only a few decades ago. Due to the recession, the median income today for   *2*

American families, in inflation-adjusted dollars, is less than it was 10 years ago. Many families have lost their savings or their homes due to unemployment. On the other hand, the wealthiest Americans have continued to increase their worth due both to their ability to keep their tax bills relatively low and their ability to earn more wealth through investments, even during a recession. Technological developments have created many billionaires. Among those are Mark Zuckerberg, founder of Facebook, and the creators of Instagram, a smart-phone app that was sold to Facebook for more than $1 billion only two years after it entered the business scene. While it is true that the wealthiest 1 percent of Americans pay a **proportionately** large share of income taxes, about 38 percent of all taxes paid, their average income is 18 times the median, and their wealth is growing.

3   How does the United States compare to the rest of the world in terms of this income inequality? We all know large numbers of truly impoverished individuals exist in many nations, but is overall income equality more likely in those nations? The Organization for Economic Cooperation and Development (OECD), an international agency dedicated to improving conditions in all nations, publishes an annual report on income inequality based on a statistic called "the **Gini Index**." The index is named after the Italian statistician who created the measure, and it measures the degree of income equality in a nation by looking at the proportions in different income categories. A Gini Index score of zero means that there is perfect equality among all incomes in a nation. The larger the score, the further the nation is from equality in incomes.

4   If we compare the score of the United States to those of all of the nations of the world, our ranking is not too low: In 2011, the United States ranked 43rd in income inequality among the 104 nations for which data were available.[a] The nation with the most inequality was Namibia, and that with the least was Sweden. Most of the nations with higher levels of income inequality were underdeveloped nations that may have a small group of very wealthy households and a multitude of very poor citizens. However, the OECD also published

the index only for its own members, mostly developed Western nations. Among this group of 22 nations, the United States is the third most unequal nation, although its ranking is close to those of Israel, the United Kingdom, Italy, and Australia. Mexico has the highest Gini score in this group and Denmark the lowest.

The issue of income inequality in America has also been the *5* subject of the research of two French economists who currently teach in the United States.[b] Both Emmanuel Saez and Thomas Piketty claim to love the United States and admire greatly the free and **entrepreneurial** nature of the country. What they find in their research is that the United States is quickly becoming more unequal than at any time in its history. Piketty says, "The United States is getting accustomed to a completely crazy level of inequality."[c] He continues, "The United States is becoming like Old Europe, which is very strange in historical perspective . . . [it] used to be very **egalitarian**, not just in spirit but in actuality." The work of these two economists, according to the *New York Times*, is being read in Washington, D.C., as well as in economic journals.

[a] Organization for Economic Development and Cooperation, "Divided We Stand: Why Inequality Keeps Rising," 2011.

[b] Emmanuel Saez and Thomas Piketty, cited in "Income Distribution in the U.S.," www.wealthandwant.com/income/income_distribution.html.

[c] Annie Lowry, "French Duo See (Well) Past Tax Rise for the Richest," *The New York Times*, April 17, 2012, A1.

From Schmidt/Shelley/Bardes/Ford, *American Government and Politics Today*, 2013-2014 Edition, 16E. © 2014 Cengage Learning

proportionately
having the correct relationship of size or quantity

Gini Index
a statistical measure of the distribution of income in a nation; higher indicates more income inequality

entrepreneurial
the quality of business risk-taking

egalitarian
believing in equality

Summarizing

Write a brief summary of "How Unequal Is American Society?" Remember that a summary focuses on the main idea and supporting points.

Reflecting

1. What main idea is developed in the text? Is it directly stated or implied?

   _____

2. What types of supporting points are provided? Name two.

   _____

3. Are both causes and effects discussed? Explain.

   _____

4. How has the essay confirmed, changed, or expanded your understanding of income inequality in the United States?

   _____

Vocabulary

Create vocabulary entries for these words. For each word, identify the pronunciation and helpful word parts, give a primary definition, and use the word in a sentence.

1. **recession** (paragraph 2, line 3)

2. **median** (paragraph 2, line 3)

3. **inequality** (paragraph 3, line 2)

Critical Thinking

- What observations can you make about areas in the world that might offer a decent quality of life for most people?
- What thoughts do you have about the income distribution in the United States?
- In the second paragraph, the writer mentions billionaires who created innovative technology that has changed how people live. Do you think that Mark Zuckerberg, the founder of Facebook, deserves to be a billionaire? Why or why not? If two people make vastly unequal contributions to society, shouldn't they have vastly unequal economic success? Support your response.
- In the final paragraph, the writer quotes an economist who says, "The United States is getting accustomed to a completely crazy level of inequality." How much inequality is a "crazy" level? How could economic inequality be reduced? Should all people be made economically equal? Explain your answer.

Writing for Enrichment

Choose one of the following writing ideas, or decide upon another idea related to the reading.

1. Write an expository paragraph about a specific example of income equality not mentioned in "How Unequal is American Society?"

2. Write an expository paragraph expanding upon one of the examples of income equality mentioned in "How Unequal is American Society?"

3. Choose a foreign country that was not mentioned in the essay. Research its ranking in the Gini Index (as described in paragraph 3 of the essay). Write an expository paragraph that compares and contrasts the ranking with the United States' ranking.

4. Write an expository paragraph about one of the topics you identified earlier in the chapter.

5. Reflect on your job, your neighborhood, your group of friends, your favorite music, or a similar topic. Then write an essay in which you explain some important feature of your topic.

When planning . . .

- Choose a topic that you care about. Writing about something that interests you helps you put more effort into your work.
- Decide on an interesting focus or feature of the topic.
- Be able to identify at least three points to explain your topic. Make sure the points clearly support the main idea for your readers.
- Review the expository samples in this chapter to see how they are developed. Some of the techniques those writers used may help you shape your own thoughts and ideas.

When writing . . .

- Pay attention to each part of your paragraph—opening, middle, and closing.
- Use a variety of strong details to support your topic sentence.

When revising and editing . . .

- Determine if your paragraph answers key questions readers have about your topic.
- Be prepared to do some additional research if necessary.
- Edit your revised writing for style and correctness.

Monkey Business Images, 2014 / Used under license from Shutterstock.com

"Use soft words and hard arguments."
—English Proverb

Reading and Writing Arguments

In everyday life, people may say "they were having an argument" to mean "they were having a quarrel."

In your college and professional life, "argument" can mean something different: an opinion or position backed by fact and sound reasoning. When political figures debate, they present arguments. When you write a position paper, you present an argument. When a military recruiter or a car salesperson or a potential employer seeks to convince you to sign a contract, that person presents an argument.

Argumentation is an essential tool for our civilization. Given our variety of personalities, backgrounds, values, and assumptions, the only way of coming to a consensus is to discuss our opinions, support them, and address any counterarguments. In this chapter, you will learn to refine your own ability to evaluate and present arguments.

Learning Outcomes

LO1 Understand arguments.
LO2 Read and respond to an argument.
LO3 Plan an argument.
LO4 Write the first draft.
LO5 Revise the writing.
LO6 Edit the writing.

What do you think?

How can soft words express hard arguments? Can hard words disguise soft arguments?

L01 Understanding Arguments

Strong arguments consider all sides of an issue, assemble all available evidence, and take a position based on careful study of the facts. Bear this in mind as you read arguments or listen to debates, speeches, and advertisements. Weigh the evidence presented and the conclusions drawn. Be critical, but don't be afraid to let an argument change your mind if the evidence points toward a new understanding.

Types of Arguments

You will encounter common types of argumentation such as editorials, personal commentaries, problem-solution essays, and position papers.

Editorial An editorial is an opinion piece written by the editor of a newspaper or other periodical.

Main Idea introduced with a counter-argument

Our state's recently adopted ban on smoking in public places may seem a restriction of personal freedom, but it is more importantly an issue of public safety. According to the Centers for Disease Control, exposure to secondhand smoke caused 34,000 heart disease-related deaths annually from 2005-2009. Nonsmokers exposed to secondhand smoke are 25-30 percent more likely than normal to develop heart disease. Currently 37 of

Supporting Facts and Details

the 50 U.S. states have at least a partial ban on public smoking. Of those states, 28 ban smoking in every establishment that serves the public. This includes restaurants and bars, as well as public workplaces. In some cases, tobacconists may be allowed a public smoking room, and hotel rooms may be exempted as "dwelling places." But the fact is that finding a legal place to smoke outside a private home is increasingly difficult. While this may

Summary restating the main idea

be irksome to people who enjoy a cigar, pipe, or cigarette, it is necessary to protect the health of nonsmokers.

Personal Commentary A personal commentary is an opinion piece written by someone other than an editor. It may appear as a blog entry or on a periodical's "Opinions" page.

Main Idea introduced with a quotation

It has been said that "when you are a hammer, every problem looks like a nail." That may explain why our political contests become more and more like advertising campaigns. Intent on raising cash for elections, parties turn to the techniques of Madison Avenue, "selling" what they believe we want to hear instead of presenting us with real issues. The

Explanation with supporting details

American voter is targeted as a consumer rather than a citizen. The same "hot-button" topics and buzz-words are trotted out each election cycle to motivate "brand loyalty," as if "Republican," "Democrat," or even "Libertarian" were alternative types of cola. Unfortunately, the problems

Call to Action

our nation faces are too complex to be "hammered" into shape. We need to evaluate each issue to select the best tool for that task.

Problem-Solution Problem-solution writing sets out to define a problem and convince readers that a particular solution or set of solutions can solve that problem.

Main Idea

Do violent media cause violent behavior? A growing body of psychological studies say this is not the correct question. Health officials

Explanation with facts and details

wouldn't claim that smoking directly causes cancer and stroke, but it does increase the risk of both. Psychologists now suggest that, in a similar way, violent media—especially "first-person shooter" video games—tend to suppress people's impulse control, making them more prone to violence on the spur of the moment. While older, more emotionally settled people are less affected, young people are especially at risk. Violent media shouldn't be banned altogether. Censorship has its own risks. But enforcing an age-based ratings system seems a clear step in the right direction. In addition, media producers should take more responsibility for their content. When the comic-book industry came under government scrutiny during the twentieth century, it voluntarily established a Comics Code Authority to rate comics and police itself. The video game industry has a similar rating system, but those ratings do not seem to be taken as seriously by

Call to Action

consumers. Perhaps it is time for a public awareness campaign to educate our citizens about the risks involved so that they will pay more attention to those ratings and enforce them with young people.

Position Paper A position paper is a short statement presenting an opinion on a subject. College instructors often assign position papers as a way of having students demonstrate their thoughts about material covered in a course.

Main Idea

I used to believe there was no way I'd ever subscribe to a music service. Why "rent" songs when I could buy them outright? However,

Explanation with details presented in time order

as my collection of CDs grew larger and larger, it became more difficult to find particular songs or CDs. Copying them to my computer was an option, but it took a lot of time and hard-drive space. And transferring those files whenever I upgraded computers was even more of a pain. So when music services started offering cloud storage of purchased songs, I quit buying CDs. The one remaining clumsiness was that different songs were in different music services, meaning I had to remember what was where and launch different software for each. Eventually, one service offered such a great monthly deal for unlimited music that I just couldn't resist. I also got the option to store what I already owned, plus an easy way to move those files. I set aside my prejudice against "renting" and became a subscriber. Now not only can I access all my music on any computer or even my smart phone, I can also try out artists on a whim and listen

Conclusion

to everything they've ever recorded. Given just how much new music is released every day and how my tastes grow and change, subscribing makes perfect sense.

L02 Reading and Responding to an Argument

If everyone had the same knowledge and understanding, there would be fewer debates. Given that we all come from different backgrounds, however, we each approach arguments from different positions. As you first read an argument text, separate facts from opinions. Then analyze the structure and content of the reading. Finally, evaluate your own reaction to the material.

Separating Facts and Opinions

A fact is a statement that can be directly proven to be true. An opinion is a personal belief that is disputable because it cannot be directly proven. Opinions often present the meaning of facts, give suggestions for policies, or predict what might happen in the future. Note how a fact (shown in the center of **Figure 12.1**) can spawn opposite opinions.

Figure 12.1 Opinions and Facts Chart

Opinions	← Facts →	Opinions
We need to build many more wind farms.	Wind energy currently accounts for only 1 percent of power supplied in the country.	Wind energy will never be able to replace fossil fuels.
Wind farms should be built in forests to double the carbon savings.	A single wind turbine can displace 2,000 tons of carbon dioxide, the same amount as one square mile of forest.	Trees should never be felled to make room for wind farms.

Practice Tell whether each piece of text below is an opinion or a fact.

1. Text messaging while driving should be banned. _____

2. Mobile devices contribute to 2,600 deaths per year. _____

4. Teenagers are the problem. _____

5. Twenty percent of adults admit to texting while driving. _____

Practice For each fact listed below, write two opposite opinions.

Opinions	← Facts →	Opinions
	Writing tutors have their hours posted in the Writing Lab.	
	Online assistance is also available.	

Analyzing Parts of an Argument

An argument consists of a main claim (the thesis), supporting claims (reasons), evidence, and recognition of counterarguments. It may also end with a call to action.

- **Main claim:** The main claim (or thesis statement) usually appears in one of the first paragraphs. It may be preceded by background information introducing the topic. *Often it is the last sentence in an opening paragraph.* A claim is a viewpoint that cannot be proven true the way a fact can but that can be supported by evidence.

  > Our country and our youth would benefit from a one- or two-year period of national service after high school.

- **Supporting claims:** A supporting claim gives a reason for accepting the main claim. Often, each middle paragraph in an essay of argumentation begins with a new supporting claim. The rest of the paragraph then gives evidence to accept the supporting claim.

  > Not only would young people gain experience, but they would also earn college grants for their service ("Mandatory").

- **Evidence:** A claim depends on evidence to show its strength. Solid evidence can be checked for its accuracy and importance. Common types of evidence include examples, facts and statistics, and expert testimony.
  - **Examples:** Besides the National Guard and Reserves, the Peace Corps and Americorps are options.
  - **Facts and statistics:** The Peace Corps is just one option, with 7,209 volunteers this year ("Fast Facts").
  - **Expert testimony:** People who have served say the experience helped them grow up and discover their potential.

- **Counterarguments:** The best arguments acknowledge opposing points of view and either concede or oppose them. Counterarguments are often introduced with words or phrases like *admittedly, granted, it is true that, I accept that,* and *no doubt.*
  - To **concede** a counterargument is to admit its truth. This shows that the writer is aware of the counterargument but believes it is outweighed by the main claim.

    > It is true that our nation is founded on the idea of personal freedom.

  - To **oppose** a counterargument is to point out its weakness.

    > Some people may object that mandatory service would violate our liberties, but the U.S. has a long history of civic responsibility.

- **Call to action:** The purpose of many arguments is to convince the reader to respond in a certain way. Including a clear call to action at the end of an argument is the best way to make sure readers know what is expected of them.

  > Tell your representative in Congress that you support a law requiring public service after high school.

Reading and Reacting to a Professional Argument

In this argumentation paragraph, the author discusses benefits of wind farming.

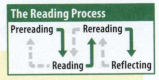

The Reading Process

Prereading → Rereading
Reading → Reflecting

About the Author

J. Robert King is a novelist and an educator who occasionally writes personal commentaries about scientific and social issues.

Before you read, answer these questions.

1. What do you know about the author?

_____

2. What does the title suggest about the author's position and purpose?

_____

3. What is your background knowledge of the topic?

_____

Support Wind Farm Energy

To **counteract** its dependence on fossil fuels, the United States must invest in wind farms for its energy needs. A wind farm is made up of a group of large wind **turbines**, which convert wind into electric energy. The benefits of wind farms are numerous. First, wind is a free and renewable source of energy. In comparison, fossil fuels like oil and coal are limited in supply and cost money to **extract** from the earth. Secondly, wind farms are a clean energy source. Unlike power plants, which **emit** dangerous pollutants, wind farms release no pollution into the air or water, meaning less smog, less acid rain, and fewer greenhouse emissions. And then there's this: The National Wind Resource Center reports that running a single wind turbine has the potential to displace 2,000 tons of carbon dioxide, or the equivalent amount that one square mile of forest trees displaces ("The Opportunity"). But despite being the fastest-growing energy source in the U.S., wind energy accounts for only 1 percent of power supplied in the country ("Renewable"). If the U.S. wants to limit carbon emissions and lessen its dependence on fossil fuels, it must act now and invest more money in wind farms. The answer is in the air.

Works Cited

"The Opportunity." Windcenter.com. NWRC, n.d. Web. 31 Jan. 2014.

"Renewable Energy Sources in the United States." nationalatlas.gov.
    National Atlas of the United States, 26 Jan. 2011. Web. 31 Jan. 2014.

---

counteract
act against

turbine
machine with angled fins that spin when a gas or liquid passes through

extract
obtain by removing

emit
give off, release

Summarizing

Write a summary of "Support Wind Farm Energy." Remember that a summary uses your own words to restate the message of the original in roughly a third of the space.

Reflecting

1. What is the main claim of the argument?

2. What supporting claims are offered?

3. What evidence and sources support those claims?

4. How are counterarguments addressed?

5. What call to action is given?

6. Do you agree or disagree with the argument? Explain your reasons.

Vocabulary

Create vocabulary entries by defining the following terms in your own words.

1. **acid rain** (line 13)   2. **greenhouse emissions** (line 13)

Critical Thinking

- The text presents only positive aspects of wind farming. Do you know of any negative aspects? If so, list them here. If not, research online to discover at least one and explain it here.
- Imagine you are the author of "Support Wind Farm Energy." Address a counterargument to building wind farms. Remember that your goal is to convince your reader that wind farming is best despite this counterargument.
- Choose another source of renewable energy and explain briefly why it is either a better solution than wind farming or not as good a solution.

L03 Planning an Argument

Your prewriting begins by selecting a topic that interests you, developing a position about it, and refining that position.

Selecting a Topic

Consider a debatable topic that you feel strongly about. It could be an issue that affects your school or community. Or you might browse newspapers, magazines, and the Internet to find current issues. Choose one that is important to you.

Practice ▸ List three or four debatable issues you could write about in an argument paragraph. Then choose one of the four topics.

_____   _____

_____   _____

Stating a Position

Once you decide on a topic, you need to state a preliminary position about it. In one sentence, write a defensible position statement using the formula in **Figure 12.2**.

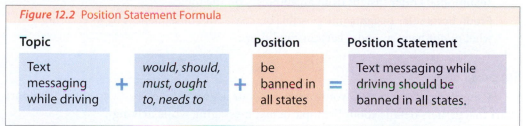

Figure 12.2 Position Statement Formula

Topic		Position	Position Statement
Text messaging while driving	+ *would, should, must, ought to, needs to* +	be banned in all states	= Text messaging while driving should be banned in all states.

Practice ▸ Write a position statement by providing the topic, selecting a verb, and indicating your position.

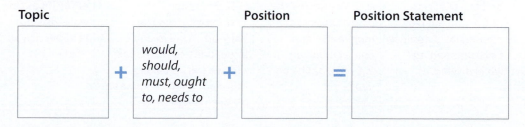

Topic		Position	Position Statement
	+ *would, should, must, ought to, needs to* +		=

Refining Your Position

With your initial position written, use the following strategies to develop and refine your opinion on the issue:

- **Research all possible positions on the issue.** Who supports each position, and why? Who opposes your position, and why?
- **Gather solid evidence regarding your issue.** Does the most compelling evidence support or oppose your position?
- **Refine your position.** At this point, your research may have given you new ideas about how to respond to your topic. Or it may have reversed your opinion. Before you are ready to write, clarify your position statement.

Gathering Details

When you take a stand on an issue, you must gather convincing support to defend your position. Four common types of details you can use are *facts, statistics, testimonials,* and *predictions.*

- **Facts** offer statements or claims of verified information.
- **Statistics** offer concrete numbers about a topic.
- **Testimonials** offer insight from an authority on the topic.
- **Predictions** offer insights into possible outcomes or consequences by forecasting what might happen under certain conditions.

Support Chart

A support chart can help you to prepare your argument. **Figure 12.3** shows a support chart that gathers details about the topic of text messaging while driving.

Figure 12.3 Support Chart

Fact	Statistic	Testimony	Prediction
At least 34 states and the District of Columbia have passed laws against text messaging while driving.	According to the U.S. Department of Transportation, mobile devices contribute to 2,600 deaths per year.	In the words of U.S. Secretary of Transportation Ray LaHood, "This is an important safety step, and we will be taking more action to eliminate distracted driving."	Roads will be safer if texting while driving is banned in all states.

Practice   Create a support chart with the research you have gathered about your issue. Try to include at least one fact, statistic, piece of testimony, and prediction. If you have not found supporting details for each category, consider doing additional research.

LO4 Writing the First Draft

After you have completed your prewriting and planning, you are ready to write your paragraph. Provided next is a sample argumentative paragraph to consider before you write.

Practice › Read the following draft of a paragraph about text messaging and driving. Be sure to pay close attention to each part of the argument.

Text Messaging and Driving Don't Mix

The **topic Sentence** states a position.

Text messaging while driving should be banned in all states because the practice is making U.S. roadways dangerous. Car crashes rank among the leading causes of death in the United States, but many blame the frequency of drinking and driving and ignore the dangers of texting and driving.

Body sentences provide evidence to support the position and address a counter-argument.

Studies by the National Highway Traffic Safety Administration show that text messaging while driving is about six times more likely to result in an accident than drunk driving is (Pennsylvania Truck Accident Lawyers). And according to the Human Factors and Ergonomics Society, mobile devices contribute to 2,600 deaths and 330,000 injuries per year ("The Use of Cell Phones"). The major danger associated with texting is the distraction it causes to the driver. A driver whose eyes are concentrating on a phone instead of the road is more likely to get in an accident. Some critics say teenage drivers are the problem, but 20 percent of adults in a recent AAA study admitted to regularly sending text messages while driving ("Text Messaging"). At least 34 states and the District of Columbia understand the aforementioned dangers and have passed bans on texting while driving ("Cell Phone").

The **closing Sentence** gives a call to action.

Let's make all of our roads a safer place; the time has come to make text messaging while driving illegal in every state.

Reflecting

1. What is your immediate reaction? Why?

2. Has your understanding of the topic changed?

3. What is the main claim of the argument?

4. What supporting claims and evidence are given?

5. What is the call to action?

Writing Tips

When writing an argument paragraph, appeal to the reader with logical reasoning and compelling evidence.

In the opening . . .

- Lead up to your claim, if necessary, by providing reasonable background.
- Make your claim firmly but respectfully.

In the middle . . .

- Give the reader plenty of solid reasons to adopt your point of view.
- Use valid research to back up your position.
- Address any counterclaims politely, providing a convincing argument against them.

In the closing . . .

- Restate your position in light of the reasons you have provided.
- If appropriate, give your reader a call to action.

The Working Parts of a Paragraph

A paragraph has three main parts, each with its own purpose. **Figure 12.4** shows how the parts work together in an argument paragraph.

Figure 12.4 **Parts of an Argumentative Paragraph**

Topic sentence: The topic sentence states your position.

Body sentences: The body sentences support the position using logical reasoning and reliable details. These sentences also address counterclaims.

Closing sentence: A closing sentence (or two) reinforces your argument and (if appropriate) encourages your reader to adopt it.

NOTE: To organize your sentences and introduce your reader to new information, use transition words that show importance, such as the following:

> first of all / to begin / secondly / another reason / the best reason / also / in addition / more importantly / most importantly / finally

Practice ▷ Prepare the first draft of your argumentative paragraph using the information you have learned so far.

L05 Revising the Writing

Start the revising process by reading your first draft two or three times to get a feel for your work so far. Then have one of your classmates read and react to your work.

Avoiding Logical Fallacies

As you revise, check for logical fallacies. A logical fallacy is a false assertion that weakens an argument. Here are five logical fallacies that should be removed from your writing.

- A **bare assertion** denies that an issue is debatable, claiming, "That's just how it is."

  Withdrawal of troops is our only option for peace.

  (This claim discourages discussion of other ways to promote peace.)

- A **threat** is a simple way to sabotage an argument, claiming, "If you don't agree with me, you'll regret it."

  If you don't accept alternative fuel sources, get ready to move back to the Stone Age.

- A **slippery slope** fallacy argues that one step will lead to unstoppable chain of events.

  If we build a skate park, vandalism is going to run rampant in our city.

- An **unreliable testimonial** is a statement made by a biased or unqualified source. A testimonial has force only if it is made by an authority.

  As TV's Dr. Daniels, I recommend Xanax for all my patients.

- A **half-truth** contains part but not all of the truth.

  Three out of five doctors recommend ibuprofen, according to a recent study.
  (What do they recommend it for? Do other surveys show the same?)

Practice ▸ Improve your writing by removing logical fallacies. Use a revising checklist like the one in **Figure 12.5** to check your ideas, organization, and voice.

Figure 12.5 Revising Checklist

Ideas

____ **1.** Does my topic sentence identify an issue and my position?

____ **2.** Do I include a variety of supporting details?

Organization

____ **3.** Do I have a topic sentence, body sentences, and a closing sentence?

Voice

____ **4.** Do I sound knowledgeable and passionate about the issue?

LO6 Editing the Writing

One important issue to check for when editing is "mechanics." Mechanics are the standards of presenting written language; capitalization and number use are two of the mechanics issues writers often encounter.

Capitalization Errors

Capitalizing proper nouns and proper adjectives (adjectives derived from proper nouns) is a basic rule of capitalization. There are times, however, when certain words are capitalized in one instance but not in another. **Table 12.1** refers to a number of these special cases.

Table 12.1 Capitalization Errors

Capitalize	Do Not Capitalize
American	un-American
January, May	winter, spring
The South is quite conservative.	Turn south at the stop sign.
Duluth City College	a Duluth college
Chancellor John Bohm	John Bohm, our chancellor
President Obama	the president of the United States
Earth (planet name)	the earth
Internet	electronic communications network

Practice In each of the following sentences, write the correction mark (≡) under letters that should be capitalized.

1. with november around the corner, it's only so long until winter engulfs minnesota.

2. Flag burning is the definition of an un-american activity.

3. I caught up with chancellor Greg Williams of the university of pittsburgh.

4. I used the internet to find out that Missouri is nicknamed the show-me state.

5. My favorite french restaurant rests in a quiet neighborhood off college avenue.

6. The west coast is known for its laid-back lifestyle.

7. Does the winter sports season begin before or after december?

8. The president of the united states lives in the white house.

Insight Different languages use capitalization differently. Even different forms of English (U.S. and British, for example) treat capitals differently.

Using Numbers

When a paragraph includes numbers or statistics, you will have to know whether to write them as words or as numerals. Here are three basic rules to follow.

Numerals or Words

In college papers, numbers from one to one hundred are usually written as words; numbers 101 and greater are usually written as numerals.

two	seven	twenty-five	103	1,489

Numerals Only

Use numerals for the following forms: decimals, percentages, pages, chapters, addresses, dates, telephone numbers, identification numbers, and statistics.

13.1	Highway 41	February 12, 2010	2.4 feet
20 percent	Chapter 6	(273) 555-2288	

Words Only

Use words to express numbers that begin a sentence.

Thirteen players suffered from food poisoning.

Practice In each of the following sentences, cross out any incorrect numbers and write the correct form.

1. My 2 cousins, Braden and Candace, live 4 miles apart on Highway Eleven.

2. 300 raffle tickets were bought at the gates.

3. The results showed twenty-five percent of participants were born before January first, 1985.

4. Please review Chapter seventeen for the test on Monday.

5. The coastal reef is two point eight knots away.

6. 15 of us are hoping to complete the three point one-mile race.

Practice ▸ Read the argumentation paragraph, looking for problems listed in the editing checklist in **Figure 12.6**. Then correct the model using correction marks. One correction has been done for you.

A Super Blow to Roscoe

For the good of the local economy ∧the Roscoe City Council must vote down a proposal to build a SuperMart store west of Highway 31. The large discount chain may slash prices, it will slash local businesses in the process. a University of Iowa study showed a group of small towns lost up to 47 percent of they're retail trade after ten years of a SuperMart moving in nearby. Grocery stores and retail

businesses were hit the hardest. If a SuperMart comes to Roscoe, local grocers like Troyer's will have to lower wages or risk clozing. A 2015 study showed how a SuperMart caused a 1.5 percent reduction in earnings for local grocery stores. Proponents of a SuperMart expansion says the store will bring new jobs, more sales tax, and great bargains. But all SuperMart will accomplish is reallocating where existing income is spent. The Roscoe City Council should look for alternatives to jump-start the community's economy vote "No" for SuperMart.

Correction Marks

ℛ delete	∧, add comma	word ∧ add word
d̳ capitalize	? ∧ add question mark	⊙ add period
∅ lowercase	,∨ insert an apostrophe	◯ spelling
∧ insert		⊓ switch

Using an Editing Checklist

Use an editing checklist to edit the remainder of your paragraph for style and correctness.

Practice Prepare a clean copy of your revised narrative and use the checklist in **Figure 12.6** to look for errors. Continue working until you can check off each item in the list.

Figure 12.6 Editing Checklist

Words

____ **1.** Have I used specific nouns and verbs?

____ **2.** Have I used more action verbs than "be" verbs?

Sentences

____ **3.** Have I used sentences with varying beginnings and lengths?

____ **4.** Have I combined short, choppy sentences?

____ **5.** Have I avoided comma splices, fragments and run-ons?

Conventions

____ **6.** Do I use correct verb forms (*he saw*, not *he seen*)?

____ **7.** Do my subjects and verbs agree (*she speaks*, not *she speak*)?

____ **8.** Have I used the right words (*their, there, they're*)?

____ **9.** Have I capitalized first words and proper nouns and adjectives?

____ **10.** Have I used commas after long introductory word groups and to separate items in a series?

____ **11.** Have I used commas after long introductory word groups?

____ **12.** Have I carefully checked my spelling?

Adding a Title

Finish the argumentation paragraph by adding an attention-getting title. Here are three simple strategies.

- **Create a slogan:**

    Support Wind Farm Energy

- **Sum up your argument:**

    Texting and Driving Don't Mix

- **Use a play on words:**

    A Super Blow to Roscoe

"If you would win a man to your cause, first convince him that you are his sincere friend."

—Abraham Lincoln

☑ Review and Enrichment

You will be reading and responding to the essay "What Exactly Is a Frivolous Lawsuit?" Use the steps in the reading process as your guide. After reading, evaluate your reaction to the argument and analyze the argument's parts (main claim, supporting claims, evidence, counterarguments, and call to action). Then use the writing exercises to create your own argumentation essay.

About the Author

Laraine Flemming is a textbook writer as well as an experienced instructor. Her first teaching experience was in a psychiatric hospital in Vinita, Oklahoma. It was there that she became convinced of the transformative power of reading. Flemming has a PhD from State University of New York in Buffalo.

Prereading

Social issues can be complicated. Each of us comes to an issue with our own beliefs based on our backgrounds, needs, and desires. Argumentation is a process that allows us to present and support our positions (opinions) on issues in a thoughtful way. Think of a local or national issue that matters to you: the shortage of student parking spaces, gender or race issues in employment, the use of drones, or another subject. Then freely write about the issue.

Consider the Traits

As you read this essay, concentrate first on the **ideas**—including the position (main claim). Then consider the **organization**—the way the argument is developed from start to finish.

_____

_____

_____

_____

What do you think?

The quotation from Abraham Lincoln indicates that part of argumentation is showing others that you care about them. How does this human connection help you persuade?

Before you read, answer these questions:

1. What do the title and beginning paragraph tell you about the essay?

_____

2. What might be the author's purpose?

_____

3. What do you expect to learn in this reading?

_____

Reading and Rereading

The court system in this country is a common topic of discussion. Essays are written about the unfairness of the courts, the selection of judges, and fair representation. "What Exactly Is a Frivolous Lawsuit?" examines lawsuits (actions brought before the courts to recover something or to seek a settlement). Pay careful attention to the position that the author develops in the essay.

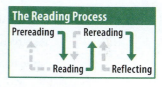

As you read, (1) identify the main idea, (2) locate each detail that supports the main idea, and (3) consider the value of this essay for you and other students.

What Exactly Is a Frivolous Lawsuit?

The lawsuit of seventy-nine-year-old Stella Liebeck, launched against McDonald's in 1994 after spilling hot coffee on herself as she went through the drive-through lane, immediately became the stuff of comedy. A *Seinfeld* episode even used it, making one of the characters sue for damages after he spilled coffee on himself. But the general attitude toward the suit, on television and off, was summed up in the response of another *Seinfeld* character, Elaine, who expressed puzzlement at the very idea of a lawsuit involving hot coffee being spilled and McDonald's being somehow liable. "Who ever heard of this anyway? Suing a company because their coffee is too hot? Coffee is supposed to be hot." In other words, the suit was a ridiculous joke.

1

What got left out of all the jokes, though, were the actual details   *2*
of the case. Liebeck suffered third-degree burns. Third-degree burns
are the most serious kind, especially for a woman of her age. Plus,
there had been at least 700 previous cases of people being scalded by
McDonald's coffee before Liebeck went to court. . . .

What Liebeck's lawyers proved was that McDonald's was   *3*
making its coffee 30 to 50 degrees hotter than other restaurants. In
fact, the Shriner Burn Institute had already warned McDonald's not
to serve coffee above 130 degrees. Yet the liquid that burned Liebeck
was the usual temperature for McDonald's brew—about 190 degrees.
As a result of Liebeck's suit, McDonald's coffee is now sold at the
same temperature as most other restaurants.

Yes, there probably are trivial lawsuits filed on a regular   *4*
basis. But Liebeck's wasn't one of them. It's actually ironic that the
"hot coffee" lawsuit, as it's come to be called, is often cited as an
illustration of why the country desperately needs **tort reform**. Yet a
closer examination of this issue suggests that citizens might want to
think twice before joining in the chorus of calls to enact tort reform.

Tort reform legislation, in place or pending, differs from state   *5*
to state. Thus one of the questions involved in the debate is how tort
reform should go forward. Should it be on a state or federal level?

In general, though, the tort reform movement focuses on   *6*
three goals: (1) the need to limit the circumstances under which
injured people may file a lawsuit after being injured by a product or
procedure, (2) the goal of making it more difficult for people injured
by a product or procedure to obtain a trial by jury, and (3) the desire
to place limits on the amount of money injured parties may be
awarded.

In the eyes of some, like political activist and organizer Jon   *7*
Greenbaum, the idea that the country is desperately in need of tort

reform is a myth. From his perspective, the right to sue corporations or companies if their products were defective or their procedures badly managed or fraudulent was a consumer victory won in the 1950s. In his eyes, now is not the time to abandon that right. He thinks implementing tort reform would be a step backward for consumers, not a step forward: "It will limit our ability to hold corporations accountable for their misdeeds. Corporate America has succeeded to a great extent by buying up our legislators and capturing regulatory bodies. We must not let them wrest control of the judicial system as well."

That, however, would not be the position of Court Koenning, the president of Citizens Against Lawsuit Abuse of Houston. For him, lawsuits demanding compensation for injury due to defective products or procedures reveal a growing canker on American society—the **abdication** of personal responsibility. As he writes, "The somebody's gotta pay attitude is pervasive, and that does not bode well for future generations. We need to reacquaint ourselves with personal responsibility and stop playing the blame game. We need to realize that every dilemma or personal disappointment is not **fodder** for a lawsuit and does not warrant a treasure trove of cash." *8*

These are all stirring sentiments. But they need to be viewed in the light of what consumers "playing the blame game" in court have actually tried to accomplish. In Los Angeles, California, consumers have gone to court to stop health insurers from canceling policies of people newly diagnosed with a serious illness. The insurance cancellations, usually based on technicalities, seem to target people who will require long-term and expensive care, for which the insurance companies would have to pay if the policies weren't cancelled. *9*

In Harrisburg, Pennsylvania, consumers turned to the courts *10* to take action against "mortgage rescue" companies who, for a fee, claimed they could help those falling behind on their payments. But after the fee was paid, no help was forthcoming. In Hartford, Connecticut, consumers also went to court against a pharmaceutical company that was blocking generic alternatives to the high-priced drugs on which the company's profits were based.

This is not to say that all personal injury complaints taken   *11* to court are worthy of respect. Did anyone really want to see the woman who sued a cosmetics company for changing the shade of her hair become a millionaire? But many of the personal injury lawsuits brought by consumers do real good, helping not just the **litigant** but the public in general. We might want to consider that fact next time we hear or read another argument in favor of tort reform because what we might be reforming is our own right to seek justice by legal means.

Sources: Court Koenning, "Starbucks 'Hot Tea' Lawsuit Highlights a Void in Personal Responsibility," www.setexasrecord.com; Jon Greenbaum, "McDonald's Hot Coffee Lawsuit and Beyond: The Tort Reform Myth Machine," CommonDreams.org

From Flemming, *Reading for Thinking*, 7E. © 2012 Cengage Learning

frivolous
not worth taking seriously, unnecessary

tort reform
laws passed to place limits on the types or amounts of awards or compensation in personal injury lawsuits

abdication
to give something up

fodder
material for creating a response or reaction; food

litigant
someone who files a lawsuit

Summarizing

Write a summary of "What Exactly Is a Frivolous Lawsuit?" Remember that a summary presents the main points in a clear, concise form using your own words.

Reflecting

1. What main idea is developed in the text?

   _____

2. How is the text organized—*chronologically, spatially,* or *logical order*? Circle one.

3. What evidence does the author use to oppose tort reform?

   _____

4. What main counterargument does the author address?

   _____

5. What point does the author make in the final few lines?

   _____

6. What side of the tort reform issue do you find most convincing?

   _____

Vocabulary

Use context clues to explain or define the following words.

1. **misdeeds** (paragraph 7)   3. **compensation** (paragraph 8)
2. **defective** (paragraphs 8 and 9)

Critical Thinking

- What side of the tort reform issue does the author seem to favor? Explain your answer with evidence from the essay.
- What side of the tort reform issue do you favor? Did your opinion change at all after reading the essay?
- What sort of implications do lawsuits have on society? How would our society be different if lawsuits were not allowed?
- What does "justice" mean to you? Should we put limits on seeking justice?
- How would you explain the purchasing term *caveat emptor* (buyer beware) after reading this essay?

Writing for Enrichment

Choose one of the following writing ideas, or decide upon an idea of your own related to the reading.

The Writing Process

- Write an argumentation paragraph explaining your reasons for pursuing a college degree.
- Consider one of your strongly held beliefs. Then argue against it in a paragraph or essay. Reflect on whether or not the process reinforces your original beliefs or makes you reconsider them.
- Write a paragraph or essay supporting the following idea: "We need to stop playing the blame game."
- Reflect on your job, your neighborhood, or your favorite pastime. Then write an essay in which you propose a solution for some important problem related to your topic.
- Write an essay that argues for or against tort reform.

When planning . . .

- Identify at least three points to support your topic. Include evidence (facts, statistics, testimonials, and predictions) to justify those supporting points.
- Address counterarguments. This makes your own position stronger.
- If your position calls for it, provide a clear call to action.

When writing . . .

- Include an opening, a middle, and a closing in your argument.
- Follow your planning notes, but remain free to expand upon new ideas.
- Keep your intended audience in mind. Picture someone in particular, and keep your voice appropriately confident and respectful.

When revising and editing . . .

- Reorganize ideas, if necessary, for better impact.
- Make sure your writing doesn't antagonize the reader by taking on a negative or condescending tone. But also make sure your writing sounds confident.
- If a point needs more support, find it. If an important counterclaim has not been mentioned, address it.
- Edit your revised writing for style and correctness.

Introduction to Research

Part 4: Introduction to Research

Lichtmeister, 2014 / Used under license from Shutterstock.com

"What is research but a blind date with knowledge?"

—Will Harvey

Lichtmeister, 2014 / Used under license from Shutterstock.com

Chapter

13

Conducting Research

In school, you may have come to think of research in terms of writing a paper. However, the word "research" actually means something larger and more general. Simply put, research is about seeking knowledge. A consumer might research computer features and prices before deciding on the best buy. A traveler might research routes and sights before planning a trip. A businessperson might research various floor plans before deciding on a new office building. A doctor might request a series of medical tests in order to research the cause of a patient's symptoms. In each case, that person might also write up the results of this research to show others—just as you show your research paper to your instructor. The main purpose, however, is to gain information.

Learning Outcomes

LO1 Understand research.

LO2 Understand and evaluate sources.

LO3 Take effective notes.

LO4 Summarize, paraphrase, and quote.

LO5 Cite sources.

LO6 Understand plagiarism.

What do you think?

Explain what you believe Will Harvey means by calling research "a blind date with knowledge." How accurately does this describe your experience with research projects?

L01 Understanding Research

In the Middle Ages, most European university students read the same classic texts. When a scholar referenced one of these texts, he could assume that his reader would be able to identify the source of the reference without being told.

In our new "Information Age," such a wealth of sources are at hand that it is critical to clearly reference where knowledge comes from.

Why Include Research in Writing

When you clearly reference your sources during writing, you accomplish three important goals:

1. **You add authority to your writing.** Identifying your sources shows just how thoroughly you have investigated your topic. It also adds the weight of experts to your thoughts and conclusions.

2. **You allow readers to follow up on the topic.** During your own research, you will often follow a trail from one source to another as you seek the information you need. By including references to your sources, you help your readers to do the same.

3. **You credit others for their work and thoughts.** All people deserve recognition for their labor and ideas. Including credit to the sources of your research is only fair. To do any less would be stealing. (This sort of intellectual theft is called *plagiarism*.)

When you credit sources of information in your writing, you present yourself as a scholar taking part in an ongoing conversation about your subject. You demonstrate your awareness of what has been said before. This gives your own conclusions validity, showing that they are based on careful consideration of that material. In turn, others can be expected to credit you for your work and ideas.

L02 Understanding and Evaluating Sources

In some fields of study, much of your research will be hands-on. Consider a chemist conducting a lab experiment or a journalist reporting on a live event.

In other fields, much of your research will involve reading and viewing other people's work and discussion. Think of a literary critic analyzing responses to a novel, or a political historian investigating documents from a particular U.S. presidency.

Research sources can be considered either *primary* or *secondary*, depending on their distance from the original events.

Understanding Primary Sources

Primary sources provide information through firsthand experiences. They involve you directly in the topic of your research:

- Conducting interviews and surveys
- Doing experiments or other hands-on activities
- Observing events
- Attending presentations (art exhibits, museum displays, political speeches)
- Studying original documents (court records, letters, journals, diaries)

Understanding Secondary Sources

Secondary sources provide information that you collect indirectly, through the work and thoughts of other people:

- Reference books (encyclopedias, atlases, and almanacs)
- Nonfiction books (biographies, histories, manuals, textbooks)
- Periodicals (magazines and journals, in print or online)
- Newspapers
- Web sites (government, nonprofit, business, and blogs)
- Documentaries

NOTE: The way a source is used can determine whether it serves as a primary source or a secondary one. For example, a survey you conduct is a primary source for you, but your survey results would be a secondary source for someone else. Similarly, the journal of a Civil War soldier would be a primary source about that person's life and thoughts, as well as of battles he took part in. Comments in that journal about other news of the time, however, would serve as a secondary source of information about those events.

Using Primary Sources

To get the most from primary sources, make sure to prepare ahead of time and take careful notes during or immediately after the event.

Interviewing

An interview is a great way to gather information from an expert on your subject. Prepare carefully to get the most from the conversation.

1. **Politely request an interview**, explaining your purpose and why you have chosen this person.
2. **Schedule the interview** in a way convenient to the other person—whether face-to-face, by phone, online, or by email.
3. **Prepare a list of important questions** ahead of time and arrange them in a sensible order.
4. **Be respectful and friendly** during the interview.
5. **Listen carefully** to the person's answers, and write them down or record them (with permission).
6. **Be prepared to reword a question** or to ask follow-up questions if needed.
7. **Thank the person** for her or his help.
8. **Review your notes soon after the interview**. If necessary, contact the person to clarify anything you are unsure about.

Conducting Surveys

For some topics, surveys can collect information from a wide range of people, to better understand common experiences or public opinion. Again, careful preparation will deliver the best results.

1. **Consider example surveys** and online survey tools when preparing your own.
2. **Follow any guidelines** common to the field of study or the class for which you are doing the survey.
3. For best results, **prepare questions that are easy to answer** and that focus on the information you need.
4. **Ask a classmate or colleague to read the survey** and to offer suggestions for improvement.
5. **Provide a clear explanation of the survey's purpose**, clear directions for filling it out, and clear instructions for how and when to return the survey to you.
6. **If possible, allow respondents to remain anonymous** to protect their privacy.
7. **Compile the responses** and consider the results and what they mean to your topic.
8. **If necessary, conduct a follow-up survey** to gain answers to any new questions raised by the original results.

Observing Events

Some topics can be studied by watching people, places, and events. When making an observation, follow these guidelines.

1. **Know what you want to accomplish**—your goal.
2. **Learn about your topic** before you observe it, so that you will best understand what is occurring.
3. **Get permission to observe** if a location or an event isn't open to the public.
4. If you will be recording the event or taking notes, **come prepared with the proper equipment**—pens, notebook, camera.
5. **If appropriate, record sights and sounds as you experience them**. For a live performance that you cannot record, plan time immediately after to write or otherwise record your impressions.
6. **Review your notes carefully** to determine what you have learned.
7. **Do any needed follow-up research** to answer questions the experience raised.

Conducting Experiments

For some fields of study, a live experiment can serve as a primary source of information. Follow the scientific process to gain the best results.

1. **Identify the question** you want to have answered by your research.
2. **Do background investigation** to learn all you can about the topic.
3. **Make a hypothesis** (an educated guess) as to what results you expect from the experiment.
4. **Test your hypothesis** by performing the experiment.
5. **Record the results**, analyze them, and draw a conclusion about your hypothesis.
6. **If needed, form a new hypothesis** and repeat the procedure.

NOTE: The final value of any primary research depends upon the quality of the questions you set out to answer and the care with which you record the results. Also imagine what questions your readers will have when reading your conclusions, and make sure you answer those questions.

Practice Working with a classmate, list two research topics that you might investigate with each of these primary source types—interviews, surveys, observations, and experiments.

Interview: _____

Survey: _____

Observation: _____

Experiment: _____

Using Secondary Sources

In many classes, your research will deal mainly with secondary sources. As secondary sources are the work of other people, they can both save you time and offer expert perspectives and analysis. On the other hand, some secondary sources can be biased or incomplete. You will have to evaluate how trustworthy each source is and how applicable it is to your purpose.

Books

Reference books and other nonfiction books are common sources of secondary information. The time and expense devoted to their publishing means they tend to be well edited and trustworthy. That is especially true of books produced by well-respected publishing houses.

- **Reference books** such as encyclopedias, atlases, and almanacs are general sources of information, and most are available both in print and online. These can serve as trustworthy starting points for research, but be aware that they often contain only general information and may not include the most recent knowledge on a subject. When using reference books, follow these guidelines.

  1. **Learn about the structure of the reference.** Check the table of contents and index, and read the introductory material. These will reveal how best to explore and document the work.
  2. **Understand what the reference covers.** Also think about what types of details it does not include.
  3. **Use precise words in searches.** Whether using an index in print works or a search feature online, note that the word "vegetarian" will lead to different information than the more specific word "vegan," for example. Familiarize yourself with the way the index or search feature works.
  4. **Take careful notes on your reading**, being sure to accurately record the information and details of how to document it.
  5. **Refer to these notes during your further research** to remind yourself what you have learned and what you still need to find out.

- **Nonfiction books** traditionally have been a main source of information in college-level research projects. They are storehouses of information about every sort of topic imaginable. When using nonfiction books, follow these guidelines:

  1. **Learn how the book is put together** and which parts are important to your research.
  2. **Use the reading process** to fully understand the text.
  3. **Take careful notes**, using a proven strategy.
  4. **Identify the source of your notes** (title and author) and the page numbers of the information.
  5. **Use quotation marks** to enclose words and ideas taken directly from the text.
  6. **Refer to the notes** as a reminder during your further research.

Periodicals

Periodicals are magazines and journals published on a regular basis (often weekly, monthly, or quarterly). Magazines usually focus on general areas of interest, and their writers may not be subject experts. Journals address professional areas of study, but they may be written in a challenging, scholarly style. One benefit of periodicals is that they provide recent information. However, this means the information may not be complete or fully tested. For the best use of periodicals, follow these guidelines.

1. **Learn about the periodical**—its purpose, structure, and features.
2. **Use the reading process** to fully understand the text.
3. **Take careful notes**, using a proven strategy.
4. **Identify the source of your notes**—the title and author of the article, page number, title of the periodical, volume number, and date.
5. **Use quotation marks** to enclose the exact words that you record.
6. **Refer to the notes as a reminder** of what you have learned and what research questions remain unanswered.

With so many periodicals available, finding the most helpful articles can be challenging. Learn about the search tools your library offers, such as EBSCOhost, LexisNexis, or another database service. Review each service's keyword search instructions for best results. When you locate promising articles, print them, save them to disk, or email them to yourself.

Web Sites

The Internet may be your starting place for research. Just make sure it isn't the only place. Like print periodicals, Internet sources can be frequently updated with the latest information. On the other hand, many Internet sources are neglected and out of date. To find the best information in such a sea of pages, follow these guidelines.

1. **Check with a librarian for special online searching options**, such as the Library of Congress, Gale's Academic OneFile, and national and state government sites.
2. **Know the basics of Internet searching.** Check each site for its particular keyword guidelines.
3. **Review several choices before deciding which to use.** Good research takes time.
4. **Check the reliability of sites that interest you.** Consider the reputation of the publisher and author, and make sure to check the publication date for timeliness.
5. **Take careful notes** or annotate copies of the information.
6. **Identify the key source of your information** (title of the article or Web page, author, name of the Web site, date of posting, and Web address).
7. **Refer to your notes often as a reminder** of what you have learned and what questions remain unanswered.

NOTE: Learn your school library's layout. The variety of resources you find there may surprise you. And don't be shy about asking your librarians questions. As information specialists, librarians can help you make the most of your time.

A Guide to Keyword Searching

The success of your computer search—whether on the Internet or in a local database—depends on your best use of search tools and the quality of your keywords. Different keywords can provide very different results.

1. Start by typing in your topic: *salmon*.
2. Add a word to call up results containing both words, though not necessarily together: *wild salmon*.
3. Enclose the phrase in quotation marks to call up just the pages containing that exact phrase: *"wild salmon."*
4. Use words or symbols to narrow or focus your search. Searching *salmon -farmed*, for example, calls up results that contain the word *salmon* but do not contain the word *farmed*.
5. Experiment with word order to receive different results: *salmon wild* versus *wild salmon*.
6. Check more than just the first page of results. What you need may be several pages deep, and browsing many results can help you to think of more specific search terms.

Practice Choose a topic, and visit your library to find (1) a book, (2) a periodical or journal, and (3) a Web site devoted to it. Write a paragraph explaining how those three sources are similar and different in their treatment of the topic.

Evaluating Sources

A recipe is only as good as its ingredients and preparation. Likewise, the quality of your research writing depends on your sources and how you use them. Follow these guidelines for choosing sources.

- **Consider the author's reputation.** Is the author a respected authority on the subject?
- **Consider the publisher's reputation.** Does the organization have a history of publishing respected materials? Universities, government offices, and long-standing companies tend to be more trustworthy than publishers with unknown names.
- **Consider the timeliness.** For many subjects, the most recent information may have greater value. For others, information that has stood the test of time may be better.
- **Consider original sources.** Where does this source draw its information from? This is especially important for evaluating persuasive materials.
- **Consider opposing viewpoints.** Not all opinions are equal, but the best sources acknowledge valid opposition. A one-sided source is often weak or biased.
- **Consider tone.** The best sources present information rationally and respectfully. Be wary of sources that rely on emotional or demeaning language.

Practice With a classmate, critique a source of your choice, noting the reputation of its author and publisher, the timeliness of its information, and the quality of its citations. Discuss how alternate viewpoints are treated and whether the tone is balanced or biased.

L03 Taking Effective Notes

Good note-taking skills help not only during your classes but also during research. Note taking helps you do the following:

- Think more deeply about your research.
- Focus your attention on essential ideas and details from your sources.
- Record your sources so that you can locate them for further research.
- Integrate sources into your research writing.
- Provide publication information for your readers.

Annotating a Text

To annotate means "to add comments or make notes in a text." (Annotate only if you own the text or are reading a photocopy.) Annotating allows you to interact with the ideas in a reading selection. Follow these suggestions:

- Write questions in the margins.
- Underline or highlight important points.
- Summarize key passages.
- Define new terms.
- Make connections between ideas.

Annotating in Action

Here is an example of one student's annotations of a paragraph from *Psychology: A Journey*, a college-level psychology textbook by Dennis Coon and John O. Mitterer.

Good question. I'd think so.

A century ago!

I don't think I could do that for science.

This seems to prove their theory.

A bad pun. But I wonder how the conclusion was wrong.

Don't feelings of hunger originate in the stomach? To find out, Walter Cannon and A.L. Washburn (1912) decided to see if stomach contractions cause hunger. In an early study, Washburn trained himself to swallow a balloon, which could be inflated through an attached tube. (You, too, will do anything for science, right?) This allowed Cannon to record the movements of Washburn's stomach. When Washburn's stomach contracted, he reported that he felt "hunger pangs." In view of this, the two scientists concluded that hunger is nothing more than the contractions of an empty stomach. (This, however, proved to be an inflated conclusion.)

From COON/MITTERER. *Psychology: A Journey*, 4E. © 2001 Cengage Learning, Inc.

Insight Annotating requires more than just highlighting or underlining, which don't record your thoughts. You should also write notes in the margin while reading.

Practice Carefully read the paragraph below. Then, if you own this book, annotate the text according to the following directions:

- Circle the main point of the paragraph.
- Underline or highlight two ideas that you either agree with, question, or find confusing. Then, for each idea, write comments in the margin.
- Circle one or two words that you are unsure of. Research those words, and then define or explain them.

The Reading Process

Prereading → Rereading → Reading → Reflecting

> With knowledge obtained from the Greeks, the Romans realized that some diseases were connected to filth, contaminated water, and poor sanitation. They began the development of sanitary systems by building sewers to carry away waste and aqueducts (waterways) to deliver clean water. They drained swamps and marshes to reduce the incidence of malaria. They created laws to keep streets clean and eliminate garbage. The first hospitals were also established in ancient Rome when physicians began caring for injured soldiers or ill people in their homes. From SIMMERS. *Diversified Health Occupations*, 7E. © 2009 Delman Learning, a part of Cengage Learning, Inc.

Outlining

Making an outline of a source helps you to grasp the structure of its contents. This can be especially useful for long, challenging texts and other complex sources. Of course, outlining is also useful for ordering your own thoughts before writing. Further, you can use an outline to keep your thoughts on track during your writing. **Figure 13.1** shows a sample outline.

Figure 13.1 Example Outline

I. **Romans obtained knowledge of disease sources from Greeks.**
   a. Filth
   b. Contaminated water
   c. Poor sanitation

II. **Romans established sanitation practices.**
   a. Sewers to carry away waste
   b. Aqueducts to bring clean water
   c. Drained swamps and marshes
   d. Created sanitation laws

III. **Romans also established hospitals.**
   a. For injured soldiers and ill people
   b. In physicians' homes

Using Clusters or Webs

Though writing has a linear flow from beginning to end, ideas aren't always connected in a straight line. A cluster or web can help you see other interconnections. To make a cluster or web, write a main idea in the center of a page, and then jot related ideas and details around it. Circle ideas and draw lines to show relationships. (See **Figure 13.2**.)

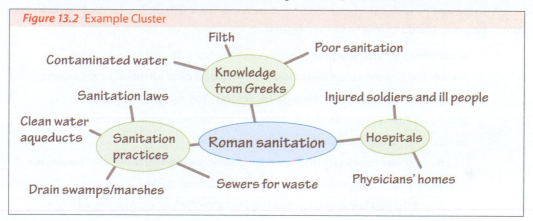

Figure 13.2 Example Cluster

Two-Column Notes (Cornell Method)

Two-column notes (see **Figure 13.3**) are great for classroom use and for review before a test. They can also be effective during your research. Use this method:

- Draw a line down a piece of paper, dividing it into a left-column one-third of the paper's width and a right column two-thirds of its width.
- Use the wide column for your main notes.
- Use the narrow column for summary headings, quotations, and citations.
- Scan the narrow column to review your information.
- Read the wide column when you need further details.

Figure 13.3 Two-Column Notes

Roman Sanitation   March 3

Comments, reactions, questions, source notes

Simmers' <u>Diversified Health Occupations</u>, pg. 5

Did they also get these strategies from Greece?

Were hospitals and home care related?

Main notes

- Romans got disease knowledge from Greeks: filth, contaminated water
- Romans set up laws and practices for sanitation: built sewers and aqueducts, drained swamps to fight disease
- Romans set up the first hospitals in physicians' homes
- Treated injured soldiers and ill people

L04   Summarizing, Paraphrasing, and Quoting

Summarizing, paraphrasing, and quoting are ways of using sources in your research.

Summarizing

A summary provides the basic ideas of a source in their original order and is usually no more than one-third the length of the original.

> **A Summary of This Chapter:** Kemper et al. say research means looking for knowledge. Documenting sources wasn't essential during Medieval times, when sources were limited. Today, though, the Information Age's expanding sources make documentation critical. Documenting sources adds authority, allows readers to follow leads, and credits others for their hard work.
>
> Sources may be primary (like interviews, surveys, observation, and experiments) or secondary (like books, periodicals, Web sites, and documentaries).
>
> Using the best keyword strategies helps to locate the best sources. But all secondary sources must be evaluated for quality. Also, using good note-taking strategies (two-column notes, outlines, and clusters) helps you understand and document information. Summarizing, paraphrasing, and quoting are ways to incorporate that information into your own writing.
>
> Two common styles for citing sources are MLA and APA format. Using these, writers can avoid plagiarism, which is using information without correctly crediting its source. Correct citation shows where ideas originated and indicates exact words borrowed from a source (291–310).

Paraphrasing

To paraphrase is to restate an idea in your own words. This shows your understanding of the idea and expresses it in your own voice.

> **A Paraphrase of the Previous Sentences:** Paraphrasing puts an idea in your own words, showing your understanding and using your voice (Kemper et al. 302).

Quoting

Quoting experts adds authority, but using too many quotations can make your writing seem a patchwork of other people's ideas. Integrate quotations smoothly by leaving out some words, but be sure to accurately represent the source.

> **A Quotation from the Previous Sentences:** Don't overuse quotations, or your paper may seem like a "patchwork of other people's ideas" (Kemper et al. 302).

Practice > Read the following excerpt and complete the bulleted activities. Give credit for the material you have borrowed.

- Write a summary of the entire selection.
- Paraphrase the paragraph.
- Write a personal response in which you incorporate a quotation from the selection.

From "How Our Skins Got Their Color"

Human skin owes its color to the presence of particles known as melanin. The primary function of melanin is to protect the upper levels of the skin from being damaged by the sun's ultraviolet rays. This radiation poses a critical problem for our kind because we lack the dense coat of hair that acts as a sunscreen for most mammals.

. . . Hairlessness exposes us to two kinds of radiation hazards: ordinary sunburn, with its blisters, rashes, and risk of infection; and skin cancers, including malignant melanoma, one of the deadliest diseases known. Melanin is the body's first line of defense against these afflictions. The more melanin particles, the darker the skin, and the lower the risk of sunburn and all forms of skin cancer. This explains why the highest rates for skin cancer are found in sun-drenched lands such as Australia, where light-skinned people of European descent spend a good part of their lives outdoors wearing scanty attire. Very dark-skinned people such as heavily pigmented Africans of Zaire seldom get skin cancer, but when they do, they get it on depigmented parts of their bodies—palms and lips.

Excerpted from *Our Kind* by Marvin Harris. Copyright (c) 1989 HarperCollins Publishers.

Claus Mikosch, 2014 / Used under license from Shutterstock.com

L05 Citing Sources

You must give credit to the sources of ideas or words that you use in your academic essays and reports. Doing so avoids *plagiarism*, which is using the words and thoughts of others without crediting them in your writing.

Academic research uses a number of different styles for citing sources. For example, the Modern Language Association (MLA) style is generally used for research in the humanities (literature, philosophy, art history), and the American Psychological Association (APA) style is generally used for research in the social sciences (sociology, psychology, political science). Check with your instructor before choosing a citation style.

Insight *Plagiarism is a serious offense that can damage your reputation. Penalties for plagiarism vary but can range from having a research paper rejected to losing financial aid to being dismissed from a university.*

Table 13.1 shows the basic guidelines for using the MLA and APA styles for crediting sources in the text of a research report.

Table 13.1 MLA and APA Guidelines

Sources	MLA	APA
Work with one author	*Author name and page number* (Waye 27)	*Author name, year of publication, and page number* (Waye, 2008, p. 27)
Work with two (or three) authors	(Waye and Joniz 27) (Sams, Banks, and Ory 31)	(Waye & Joniz, 2008, p. 27) (Sams, Banks, & Ory, 2010, p. 31)
Work with four (or five) authors	(Waye et al. 27)	(Waye, Joniz, Damik, & Martin, 2008, p. 27)
Work with six or more authors	(Waye et al. 27)	(Waye et al., 2008, p. 27)
Author identified within the sentence	According to Mariah Waye, fishery expert, wild salmon need human help (27).	According to Mariah Waye, fishery expert, wild salmon need human help (2008, p. 27).
Work with no author specified	*First main word(s) of the title and page number:* ("Salmon in Crisis" 27)	*First main word(s) of the title, date, and page number:* ("Salmon in Crisis," 2008, p. 27)
Work with no page number specified (as in a Web page)	*Author name only (or first main word[s] of title if no author is specified):* (Waye)	*Author name (or first main word[s] of title if no author is specified) and date:* (Waye, 2008)

Using In-Text Citations

You can learn more about basic documentation by studying the following passages from a research report, demonstrating first the MLA style and then the APA style.

MLA Style

Source is cited in the sentence. → **According to the Consumer Product Safety Commission**, almost 25,000 children are treated in hospital emergency rooms each year as a result of shopping-cart injuries. The National Safe Kids Campaign says "the number of children ages 5 and under injured in shopping-cart incidents

Title only; this Web site names no author. → has increased more than 30 percent since 1985" (**"Secure Children"**).

B. Potential Injuries

Shopping-cart injuries include cuts, bruises, fractures, internal injuries, and head injuries—even skull fractures. In fact, children have

Four authors, with page number → died as a result of shopping-cart falls (**Smith et al. 161**). For the sake of our customers, Jonesville Home Mart needs to take steps to ensure shopping-cart safety.

C. Solutions

A solution to this problem comes from a sister store in Anchorage,

Single author, with page number → which has made safety its motto (**Clepper 47**). Like this store, Jonesville . . .

APA Style

According to the Consumer Product Safety Commission, almost 25,000 children are treated in hospital emergency rooms each year as a result of

Online material with no page numbers specified → shopping-cart injuries (**2009**). The National Safe Kids Campaign says "the number of children ages 5 and under injured in shopping-cart incidents has increased more than 30 percent since 1985" (**"Secure Children," 2009**).

B. Potential Injuries

Shopping-cart injuries include cuts, bruises, fractures, internal injuries, and head injuries—even skull fractures. In fact, children have

Four authors, with year and page number → died as a result of shopping-cart falls (**Smith, Dietrich, Garcia, & Shields, 2010, p. 161**). For the sake of our customers, Jonesville Home Mart needs to take steps to ensure shopping-cart safety.

C. Solutions

A solution to this problem comes from a sister store in Anchorage,

Single author, with year and page number → which has made safety its motto (**Clepper, 2010, p. 47**). Like this store, Jonesville . . .

Creating a Source List

At the end of your report, you must list your sources—in either a **works-cited list** (MLA) or a **references list** (APA)—so that your reader can locate them. **Table 13.2** shows the differences between the styles. In both the MLA and APA formats, any source listed must also be cited in your paper, and any source cited in your paper must also appear in the source list. The exception, in APA format, is personal communication such as interviews and email, which should be cited in text but not included in the references list.

Whether your sources are books, magazine articles, pamphlets, or Web sites, the citations should include all of the following elements that are available:

1. **Author name(s)**
2. **Title** (When including two parts of a publication, list the smaller part first, in quotes; the larger part next, in italics.)
   - "Book chapter." *Book title.*
   - "Magazine article." *Magazine title.*
   - "Web site article." *Web site title.*
3. **Publication facts** (the date, the place of publication, and the publisher; or appropriate Web information)

Table 13.2 MLA and APA Source List Differences

	Author	Title	Publication Facts
MLA	Give the name that appears on the title page.	Capitalize all important words.	Place the date after the publication information, followed by the medium—Print, Web, CD-ROM, etc.
	Waye, Mariah S. *Environmental Watch: Salmon in Danger.* New York: Pudding Press, 2010. Print.		
APA	Use initials for the first and middle names.	Capitalize only the first word in a title, the first word in a subtitle, and any proper nouns. Capitalize titles of periodicals normally.	Place the date after the author's name.
	Waye, M. S. (2010). *Environmental watch: Salmon in danger.* New York, NY: Pudding Press.		

works-cited list
list of sources prepared according to MLA style

references list
list of sources prepared according to APA style

MLA Style

Works Cited

Magazine article — Clepper, Irene. "Safety First: Alaska Retailer Attracts Customers with Safe-and-Sound Seminars." *Playthings* 97 (2010): 46-47. Print.

Web article — Consumer Product Safety Commission. "Shopping Cart Injuries: Victims 5 years old and younger." CPSC. 25 July 2012. Web. 22 Sept. 2014.

Web article — "Secure Children Properly in Shopping Carts." Texas Medical Center. 2009. Web. 22 Sept. 2014.

Book — Shelov, Steven P., ed. *Caring for Your Baby and Young Child: Birth to Age 5.* 5th ed. New York: Bantam, 2009. Print.

Article, four authors — Smith, Gary A., et al. "Injuries to Children Related to Shopping Carts." *Pediatrics* 97 (2010): 161-65. Print.

APA Style (for the same sources)

References

Magazine article — Clepper, I. (2010). Safety first: Alaska retailer attracts customers with safe-and-sound seminars. *Playthings*, 97, 46-47.

Web article — Consumer Product Safety Commission. (2012). Shopping cart injuries: Victims 5 years old and younger. Retrieved September 22, 2014 from https://www.cpsc.gov/en/Media/Documents/Research--Statistics /Injury-Statistics/Public-Facilities-and-Products/Shopping-Cart-Injuries-Victims-5-years-old-and-younger

Web article — Secure children properly in shopping carts. (2009). Retrieved September 22, 2014, from http://www.tmc.edu/tmcnews/06_15_00/page_16.html

Book — Shelov, S. P. (Ed.). (2009). *Caring for your baby and young child: Birth to age 5.* New York, NY: Bantam.

Article, four authors — Smith, G. A., Dietrich, A., Garcia, T., & Shields, B. (2010). Injuries to children related to shopping carts. *Pediatrics*, 97, 161-165.

NOTE: For more examples visit the Purdue Online Writing Lab at owl.english.purdue.edu.

L06 Understanding Plagiarism

The following essay and examples taken from it demonstrate ways that a careless writer might plagiarize a source, even if accidentally. You can avoid these errors in your own writing by keeping careful notes, with quotation marks around exact words, and with source information for your works-cited page or references list.

A Good, Old-Fashioned Book
By Marcus Connerley

With the rise of ebooks, a common debate crops up on social media sites. Someone mentions a favorite title, and someone else responds, "I'll wait till it's an ebook." Or someone mentions that a particular ebook is free today, and someone else says, "I read only 'real' books." Another person points out that ebooks save space; you can carry a library in a pocket. Then another commenter responds that carrying one book at a time is enough. Inevitably, someone mentions the delightful smell of paper and glue. "Give me an old-fashioned book," that person says. "Ebooks aren't real books."

Rakic, 2014 / Used under license from Shutterstock.com

Did a similar debate rage over the switch from vellum scrolls to bound volumes? Or from clay tablets to scrolls? Actually, each new publishing technology has faced resistance and criticism.

Many authors predicted that the rise of paperbacks would destroy publishing. Even George Orwell argued that "if other publishers had any sense, they would combine against them and suppress them" ("Penguin Profile: Company History"). Just a few centuries earlier, the rise of printing itself gave authorities fear. As the governor of Virginia in the late 1600s put it, "learning has brought disobedience, and heresy, and sects into the world, and printing has divulged them, and libels against the best government" (Schweiger).

If each new publishing technology is destined to bring criticism, if the old ways are best, maybe we should just go back to making cave paintings. After all, that is the oldest form of human recording (Thurman). Cave paintings certainly had their advantages. For example, you never had to worry about someone borrowing and forgetting to return them.

Works Cited

"Penguin Profile: Company History." Penguin Press Office. 2013. Penguin.co.uk. Web. 6 Nov. 2014.

Schweiger, Beth Barton. "The Literate South: Reading Before Emancipation." *Journal of the Civil War Era* 3 (2013): 331-359. Print.

Thurman, Judith. "Letter from Southern France: First Impressions." *New Yorker* 23 June 2008: 58-67. Print.

Common Types of Plagiarism

The highlighted examples of plagiarism below are linked to "A Good, Old-Fashioned Book," the article from which the information was taken.

Copying Text Without Credit

Here the writer copies word for word from the original source without giving any credit.

> Nowadays, with ebooks, a common debate crops up on social media sites. One person mentions a favorite title, and someone else says he'll wait till it's an ebook. Someone else says, "I read only 'real' books." Someone points out that ebooks save space; you can carry a library in a pocket. Inevitably, someone mentions the delightful smell of paper and glue and says, "Ebooks aren't real books."

Neglecting Quotation Marks

Here the writer credits the source but forgets to place quotation marks around exact words borrowed from it.

> Marcus Connerley points out that many authors predicted that the rise of paperbacks would destroy publishing. He notes that even George Orwell argued that if other publishers had any sense, they would combine against them and suppress them; and that just a few centuries earlier, the rise of printing itself gave authorities fear.

Paraphrasing Ideas Without Citing Them

Here the writer paraphrases information from a specific passage without identifying the source.

> If the old ways really are the best, that would mean we should go back to painting on cave walls. Cave paintings are the oldest form of publishing, and even they have advantages. You don't have to worry, for instance, that someone will borrow yours and forget to return them.

Insight Other types of source abuse include *self-plagiarism* and *copyright violation*. Self-plagiarism means using material you have written elsewhere without giving credit. In school, this generally involves using a paper in more than one class without permission. In professional life, it can mean neglecting to cite your previously published work. Copyright violation means using text, images, or audio files without permission and credit. It can result in criminal charges and lawsuits.

☑ Reviewing the Chapter

Understand Research

1. Explain at least two reasons for including research in your writing.

   _____

   _____

Understand and Evaluate Sources

2. Define "primary source" and provide at least two examples.

   _____

   _____

3. Define "secondary source" and provide at least two examples.

   _____

4. List at least three things to consider when evaluating a source.

   _____

   _____

Take Effective Notes

5. List at least two methods of taking notes.

   _____

Summarize, Paraphrase, and Quote

6. What is the difference between a quotation and a paraphrase?

   _____

Cite Sources

7. What are two common documentation styles?

   _____

Understand Plagiarism

8. Define plagiarism.

   _____

Sentence Workshops

Part 5: Sentence Workshops

Alexander A.Trofimov, 2014 / Used under license from Shutterstock.com

Chapter 14

"Grasp the subject; the words will follow."
—Cato the Elder

Sentence Basics

The basics of sentences really are basic. A sentence is the connection between a noun and a verb (or a subject and a predicate), with all of the other words modifying those two parts. These are the building blocks of thought.

In the pages that follow, you will explore the ins and outs of subjects and predicates, as well as the words, phrases, and clauses that describe them. Fear not. These are sentence basics, and we'll make sure they are easy to understand.

Learning Outcomes

LO1 Subjects and Predicates (Verbs)
LO2 Special Types of Subjects
LO3 Special Types of Predicates
LO4 Adjectives
LO5 Adverbs
LO6 Prepositional Phrases
LO7 Clauses

What do you think?

Read the quotation above from Cato the Elder. How does grasping the subject of a sentence (or of a longer piece of writing) help you write the rest of the words?

L01 Subjects and Predicates (Verbs)

The subject of a sentence tells what the sentence is about. The predicate of a sentence tells what the subject does or is. Subjects are usually nouns, and predicates are usually verbs.

Parrots talk.

Subject: what the
sentence is about

Predicate: what
the subject does

► Simple Subject and Simple Predicate

The simple subject is the subject without any modifiers, and the simple predicate is the verb and any helping verbs without modifiers or objects. Modifiers add information to the subject and predicate.

The red and black parrot is singing the song loudly.

simple subject   simple predicate

► Complete Subject and Complete Predicate

The complete subject is the subject with modifiers, and the complete predicate is the verb with modifiers and objects. (The modifiers are indicated in red in the next example.)

The red and black parrot is singing the song loudly.

complete subject   complete predicate

In this example, the words "red and black" modify, or give more information about, the parrot. The words "the song loudly" give more information about the parrot's singing.

► Implied Subject

In commands, the subject *you* is implied. Commands are the only type of sentence in English that can have an implied subject.

(You)   Start singing!

implied subject   complete predicate

► Inverted Order

Most often in English, the subject comes before the predicate. However, in questions and sentences that begin with *here* or *there*, the subject comes after the predicate.

subject   subject

Why are you so loud?   Here is a cracker.

predicate   predicate

Practice ▸ For the following sentences, identify and label the simple subject (SS) and simple predicate (SP). Then write a similar sentence of your own and identify the simple subject and simple predicate in the same way.

1. In the wild, parrots gather in large groups.

   _____

2. In captivity, a parrot needs constant companionship.

   _____

3. Without enough attention, some parrots pluck their feathers.

   _____

4. A caring pet owner understands the parrot's need for attention.

   _____

5. Why do parrots live so long?

   _____

Practice ▸ For the following sentences, identify and label the complete subject (CS) and complete predicate (CP). Then write a similar sentence of your own and identify the complete subject and complete predicate in the same way.

1. A typical pet parrot can live to be 80 years old.

   _____

2. A baby parrot could outlive the pet owner.

   _____

3. Parrot owners often place their parrots in their wills.

   _____

4. There must be an explanation.

   _____

---

simple subject
the subject without any modifiers

simple predicate
the verb and any helping verbs without modifiers or objects

complete subject
the subject with modifiers

complete predicate
the verb with modifiers and objects

implied subject
the word *you* implied in command sentences

L02   Special Types of Subjects

As you work with subjects, watch for these special types.

▶ Compound Subjects

A **compound subject** is two or more subjects connected by *and* or *or*.

My <u>brother</u> and <u>sister</u> run well. <u>Dajohn, Larinda,</u> or <u>I</u> will win the race.

       compound subject   compound subject

▶ Infinitives as Subjects

An **infinitive** can function as a subject. An infinitive is a verb form that begins with *to* and may be followed by objects or modifiers.

            infinitive

<u>To complete a one-and-a-half flip</u> is my goal.

     infinitive subject with modifiers

▶ Gerunds as Subjects

A **gerund** can function as a subject. A gerund is a predicate form that ends in *ing* and may be followed by objects or modifiers.

<u>Swimming</u> is his favorite sport.   <u>Handing him the goggles</u> would be nice.

   gerund subject   gerund subject with modifiers

▶ Noun Clauses as Subjects

A **noun clause** can function as a subject. The clause itself has a subject and a verb but cannot stand alone as a sentence. Noun clauses are introduced by words like *what, that, when, why, how, whatever,* or *whichever.*

<u>Whoever wants to go swimming</u> must remember to bring a swimsuit.

     noun clause subject

<u>Whatever remains of the afternoon</u> will be spent at the pool.

     noun clause subject

Insight   Note that each of these special subjects functions as a noun. A sentence is still, at root, the connection between a noun and a verb.

Say It   Pair up with a partner and read each sentence aloud. Take turns identifying the type of subject—compound subject, infinitive subject, gerund subject, or noun-clause subject. Discuss your answers.

1. Swimming across the pool underwater is challenging.
2. To get a lifesaving certificate is hard work.
3. Whoever gets a certificate can be a lifeguard.
4. You and I should go swimming sometime.

Practice   For the following sentences, identify the complete subject as a compound subject (CPS), infinitive (I), gerund (G), or noun clause (NC). Then write a similar sentence of your own and identify the complete subject in the same way.

1. To clean the car thoroughly requires a vacuum.

   _____

2. Wishing for better weather won't stop the rain.

   _____

3. The river and the lake are flooding into the streets.

   _____

4. Whoever needs to set the table should get started now.

   _____

5. Shoes, shirts, and pants are required in this restaurant.

   _____

6. Reading us the riot act is not the best way to win us over.

   _____

---

compound subject
two or more subjects connected by *and* or *or*

infinitive
a verb form that begins with *to* and can be used as a noun (or as an adjective or adverb)

gerund
a verb form that ends in *ing* and is used as a noun

noun clause
a group of words that begin with words like *that, what, whoever, whatever, why,* or *when* and contain a subject and a verb but are unable to function as a sentence

L03   Special Types of Predicates

As you work with predicates, watch for these special types.

▶ Compound Predicates

A **compound predicate** consists of two or more verbs joined by *and* or *or*.

I <u>sang</u> and <u>danced</u>. The audience <u>laughed, clapped,</u> or <u>swayed</u>.

compound predicate   compound predicate

▶ Predicates with Direct Objects

A **direct object** follows a transitive verb and tells what or who receives the action of the verb. A **transitive verb** is an action verb that transfers action to a direct object.

I sang a song. I danced a few dances. I told some jokes.

direct object   direct object   direct object

▶ Predicates with Indirect Objects

An **indirect object** comes between a transitive verb and a direct object and tells to whom or for whom an action was done.

I sang Jim his favorite song. I told Ellen her favorite joke.

indirect object   indirect object

▶ Passive Predicates (Verbs)

When a verb is **passive**, the subject of the sentence is being acted upon rather than acting. Often, the actor is the object of the **preposition** in a phrase that starts with *by*. To make the sentence **active**, rewrite it, turning the object of the preposition into the subject.

Passive

Teri was serenaded by Josh.

subject   passive verb   object of the
                          preposition

Active

Josh serenaded Teri.

subject   active verb   direct object

Say It Pair up with a partner and read each sentence. Take turns identifying the sentence as active or passive. If the sentence is passive, speak the active version out loud.

1. I threw out my back.
2. My friends were warned by the bouncer.
3. A camera crew was escorted to the exit by the guard.

Practice For the following sentences, identify and label any compound predicate (CPP), direct object (DO), and indirect object (IO) that you find. Then write a similar sentence of your own and identify the same items.

1. Everyone danced and sang.

   _____

2. The DJ played dance music.

   _____

3. I gave him a request.

   _____

4. The crowd twisted and shouted.

   _____

Practice For the following sentences, identify and label the simple subject (S), the passive predicate (PP), and the object of the preposition *by* (O). Then rewrite each sentence, making it active.

1. Many songs were played by the DJ.

   _____

2. A good time was had by the partygoers.

   _____

compound predicate
two or more predicates joined by *and* or *or*

direct object
a word that follows a transitive verb and tells what or who receives the action of the verb

indirect object
a word that comes between a

transitive verb and a direct object and tells to whom or for whom an action was done

passive
the voice created when a subject is being acted upon

active
the voice created when a subject is acting

transitive verb
an action verb that transfers action to a direct object

preposition
a word or group of words that is used with a noun, pronoun, or noun phrase to show direction, location, time, or to introduce an object

L04 Adjectives

To modify a subject (or another type of noun), use an adjective. You may also use a phrase or clause that acts as an adjective.

Adjectives answer these basic questions: *which? what kind of? how many? how much?*

To modify the noun books, ask . . .

> *Which* books? ⟶ **hardbound** books
>
> *What kind* of books? ⟶ **old** books
>
> *How many* books? ⟶ **five** books

> **five old hardbound** books

▶ Adjective Phrases and Clauses

Phrases and clauses can also act as adjectives to modify nouns. A phrase is a group of words that lacks a subject or predicate or both. A clause is a group of words that has a subject and a predicate but does not form a complete sentence.

To modify the noun books, ask . . .

> *What kind of* books? ⟶ books **about women's issues**
>
>   ⟶ books **that are out of date**
>
> *Which* books? ⟶ books **that my mother gave me**

> The **out-of-date** books **that my mother gave me about women's issues**
> rest on the top shelf.

Insight   If a group of words answers one of the basic adjective questions, the words are probably functioning as an adjective.

Say It   Pair up with a classmate to find adjectives—words, phrases, or clauses—that modify the following nouns. Take turns asking the questions while the other person answers.

1. **Cars**
   Which cars?
   What kind of cars?
   How many cars?

2. **Trees**
   Which trees?
   What kind of trees?
   How many trees?

Practice   For each noun, answer the questions using adjectives—words, phrases, or clauses. Then write a sentence using two or more of your answers. An example is provided for you.

1. **Dogs**

   Which dogs? ___Labrador dogs___

   What kind of dogs? ___black dogs___

   How many dogs? ___two dogs___

   Sentence: ___Two black Labrador dogs played in the yard.___

   _____

2. **Classes**

   Which classes? _____

   What kind of classes? _____

   How many classes? _____

   Sentence: _____

   _____

3. **Ideas**

   Which ideas? _____

   What kind of ideas? _____

   How many ideas? _____

   Sentence: _____

   _____

L05 Adverbs

To modify a verb, use an adverb. You may also use phrase or clause that acts as an adverb.

Adverbs answer these basic questions: *how? when? where? why? how long? how often?*

To modify the verb jumped, ask . . .

How did they jump? ⟶	jumped **eagerly**
When did they jump? ⟶	jumped **today**
Where did they jump? ⟶	jumped **here**
How often did they jump? ⟶	jumped **often**

Today children **often** jumped **here eagerly**.

▶ ## Adverb Phrases and Clauses

Phrases and clauses can also act as adverbs to modify verbs.

To modify the verb jumped, ask . . .

When did they jump? ⟶	jumped **before lunchtime**
Where did they jump? ⟶	jumped **on the trampoline**
Why did they jump? ⟶	jumped **to get some exercise**
How long did they jump? ⟶	jumped **for an hour**

To get some exercise before lunchtime, the children jumped **on the trampoline for an hour**.

Insight Read the last sentence aloud. Though it may look imposing on the page, it sounds natural, probably because adverbs are a common part of our speech. Experiment with these modifiers in your writing as well.

Practice For each verb, answer the questions using adverbs—words, phrases, or clauses. Then write a sentence using three or more of your answers.

1. **Sang**

   How did they sing? _____

   When did they sing? _____

   Where did they sing? _____

   Why did they sing? _____

   How long did they sing? _____

   How often did they sing? _____

   Sentence: _____

   _____

2. **Ate**

   How did they eat? _____

   When did they eat? _____

   Where did they eat? _____

   Why did they eat? _____

   How long did they eat? _____

   How often did they eat? _____

   Sentence: _____

   _____

L06 Prepositional Phrases

One of the simplest and most versatile types of phrases in English is the **prepositional phrase**. A prepositional phrase can function as an adjective or an adverb.

▶ Building Prepositional Phrases

A prepositional phrase is a preposition followed by an object (a noun or pronoun) and any modifiers.

Preposition	**+**	Object	**=**	Prepositional Phrase
at		noon		at noon
in		an hour		in an hour
beside		the green clock		beside the green clock
in front of		my aunt's vinyl purse		in front of my aunt's vinyl purse

As you can see, a propositional phrase can be just two words long, or many words long. As you can also see, some prepositions are themselves made up of more than one word. **Table 14.1** shows a list of common prepositions.

Table 14.1 Prepositions

aboard	back of	except for	near to	round
about	because of	excepting	notwithstanding	save
above	before	for	of	since
according to	behind	from	off	subsequent to
across	below	from among	on	through
across from	beneath	from between	on account of	throughout
after	beside	from under	on behalf of	'til
against	besides	in	onto	to
along	between	in addition to	on top of	together with
alongside	beyond	in behalf of	opposite	toward
alongside of	but	in front of	out	under
along with	by	in place of	out of	underneath
amid	by means of	in regard to	outside	until
among	concerning	inside	outside of	unto
apart from	considering	inside of	over	up
around	despite	in spite of	over to	upon
as far as	down	instead of	owing to	up to
aside from	down from	into	past	with
at	during	like	prior to	within
away from	except	near	regarding	without

Insight A preposition is pre-positioned before the other words it introduces to form a phrase. Other languages have post-positional words that follow their objects.

Practice For the following items, create a prepositional phrase by writing a preposition and an object (and any modifiers). Then write a sentence using the prepositional phrase. One example is provided for you.

1.

Preposition	+	**Object** (and any modifiers)
underneath		*the dining table*

Sentence: _Our dog often sleeps under the dining room table._

2.

Preposition	+	**Object** (and any modifiers)

Sentence: _____

3.

Preposition	+	**Object** (and any modifiers)

Sentence: _____

4.

Preposition	+	**Object** (and any modifiers)

Sentence: _____

5.

Preposition	+	**Object** (and any modifiers)

Sentence: _____

---

prepositional phrase
a group of words beginning with a preposition and including an object (noun or pronoun) and any modifiers

L07 Clauses

A clause is a group of words with a subject and a predicate. If a clause can stand on its own as a sentence, it is an **independent clause**; but if it cannot, it is a **dependent clause**.

▶ Independent Clause

An independent clause has a subject and a predicate and expresses a complete thought. It is the same as a simple sentence.

Clouds piled up in the stormy sky.

▶ Dependent Clause

A dependent clause has a subject and a predicate but does not express a complete thought. Instead, it is used as an **adverb clause**, an **adjective clause**, or a **noun clause**.

> **Say It** Read the dependent clauses (in red) out loud. Can you hear how they sound incomplete? A dependent clause must connect with an independent clause to form a complete thought and make sense.

- An **adverb clause** begins with a subordinating conjunction (see **Table 14.2**) and functions as an adverb. To be complete, it must be connected to an independent clause.

Table 14.2 Subordinating Conjunctions

after	because	in order that	though	where
although	before	provided that	unless	whereas
as	even though	since	until	while
as if	given that	so that	when	
as long as	if	that	whenever	

Because I have 19 pets, I have a big pet-food bill.
adverb clause (dependent)

- **An adjective clause** begins with a relative pronoun (*which, that, who*) and functions as an adjective, so it must be connected to an independent clause to be complete.

My oldest pet is a cat that thinks he is a person.
adjective clause (dependent)

- **A noun clause** begins with words like those in **Table 14.3** and functions as a noun. It is used as a subject or an object in a sentence.

Table 14.3 Subordinating Conjunctions

how	what	whoever	whomever
that	whatever	whom	why

My cat doesn't care about what I think.
noun clause (dependent)

Practice For the following sentences, identify and label any adverb clauses (ADVC), adjective clauses (ADJC), or noun clauses (NC). Then write a similar sentence of your own and identify the clauses.

1. I know a woman who has 15 cats.

   _____

2. The number is so high because she takes care of shelter kittens.

   _____

3. When a pregnant cat is dropped off at the shelter, this woman takes her home.

   _____

4. She provides what the mother and the kittens need.

   _____

5. Whatever cat comes to her receives good care.

   _____

6. People who are cruel to animals should not have pets.

   _____

7. When I visit my friend, I see plenty of kittens.

   _____

8. All are safe, provided that they don't escape.

   _____

9. My friend has a shirt that has the words "Cat Lady" printed on it.

   _____

10. Though others might scoff, my friend is proud of what she does.

   _____

independent clause	**adverb clause**	**noun clause**
a group of words with a subject and predicate that expresses a complete thought	a dependent clause beginning with a subordinating conjunction and functioning as an adverb	a dependent clause beginning with a word like *what, how, that,* or *why* and functioning as a noun
dependent clause	**adjective clause**	
a group of words with a subject and predicate that does not express a complete thought	a dependent clause beginning with a relative pronoun and functioning as an adjective	

🌐 Real-World Application

Practice ▶ In the following email, identify the <u>simple subjects</u>, <u>simple predicates</u>, and (dependent clauses). (Use underlining and circling as shown.)

✉   📎   📇   📝   ● ● ●

To: Robert Pastorelli

Subject: Meeting to Discuss Benefits and Policies

Dear Robert:

I am pleased that you have accepted the production manager position at Rankin Technologies. I believe that you will find many opportunities for professional growth with us.

Our Human Resources Department is here to help you grow. To that end, I would like to discuss Rankin's benefit package, policies, and procedures. Specifically, I would like to share the following information:

- Profit-sharing plan
- Medical-plan benefits for you and your family
- Procedures for submitting dental and optometry receipts
- Counseling services
- Continuing-education programs
- Advancement policies and procedures
- Workplace policies

On Friday, I will arrange a convenient time for your orientation meeting. In the meantime, if you have questions, please contact me at extension 3925 or simply reply to this message.

Sincerely,

Julia

Chapter

15

"A complex system that works is invariably found to have evolved from a simple system that works."

—John Gaule

Simple, Compound, and Complex Sentences

A two-by-four is a simple thing—a board with standard dimensions. But two-by-fours can be used to create everything from a shed to a mansion. It's the way that the boards are connected and combined that determines the proportions of the final structure.

A sentence can be a simple thing as well, just a subject and a predicate. But you can also connect sentences to create compound or complex types. Using a variety of these types is important to developing your writing skill.

Learning Outcomes

LO1 Simple Sentences

LO2 Simple Sentences with Compound Subjects

LO3 Simple Sentences with Compound Predicates

LO4 Compound Sentences

LO5 Complex Sentences

LO6 Complex Sentences with Relative Clauses

What do you think?

If you could build anything out of two-by-fours, what would you build? If you could build anything out of sentences, what would you build? Why?

L01 Simple Sentences

A **simple sentence** consists of a subject and a predicate. The subject is a noun or pronoun that names what the sentence is about. The predicate is a verb that tells what the subject does or is.

My friend played.
Subject   Predicate

▶ Modifiers

Other words can modify the subject. Words that modify the subject answer the adjective questions: *which? what kind of? how many? how much?*

> My **best** friend played. (The words tell *which friend*.)

Other words can also modify the verb. These words and phrases answer the adverb questions: *how? when? where? why? how long? how often?*

> My best friend played **all afternoon and into the evening**. (The phrases tell *when my friend played*.)

▶ Direct and Indirect Objects

The verb may also be followed by a **direct object**, a noun or pronoun that receives the action of the verb. The direct object answers the question *what?* or *whom?*

> My best friend played **basketball**. (The word tells *what my friend played*.)

A noun or pronoun that comes between the verb and its direct object is called an **indirect object**. The indirect object tells *to whom* or *for whom* an action is done.

> My best friend passed **me** the basketball. (The word tells *to whom my friend passed the basketball*.)

---

simple sentence
a subject and a predicate that together form a complete thought

direct object
a noun or pronoun that follows a verb and receives its action

indirect object
a noun or pronoun that comes between a verb and a direct object, telling *to whom* or *for whom* an action is done

Practice For the following items, write a noun for the subject, a verb, and words to answer the question. Then put the words together to form a sentence.

1.

Subject		Verb
	+	

Which? _____

Simple Sentence: _____

2.

Subject		Verb
	+	

What kind of? _____

Simple Sentence: _____

3.

Subject		Verb
	+	

Where? _____

Simple Sentence: _____

4.

Subject		Verb
	+	

How? _____

Simple Sentence: _____

L02 Simple Sentences with Compound Subjects

A simple sentence can have a **compound subject** (two or more subjects).

► Two Subjects

To write a simple sentence with two subjects, join them using *and* or *or*.

One Subject:	Chan works at the animal shelter.
Two Subjects:	Chan and Lynn will clean cages today.
	Chan or Lynn will clean cages today.

One Subject:	The manager must supervise the volunteers.
Two Subjects:	The manager and receptionist must supervise the volunteers.
	The manager or the receptionist must supervise the volunteers.

► Three or More Subjects

To write a simple sentence with three or more subjects, create a series. Use commas between all subjects and place *and* or *or* before the last subject.

Three Subjects:	Chan, Lynn, and I love animals.
Five Subjects:	Chan, Lynn, the manager, the receptionist, and I encourage people to adopt pets from the shelter.

When a compound subject is joined by *and*, the subject is plural and requires a plural verb. When a compound subject is joined by *or*, the verb should match the last subject.

Chan and Lynn plan to work weekends at the shelter during school.

Chan or Lynn plans to work weekends at the shelter during school.

---

compound subject
two or more subjects joined by *and* or *or*

Insight Using a compound subject does not make the sentence compound. As long as all of the subjects connect to the same predicate, the thought is still a simple sentence.

Say It   Speak each of the following sentences out loud.

1. Chan *volunteers* regularly.
2. Chan *and* Lynn *volunteer* regularly.
3. Chan *or* Lynn *volunteers* once a month.
4. Chan, Lynn, *and* Dave *help* at the shelter each week.
5. Chan, Lynn, *or* Dave *helps* at the shelter each week.

Practice   Write a subject in each box. Then write a sentence using a compound subject joined by *and* or *or.*

1.

Subject	Subject

   Simple Sentence: _____

2.

Subject	Subject

   Simple Sentence: _____

3.

Subject	Subject	Subject

   Simple Sentence: _____

4.

Subject	Subject	Subject

   Simple Sentence: _____

5.

Subject	Subject	Subject	Subject

   Simple Sentence: _____

6.

Subject	Subject	Subject	Subject

   Simple Sentence: _____

L03 Simple Sentences with Compound Predicates

A simple sentence can have a **compound predicate** (two or more verbs).

▶ Two Verbs

To create a compound predicate, join two verbs using *and* or *or*.

One Verb: The tornado roared.

Two Verbs: The tornado roared and twisted.

Remember that the predicate often includes words that modify or complete the verbs.

One Verb plus Other Words: A tornado tore through our town.

predicate

Two Verbs plus Other Words: A tornado tore through our town and damaged buildings.

compound predicate

▶ Three or More Verbs

To make a compound predicate with three or more verbs, use a series. Put commas between all the verbs and place *and* or *or* before the last verb.

Three Verbs: The tornado roared, twisted, and shuddered.

Five Verbs: People shouted, ran, gathered, hid, and waited.

Each verb in a series can also include modifiers or completing words. In the example that follows, the underlined material forms the compound predicate. The red words are verbs. The black words that are underlined modify the verb that comes before them.

The tornado tore apart a warehouse, ripped the roofs from homes, and flattened trailers in a local park.

Insight   A compound predicate does not make the sentence compound. As long as all the verbs connect to the same subject, the thought is still a simple sentence.

Practice > For the following subject, write a verb in each box. Then write a simple sentence joining the verbs with *and* or *or* to make a compound predicate. You may also add modifiers and completing words.

1. The hailstorm

Verb

Verb

_____

2. Driving rain

Verb

Verb

_____

3. A news crew

Verb

Verb

_____

4. Good neighbors

Verb

Verb

Verb

_____

---

compound predicate
two or more predicates joined by *and* or *or*

L04 Compound Sentences

A **compound sentence** is made by joining simple sentences with a **coordinating conjunction**: *and, but, or, nor, for, so,* or *yet.*

► Compound of Two Sentences

Most compound sentences connect two simple sentences, or independent clauses. Connect the sentences with a comma and a coordinating conjunction between them.

Two Sentences: We drove all night. The sun rose behind us.

Compound Sentence: We drove all night, and the sun rose behind us.

You can also join two sentences with a semicolon.

Compound Sentence: We drove all night; the sun rose behind us.

► Compound of Three or More Sentences

You may also join three or more short sentences to form a compound sentence.

Three Sentences: I drove. Janice navigated. Paulo slept.

Compound Sentence: I drove, Janice navigated, and Paulo slept.

Joining several sentences with semicolons works well for sharing a long, involved process.

I took the shift from Williamsburg to Monticello; Janice drove from Monticello to Louisville; Paulo brought us from Louisville to Indianapolis.

NOTE: Remember that a compound sentence is made of two or more simple sentences. Each part must have its own subject and verb.

---

compound sentences
two or more simple sentences joined with a coordinating conjunction or semicolons

coordinating conjunction
a word that joins grammatically equal parts of a sentence

Practice Write a simple sentence to answer each prompt; then combine the sentences to form a compound sentence.

1. What did you do on a road trip? _____

    What did a different person do? _____

    Compound sentence: _____

    _____

2. What do you like to eat? _____

    What does a friend like to eat? _____

    Compound sentence: _____

    _____

3. What did you do last weekend? _____

    What did a friend do? _____

    What did a relative do? _____

    Compound sentence: _____

    _____

4. Where do you want to go? _____

    Where does a friend want to go? _____

    Where does a relative want to go? _____

    Compound sentence: _____

    _____

5. What is your favorite place? _____

    What is a friend's favorite place? _____

    What is relative's favorite place? _____

    Compound sentence: _____

    _____

L05 Complex Sentences

A **complex sentence** shows a dependent relationship between two ideas. Instead of joining two sentences as equal ideas, a complex sentence shows how one idea depends on the other.

► Using a Subordinating Conjunction

You can create a complex sentence by placing a **subordinating conjunction** before the clause that is less important. **Table 15.1** shows common subordinating conjunctions:

Table 15.1 Common Subordinating Conjunctions			
after	before	so that	when
although	even though	that	where
as	if	though	whereas
as if	in order that	till	while
as long as	provided that	'til	
because	since	until	

The subordinating conjunction shows how one sentence (the dependent clause) depends on the other (the independent clause) to make sense. Remember, a clause is a group of words with a subject and a verb. A dependent clause does not express a complete thought, while an independent clause does.

Two Simple Sentences:	We looked repeatedly. We found no instructions.
Complex Sentence:	Though we looked repeatedly, we found no instructions.
	<u>dependent clause</u> <u>independent clause</u>

NOTE: The subordinating conjunction begins the dependent clause, but the two clauses can be in either order. When the dependent clause comes second, it is usually not separated by a comma.

Complex Sentence:	We found no instructions though we looked repeatedly.

► Compound-Complex Sentences

You can create a **compound-complex sentence** by placing a subordinating conjunction before a simple sentence and connecting it to a compound sentence.

Simple Sentence:	We didn't own a car.
Compound Sentence:	I rode my bike, and Jane took the bus.
Compound-Complex:	Since we didn't own a car, I rode my bike, and Jane took the bus.

Practice Write a simple sentence to answer each prompt. Then select a subordinating conjunction from **Table 15.1**, place it at the beginning of one sentence, and combine the two sentences into a single complex sentence.

1. What did you look for? _____

   What did you find? _____

   Complex sentence: _____

   _____

2. Who helped you? _____

   Who did not help? _____

   Complex sentence: _____

   _____

3. What do you need? _____

   What did you get? _____

   Complex sentence: _____

   _____

4. What did you see? _____

   What did a friend see? _____

   Complex sentence: _____

   _____

5. Whom did you meet? _____

   Whom did you avoid? _____

   Complex sentence: _____

   _____

complex sentence
a sentence with one independent clause and one or more dependent clauses

compound-complex sentence
a sentence with two or more independent clauses and one or more dependent clauses

subordinating conjunction
word or word groups that connect clauses of different importance

L06 Complex Sentences with Relative Clauses

In a complex sentence, one clause depends on the other. You've seen how a dependent clause can start with a subordinating conjunction. Another type of dependent clause starts with a relative pronoun.

A **relative clause** is a group of words that begins with a **relative pronoun** (*that, which, who, whom*) and includes a verb and any words that modify or complete it.

> **Relative Clauses:**   that you won't want to miss
> who just graduated
> which should be spectacular

Each relative clause example has a subject and a verb, but not one of the clauses is a complete sentence. They all need to be connected to an independent clause to complete their meaning.

> **Complex Sentences:**   I'm throwing a party that you won't want to miss.
> It's for Ben, who just graduated.
> The plan includes fireworks, which should be spectacular.

▶ *That* and *Which*

The pronoun *that* signals information that is necessary to the meaning of the sentence. The pronoun *which* signals information that is not necessary, so the clause is set off with a comma.

> **That:** Please reserve the room that we will use. (The clause beginning with *that* defines the room.)

> **Which:** The meeting is at 2 p.m., which is our usual starting time. (The clause beginning with *which* just adds information about the time.)

▶ *Who* and *Whom*

The pronoun *who* is the subject when it introduces a clause, and *whom* is either a direct object of a clause it introduces or an object of a preposition. Remember, the direct object receives the action of a verb.

> **Who:** I spoke to the woman who will present the report. (*Who* is the subject of the clause in red.)

> **Whom:** I greeted the new employees, whom I invited. (*Whom* is the direct object of the verb *invited*.)

> The new manager, whom I communicated with, previously worked in the banking industry. (*Whom* is the object of the preposition *with*.)

Practice For each item, write a relative clause beginning with the pronoun provided. Then write a complex sentence that includes the relative clause. (If you need a topic idea, consider writing about a party, concert, or family gathering you attended.)

1. Relative clause (that): _____

   Complex sentence: _____

   _____

2. Relative clause (who): _____

   Complex sentence: _____

   _____

3. Relative clause (which): _____

   Complex sentence: _____

   _____

4. Relative clause (whom): _____

   Complex sentence: _____

   _____

5. Relative clause (that): _____

   Complex sentence: _____

   _____

6. Relative clause (which): _____

   Complex sentence: _____

   _____

7. Relative clause (who): _____

   Complex sentence: _____

   _____

---

relative clause
a group of words that begins with a relative pronoun and includes a verb but cannot stand alone as a sentence

relative pronoun
a word (*that, which, who, whom*) that begins a relative clause and connects the clause to another word in the sentence

🌐 Real-World Application

Practice ▶ Read the following invitation to a party. Note how every sentence is a simple sentence. Rewrite the invitation, combining some sentences into compound or complex sentences to improve the flow.

✉ 📎 👤📇 📝   ● ● ●

To:	Ms. Jamison
Subject:	Party Invite

Dear Ms. Jamison:

You are invited to a party. The party celebrates my promotion to store manager. I've been working toward this promotion all year. The store owner notified me yesterday. You've been a great support. I want to share my appreciation with you.

The party will be Tuesday, July 13, at 8:00 p.m. It is at the Lucky Star restaurant. I've invited my colleagues and friends. Please don't bring a gift. Just bring an appetite and a party spirit. I will provide beverages and cake. This is a big step for me. I hope to see you there.

Sincerely,

Randy Lowe

Dear Ms. Jamison:

_____

_____

_____

_____

_____

_____

_____

_____

_____

_____

Chapter

16

"Men keep agreements when it is to the advantage of neither to break them."
—Solon

Agreement

When people come to an agreement, they can begin to work together. Until an agreement is reached, the people most often work against each other or, perhaps, have no working relationship at all.

The same goes for subjects and verbs. If the verb does not agree with the subject in number, both being either singular or plural, these two sentence parts cannot work together. And the same happens when pronouns and antecedents don't agree. Sentences break down.

This chapter helps you recognize and correct agreement errors. It also focuses on a few other pronoun problems. After you review the information and complete the exercises, you will be prepared to write well-connected sentences that work.

Learning Outcomes

LO1 Subject-Verb Agreement
LO2 Agreement with Compound Subjects
LO3 Agreement with *I* and *You*
LO4 Agreement with Indefinite Pronouns
LO5 Pronoun-Antecedent Agreement
LO6 Other Pronoun Problems

What do you think?

What are some ways sentences can agree? What results may occur if they don't agree?

L01 Subject-Verb Agreement

A verb must **agree in number** with the subject of the sentence. If the subject is singular, the verb must be singular. If the subject is plural, the verb must be plural.

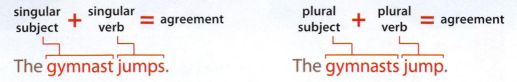

Plural subjects often end in *s*, but plural verbs usually do not. Also note that only present-tense verbs and certain *be* verbs have separate singular and plural forms. **Table 16.1** shows the singular and plural forms of common present- and past-tense verbs. Present-tense verbs indicate that an action is currently happening. Past-tense verbs indicate that an action has already happened.

Table 16.1 Singular and Plural Forms of Common Verbs

Present:	Singular	Plural	Past:	Singular	Plural
	walks	walk		walked	walked
	sees	see		saw	saw
	eats	eat		ate	ate
	is/am	are		was	were

- To make most verbs singular, add just an *s*.

  listen—listen**s**   hear—hear**s**   swim—swim**s**

- The verbs *do* and *go* are made singular by adding an *es*.

  do—do**es**   go—go**es**

- When a verb ends in *ch*, *sh*, *x*, or *z*, make it singular by adding *es*.

  pitch—pitch**es**   wish—wish**es**   fix—fix**es**   buzz—buzz**es**

- When a verb ends in a consonant followed by a *y*, change the y to *i* and add *es*.

  try—tri**es**   fly—fli**es**   cry—cri**es**   quantify—quantifi**es**

---

agree in number
match, as when a subject and verb are
both singular or both plural.

Say It   Read the following word groups aloud, emphasizing the words in *italics*.

1. The alarm *rings*   /   The alarms *ring*   /   The dog *barks*   /   The dogs *bark*
2. The man *is*   /   The men *are*   /   The woman *is*   /   The women *are*
3. She *sits*   /   They *sit*   /   He *walks*   /   They *walk*
4. The woman *tries*   /   The women *try*   /   The man *does*   /   The men *do*

Practice   For the following sentences, write the correct form of the verb in parentheses.

1. The person at the help desk _____ knowledgeable. (are)

2. Tech assistants _____ more about computers than most. (know)

3. Any question _____ a quick answer. (receive)

4. One student _____ about the "any" key. (ask)

5. The instructions _____ to press the "any" key. (say)

6. One tech helper _____ the word "any" to space bars. (tape)

7. The label _____ help many students. (do)

8. The tech also _____ computers that break down. (fix)

Practice   Correct any agreement errors you find by crossing out the verb and writing the correct present-tense verb.

Those who study computer science has a challenging career. Since computer technology change so quickly, the things students learns when they is starting out will probably be outdated by the time they graduates. Memory capacity double every few years, and high-speed connections creates new possibilities. Innovations on the Web and in handheld devices drives change in all areas. One computer-science major confess, "Students doesn't have the luxury of being amazed by new technology. As soon as they hears about a new software or hardware development, they has to check it out and get on board—or they gets left behind."

Practice   For each plural verb, write one sentence using the verb in its singular form.

1. fly
2. do
3. fish
4. wax

L02 Agreement with Compound Subjects

Sentences with **compound subjects** have special agreement rules.

- When a sentence has two or more subjects joined by *and*, the verb should be plural.

plural subject **+** **plural verb** **=** agreement

Bill and Sue try new hairstyles.

- When a sentence has two or more subjects joined by *or* or *nor*, the verb should agree with the last subject.

or

singular subject **+** **singular verb** **=** agreement

Either Bill or Sue carries a hairbrush.

The sentence has two subjects joined by *or*. The second subject (*Sue*) is singular, so a singular verb (*carries*) is needed for the sentence to agree.

plural subject **+** **plural verb** **=** agreement

Neither the couple nor their friends look ordinary.

The sentence has two subjects joined by *nor*. The second subject (*friends*) is plural, so a plural verb (*look*) is needed for the sentence to agree.

Say It   Read the following sentences aloud, emphasizing the words in *italics*.

1. The woman *and* man *talk*. The woman *or* man *talks*.
2. A mouse *and* gerbil *run*. A mouse *or* a gerbil *runs*.
3. Either Sarah *or* Steve *phones*. Neither Sarah *nor* Steve *phones*.
4. Jim *or* Patty *responds*.
5. A man, woman, *and* child *arrive*. A man, a woman, *or* a child *arrives*.

---

compound subject
two or more subjects that share the same verb or verbs

Practice For the following sentences, write the correct form of the verb in parentheses.

1. Either the office manager or the secretary _____ to multitask. (have)

2. The secretary or manager _____ the phone. (answer)

3. Calls and faxes _____ every few minutes. (arrive)

4. Customer service and satisfaction _____ important. (are)

5. Neither the secretary nor the manager _____ the rush. (mind)

6. Either a new contact or a sale _____ with each call. (come)

7. Either the manager or the secretary _____ visitors as well. (greet)

8. A friendly smile and a polite word _____ conversation. (encourage)

9. Praise or complaints _____ the same professional reply. (receive)

10. Not only the manager but also the secretary _____ voted employee of the month. (were)

Practice Correct any agreement errors you find by crossing out the verb and writing the correct present-tense verb.

Multitasking is doing more than one thing at a time. People who multitask and people who don't disagrees about its value. Many stay-at-home parents and in-home baby-sitters cooks, cleans, and takes care of children at the same time. Office workers and blue-collar workers, on the other hand, often focuses on one job at a time. Which approach works best? Sometimes the stay-at-home parent or baby-sitter have dinner on the table, a clean house, and happy kids at the end of a day. And the admin assistant or machine operator have one job done well and another underway at quitting time. So both approaches can work. It seems that the tasks themselves, the people who perform them, and other factors plays a role. The debate about multitasking continues.

Practice Write a sentence with a compound subject joined by *and*. Write a sentence with a compound subject joined by *or*. Check subject-verb agreement.

L03 Agreement with *I* and *You*

The pronouns *I* and *you* usually take plural verbs, even though they are singular.

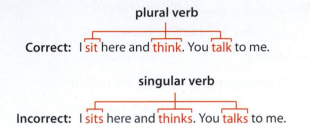

plural verb

Correct: I sit here and think. You talk to me.

singular verb

Incorrect: I sits here and thinks. You talks to me.

NOTE: The pronoun *I* takes the singular verbs *am* and *was*. **Do not** use *I* with *be* or *is*. **Table 16.2** shows when to use *am, is, are, was,* and *were*.

Correct: I am glad. I was hoping to go.
I am excited to see the show.

Incorrect: I are glad. I were hoping to go.
I is excited to see the show.

Table 16.2 Using *am, is, are, was,* and *were*

Present:	Singular	Plural	Past:	Singular	Plural
	I *am*	we *are*		I *was*	we *were*
	you *are*	you *are*		you *were*	you *were*
	he *is*	they *are*		he *was*	they *were*
	she *is*			she *was*	
	it *is*			it *was*	

Insight The word *am* exists for one reason only—to be used with the word *I*. There is no other subject for the verb *am*. In academic or formal writing, *I* should never be used with *be* or *is*. Think of René Descartes saying, "I think, therefore I am."

Say It Read the following sentences aloud, emphasizing the words in *italics*.

1. I *walk* / You *walk* / She *walks* / They *walk*
2. I *drive* / You *drive* / He *drives* / They *drive*
3. I *do* / You *do* / He *does* / They *do*
4. I *am* / You *are* / She *is* / They *are*

Practice For the following sentences, write the correct form of the verb in parentheses. (Do not change the tense.)

1. I _____ as hard as he _____ . (work)

2. You _____ as beautifully as she _____ . (sing)

3. The group _____ together, or you _____ alone. (decide)

4. My brother _____ guitar, while I _____ piano. (play)

5. I _____ you if you _____ me. (forgive)

6. I _____ just as loudly as she _____ . (applaud)

7. I _____ tired, but he _____ tired too. (are)

8. You _____ full of energy, and she _____ also. (are)

9. Yesterday, I _____ late, but you _____ late too. (were)

10. You _____ my friend; I hope I _____ yours. (are)

Practice Correct any agreement errors you find by crossing out the verb and writing the correct verb.

I wants to thank you for yesterday. I is still thinking about the art exhibit. You knows so much about art, and you makes it so interesting when you talks about it. You am my new favorite tour guide. I be ready to visit the art institute again whenever you wants.

I thinks my favorite painters are the Impressionists, especially Monet and Manet. I weren't aware they were separate people until yesterday. You was kind to point that out, and I be glad to know that now.

Thanks again for the guided tour. You is generous with your time, and I is always happy to hear what you says about art. Next time you is going to the institute, please give me a call.

Practice Write two sentences using *I* as the subject. Then write two more using *you* as the subject. Check your subject-verb agreement.

L04   Agreement with Indefinite Pronouns

An **indefinite pronoun** is intentionally vague. Instead of referring to a specific person, place, or thing, an indefinite pronoun refers to something general or unknown.

► Singular Indefinite Pronouns

Singular indefinite pronouns (see **Table 16.3**) take singular verbs:

Someone donates $10 a week.

No one knows who it is.

Everyone appreciates the generosity.

Table 16.3 Singular Indefinite Pronouns

someone	somebody	something
anyone	anybody	anything
no one	nobody	nothing
everyone	everybody	everything
one	each	either / neither

Note that indefinite pronouns that end in *one, body,* or *thing* are singular, just as these words themselves are singular. Just as you would write "That thing is missing," you would write "Something is missing."

Using *one, each, either,* and *neither* as subjects can be tricky because these words are often followed by a prepositional phrase that contains a plural object. The verb must still be singular.

One of our roommates **is** generous.
    prepositional phrase

Each of us **wants** to know who it is.
    prepositional phrase

Remember that a compound subject joined with *or* needs a verb that matches the last subject.

Something or someone is behind the curtain.

Say It   Read the following word groups aloud, emphasizing the words in *italics*.
1. Someone *is*   /   Somebody *has*   /   Something *does*
2. Anyone *is*   /   Anybody *has*   /   Anything *does*
3. One of the books *is*   /   Each of the books *has*   /   Either of the books *does*

---

indefinite pronoun
a special type of pronoun that does not refer to a
specific person, place, or thing

Practice For the following sentences, write the correct form of the verb in parentheses. (Do not change the tense.)

1. Someone _____ a new muffler. (need)

2. Each of the cars _____ repair. (need)

3. Something _____ when I turn the ignition. (rattle)

4. Either of the garages _____ good work. (do)

5. Neither of the options _____ very affordable. (are)

6. Somebody _____ to fix the tailgate. (have)

7. Nobody _____ to drive a noisy car. (want)

8. Nobody or nothing _____ me from fixing my car. (deter)

9. Either of the repair jobs _____ a fortune. (cost)

10. One of my paychecks _____ each time I make repairs. (vanish)

Practice For the following sentences, write a sentence using the indefinite pronoun as a subject. Choose present-tense verbs and check subject-verb agreement.

1. Everyone _____

_____

2. Each _____

_____

3. No one _____

_____

4. Anything _____

_____

5. One _____

_____

6. Either _____

_____

Other indefinite pronouns are plural, and some indefinite pronouns can be singular *or* plural depending on how they are used.

► Plural Indefinite Pronouns

Plural indefinite pronouns take plural verbs (see **Table 16.4**).

> **Both** of us **run** marathons.
>
> **Many** of our friends **cheer** for us.
>
> **Several** of the spectators **hold** signs.

Table 16.4 Plural Indefinite Pronouns

both	many
few	several

► Singular or Plural Indefinite Pronouns

Some indefinite pronouns are singular or plural (see **Table 16.5**). If the object of the prepositional phrase following the pronoun is singular, the pronoun takes a singular verb; if the object is plural, the pronoun takes a plural verb.

NOTE: The *object* of the prepositional phrase is the noun that follows the preposition. It is needed to complete the phrase's meaning.

Table 16.5 Singular or Plural Indefinite Pronouns

all	most
any	none
half	some
part	

All of the **pizza is** gone.
indefinite pronoun / singular object / singular verb

All of the **pizzas are** gone.
indefinite pronoun / plural object / plural verb

Notice the shift in meaning, depending on the prepositional phrase. "All of the pizza" means that one pizza is gone. "All of the pizzas" means that many pizzas are gone. Here's another example.

> **Half** of the **mortgage is** paid off.
>
> **Half** of the **mortgages are** paid off.

In the first sentence, half of one mortgage is paid off. In the second sentence, half of a number of mortgages are paid off.

Say It   Read the following word groups aloud, emphasizing the words in *italics*.
1. Both *are*   /   Few *have*   /   Many *do*   /   Several *were*
2. All of the budget *is*   /   Any of the budgets *are*   /   Half of the budget *does*
3. Part of the pie *is*   /   Most of the pies *are*   /   None of the foods *are*

Practice For the following sentences, write the correct form of the verb in parentheses. (Do not change the tense.) Check your work by saying each sentence aloud, emphasizing the underlined verbs.

1. One of us _____ the living room, but both of us _____ the kitchen. (clean)

2. All of the book _____ scary, but all of the scary parts _____ fun. (were)

3. Some of the Facebook pages _____ personal updates, and part of each page _____ photos. (contain)

4. Everyone _____ to be famous, but few _____ to be followed day and night. (want)

5. One of my friends _____ a Webcast show, and some of my roommates _____ a radio show. (broadcast)

6. Either _____ a valuable idea, and neither _____ expensive. (is)

7. Most of the exam _____ lecture material, and most of the essays _____ student research. (address)

8. Half of the final grade _____ performance based, so most of the students _____ working hard on their projects. (is)

9. Most of us _____ the lions pace, though some of the lions _____ us. (watch)

10. Half of the car _____ submerged, and half of the spectators _____ gasping. (was)

Practice For the following items, write a sentence using the indefinite pronoun as the subject. Choose present-tense verbs and check subject-verb agreement.

1. Several _____

2. Few _____

3. All _____

4. Most _____

5. Part _____

L05 Pronoun-Antecedent Agreement

A pronoun must agree in **person**, **number**, and **gender** with its **antecedent** (see **Table 16.6**). The antecedent is the noun that the pronoun refers to or replaces.

antecedent
(third-person, singular, masculine) **+** **pronoun** (third-person, singular, masculine) **=** **agreement**

The **man** went to lunch but forgot **his** car keys.

Table 16.6 Pronoun-Antecedent Agreement

	Singular	Plural
First Person:	I, me, my, mine	we, us, our, ours
Second Person:	you, your, yours	you, your, yours,
Third Person:		
masculine	he, him, his	they, them, their, theirs
feminine	she, her, hers	they, them, their, theirs
neuter	it, its	they, them, their, theirs

▶ Two or More Antecedents

When two or more antecedents are joined by *and*, the pronoun should be plural.

> Juan and Maria will perform their dance.

When two or more singular antecedents are joined by *or* or *nor*, the pronoun or pronouns should be singular.

> Either Maria or Juan choreographed the dance, so she or he has planned a short introduction.
> Neither Maria nor Juan missed her or his steps.

NOTE: Avoid sexism when choosing a pronoun to replace a general noun. Don't assume the pronoun refers to only males or only females.

> **Sexist:** Each student should bring his transcript.
> **Correct:** Each student should bring her or his transcript.
> **Correct:** Students should bring their transcripts.

Ocean/Corbis

Practice In the following sentences, write the pronoun that agrees with the underlined word or words.

1. The <u>cha-cha-cha</u> began in Cuba, and _____ got its name from the shuffling sound of the dancers' feet.

2. In the 1950s, <u>Monsieur Pierre</u> traveled to Cuba, where _____ studied dance styles and created the ballroom rumba.

3. <u>Pepe Sanchez</u> is the father of the Cuban bolero, even though _____ was not trained as a musician or dancer.

4. The <u>paso doble</u> came from bullfight music, so _____ depicts the lead dancer as the bullfighter and the follower as the cape.

5. In the early twentieth century, <u>Brazilians</u> created the samba, and _____ danced three steps for each two-count measure.

6. The <u>tango</u> had _____ start in Argentina and Uruguay.

7. Stiff and stylized, the tango is performed with the <u>man</u> holding _____ arms in a rigid frame and the <u>woman</u> matching _____ steps to her partner's.

8. Salsa dancing combines other <u>styles</u> and blends _____ together like the ingredients in hot sauce.

9. Salsa dancing requires hip <u>movements</u>, and _____ usually involve side-to-side dips and swaying.

10. Northern European dancing, however, calls for straight hips and leaping, hopping <u>movements</u>; _____ may help the dancers stay warm.

Practice Rewrite each of the following sentences to avoid sexism.

1. Every dancer should put on his shoes.

   _____

2. Each dancer must keep track of her equipment.

   _____

3. One of the applicants will have his application accepted.

   _____

---

person
the person speaking (first person—*I, we*), the person being spoken to (second person—*you*), or the person being spoken about (third person—*he, she, it, they*)

number
indication of whether a word is singular or plural

gender
masculine, feminine, neuter, or indefinite

antecedent
the noun that a pronoun refers to or replaces

L06 Other Pronoun Problems

▶ Missing Antecedent

If no clear antecedent is provided, the reader doesn't know what or whom the pronoun refers to.

Confusing: In Wisconsin, they produce many types of cheese.
(To whom does the pronoun "they" refer?)

Clear: In Wisconsin, cheese makers produce many types of cheese.

▶ Vague Pronoun

If the pronoun could refer to two or more words, the passage is ambiguous.

Indefinite: Ben told his son to use his new surfboard.
(To whom does the pronoun "his" refer, Ben or his son?)

Clumsy: Ben told his son to use Ben's new surfboard.

Clear: Ben loaned his new surfboard to his son.

▶ Incorrect Case

Pronouns have three cases. That means they can be used in three ways—as subjects, objects, or possessives. **Table 16.7** outlines which pronouns to use in each case. One common error is using an object pronoun as a subject.

Table 16.7 Cases of Personal Pronouns

Subject	Object	Possessive
I	me	my, mine
we	us	our, ours
you	you	your, yours
he	him	his
she	her	her, hers
it	it	its
they	them	their, theirs

Incorrect: Them are too big.
Her and me need smaller shoes.

Correct: They are too big.
She and I need smaller shoes.

Also remember to use *my* before the thing possessed and *mine* afterward: *my cat*, but *that cat is mine*. Do the same with *our/ours*, *your/yours*, *her/hers*, and *their/theirs*.

▶ Double Subject

If a pronoun is used right after the subject, an error called a double subject occurs.

Incorrect: My grandmother, she is a good baker.

Correct: My grandmother is a good baker.

Practice ▶ In the following sentences, write the correct pronoun from the choices in parentheses.

1. _____ want to give _____ some advice.
   (I, me, my, mine)   (you, your, yours)

2. _____ should watch _____ and learn what _____ does.
   (you, your, yours)   (he, him, his)   (he, him, his)

3. _____ will lend _____ the book. It is _____ .
   (she, her, hers)   (I, me, my, mine)   (she, her, hers)

4. _____ grant _____ permission for _____ to go.
   (I, me, my, mine)   (I, me, my, mine)   (she, her, hers)

5. _____ watched _____ dog do tricks for _____ .
   (we, us, our, ours)   (we, us, our, ours)   (we, us, our, ours)

Practice ▶ Rewrite each of the following sentences, correcting the pronoun problems.

1. David and Jerry took his car to the shop.

   _____

2. Clare needed to work with Linda, but she had no time.

   _____

3. After we drove a hundred miles, it gave out.

   _____

4. When are they going to make an effective vaccine?

   _____

5. Bill and Sarah, they went to the movies.

   _____

6. Him and her like action films.

   _____

ambiguous
unclear, confusing

🌎 Real-World Application

Practice In the following email, correct the agreement errors.

✉ 📎 📇 📝   ● ● ●

To: Donald Keebler

Subject: Thank You from Hope Services

Dear Mr. Keebler:

Everyone at Hope Services want to thank you for helping us choose the right sound system. I is especially thankful for the convenient installation.

We believe the system meets their needs. Being able to adjust sound input and output for different uses has been wonderful. The setup help staff in the family room as they do play-based assessments. Team members can tune in to various conversations as if them were in the room themselves. As a result, children who may feel overwhelmed by too many people in the room relaxes and plays naturally. In addition, parents can listen in on sessions in the therapy room as therapists model constructive one-on-one communication methods with children.

You does excellent work, Donald. I are happy to recommend yours services to anyone needing sound equipment.

Yours friend,

Elizabeth

wellphoto, 2014 / Used under license from Shutterstock.com

Chapter

17

"Another way to look at sentences is to see them as carriers of 'news.'"

—Scott Rice

Sentence Problems

Mathematics is full of problems. The whole point of math is to puzzle out a solution. And for each problem, there should be only one or, occasionally, a small set of right answers.

Writing is different. Sentences should not be full of problems. If a reader has to puzzle out the meaning of a sentence, the sentence is a problem. Sometimes a shift has occurred in person, tense, or voice. At other times, a modifier is misplaced or dangling. The result can be a sentence that confuses instead of communicates.

This chapter focuses on correcting these kinds of sentence problems.

Learning Outcomes

LO1 Common Fragments
LO2 Tricky Fragments
LO3 Comma Splices
LO4 Run-On Sentences
LO5 Rambling Sentences
LO6 Dangling and Misplaced Modifiers
LO7 Shifts in Sentence Construction

What do you think?

How do sentence problems impact the sentence's ability to be a carrier of news?

L01 Common Fragments

In everyday speech and informal writing, sentence fragments are occasionally used and understood. In classroom conversations and writing assignments, fragments should be avoided because they are often misunderstood.

► Missing Parts

A sentence requires a subject and a verb. If one or the other or both are missing, the sentence is a fragment. A fragment can be fixed by supplying the missing part.

Fragment:	Went to the gym.
Fragment + Subject:	We went to the gym.

Fragment:	Everyone at the community center.
Fragment + Verb:	Everyone at the community center is playing basketball.

Fragment:	For the sake of student safety.
Fragment + Subject and Verb:	The attendant locks the doors for the sake of student safety.

► Incomplete Thoughts

A sentence also must express a complete thought. Some fragments have a subject and a verb but do not express a complete thought. These fragments can be corrected by providing words that complete the thought.

Fragment:	The bay is.
Completing Thought:	The bay is beautiful.

Fragment:	If we arrive in time.
Completing Thought:	If we arrive in time, we may see the sunset.

Fragment:	That are near the shore.
Completing Thought:	Let's sit on the benches that are near the shore.

Say It   Read these fragments aloud. Then read each one again, but this time supply the necessary words to form a complete thought.

1. The movie theaters are.
2. When the game starts.
3. That friend is.
4. Where you may find open seats.
5. The mascot was.

Practice Add words to turn the following fragments into complete sentences.

1. Groceries for our special meal.

_____

2. While I made the pasta.

_____

3. Finished everything within 45 minutes.

_____

4. Easily, the best meal ever.

_____

Practice The following paragraph contains numerous fragments. Either add what is missing or combine fragments with other sentences to make them complete. Use the correction marks shown.

The kitchen needs to be painted. Everyone who uses the kitchen. Should help

paint. Need lots of help. If you have time on Saturday, plan to paint. Ben and I

will. The supplies we need. When we are finished. The kitchen will look much

better. And be cleaner. Can't guarantee the food will taste any better.

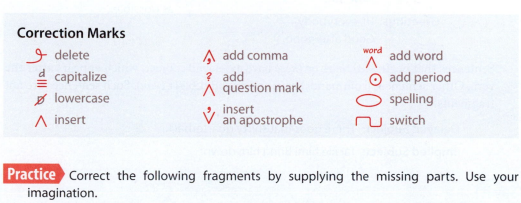

Correction Marks

- ⌿ delete
- ᵈ capitalize
- ⌿ lowercase
- ∧ insert

- ⋀ add comma
- ? add question mark
- ⌄ insert an apostrophe

- word∧ add word
- ⊙ add period
- ◯ spelling
- ⊓ switch

Practice Correct the following fragments by supplying the missing parts. Use your imagination.

1. the front hall of the dorm.

2. When I arrived.

3. Was filled with new students.

L02 Tricky Fragments

Some fragments are more difficult to find and correct. They creep into our writing because they are often part of the way we talk.

► Absolute Phrases

An absolute phrase may look like a sentence, but it isn't. An absolute phrase can be made into a sentence by adding a helping verb or by connecting the phrase to a complete sentence.

> **Absolute Phrase**
> **(Fragment):** Its engine sputtering
>
> **Absolute Phrase +**
> **Helping Verb:** Its engine was sputtering.
>
> **Absolute Phrase +**
> **Complete Sentence:** Its engine sputtering, the lawn mower kept running.

► Informal Fragments

Fragments that are commonly used in speech should be eliminated from formal writing. Avoid the following types of fragments unless you are writing dialogue.

> **Interjections:** Hey! Yeah!
>
> **Exclamations:** What a nuisance!
> How fun!
>
> **Greetings:** Hi, everybody.
> Good afternoon.
>
> **Questions:** How come? Why not? What?
>
> **Answers:** About three or four. As soon as possible.

Sentences that begin with *here* or *there* have a delayed subject, which appears after the verb. Other sentences (commands) have an implied subject (*you*). Such sentences are not fragments.

> **Delayed Subject:** There goes that shifty quarterback.
>
> **Implied Subject:** Tackle him! Bring him down!

Say It   Read each fragment aloud. Then add words to form a complete thought.

1. Are three types of computer tablets.
2. The students nodding off.
3. About five in the morning.
4. Is my favorite song right now.
5. My friend working in the cafeteria.

Practice ▶ Rewrite each of the following fragments, making it a sentence.

1. Their hearts melting at the sight of the orphaned pets.

_____

2. The dogs yelping hellos and wagging their tails.

_____

3. Our cats and dogs chasing each other and playing together.

_____

4. Are many benefits to pet ownership.

_____

5. The vet's office teeming with a variety of pets.

_____

Practice ▶ The following paragraphs contain a number of informal fragments. Identify and cross out each one. Reread each paragraph and listen for the differences.

      Dogs and cats have been our companions for a long time. Awesome! Dogs descended from wolves roaming around during the last Ice Age. What then? Humans killed the wolves that stole their food. Poor things. But a wolf that was neither afraid of humans nor aggressive might be spared. Living alongside people, the wolves slowly became domesticated.

      Domesticated cats arrived later as humans became farmers. "Barn cats" were probably the first pet cats. At last! They ate the mice and rats that fed on stored grains. The farmers approved. Perfect.

      That's why dogs take walks and cats stay home. Maybe. Dogs joined us when we walked everywhere, and cats showed up when we were staying put.

absolute phrase
a group of words with a noun and a participle (a word ending in *ing*) and the words that modify them

helping verb
verb that works with a main verb to form a sentence

delayed subject
a subject that appears after the verb, as in a sentence that begins with *here* or *there* or a sentence that asks a question

implied subject
the word *you*, assumed to begin command sentences

L03 Comma Splices

Comma splices occur when two sentences are connected with only a comma. A comma splice can be fixed by adding a coordinating conjunction (*and, but, or, nor, for, so,* or *yet*) or a subordinating conjunction (*while, after, when, before, because, although*). The two sentences can also be joined by a semicolon (;) or separated by a period.

Comma Splice: The winners were announced, we were not mentioned.

Corrected by adding a coordinating conjunction:	The winners were announced, but we were not mentioned.
Corrected by adding a subordinating conjunction:	When the winners were announced, we were not mentioned.
Corrected by replacing the comma with a semicolon:	The winners were announced; we were not mentioned.

Insight A comma without a conjunction is not strong enough to join two sentences. A semicolon can join two related sentences, or a period can separate them.

Comma Splice: Our instructor praised our efforts, he thought we deserved an award.

Corrected by adding a coordinating conjunction:	Our instructor praised our efforts, for he thought we deserved an award.
Corrected by adding a subordinating conjunction:	Our instructor praised our efforts because he thought we deserved an award.
Corrected by replacing the comma with a period:	Our instructor praised our efforts. He thought we deserved an award.

---

comma splice
a sentence error that occurs when two sentences are connected with only a comma

Practice Correct the following comma splices by adding a coordinating conjunction (*and, but, yet, or, nor, for, so*), by adding a subordinating conjunction (*when, while, because, before, after*), or by replacing the comma with a semicolon or period. Use the approach that makes the sentence read most smoothly.

1. Contests usually have many participants, very few actually win.

2. Businesses run contests for one reason, they are advertising.

3. The business gives away a few prizes, it brings in many names and addresses.

4. Most people enter a contest for one reason, they want the prize, of course.

5. A business should contact entrants, they provide a marketing opportunity.

6. Bill and I entered the contest, we both were disappointed.

7. Then we received discount coupons, we were happy.

8. Winning is a long shot, there are other benefits to entering.

9. We each used our coupons the discount was significant.

10. We're on the lookout for another contest, maybe we'll have better luck in the future.

Practice Rewrite the following paragraph, correcting any comma splices that you find.

Braille is a system of communication, it is used by the blind. It was developed by Louis Braille in 1824. The system uses combinations of small raised dots to create an alphabet. The dots are imprinted on paper, they can be felt. A blind person reads the page by running his or her fingers across the dots. The basic unit is called a cell, a cell is two dots wide and three dots high. Numbers, punctuation marks, and written music can be expressed with this system. Braille has allowed the blind to read, it is truly a great invention.

L04 Run-On Sentences

A **run-on sentence** occurs when two sentences are joined without punctuation or a connecting word. A run-on can be corrected by adding a comma and a conjunction or by inserting a semicolon or period between the two sentences.

Run-On: I was feeling lucky I was totally wrong.

Corrected by adding a comma and coordinating conjunction: I was feeling lucky, but I was totally wrong.

Corrected by adding a subordinating conjunction and a comma: Although I was feeling lucky, I was totally wrong.

Corrected by inserting a semicolon: I was feeling lucky; I was totally wrong.

Insight Run-ons and comma splices are very similar. As such, they can be corrected in the same basic ways.

Run-On: I signed up for the contest I had to write a story about robotic life.

Corrected by adding a comma and coordinating conjunction: I signed up for the contest, so I had to write a story about robotic life.

Corrected by adding a subordinating conjunction and a comma: When I signed up for the contest, I had to write a story about robotic life.

Corrected by inserting a period: I signed up for the contest. I had to write a story about robotic life.

Practice > Correct the following run-on sentences. Use the approach that makes the sentence read most smoothly.

1. John McCarthy coined the term *artificial intelligence* this field deals with the intelligence of machines.

2. Thinking machines first appeared in Greek myths they have been a common feature in fiction since the 1800s.

3. True artificial intelligence could become a reality an electronic brain could be produced.

4. Scientists had computers solving algebra word problems people knew these machines could do incredible things.

5. Reports criticized the artificial intelligence movement funding for research stopped.

6. Funding is very strong again artificial intelligence plays an important role in the technology industry today.

7. Computers solve problems in one way human beings solve them in other ways.

8. People can acquire a great deal of basic knowledge it is not so easy to build this knowledge into machines.

Practice > Correct any run-on sentences that you find in the following paragraph. Use correction marks.

Smart Cars look like little water bugs they are only eight feet long and five feet wide. You can fit two or three of these "bugs" in one parking space. Smart Cars are popular in Europe you see them zipping around the United States, too. Some Smart Cars run on a three-cylinder engine they can still go from zero to 60 in about 15 seconds. They get 33 miles per gallon in the city and 41 miles per gallon on the highway.

run-on sentence
a sentence error that occurs when two sentences are joined without punctuation *or* a connecting word

L05 Rambling Sentences

A rambling sentence occurs when many separate ideas are connected by one *and*, *but*, or *so* after another. The result is an unfocused sentence that goes on and on. To correct a rambling sentence, break it into smaller units, adding and cutting words as needed.

Rambling: The start of the half-marathon was cold, but I came prepared with layers of athletic shirts and cold-weather running tights, so I was ready to run, and about three miles into the race, the chilly weather started to feel good, and I ran faster and stronger than I normally would, so all in all, I have no complaints, and the weather was perfect.

Corrected: The start of the half-marathon was cold, but I came prepared with layers of athletic shirts and cold-weather running tights. About three miles into the race, the chilly weather started to feel good. It helped me run faster and stronger than I normally do. All in all, I have no complaints; the weather was perfect.

Say It   Read the following rambling sentences aloud. Afterward, circle all of the connecting words (*and, but, so*). Then think of a way to break each rambling sentence into smaller units. Say the new sentences out loud.

1. You should update the privacy settings on all your social media accounts and make sure you don't report too much personal information on your profiles, but you can still enjoy social media, but just do so carefully.

2. Did you know that in 1914, two years after the *Titanic* sank, the International Ice Patrol was formed and their job was to report icebergs but the United States decided this job should be the responsibility of the U.S. Coast Guard?

---

rambling sentence
a sentence error that occurs when many separate ideas
are connected by one *and*, *but*, or *so* after another

Michael D Brown, 2014 / Used under license from Shutterstock.com

Practice Correct the following rambling sentences by dividing them into separate sentences.

1. The cat entered silently through the window and next he jumped onto a chair and darted behind the curtain so he could hide from everyone and then he curled up and relaxed for a while.

_____

_____

_____

2. I went to the dentist yesterday and when I got there, I had to wait forever to see him and when he finally examined my teeth, he found two cavities and now I have to go back next week to get fillings and I don't want to go.

_____

_____

_____

3. We use trampolines for entertainment but they were used for other purposes a long time ago and Eskimos once used a form of a trampoline made from skins to watch for whales and seals and I think that is a much better way to use a trampoline than to just jump up and down on it so I wonder what practical way we can use them today.

_____

_____

_____

_____

Practice Write a rambling sentence about a topic of your own choosing. Afterward, exchange your work with a classmate and correct each other's rambling sentence.

_____

_____

_____

_____

_____

L06   Dangling and Misplaced Modifiers

▶ Dangling Modifiers

A modifier is a word, phrase, or clause that functions as an adjective or adverb. When the reader cannot find the word that is being described by the modifier, the modifier is called a **dangling modifier**. This error can be corrected by inserting the missing word or rewriting the sentence.

> **Dangling Modifier:** After buckling the fancy red collar around his neck, my dog pranced proudly down the street.
> *(The dog could buckle his own collar?)*
>
> **Corrected:** After I buckled the fancy red collar around his neck, my dog pranced proudly down the street.

> **Dangling Modifier:** Trying desperately to chase a rabbit, I was pulled toward the bushes. *(I was chasing the rabbit?)*
>
> **Corrected:** Trying desperately to chase a rabbit, my dog pulled me toward the bushes.

▶ Misplaced Modifiers

When a modifier is placed beside a word that it does not modify, the result is an amusing or **illogical** statement. The reader must ask, "Who or what is actually being described?" The **misplaced modifier** can be corrected by moving it next to the word that it modifies.

> **Misplaced Modifier:** Share the document that is attached with Jill.
> *(The document is attached with Jill?)*
>
> **Corrected:** Share the attached document with Jill.

> **Misplaced Modifier:** At the game I noticed a beautiful bronze man's watch.
> *(Is the man or the watch bronze?)*
>
> **Corrected:** At the game I noticed a man's beautiful bronze watch.

Avoid placing any adverb modifiers between a verb and its direct object.

> **Misplaced:** You need to give quickly the report to your boss.
>
> **Corrected:** You need to quickly give the report to your boss.

Also, do not separate two-word verbs with an adverb modifier.

> **Misplaced:** The application should be filled carefully out.
>
> **Corrected:** The application should be filled out carefully.

Say It   Read the following sentences aloud, noting the dangling or misplaced modifier in each one. Then think of a way to correct the errors, and say the new sentences aloud.

1. The new dog park makes good use of vacant property called Dog Heaven.

2. You will usually find an old basset hound running around the park with extremely stubby legs.

Practice   Rewrite the following sentences, correcting the misplaced and dangling modifiers.

1. We saw a buck and a doe on the way to marriage counseling.

   _____

2. The car was reported stolen by the police.

   _____

3. We have new phones for hard-of-hearing people with loud ring tones.

   _____

4. Please present the proposal that is attached to Mr. Brumbly.

   _____

5. I drove with Jennie to the place where we live in a Buick.

   _____

Practice   For each sentence, correct the placement of the adverb.

1. Provide promptly the form to Human Resources.

   _____

2. We will initiate immediately your new insurance.

   _____

3. Please fill carefully out the form.

   _____

dangling modifier	**illogical**	**misplaced modifier**
a modifying word, phrase, or clause that appears to modify the wrong word or a word that isn't in the sentence	without logic; senseless, false, or untrue	a modifying word, phrase, or clause that has been placed incorrectly in a sentence, often creating an amusing or illogical idea

L07 Shifts in Sentence Construction

▶ Shift in Person

A **shift in person** is an error that occurs when first, second, or third person are improperly mixed in a sentence.

Shift in Person: Once you feel better, you can do everything an individual loves to do.
(The sentence improperly shifts from second person—*you*—to third person—*individual*.)

Corrected: Once you feel better, you can do everything you love to do.

▶ Shift in Tense

A **shift in tense** is an error that occurs when more than one verb tense is improperly used in a sentence.

Shift in Tense: I searched everywhere before I find my essay.
(The sentence improperly shifts from past tense—*searched*—to present tense—*find*.)

Corrected: I searched everywhere before I found my essay.

▶ Shift in Voice

A **shift in voice** is an error that occurs when active voice and passive voice are mixed in a sentence.

Shift in Voice: As you search for your essay, your keys may also be found.
(The sentence improperly shifts from active voice—*search*—to passive voice—*may be found*.)

Corrected: As you search for your essay, you may also find your keys.

Say It Read the following sentences aloud, paying careful attention to the improper shift each contains. Then think of a way to correct the errors, and say the new sentences aloud.

1. Margo drinks plenty of fluids and got plenty of rest.
2. Landon is running again, and many new routes are being discovered by him.
3. When you are ready to work, a person can search for jobs online.
4. Charley served as a tutor in the writing lab and helps English language learners with their writing.

Practice Rewrite the following sentences, correcting any improper shifts in construction.

1. I jogged along the wooded path until I feel exhausted.

   _____

2. As we drove to the movie theater, favorite comedies had been discussed by us.

   _____

3. When you drop off my toolbox, can he or she also return my grill?

   _____

Practice Correct the improper shifts in person, tense, or voice in the following paragraph. Use the correction marks shown when you make your changes.

> When you think about today's technology, the first word that comes to mind was convenience. For instance, if you traveled before the creation of the Internet, printed maps were used by you. And if you were traveling out of state, a person needed to purchase other state maps from a gas station or convenience store. You would unfold each map and the best possible route was planned by you. Now you have access to digital maps, personal navigation systems, and Web sites to find your way. You probably enjoy the ease and speed of the new technology and thought the old methods are tiresome.

Correction Marks

ℓ delete	⋏ add comma	word ⋏ add word
d capitalize	? ⋏ add question mark	⊙ add period
lowercase	' ⋁ insert an apostrophe	◯ spelling
⋏ insert		⊓ switch

shift in person
an error that occurs when first, second, and third person are improperly mixed in a sentence

shift in tense
an error that occurs when more than one verb tense is improperly used in a sentence

shift in voice
an error that occurs when active voice and passive voice are mixed in a sentence

🌍 Real-World Application

Practice ▸ Correct any sentence fragments in the following business memo. Use the correction marks shown.

November 14, 2015

Ms. Colleen Turner
Human Resource Director
Western Printing Company
Racine, WI 53001

Dear Ms. Turner:

In response to your advertisement in the Racine Standard Press on November 12. I am writing to apply for the position of graphic designer. Have worked as a designer for Alpha Publications in Brookfield, Wisconsin, for the past three years.

I work with a team of designers. Create business handbooks and workbooks. Including the award-winning handbook Write for Business. Our team each product from design conception to preparation of the final disk.

My special skills are. Coloring illustrations and incorporating graphics in page design. I also have experience with several design software programs. Adobe InDesign, Photoshop, and Illustrator.

I have enclosed my résumé. For more information about my qualifications and training. I look forward to hearing from you. Can reach me at (200) 555-6655 or at aposada@atz.com. Thank you for your consideration.

Sincerely,

Anna Posada

Enclosed: résumé

Correction Marks

ℛ delete	⋏, add comma	word ⋀ add word	
d̲ capitalize	? ⋀ add question mark	⊙ add period	
ℓ̸ lowercase	', ⋁ insert an apostrophe	◯ spelling	
⋀ insert		⊓ switch	

Practice In the following sales letter, use correction marks to fix any comma splices or run-on sentences.

🌸 Dale's Garden Center

405 Cherry Lane
Flower City, IL 53185

February 1, 2015

Dear Gateway College Student:

Did any of your science instructors ever tell you that plants can talk? Well, they can Dale's flowers speak the language of romance.

With Valentine's Day just two weeks away, let Dale's flowers give you the words to share with your sweetheart. Red roses share your love in the traditional way, a Southern Charm Bouquet says the same thing with a little more class. Or send "poetry" by choosing our Valentine Special in a porcelain vase!

Check out the enclosed selection guide then place your order by phoning 1-800-555-LEAF. If you call by February 13, we promise delivery of fresh flowers on Valentine's Day.

Let Dale's flowers help you start a conversation that could last a lifetime!

Sincerely,

Dale Brown

P.S. Long-distance romances are not a problem, we deliver flowers anywhere in the world.

Practice Fix the following comma splice and run-on sentence. Write your corrected sentence on the lines provided.

1. Carnations are popular, they are colorful and reasonably priced.

_____

2. A room can be stale flowers can make it fresh and fragrant.

_____

Practice Correct any dangling modifiers, misplaced modifiers, or shifts in construction in the following message. (Only one sentence is free of errors.) Use the correction marks shown.

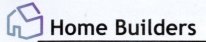 **Home Builders**

1650 Northwest Boulevard • St. Louis, MO 63124
314-555-9800 • FAX 314-555-9810 • www.homebuilders-stl.org

February 15, 2015

Philip Tranberg
1000 Ivy Street
Saint Louis, MO 63450

Dear Philip:

You show a strong interest in Home Builders and the desire to provide people with affordable housing is expressed by you.

First review the enclosed list in Missouri of Home Builders affiliates. Each affiliate handles its own projects and will assign volunteers to work groups. Then check for additional affiliates about Home Builders campus chapters in the enclosed brochure. Joining or starting a chapter is talked about in this brochure. If you have other questions, I may contact the campus coordinator at the address printed on the brochure.

Again, thank you for your interest in providing affordable housing with Home Builders.

Sincerely,

Matthew Osgoode

Enclosures

Correction Marks

℘ delete	⋀, add comma	ᵂᵒʳᵈ⋀ add word
≡ᵈ capitalize	? ⋀ add question mark	⊙ add period
⌿ lowercase	, ⱽ insert an apostrophe	◯ spelling
⋀ insert		⊓ switch

Practice ▶ Rewrite the following sentences, fixing misplaced modifiers, dangling modifiers, and improper shifts in construction.

1. The dogs kept grabbing food off my parents' kitchen counter, so they started hiding the food in the microwave.

   _____

2. The email will shortly arrive.

   _____

3. I spotted a deer and a wild turkey on vacation.

   _____

4. The store sells baseball hats for trendy teens with gold sequins.

   _____

5. When you approach a stop sign, they should be wary of pedestrians.

   _____

6. The police officer apprehended the male suspect and takes him to a holding cell.

   _____

7. After she repairs the roof, other problems may be repaired.

   _____

8. Kimberly does yoga daily and ate well.

   _____

9. Move carefully the china off of the shelf.

   _____

10. When people give restaurant reviews, he or she should evaluate fairly.

    _____

11. I gave my coworker my new address in human resources.

    _____

12. In preparation for the Olympics, Michael Phelps swam up to eight hours a day and maintains a strict diet.

    _____

Practice Rewrite the following passages, fixing any fragments or comma splices.

1. The dancer bowed. After completing her routine.

   _____

2. Our group discussed the next steps in the project, we came to a consensus.

   _____

3. Will debate the merits of the new foreign policy.

   _____

4. Came to an understanding to resolve the issue.

   _____

5. The review lauded the lead actor, it was the supporting actress who stole the show.

   _____

Practice Each of the following sentences contains a sentence problem. Circle the type of sentence problem. Then rewrite the sentence to fix the problem.

1. Gregor Mendel's pea-plant experiments are famous they helped establish many of the rules of genetics and heredity.

   run-on sentence   _comma splice_   _rambling sentence_

   _____

   _____

2. At one time people thought the world was flat, a round Earth was unthinkable.

   run-on sentence   _comma splice_   _rambling sentence_

   _____

3. It's helpful to check your passport's expiration date before traveling abroad, and you should pack only essential items, and if you are going to a country with a foreign language, you should learn some basic greetings and phrases.

   run-on sentence   _comma splice_   _rambling sentence_

   _____

   _____

   _____

Word Workshops

Part 6: Word Workshops

gary718, 2014 / Used under license from Shutterstock.com

Chapter 18

"Look around you. Everything you see you can name. Each of those names fits the definition of a noun."
—Elizabeth O'Brien

Noun

A noun names a person, place, or thing. The words *man*, *lakefront*, and *sculpture*, for example, are nouns. Did you know that nouns can also name ideas? The words *beauty*, *artistry*, and *mathematics* are examples. You can't see these things, but they are real. And they can change the world.

At one point, the sculpture *Cloud Gate* was only an idea in the mind of Anish Kapoor. Several years and $26 million later, Cloud Gate became a real thing—looking like a giant, polished drop of mercury hovering above the ground along the Chicago lakefront. The sculpture is shown in the opening photograph of this chapter.

In this chapter, you will learn to understand and use the nouns that name the people, places, things, and ideas in your world.

Learning Outcomes

- **LO1** Classes of Nouns
- **LO2** Number of Nouns
- **LO3** Count and Noncount Nouns
- **LO4** Articles with Nouns
- **LO5** Other Noun Markers

What do you think?

What do you most like to work with—people, places, things, or ideas? Why?

L01   Classes of Nouns

All nouns are either *common* or *proper*. They can also be *collective*, *concrete*, or *abstract*.

► Common or Proper

A **common noun** names a general person, place, thing, or idea. It is not capitalized. A **proper noun** names a specific person, place, thing, or idea and is capitalized. **Table 18.1** shows common and proper nouns.

Table 18.1 Common and Proper Nouns

	Common Nouns	Proper Nouns
Person:	singer	Beyonce
Place:	memorial	Vietnam Veterans Memorial
Thing:	car	Ford
Idea:	holiday	Presidents' Day

► Collective

A **collective noun** names a group or unit of people, animals, or things: *team*, *crowd*, *family*, *flock*, *committee*, *audience*.

► Concrete or Abstract

A **concrete noun** can be seen, heard, smelled, tasted, or touched. An **abstract noun** (a condition, an idea, or a feeling) cannot be sensed. **Table 18.2** demonstrates each type.

Table 18.2 Concrete and Abstract Nouns

Concrete Nouns	Abstract Nouns
cathedral	faith
smile	happiness
hospital	health

L02   Number of Nouns

The **number** of a noun indicates whether it is singular (one) or plural (more than one). **Table 18.3** shows singular and plural nouns.

Table 18.3 Singular and Plural Nouns

Singular Nouns	Plural Nouns
friend	friends
dish	dishes
plate	plates
goose	geese
foot	feet

NOTE: Form the plural of most nouns by adding *s*. For nouns ending in *ch, s, sh, x* or *z*, add *es*. Also note that some nouns take a special spelling in the plural form.

Practice In the following sentences, identify the underlined nouns as common (C) or proper (P). Also indicate if the underlined noun is collective (CL).

1. Waterfalls capture the imagination.

2. Niagara Falls is the most powerful set of falls in North America.

3. Niagara Falls is nearly 4,400 feet wide, but Victoria Falls is well over 5,500 feet wide.

4. Every second, 85,000 gallons of water rush over Niagara Falls.

5. The tallest cascade is Angel Falls in Venezuela.

6. A team of explorers led by Ruth Robertson in 1949 measured the height of Angel Falls at 3,212 feet.

7. In 1937, Jimmie Angel crash-landed on the falls; a crew had to bring the plane down.

8. The staff that created the movie *Up* modeled Paradise Falls after Angel Falls.

9. Students from our animation class went to the Rialto Cinema Center to see the film.

10. The audience seemed to love the experience.

Practice Identify each word as concrete (CT) or abstract (A).

truck _____   grace _____   talent _____   transportation _____

garage _____   road _____   faith _____   porch _____

Practice Write the plural version of any singular nouns. Write the singular version of any plural nouns.

desk _____   daughters _____   wish _____   museum _____

church _____   coaches _____   knobs _____   gas _____

---

common noun
noun that names a general person, place, thing, or idea; not capitalized as a name

proper noun
noun that names a specific person, place, thing, or idea; capitalized

collective noun
noun that names a group or unit

concrete noun
noun referring to something that can be sensed

abstract noun
noun that names an idea, a condition, or a feeling—something that cannot be sensed

number of noun
indicates whether a noun is singular (one) or plural (more than one)

L03 Count and Noncount Nouns

Some nouns name things that can be counted, and other nouns name things that cannot be counted. Different rules apply to each type.

► Count Nouns

A **count noun** names something that can be counted—*pencils, students, eggs, houses*. It can be singular or plural and be preceded by a number or an article (*a, an,* or *the*): *one* pencil, *a* student, *an* egg, *the* house. **Table 18.4** shows singular and plural count nouns.

Table 18.4 Count Nouns

Singular	Plural
grape	grapes
dog	dogs
car	cars
idea	ideas

> Insight Many native English speakers, although unaware of count and noncount nouns, naturally use these nouns correctly. Take time to notice how these speakers use count and noncount nouns.

► Noncount Nouns

A **noncount noun** names something that cannot be counted. It is used in singular form and can be preceded by *the*, but rarely by *a* or *an*. **Table 18.5** lists noncount nouns by category.

The **homework** involves **reading** and **writing**.

Table 18.5 Noncount Nouns

Substance	Foods	Activities	Science	Languages	Abstractions
wood	water	reading	oxygen	Spanish	justice
cloth	milk	boating	weather	English	harm
ice	wine	smoking	heat	Mandarin	publicity
plastic	sugar	dancing	sunshine	Farsi	advice
wool	rice	swimming	electricity	Greek	happiness
steel	meat	soccer	lightning	Latin	health
aluminum	cheese	hockey	biology	French	joy
metal	flour	photography	history	Japanese	love
leather	pasta	writing	mathematics	Afrikaans	anger

► Two-Way Nouns

Two-way nouns can function as either count or noncount nouns.

Please leave the **paper** on my desk. (count noun)

The sculpture is made of **paper**. (noncount noun)

Practice Read the following list of nouns and sort the words into columns of count and noncount nouns.

door	tablecloth	French	sunshine
heat	cherry	happiness	flour
swimming	vacation	photography	tablespoon
wool	wagon	ruler	

Count Nouns

_____

_____

_____

_____

_____

_____

_____

Noncount Nouns

_____

_____

_____

_____

_____

_____

_____

Practice Read the following paragraph and correct the noun errors. The first line has been corrected for you.

There are different activities for ~~four~~ different weather. For days with sunshines, outdoor activities are best. Some people enjoy swimmings, others like boatings, and even more play soccers. For days in the spring or fall, quieter activities work well. Writing poetries and enjoying photographies are good pastimes, as well as dancings. During the winter, there are readings and homeworks to do. The key to happinesses is to enjoy whatever you are doing.

---

count noun
a noun that names things that can be counted (*pens*, *votes*, *people*)

noncount noun
a noun that names things that cannot be counted (*ice*, *plastic*, *sunshine*)

two-way nouns
a noun that can function as either a count or a noncount noun (*glass*, *light*, *paper*)

L04   Articles with Nouns

Articles show whether a noun refers to a specific thing or to a general thing. Articles are either definite or indefinite.

► Definite Article

The **definite article** is the word *the*. It signals that the noun refers to one specific person, place, thing, or idea.

> Look at the rainbow.
> (*Look at a specific rainbow.*)

The can be used with most nouns, but usually not with proper nouns.

> **Incorrect:** The Fluffy jumped off the laptop.
> **Correct:** Fluffy jumped off the laptop.

> ## Insight
> If your native language does not use articles, pay close attention to the way native English speakers use *the* when referring to a specific thing. Note, however, that *the* is not usually used with proper nouns.

► Indefinite Articles

The **indefinite articles** are the words *a* and *an*. They signal that the noun refers to a general person, place, thing, or idea. The word *a* is used before nouns that begin with consonant sounds, and the word *an* is used before nouns that begin with vowel sounds.

> Chan needs a laptop.
> (*He'll take any laptop.*)

Don't use *a* or *an* with noncount nouns or with plural count nouns.

> **Incorrect:** Pass me a cheese.
> **Correct:** Pass me the cheese.

If a word begins with an *h* that is pronounced, use *a*. If the *h* is silent, use *an*.

> **Incorrect:** It is a honor.
> **Correct:** It is an honor.

> **Incorrect:** An hen lays eggs.
> **Correct:** A hen lays eggs.

Practice ▶ Add the appropriate indefinite article (*a* or *an*) to the following words. The first one has been done for you.

1. __an__ anthill	6. _____ ad	11. _____ euro	
2. _____ pear	7. _____ heap	12. _____ honest man	
3. _____ hog	8. _____ honor	13. _____ idea	
4. _____ hour	9. _____ dolphin	14. _____ exaggeration	
5. _____ apple	10. _____ egg	15. _____ handshake	

Practice ▶ In the following paragraph, delete or replace any articles that are incorrectly used. The first sentence has been done for you.

Scientists wonder whether ~~a~~ *the* planet Neptune collided with ~~the~~ *a* "super-Earth" when ~~a~~ *the* solar system was forming. The Neptune emits much more radiation than the Uranus, though they are otherwise twins in a solar system. Extra radiation may be left over from this collision with the planet twice the size of an Earth. The Neptune's large moon, Triton, rotates opposite to a planet's spin. This fact shows that a Triton was probably the super-Earth's moon and was captured after the collision. If scientists are right, the Neptune holds another planet inside its gassy belly.

---

article
the most common type of noun marker (*a, an,* or *the*)

definite article
the word *the,* used to mark a noun that refers to a specific person, place, or thing

indefinite article
the words *a* or *an,* used to mark a noun that refers to a general person, place, or thing

L05   Other Noun Markers

▶ Possessives

A **possessive** is the possessive case of a noun or pronoun showing ownership of another noun. Possessives are formed by adding an apostrophe-*s* to singular nouns and an apostrophe to plural nouns. **Table 18.6** lists possessive pronouns.

- **Dave's** email came back, but **Ellen's** didn't.
- **Milwaukee's** harbor is calm.
- The **Smiths'** house needs painting.
- That is **my** car. That car is **mine**.
- It's **your** book. The book is **yours**.

Table 18.6 Possessive Pronouns

	Singular		Plural	
	Before Noun	After Noun	Before Noun	After Noun
First Person	my	mine	our	ours
Second Person	your	yours	your	yours
Third Person	his	his	their	theirs
	her	hers	their	theirs
	its	its	their	theirs

▶ Indefinite Adjectives

An **indefinite adjective** marks a general noun. Some indefinite adjectives mark count nouns, and others mark noncount nouns. **Table 18.7** shows how to use indefinite pronouns.

- **All** people are welcome to join. **Much** celebrating will be done.

Table 18.7 Indefinite Adjectives

With Count Nouns			With Noncount Nouns		With Count or Noncount		
each	either	several	much	little	all	any	more
few	many	neither			most	enough	some

▶ Demonstrative Adjectives

A **demonstrative adjective** marks a specific noun. The words *this* and *that* (singular) or *these* and *those* (plural) demonstrate exactly which one is meant.

- **These** songs are by **that** artist.
- **This** song includes **those** lyrics.

▶ Quantifiers

A **quantifier** tells *how many* or *how much* of something. **Table 18.8** shows examples.

Table 18.8 Quantifiers

With Count Nouns		With Noncount Nouns		With Count or Noncount		
each	nine	a bag of	a little	no	a lot of	most
several	every	a bowl of	much	not any	lots of	all
a number of	many	a piece of	a great deal of	some	plenty of	
both	a few					

Practice Identify the appropriate noun marker in parentheses for each sentence.

1. Please leave (*your, yours*) phone number after the beep.

2. Is this phone number (*your, yours*)?

3. How (*many, much*) students are allowed in the class?

4. The professor did not give us (*any, each*) homework.

5. I want to buy (*this, these*) shirts.

6. The resident assistant didn't like (*that, those*) idea.

7. After making the dough, we had (*several, a little*) flour left.

8. I liked (*a number of, much*) the suggestions.

9. The proposal was originally (*her, hers*).

10. Let's make sure to return (*their, theirs*) pillows.

Practice Cross out and replace any noun marker that is used incorrectly. The first one has been done for you.

What is ~~yours~~ *your* major? You probably have heard that much times. But taking a little courses in one area does not mean it is yours major. Much students don't choose a major until theirs junior year. This students have to explore theirs options before making up theirs minds. That delay isn't a problem. Those exploration is the point of undergraduate study. Until you know for sure a major is your, you should "taste-test" much fields. In mine junior year, I was told I would not graduate unless I picked mine major. I added up mine hours, and that total showed I was closest to English. Two weeks later, the head of the English Department called and said, "I thought we should meet since you are one of mine majors."

possessive	**demonstrative adjective**
the possessive case of a noun or pronoun, showing ownership of another noun	a demonstrative pronoun (*this, that, these, those*) used as an adjective to mark a specific noun
indefinite adjective	**quantifier**
an indefinite pronoun (*many, much, some*) used as an adjective to mark a general noun	a modifier that tells *how many* or *how much*

🌐 Real-World Application

Practice ▶ Correct any errors with nouns, articles, or other noun markers in the following promotional email.

✉ 📎 👤 🖉   ● ● ●

To: Nina Petri; Bryan Neshek; Marcos Zimka; Sonya Michaels

Subject: Project Details

Dear Team:

A date for ours cleanup of Riverway park is coming up fast. On April 3, we should meet at riverway's picnic shelter by 8:00 a.m. I know we have discussed these project much times, but here are the specific instructions:

1. Bring an pair of work gloves and two large garbage bag.

2. Wear boots or athletic shoes to protect your foots.

3. Pack an bag lunch and bottled water. (Can you still bring yours cooler, Nina?)

4. Be ready to walk through the Park and pick up trash for four hour.

The farmington city council is grateful for ours willingness to clean up the park. They want us to come to their next meeting and discuss much projects! Visiting a residents at Merrybrook nursing home and helping the animal shelter with an fund-raiser are two thing they mentioned.

If you have other ideas, please email them to me. I'd like to propose several projects at the meeting on may 4. I'll let you know a exact time of that Council meeting later on. Meanwhile, the important job of cleaning up a park is ours first priority. Thanks again for participating.

A few community spirit goes a long way!

Sincerely,

Fatima Reyes

paul prescott, 2014 / Used under license from Shutterstock.com

Chapter

19

"A pronoun is an understudy standing in for the occasionally overworked noun."

—Anonymous

Pronoun

Mannequins are everywhere—selling dresses, shirts, suits, shorts, and more. After all, it would be unreasonable to ask real people to stand around all day and all night showing off clothing.

Just as mannequins stand in for people, pronouns stand in for nouns. Writing that has no pronouns quickly becomes overloaded with nouns, which makes it repetitive and hard to read. This chapter explains pronouns and how to use them correctly in your writing.

Learning Outcomes

LO1 Personal Pronouns
LO2 Pronoun-Antecedent Agreement
LO3 Indefinite Pronouns
LO4 Relative Pronouns
LO5 Other Pronoun Types

What do you think?
How does a pronoun "stand in" for a noun?

L01 Personal Pronouns

A **pronoun** takes the place of a noun or another pronoun. **Personal pronouns** indicate whether the person is speaking (first person), is being spoken to (second person), or is being spoken about (third person). **Table 19.1** lists the personal pronouns.

Table 19.1 Personal Pronouns

	Singular			Plural		
Person	**Nom.**	**Obj.**	**Poss.**	**Nom.**	**Obj.**	**Poss.**
First (speaking)	I	me	my/mine	we	us	our/ours
Second (spoken to)	you	you	your/yours	you	you	your/yours
Third (spoken about)						
masculine	he	him	his	they	them	their/theirs
feminine	she	her	her/hers	they	them	their/theirs
neuter	it	it	its	they	them	their/theirs

Nom. = nominative case / **Obj.** = objective case / **Poss.** = possessive case

► Case of Pronouns

The **case** of a pronoun indicates how it can be used.

- **Nominative** pronouns are used as subjects or as subject complements. Subject complements follow the linking verbs (*am, is, are, was, were, be, being,* or *been*) and refer to the subject. The subject complement in the following example follows the linking verb "was" and refers to the subject "person."

    I was nominated, but the person selected was she.
    subject   subject   subject complement

- **Objective** pronouns are used as direct objects, indirect objects, or objects of prepositions.

    The professor lectured us about it.
                            direct object   object of the preposition

- **Possessive** pronouns show ownership.

    My notebook has fewer notes than hers.
    possessive   possessive

► Gender

Pronouns can be **masculine**, **feminine**, or **neuter**.

    She helped him with it.
    feminine   masculine   neuter

Say It Read the following word groups aloud.

1. *I* am / *You* are / *He* is / *She* is / *It* is / *We* are / *They* are
2. Help *me* / Help *you* / Help *him* / Help *her* / Help *it* / Help *us* / Help *them*

Practice For each sentence, select the correct personal pronoun in parentheses.

1. The dorm cafeteria is where (*I, me, my*) friends gather.

2. (*We, Us, Our*) talk about classes and also about each other.

3. I told Emily that I would help (*she, her, hers*) with her homework.

4. I have a heavy schedule, but not as heavy as (*she, her, hers*).

5. (*I, Me, My, Mine*) 18 credits require less work than (*she, her, hers*) 20.

Practice Correct the pronoun errors in this paragraph.

I asked me sons if them would like to take a walk around Lake Geneva. Them asked how us could walk around the lake. I told they that a path goes all the way around the lake, and its is open to the public. My sons said that them wanted to go, but them wondered how far the walk was. Me told they that it was about 30 miles. They mouths dropped open. They couldn't figure out what to say to I. My sons and me looked at each other. Then I said them needed to get theirs backpacks and shoes. They told me that they had changed their minds. But I convinced they, and us hiked all the way around Lake Geneva. When it was over, I wished I had listened to they. My legs hurt so much!

---

pronoun
a word that takes the place of a noun or other pronoun

personal pronoun
a pronoun that indicates whether the person is speaking, is spoken to, or is spoken about

nominative pronoun
used as a subject or subject complement

objective pronoun
used as a direct object, an indirect object, or an object of a preposition

possessive pronoun
used to show ownership

gender
masculine (male), feminine (female), or neuter (neither male nor female)

L02 Pronoun-Antecedent Agreement

The **antecedent** is the word that a pronoun refers to or replaces. A pronoun and its antecedent agree when they have the same person, number, and gender.

Linda asked to borrow a pen but then found hers.

Third-person: singular feminine

► Agreement in Person

A pronoun needs to match its antecedent in **person** (first, second, or third).

third person   second person

Incorrect: If people look hard, you might find some good deals.

Correct: If you look hard, you might find some good deals.

Correct: If people look hard, they might find some good deals.

► Agreement in Number

A pronoun needs to match its antecedent in **number** (singular or plural).

singular   plural

Incorrect: Each student should bring their assignment.

Correct: Students should bring their assignments.

Correct: Each student should bring her or his assignment.

► Agreement in Gender

A pronoun needs to match its antecedent in **gender** (masculine, feminine, or neuter).

feminine   masculine

Incorrect: Janae will present his speech.

Correct: Janae will present her speech.

---

antecedent
the word that a pronoun refers to or replaces

pronoun-antecedent agreement
matching a pronoun to its antecedent in person, number, and gender

person
first (speaking), second (spoken to), third (spoken about)

number
singular or plural

Practice Rewrite each sentence to correct the agreement in person error.

1. If both of you go to the job fair, they will probably find job opportunities.

_____

2. We went to the fair last year, and they landed some good jobs.

_____

3. If the graduates fill out applications, you may find jobs.

_____

4. I hope to find a job where you can use your training.

_____

Practice Rewrite each sentence to correct the agreement in number error.

5. Each applicant should put their name on the sign-in list.

_____

6. An interviewer will arrive, and they will talk to each applicant.

_____

7. Applicants should supply his contact information.

_____

Practice Rewrite each sentence to correct the agreement in gender error.

8. If Lionel goes, she can drive others.

_____

9. Emily said he was going.

_____

10. The hall is big, and she sits at a major intersection.

_____

L03 Indefinite Pronouns

An **indefinite pronoun** does not have an antecedent, and it does not refer to a specific person, place, thing, or idea. These pronouns pose unique issues with subject-verb and pronoun-antecedent agreement.

▶ Singular Indefinite Pronouns

The indefinite pronouns in **Table 19.2** are singular. When they are used as subjects, they require a singular verb. As antecedents, they must be matched to singular pronouns.

Table 19.2 Personal Pronouns

each	anyone	somebody	everything
either	someone	everybody	nothing
neither	everyone	nobody	
another	no one	anything	
one	anybody	something	

<u>Someone is</u> supposed to empty the dishwasher.
singular subject   singular verb

<u>No one</u> has said <u>he</u> or <u>she</u> will take responsibility.
singular antecedent   singular pronouns

▶ Plural Indefinite Pronouns

The indefinite pronouns in **Table 19.3** are plural. As subjects, they require a plural verb, and as antecedents, they require a plural pronoun.

Table 19.3 Plural Indefinite Pronouns

both	several
few	many

A <u>few</u> of the housemates <u>leave</u> dirty dishes everywhere.
plural subject   plural verb

<u>Several</u> of their friends said <u>they</u> are fed up.
plural antecedent   plural pronoun

▶ Singular or Plural Indefinite Pronouns

The indefinite pronouns in **Table 19.4** can be singular or plural, depending on the object of the preposition in the phrase that follows them.

Table 19.4 Singular or Plural Indefinite Pronouns

all	most	some
any	none	

plural object
<u>All</u> of the <u>pies were</u> eaten.
singular / plural   plural verb

singular object
<u>All</u> of the <u>pie was</u> eaten.
singular / plural   singular verb

Practice ▸ Rewrite each sentence to correct the agreement errors. (*Hint:* All of the sentences are about a group of male roommates.)

1. Everyone needs to wash their own dishes.

    _____

2. No one are exempt.

    _____

3. Anyone not washing their dishes must wash everyone else's.

    _____

4. Nothing short of illness are an excuse.

    _____

5. Few is arguing with the new policy.

    _____

6. Several says it is about time.

    _____

7. Many expresses their appreciation.

    _____

8. For a week, all of the dishes has been washed.

    _____

9. Ted made sure all of his plates was washed and put away.

    _____

10. Most of the roommates agrees that this works.

    _____

11. Most of the morning are spent cleaning up.

    _____

12. None of the dishes is left lying about.

    _____

13. None of the food are left to eat either, since everybody have forgotten to go shopping.

    _____

indefinite pronoun
a pronoun that does not refer to a specific person, place, thing, or idea

L04 Relative Pronouns

A **relative pronoun** (*who, whom, which, whose, whoever, whomever, that*) introduces a dependent clause. (The dependent clauses in the examples that follow are indicated by **bold** type.)

> I would like to meet the person **who invented the World Wide Web.**

- **Who/Whoever** and **Whom/Whomever**—These pronouns refer to people. *Who* and *whoever* are used as subjects, while *whom* and *whomever* are used as objects.

  > I want to thank **whoever chose the playlist.** The person **whom I thanked** has terrific taste in music.

- **That** and **Which**—These pronouns usually refer to things. Clauses beginning with *that* are not set off with commas, while those that begin with *which* are set off with commas.

  > I read a book **that told of Teddy Roosevelt's Amazon journey.** I liked *River of Doubt*, **which I purchased for $29.**

- **Whose**—This pronoun indicates ownership or connection.

  > The mechanic **whose hand was cut** was fixing our car.

L05 Other Pronoun Types

Other types of pronouns have specific uses in your writing.

- An **interrogative pronoun** asks a question (*who, whose, whom, which, what*).

  > Who will make the salads? What is your favorite dressing?

- A **demonstrative pronoun** points to a specific thing (*this, that, these, those*).

  > This is the new table. These are the old chairs.

- A **reflexive pronoun** reflects back to the subject of a sentence (*myself, ourselves, yourself, yourselves, himself, herself, itself, themselves*).

  > We emailed ourselves the vacation photos.

- An **intensive pronoun** emphasizes the noun or pronoun it refers to (*myself, ourselves, yourself, yourselves, himself, herself, itself, themselves*).

  > I myself studied three hours for the test.

- A **reciprocal pronoun** refers to the individuals within a plural antecedent (*each other, one another*).

  > The teachers respect one another.

Practice For each sentence, select the correct relative pronoun.

1. Theo Jansen is an engineer and artist (*who, whom*) is creating new life.

2. He builds sculptures (*that, which*) harness the wind to walk.

3. Theo refers to his sculptures as animals, (*that, which*) is unusual for an engineer.

4. These animals are built of plastic pipe, (*that, which*) is inexpensive and strong.

5. Another engineer and artist (*who, whom*) Jansen admires is Leonardo da Vinci.

6. Theo's creations are on display for (*whoever, whomever*) is on the beach.

7. His most famous creation is the Strandbeest, (*that, which*) has wings on top.

8. The wings pump air into plastic bottles, (*that, which*) store it up.

9. The air powers "muscles" (*that, which*) are made of sliding tubes.

10. With its muscles activated, the beast walks, (*that, which*) is amazing to see.

Practice Write the type of each underlined pronoun: *interrogative, demonstrative, reflexive, intensive,* or *reciprocal.*

1. <u>This</u> is the reason we should have filled the tank. _____

2. <u>What</u> should we use to pay for gas? _____

3. I <u>myself</u> expected you to bring money. _____

4. You should pat <u>yourself</u> on the back. _____

5. <u>That</u> is all the money you have? _____

6. The change <u>itself</u> won't be enough. _____

7. <u>Who</u> buys $1.73 worth of gas? _____

8. <u>That</u> won't get us far. _____

9. Let's cooperate with <u>one another</u> and pool our money. _____

---

relative pronoun
a pronoun that begins a relative clause, connecting it to a sentence

relative clause
a type of dependent clause that begins with a relative pronoun

Real-World Application

Practice Correct any pronoun errors in the letter that follows.

◪ Rankin Technologies

401 South Manheim Road, Albany, NY 12236 ▪ Ph: 708.555.1980 ▪ Fax: 708.555.0056

April 28, 2015

Mr. Henry Danburn
Construction Manager
Titan Industrial Construction, Inc.
P.O. Box 2112
Phoenix, AZ 85009-3887

Dear Mr. Danburn:

Thank you for meeting with I last week at the National Convention in Las Vegas. I want to follow up on ours discussion of ways in which Rankin Technologies could work with Titan Industrial Construction.

Enclosed is the information that your requested. I believe this material demonstrates which Rankin Technologies would be a solid match for yours projects in western Illinois.

You yourselves are the construction manager for the Arrow Mills renovation project in California. Rankin did the electrical installation on that project initially, and us would be very interested in working with you on the renovation. Someone whom is familiar with our work at Arrow Mills is Mike Knowlan. She is the plant manager and can be reached at 606-555-6328.

Us are excited about working with yous on any future projects and on the Arrow Mills project in particular. Please call I with any questions (708-555-1980).

Sincerely,

James Gabriel

James Gabriel
Vice President
Enclosures: 5

"I think I am a verb."

— R. Buckminster Fuller

Chapter

20

Verb

Of course, we call ourselves human beings, but a few people have suggested we should think of ourselves as "human doings." They would argue that our actions define our existence.

Whether you call yourself a human being or a human doing, you can still think of yourself as a verb. Verbs express both states of being and actions. They give a sentence energy, movement, and meaning. This chapter examines these amazing words and explains how to use them.

Learning Outcomes

LO1 Classes of Verbs
LO2 Number and Person
LO3 Voice
LO4 Basic Tenses
LO5 Progressive-Tense Verbs
LO6 Perfect-Tense Verbs
LO7 Verbals
LO8 Verbals as Objects

What do you think?

Are you a human being or a human doing? Why?

L01 Classes of Verbs

Verbs show action or express a state of being.

► Action Verbs

Verbs that show action are called **action verbs**. Some action verbs are **transitive**, which means that they transfer action to a direct object.

> Bill clutches the pillow.
> (The verb *clutches* transfers action to the direct object *pillow*.)

Others are **intransitive** and do not transfer action to a direct object.

> Bill sleeps.
> (The verb *sleeps* does not transfer action to a direct object.)

► Linking Verbs

Verbs that link the subject to a noun, a pronoun, or an adjective are **linking verbs**. They express a state of being. **Table 20.1** lists common linking verbs. Three of the verbs in this table—*be, being,* and *been*—require a helping verb. All of the other ones can be used alone.

> Bill is a heavy sleeper.
> (The linking verb *is* connects *Bill* to the noun *sleeper*.)

> He seems weary.
> (The linking verb *seems* connects *He* to the adjective *weary*.)

Table 20.1 Linking Verbs

is	was	being	seem	look	sound
am	were	been	grow	smell	appear
are	be	become	feel	taste	remain

NOTE: The linking verbs *grow, feel, look, smell, taste, sound, appear,* and *remain* can also function as action verbs.

> The bread sticks smell good.
> (*Smell* used as a linking verb)
>
> The roommates smell pizza.
> (*Smell* used as an action verb)

> The cake tastes stale.
> (*Tastes* used as a linking verb)
>
> Brad tastes the pie.
> (*Tastes* used as an action verb)

▶ Helping Verbs

A **helping** (or auxiliary) verb works with an action or a linking verb to form a certain tense, mood, or voice. **Table 20.2** lists common helping verbs.

> Bill **will** go grocery shopping if he has enough time.
> (The helping verb *will* works with the main verb *go* to form a special tense.)

Table 20.2 Helping Verbs

am	have	are	is	be	may
been	might	being	must	can	shall
could	should	did	was	do	were
does	will	had	would	has	

Practice   For the following sentences, identify the underlined verbs as transitive action verbs (T), intransitive action verbs (I), linking verbs (L), or helping verbs (H).

1. I <u>need</u> eight hours of sleep per night, but I often <u>get</u> only six.

2. This weekend, I <u>will be</u> getting even less sleep.

3. One of my favorite bands is <u>playing</u> in town.

4. They <u>rock</u>, and whenever I <u>see</u> a concert of theirs, I hardly <u>sleep</u>.

5. I <u>am</u> eager, but after the weekend, I <u>will</u> be worn out.

6. The problem with having too much fun on the weekend <u>is</u> the week after.

7. Maybe I <u>should</u> go to bed earlier so that I <u>can</u> store up sleep.

8. I <u>feel</u> awake now, but next week I will <u>look</u> weary.

---

action verb
word that expresses action

transitive verb
action verb that transfers action to a direct object

intransitive verb
action verb that does not transfer action to a direct object

linking verb
verb that connects the subject with a noun, a pronoun, or an adjective in the predicate

helping (auxiliary) verb
verb that works with a main verb to form a certain tense, mood, or voice

L02   Number and Person

Verbs reflect number (singular or plural) and person (first person, second person, or third person).

► Number

The **number** of the verb indicates whether the subject is singular or plural. Third-person present-tense singular verbs end in *s*; third-person present-tense plural verbs do not end in *s*.

> **Singular:** The "Gettysburg Address" speaks of those who "gave the last full measure of devotion."
>
> **Plural:** Many historians speak of it as the greatest American speech.

► Person

The **person** of a verb indicates whether the subject is speaking, being spoken to, or being spoken about. **Table 20.3** shows the number and person of *be* verbs.

Table 20.3 Be Verbs (Number and Person)

	Singular	Plural	Singular	Plural
First Person:	(I) am	(we) are	(I) was	(we) were
Second Person:	(you) are	(you) are	(you) were	(you) were
Third Person:	(he, she, it) is	(they) are	(he, she, it) was	(they) were

NOTE: The pronoun *I* takes a special form of the *be* verb—*am*—in present tense and is paired with *was* in past tense.

> **Incorrect:** I is excited about going to Gettysburg.
>
> **Correct:** I am excited about going to Gettysburg.

> **Incorrect:** I were hoping to go with you.
>
> **Correct:** I was hoping to go with you.

> **Incorrect:** You is going to the Gettysburg National Military Park.
>
> **Correct:** You are going to the Gettysburg National Military Park.

> **Incorrect:** You was my first choice.
>
> **Correct:** You were my first choice.

---

number
singular or plural

person
first (subject is speaking), second (subject is spoken to), third (subject is spoken about)

Practice For the following sentences, provide the present-tense verb (*is, am, are*) that agrees with the subject in person and number.

1. We _____ interested in going to Gettysburg.

2. It _____ a town in Pennsylvania where a great battle took place.

3. You _____ welcome to come on the trip with us.

4. Little Round Top _____ a hill where the fighting was focused.

5. The Union troops _____ memorialized in statues on the hill.

6. You _____ standing on a piece of American history.

7. Pickett's Charge _____ considered General Lee's greatest mistake.

8. Troops from both sides _____ buried in the cemetery.

9. I _____ eager to see where Lincoln gave the "Gettysburg Address."

10. We _____ hoping to spend two days in Gettysburg.

Practice Rewrite the following sentences, correcting the present-tense verbs to agree with their subjects in number and person.

1. I listens as the tour guide describe the last day of battle.

_____

2. Rifle shots hails down on the Confederate soldiers.

_____

3. General Pickett order them to charge Little Round Top.

_____

4. Flying lead kill many Southern soldiers.

_____

5. The Union troops repels the charge and wins the day.

_____

6. President Lincoln deliver the "Gettysburg Address."

_____

L03 Voice

The **voice** of the verb indicates whether the subject is acting or being acted upon.

► Active Voice and Passive Voice

In **active voice**, the subject is acting. In **passive voice**, the subject is being acted upon. **Table 20.4** gives examples of active and passive voice.

Active: The usher led us to our seats.

Passive: We were led by the usher to our seats.

Table 20.4 Active Voice and Passive Voice

	Active Voice		Passive Voice	
	Singular	**Plural**	**Singular**	**Plural**
Present Tense	I see you see he/she/it sees	we see you see they see	I am seen you are seen he/she/it is seen	we are seen you are seen they are seen
Past Tense	I saw you saw he saw	we saw you saw they saw	I was seen you were seen it was seen	we were seen you were seen they were seen
Future Tense	I will see you will see he will see	we will see you will see they will see	I will be seen you will be seen it will be seen	we will be seen you will be seen they will be seen
Present Perfect Tense	I have seen you have seen he has seen	we have seen you have seen they have seen	I have been seen you have been seen it has been seen	we have been seen you have been seen they have been seen
Past Perfect Tense	I had seen you had seen he had seen	we had seen you had seen they had seen	I had been seen you had been seen it had been seen	we had been seen you had been seen they had been seen
Future Perfect Tense	I will have seen you will have seen he will have seen	we will have seen you will have seen they will have seen	I will have been seen you will have been seen it will have been seen	we will have been seen you will have been seen they will have been seen

Active voice is preferred for most writing because it is direct and energetic.

Active: We gave the band a standing ovation.

Passive: The band was given a standing ovation by us.

Passive voice is preferred when the focus is on the receiver of the action or when the subject is unknown.

Passive: A rose was thrown onstage.

Active: Someone threw a rose onstage.

skyboysv, 2014 / Used under license from Shutterstock.com

Practice Read the following sentences, changing passive verbs to active verbs. Think about who or what is performing the action and make that the subject. One example is given.

1. The concert was attended by three thousand fans.
   Three thousand fans attended the concert.

2. A good time was had by everyone.

3. The ten greatest hits were played by the band.

4. Three concert T-shirts were bought by my friends and me.

5. The opening acts were tolerated by the crowd.

6. The air was electrified by the appearance of the main act.

7. I was not disappointed by their performance.

8. My short friend's view was blocked by a tall guy.

9. The guy was asked by my friend to switch seats.

10. Every new song was cheered for by the crowd.

---

voice
active or passive

active voice
voice created when the subject is performing the action of the verb

passive voice
voice created when the subject is receiving the action of the verb

L04 Basic Tenses

Basic verb tenses tell whether action happens in the present, future, or past.

■ **Present-tense verbs** express action that is happening now or routinely: *help, look, try.*

Cruise ships arrive often in Cabo San Lucas, Mexico.

■ **Future-tense verbs** express action that will happen later: *will help, will look, will try.*

Many tourists will visit Cabo San Lucas this year.

■ **Past-tense verbs** express action that has already happened: *helped, looked, tried.*

We traveled to Mexico last winter.

▶ Irregular Verbs

Most verbs form the past tense by adding *ed*, but irregular verbs form the past tense by changing the verb itself. **Table 20.5** shows the past tense of irregular verbs.

Table 20.5 Present and Past Tense of Irregular Verbs

Pres.	Past	Pres.	Past	Pres.	Past	Pres.	Past	Pres.	Past	Pres.	Past
am, are	was, were	come	came	find	found	hear	heard	see	saw	steal	stole
become	became	dig	dug	fly	flew	hide	hid	shake	shook	swim	swam
begin	began	do	did	forget	forgot	keep	kept	shine	shone	swing	swung
blow	blew	draw	drew	freeze	froze	know	knew	shrink	shrank	take	took
break	broke	drink	drank	get	got	lead	led	sing	sang	teach	taught
bring	brought	drive	drove	give	gave	pay	paid	sink	sank	tear	tore
buy	bought	eat	ate	go	went	ride	rode	sit	sat	think	thought
can	could	fall	fell	grow	grew	ring	rang	sleep	slept	throw	threw
catch	caught	feel	felt	hang	hung	rise	rose	speak	spoke	wear	wore
choose	chose	fight	fought	have	had	run	ran	stand	stood	write	wrote

▶ Present Tense in Academic Writing

Use present-tense verbs to discuss fictional events in literature.

In the short story, the young man dreams of seeing the world.

Also use present-tense verbs (*writes, reports, asserts*) when quoting or summarizing material from periodicals.

The university newsletter reports that many students travel abroad after graduating.

Practice For the following sentences, supply the present-tense form of the verb indicated in parentheses.

1. Many visitors _____ in Cabo's warm waters. (snorkeled)

2. White, sandy beaches _____ many swimmers. (attracted)

3. Parasailors _____ overhead from parachutes. (flew)

4. Waves _____ if winds are strong. (picked up)

5. Boats _____ people from cruise ships to shore. (ran)

Practice For each verb, write the correct past-tense form.

1. give _____

2. shop _____

3. trick _____

4. type _____

5. teach _____

6. cry _____

7. sing _____

8. soap _____

9. cap _____

10. cope _____

11. try _____

12. fly _____

13. think _____

14. grip _____

Practice Write a sentence of your own, using the verb in the tense given in parentheses.

1. enjoy (present) _____

2. swim (future) _____

3. realize (present) _____

4. complete (future) _____

present tense
verb tense expressing action that is happening now

past tense
verb tense expressing action that has already happened

future tense
verb tense expressing action that will happen later

L05 Progressive-Tense Verbs

The basic tenses tell when action takes place—in the past, present, or future. The progressive tenses indicate that action is ongoing.

■ **Progressive tenses** are formed by using a helping verb along with the *ing* form of the main verb. Each progressive tense uses a helping verb in the appropriate basic tense—either past, present, or future.

> In 1804, one billion people were sharing the globe.
> (past progressive)

> Currently, about seven billion people are living on Earth.
> (present progressive)

> In 2040, about nine billion people will be calling this planet home.
> (future progressive)

Forming Progressive Tense						
Past:	was/were	+	main verb	+	ing
Present:	am/is/are	+	main verb	+	ing
Future:	will be	+	main verb	+	ing

Insight   **Avoid** using the progressive tense with . . .

■ Verbs that express thoughts, attitudes, and desires: *know, understand, want, prefer*
■ Verbs that describe appearances: *seem, resemble*
■ Verbs that indicate possession: *belong, have, own, possess*

> **Incorrect:** I am knowing your name.
>
> **Correct:** I know your name.

> **Incorrect:** The dog was seeming sick.
>
> **Correct:** The dog seemed sick.

---

progressive tense
verb tense that expresses ongoing action

Andresr, 2014 / Used under license from Shutterstock.com

Practice Rewrite each sentence three times, changing the tenses as requested in parentheses.

- Vaccinations improve health.

1. (present progressive) _____

_____

2. (past progressive) _____

_____

3. (future progressive) _____

_____

- Increased food production helps economies.

4. (present progressive) _____

_____

5. (past progressive) _____

_____

6. (future progressive) _____

_____

- Improved public-health programs lead to lower mortality rates.

7. (present progressive) _____

_____

8. (past progressive) _____

_____

9. (future progressive) _____

_____

L06 Perfect-Tense Verbs

The perfect tenses tell that action is finished, not ongoing, whether in the past, present, or future.

Perfect tenses are formed by using a helping verb along with the past-tense form of the main verb. Each uses a helping verb in the appropriate basic tense—either past, present, or future.

By 1804, the world population **had reached** one billion. (past perfect)

We **have added** another billion people in the last 13 years. (present perfect)

In 13 more years, we **will have welcomed** another billion. (future perfect)

	Forming Perfect Tense		
Past:	had	+	past-tense main verb
Present:	has/have	+	past-tense main verb
Future:	will have	+	past-tense main verb

▶ Perfect Tense with Irregular Verbs

To form the perfect tenses with irregular verbs, use the past participle instead of the past-tense form. **Table 20.6** shows the past participles of common irregular verbs.

Table 20.6 Present Tense and Past Participles of Irregular Verbs

Pres.	Past Part.	Pres.	Past Part.	Pres.	Past Part.	Pres.	Past Part.	Pres.	Past Part.	Pres.	Past Part.
am, are	been	dig	dug	fly	flown	hide	hidden	see	seen	stand	stood
become	become	do	done	forget	forgotten	keep	kept	shake	shaken	steal	stolen
begin	begun	draw	drawn	freeze	frozen	know	known	shine	shone	swim	swum
blow	blown	drink	drunk	get	gotten	lead	led	show	shown	swing	swung
break	broken	drive	driven	give	given	pay	paid	shrink	shrunk	take	taken
bring	brought	eat	eaten	go	gone	prove	proven	sing	sung	teach	taught
buy	bought	fall	fallen	grow	grown	ride	ridden	sink	sunk	tear	torn
catch	caught	feel	felt	hang	hung	ring	rung	sit	sat	throw	thrown
choose	chosen	fight	fought	have	had	rise	risen	sleep	slept	wear	worn
come	come	find	found	hear	heard	run	run	speak	spoken	write	written

---

perfect tense
verb tense that expresses completed action

Practice Rewrite each sentence three times, changing the tense as requested in parentheses.

- According to scientists, the earth circles the sun more than 4.5 billion times.

1. (past perfect) _____

_____

2. (present perfect) _____

_____

3. (future perfect) _____

_____

- The sun lives half of its lifetime.

4. (past perfect) _____

_____

5. (present perfect) _____

_____

6. (future perfect) _____

_____

- Two stars within our galaxy go supernova.

7. (past perfect) _____

_____

8. (present perfect) _____

_____

9. (future perfect) _____

_____

L07 Verbals

A **verbal** is formed from a verb but functions as a noun, an adjective, or an adverb. Each type of verbal—gerund, participle, and infinitive—can appear alone or can begin a **verbal phrase**.

► Gerund

A **gerund** is a verb ending in *ing*, and it functions as a noun.

> Swimming is my favorite pastime. (subject)
>
> I love swimming. (direct object)

A **gerund phrase** begins with a gerund and includes any objects and modifiers.

> Swimming laps at the pool builds endurance. (subject)
>
> I prefer swimming laps at the pool rather than at the lake. (direct object)

► Participle

A **participle** is a verb ending in *ing* or *ed*, and it functions as an adjective.

> The excited students received their lifesaving certification. (*excited* modifies *students*)
>
> What an exciting day! (*exciting* modifies *day*)

A **participial phrase** begins with a participle and includes any objects and modifiers.

> Exciting the young swimmers, I said we were diving today.

► Infinitive

An **infinitive** is formed from *to* and a present-tense verb, and it functions as a noun, an adjective, or an adverb.

> To teach is a noble profession. (subject)
>
> This is an important point to remember. (adjective)
>
> The students are eager to learn. (adverb)

An **infinitive phrase** begins with an infinitive and includes any objects or modifiers.

> I plan to teach swimming skills step-by-step.

Practice Identify each underlined verbal or verbal phrase by selecting the correct choice in parentheses (gerund, participle, infinitive).

1. <u>Jogging</u> is excellent exercise. (gerund, participle, infinitive)

2. You should plan <u>to jog</u> three times a week. (gerund, participle, infinitive)

3. Friends <u>jogging</u> together can also be fun. (gerund, participle, infinitive)

4. Try <u>to wear</u> good shoes. (gerund, participle, infinitive)

5. <u>Avoiding</u> joint injury is important. (gerund, participle, infinitive)

6. <u>Toned</u> by exercise, your muscles will be stronger. (gerund, participle, infinitive)

Practice Complete the following sentences by supplying the type of verbal (or verbal phrase) requested in parentheses.

1. The exercise I would choose is _____ . (gerund)

2. _____ , I would lose weight. (participle)

3. _____ is a good toning exercise. (infinitive)

4. I would also like to try _____ . (gerund)

5. When exercising, remember _____ . (infinitive)

6. _____ , I'll be in great shape. (participle)

Practice For each verbal phrase, write a sentence that correctly uses it.

1. to lift weights _____

2. running a marathon _____

3. filled with anticipation _____

verbal
a construction formed from a verb but functioning as a noun, an adjective, or an adverb

verbal phrase
phrase beginning with a gerund, a participle, or an infinitive

gerund
verbal ending in *ing* and functioning as a noun

gerund phrase
phrase beginning with a gerund and including objects and modifiers

participle
verbal ending in *ing* or *ed* and functioning as an adjective

participial phrase
phrase beginning with a participle and including objects and modifiers

infinitive
verbal beginning with *to* and functioning as a noun, an adjective, or an adverb

infinitive phrase
phrase beginning with an infinitive and including objects and modifiers

L08 Verbals as Objects

Though both infinitives and gerunds can function as direct objects, some verbs take infinitives but not gerunds, and others take gerunds but not infinitives.

► Gerunds as Objects

Verbs that tell something real or true use **gerunds** as direct objects. **Table 20.7** lists verbs that are followed by gerunds.

Table 20.7 Verbs Followed by Gerunds				
admit	miss	discuss	regret	imagine
deny	recommend	finish	consider	recall
enjoy	avoid	quit	dislike	

I enjoy **playing** cards.   I dislike **losing** a poker hand.

not I enjoy to play cards.   **not** I dislike to lose a poker hand.

► Infinitives as Objects

Verbs that tell something you hope for or intend use **infinitives** as direct objects. **Table 20.8** lists verbs that are followed by infinitives.

Table 20.8 Verbs Followed by Infinitives					
agree	volunteer	promise	need	fail	hesitate
demand	appear	want	refuse	offer	plan
hope	deserve	attempt	wish	seem	tend
prepare	intend	endeavor	consent	decide	

I attempt **to win** every hand.   I need **to get** a better poker face.

not I attempt winning every hand.   **not** I need getting a better poker face.

► Gerunds or Infinitives as Objects

Some verbs use either gerunds or infinitives as direct objects. **Table 20.9** lists verbs that can be followed by either gerunds or infinitives.

Table 20.9 Verbs Followed by Gerunds or Infinitives				
begin	love	stop	like	start
hate	remember	continue	prefer	try

I love **playing** poker.   **or** I love **to play** poker.

Practice For the following sentences, select the appropriate verbal in parentheses.

1. I enjoy (to play, playing) canasta.

2. We should plan (to play, playing) canasta this weekend.

3. In canasta, you need (to get, getting) seven-card melds.

4. You and a partner endeavor (to meld, melding) suits.

5. You and your partner can discuss (to go, going) out.

6. The rules recommend (to keep, keeping) other table talk down.

7. I recall (to win, winning) three hands in a row.

8. If you lose a hand, you'll regret (to have, having) wild cards.

9. If you fail (to use, using) a wild card, it costs 50 points.

10. You'll dislike (to get, getting) penalized 50 points.

Practice For the following verbs, write your own sentence using the verb followed by a gerund or an infinitive, as appropriate.

1. deny

_____

2. promise

_____

3. refuse

_____

4. consider

_____

5. recommend

_____

6. avoid

_____

gerund
verbal ending in *ing* and functioning as a noun

infinitive
verbal beginning with *to* and functioning as a noun, an adjective, or an adverb

🌐 Real-World Application

Practice Rewrite the following paragraph, changing passive verbs to active verbs.

Your request to send all the sales representatives to the software training seminar in Cincinnati was reviewed by me. Your idea that this training would help your staff is agreed to by all the managers. Our training budget was reviewed by Matt to see if the seminar could be afforded by us.

_____

_____

_____

Practice In the following paragraph, change future-perfect verbs into past-perfect verbs.

We will have used a large portion of our budget to upgrade design software for the engineering staff. In addition, we will have made prior commitments to train office staff in August. As a result, we will not have reserved enough money to send all sales representatives to Cincinnati.

Practice In the following paragraph, correct misused verbals.

I want exploring other solutions with you. Do you recommend to send two representatives who then could train others? I recall to do that in previous situations. All the managers hope finding a satisfactory compromise for you.

Darren Brode, 2014 / Used under license from Shutterstock.com

Chapter 21

Adjective and Adverb

"If you need three adjectives to describe something, then you've probably chosen the wrong something."

—Roger Rosenblatt

All right, so you have a car. Lots of people have cars. It's a vintage Volkswagen Beetle? Nice. And it's decked out with custom paint, dashboard toys, and bumper stickers that say "smile," "laugh," and "let flow"? You call it your "crazy, hippy, dippy, vintage buggy"? Wow, do you have a car!

The owner of the car above has totally modified it and then has used strings of modifying words and phrases to describe it. That's what adjectives and adverbs do. They add color, texture, shape, size, and many more vivid details to each description. Remember, though, that too many modifiers can overload a sentence—much as too many ornaments can overwhelm a car.

Learning Outcomes

LO1 Adjective Basics
LO2 Adjective Order
LO3 Adverb Basics
LO4 Adverb Placement

What do you think?

What is Roger Rosenblatt trying to say? Can too many adjectives overload a sentence?

L01 Adjective Basics

An **adjective** is a word that modifies a noun or pronoun. Even **articles** such as *a, an,* and *the* are adjectives, indicating whether you mean a general or specific thing. Adjectives answer these basic questions: *which? what kind of? how many? how much?*

Adjectives often appear before the word they modify.

> She drives an new red truck.

A **predicate adjective** appears after the noun it modifies and is linked to the word by a linking verb.

> Her truck is new and red.

Proper adjectives are formed from proper nouns and are capitalized.

> She drives an American truck.

 Forms of Adjectives

Adjectives have three forms: positive, comparative, and superlative.

- **Positive adjectives** describe a noun or pronoun without making a comparison.

  > Keats is a friendly dog.

- **Comparative adjectives** compare two nouns or pronouns.

  > Keats is friendlier than our cat, Yeats.

- **Superlative adjectives** compare three or more nouns or pronouns.

  > He is the friendliest dog you will ever meet.

NOTE: Create the comparative form of most one- or two-syllable words by adding *er,* and create the superlative form by adding *est.* For words of three syllables or more, use *more* (or *less*) to create comparatives and *most* (or *least*) to create superlatives. The adjectives *good* and *bad* have special comparative and superlative forms. **Table 21.1** shows examples of the forms.

Table 21.1 Forms of Adjectives

Positive	Comparative	Superlative
big	bigger	biggest
happy	happier	happiest
wonderful	more wonderful	most wonderful

Positive	Comparative	Superlative
good	better	best
bad	worse	worst

Practice For the following sentences, identify the underlined adjectives as positive (P), comparative (C), or superlative (S).

1. We once had a <u>beautiful</u> collie with a <u>long</u>, <u>shiny</u> coat.

2. She was <u>smarter</u> than our last dog, perhaps the <u>smartest</u> pet we've owned.

3. She thought she was the <u>alpha</u> female and my wife was the <u>beta</u> female.

4. My wife became even <u>more unhappy</u> when the dog tore up her <u>best</u> couch.

5. My wife was <u>happiest</u> on the day we gave the dog to a farmer.

Practice Read the following paragraph and correct adjective errors. The first one has been done for you.

Did you know there is an ~~I~~ntelligence test for dogs? It includes Various tasks to check the dog's Adaptive intelligence, or problem-solving ability. The most smartest dogs can quickly find a treat under one of three buckets, get a treat from under a piece of furniture, find their Favorite spot after a room is rearranged, and get a towel off their heads. In tests, border collies, poodles, and German shepherds have tested as the most smartest, and Afghan hounds, British bulldogs, and chow chows tested at the most low end. Even if they aren't the intelligentest, these dogs might still be the most cuddliest.

---

adjective
word that modifies a noun or pronoun

articles
the adjectives *a*, *an*, and *the*

predicate adjective
adjective that appears after a linking verb and describes the subject

positive adjective
adjective that modifies a noun or pronoun without making a comparison

comparative adjective
adjective that compares two nouns or pronouns

superlative adjective
adjective that compares three or more nouns or pronouns

L02 Adjective Order

Adjectives describe in different ways. Some adjectives refer to time; some refer to shape, size, color, and other features. English uses a specific order for adjectives when several of them appear before a noun. **Table 21.2** shows the correct order of different adjectives.

Table 21.2 Adjective Order

Begin with . . .

1.	articles	a, an, the
	demonstrative adjectives	that, this, these, those
	possessives	my, our, her, their, Kayla's

Then position adjectives that tell . . .

2.	time	first, second, next, last
3.	how many	three, few, some, many
4.	value	important, prized, fine
5.	size	giant, puny, hulking
6.	shape	spiky, blocky, square
7.	condition	clean, tattered, repaired
8.	age	old, new, classic
9.	color	blue, scarlet, salmon
10.	nationality	French, Chinese, Cuban
11.	religion	Baptist, Buddhist, Hindu
12.	material	cloth, stone, wood, bronze

Finally place . . .

13.	nouns used as adjectives	baby [seat], shoe [lace]

Example:

We set sail in a stunning old French shrimp ship.

(**1** + **4** + **8** + **10** + **13** + **noun**)

Insight Even though there is an accepted order for multiple adjectives, avoid stacking too many modifiers in front of a noun.

► Adjective Phrases and Clauses

There are many single-word adjectives to describe things, but several kinds of phrases (prepositional, participial, infinitive) and adjective clauses also serve this purpose.

Todd cleans the boats docked in the harbor. (participial phrase—answers *Which boats?*)

Ships that are battered and worn float in the distance. (adjective clause—answers *What kind of ships?*)

Practice ▶ Rearrange each set of adjectives and articles so that they are in the correct order. Then insert them to create a complete sentence. The first one has been done for you.

1. purple   rectangular   this

   Look at _____ *this rectangular purple* _____ carton.

2. your   Mexican   beautiful

   Please bring _____ guitar.

3. wooden   worn-out   many

   The box holds _____ blocks.

4. precious   the   Islamic

   The curator examined _____ mosaic.

5. traditional   several   Russian

   Lisa bought _____ dolls.

6. stone   chess   Doug's

   Who has seen _____ pieces?

7. broken-down   that   old

   I'm selling _____ sedan.

8. felt   his   pin-striped

   Dan wore _____ fedora.

9. old   the   mossy

   We sat quietly in _____ temple.

10. original   three   piano

    Lucy composed _____ pieces.

11. first   our   real

    This is _____ vacation.

L03 Adverb Basics

An **adverb** modifies a verb (or **verbal**), an adjective, an adverb, or a whole sentence. An adverb answers these basic questions: *how? when? where? why? to what degree? how often? how long?*

> Insight Intensifying adverbs such as *very* and *really* should be used sparingly. Also, in academic writing, it is better to use a precise, vivid verb than to prop up an imprecise verb with an adverb.

He danced boldly.
(*Boldly* modifies the verb *danced*.)

He laughed very loudly.
(*Very* modifies the adverb *loudly*, which modifies the verb *laughed*.)

Apparently he has had dance training.
(*Apparently* modifies the whole sentence.)

NOTE: Most adverbs end in *ly*. Some can be written with or without the *ly*, but when in doubt, use the *ly* form.

loud ⟶ loud**ly**   tight ⟶ tight**ly**   deep ⟶ deep**ly**

► Forms of Adverbs

Adverbs have three forms: positive, comparative, and superlative.

- **Positive adverbs** describe without comparing.

  He danced skillfully.

- **Comparative adverbs** (*-er, more,* or *less*) compare two actions.

  He danced more skillfully than his brother danced.

- **Superlative adverbs** (*-est, most,* or *least*) compare three or more actions.

  He danced the most skillfully of any of those trying out for the play.

NOTE: Some adverbs have special comparative or superlative forms.

well ⟶ better ⟶ best   badly ⟶ worse ⟶ worst

Practice ▸ For the following sentences, provide the correct form of the adverb in parentheses—positive, comparative, or superlative.

1. I like to dance _____ (fast).

2. I dance _____ (fast) than any of my friends dance.

3. My moves are the _____ (fast) of anyone on the floor.

4. My brother moves _____, (well) too.

5. He dances _____ (well) than most people.

6. But out of all my family members I dance _____ (well).

7. I usually ask the band to play _____ (quickly).

8. They sometimes play _____ (quickly) than I like.

9. Out of all the bands at the festival, Absolute Zero played _____ (quickly).

10. At extremely fast tempos, I sometimes dance _____ (badly).

Practice ▸ For the following sentences, choose the correct adjective or adverb in parentheses. Then underline the word each adjective or adverb modifies.

1. I hope this turns out to be a (good, well) movie.

2. I hope the actors perform (good, well).

3. I don't want to spend money on a (bad, badly) movie.

4. I want (bad, badly) to see this movie.

5. If my kid brother comes along, he might behave (bad, badly).

6. If I buy him some candy, he may behave (good, well).

7. That guy has a (bad, badly) attitude.

8. The usher has done (good, well) to ask him to leave.

---

adverb
word that modifies a verb, a verbal, an adjective, an adverb, or a whole sentence

verbal
word formed from a verb but functioning as a noun, an adjective, or an adverb

positive adverb
adverb that modifies without making a comparison

comparative adverb
adverb that compares two actions

superlative adverb
adverb that compares three or more actions

L04 Adverb Placement

Adverbs should be placed in a way that makes the meaning of the sentence plain.

- **How Adverbs:** These can appear in several places but not between a verb and a direct object.

  Furiously we paddled the raft.   We paddled the raft furiously.

  We furiously paddled the raft.   `not` We paddled furiously the raft.

- **When Adverbs:** Place these at the beginning or end of the sentence.

  We went rafting yesterday. Today we'll go again.

- **Where Adverbs:** Place these after the verb they modify but not between the verb and the direct object. (**NOTE:** Prepositional phrases often function as where adverbs.)

  Our guide shouted instructions from the back of the boat.

  `not` Our guide shouted from the back of the boat instructions.

- **Adverbs of *Degree*:** Place these right before the adverb or adjective they modify.

  I learned very quickly to hang on tight. This tip was most helpful.

- **How Often Adverbs:** Place these right before an action verb, between the verb and its helping verb (if it has one).

  I often dreamed about going white-water rafting.

  Before that trip, I had never gotten to go.

▶ Adverb Phrases and Clauses

There are many single-word adverbs to choose from when you write, but certain phrases (prepositional and infinitive) and adverb clauses also serve this purpose.

  After the rain stopped, the children ran outside. (adverb clause—answers *when?*)

  The children splashed in the puddles. (prepositional phrase—answers *where?*)

  They splashed each other to cool off. (infinitive phrase—answers *why?*)

NOTE: Adverb clauses are dependent clauses, meaning they must connect to an independent clause to form a complete sentence.

Practice ▸ For the following sentences, insert the adverb (in parentheses) in the most appropriate position. The first one has been done for you.

1. The instructor *often* reminded us to stay alert. (often)

2. He began our training by explaining the equipment. (thoroughly)

3. He said it is important to wear a helmet. (especially)

4. The instructor was careful about safety. (very)

5. He told us that people fall out of the raft. (sometimes)

6. The rapids chattered all around us. (soon)

7. We went over challenging rapids. (frequently)

8. The water was moving fast. (extremely)

9. I would recommend that guide. (highly)

10. I will go rafting again. (definitely)

Practice ▸ In the following paragraph, move adverbs into their correct positions. The first one has been done for you.

Adrenaline junkies seek often thrills by putting themselves in danger. Dangerous situations trigger usually the release of adrenaline. Adrenaline is a hormone that causes typically the heart rate to increase. It triggers also the fight-or-flight response. Adrenaline junkies enjoy very much this feeling and seek often it out through high-risk activities. They try frequently skydiving or bungee jumping. Some go repeatedly white-water rafting to get their thrills.

🌎 Real-World Application

Practice ▸ In the following document, correct the use of adjectives and adverbs.

Verdant Landscaping

1500 West Ridge Avenue
Tacoma, WA 98466

January 6, 2014

Ms. Karen Bledsoe

Blixen Furniture

1430 North Bel Air Drive

Tacoma, WA 98466-6970

Dear Ms. Bledsoe:

We miss you! Verdant Landscaping has been scheduled not to care for your grounds since fall 2008. You were a valued customer. Did our service fall short in some way? Whatever prompted you to make a change, we would like to discuss ways we could serve you gooder.

During the past year, Verdant has added important these new three services: A full-time landscape architect helps expertly you improve your grounds with flower beds, hardy shrubs, and blooming trees. A tree surgeon can help at a moment's notice you take care of diseased or damaged trees. And our lawn crews offer now mulching services. We provide the most good service and value at the most good price!

I'd like to call next week you to discuss whatever concerns you may have and to offer you a 10 percent discount on a lawn-service new agreement. I can answer at that time any questions you may have about our new services as they are described in the enclosed brochure.

Sincerely,

Stephen Bates

Stephen Bates

Customer Service

Enclosure: Brochure

"Take hold lightly; let go lightly. This is one of the great secrets of felicity in love."

—Spanish Proverb

Chapter 22

Conjunction and Preposition

Every relationship is different. Some people have an equal relationship, like wives and husbands or brothers and sisters. Some people have unequal relationships, like mothers and daughters or fathers and sons. And the very young or very old are often dependent on middle-aged family members.

Ideas have relationships, too. Sometimes ideas are equal—you can tell by the conjunction that connects them. At other times, one idea depends on another. There are conjunctions for those situations, too. And there are also prepositions that create special relationships between nouns and other words.

Conjunctions and prepositions express relationships between ideas in your writing. Using them carefully allows you to share exact, clear messages.

Learning Outcomes

LO1 Coordinating and Correlative Conjunctions
LO2 Subordinating Conjunctions
LO3 Common Prepositions
LO4 *By, At, On,* and *In*

What do you think?

What kind of relationship does the photo suggest?

L01 Coordinating and Correlative Conjunctions

A **conjunction** is a word or word group that joins parts of a sentence—words, phrases, or clauses.

► Coordinating Conjunctions

A **coordinating conjunction** joins grammatically equal parts—a word to a word, a phrase to a phrase, or a clause to a clause. (A clause is a word group that has a subject and a predicate. **Table 22.1** lists coordinating conjunctions.)

Table 22.1 Coordinating Conjunctions						
and	but	or	nor	for	so	yet

- **Equal importance:** A coordinating conjunction shows that the two things joined are of equal importance.

  Ted and Jana like rhythm and blues.
  (*And* joins equal words.)

  I have R&B songs on my iPod and on CDs.
  (*And* joins the phrases *on my iPod* and *on CDs*.)

  I want to download more, but I am not connected to wifi.
  (*But* joins the two clauses, with a comma after the first.)

- **Items in a series:** A coordinating conjunction can join more than two equal parts.

  Ted, Jana, and I are planning to attend an R&B festival.
  (*And* joins *Ted*, *Jana*, and *I*, three parts of a compound subject. A comma follows each word except the last.)

  We will drive to the fest, check out the acts, and buy our tickets.
  (*And* joins three parts of a compound verb.)

► Correlative Conjunctions

Correlative conjunctions consist of a coordinating conjunction and another word. They connect related ideas that work together: word to word, phrase to phrase, or clause to clause. **Table 22.2** lists correlative conjunctions.

Table 22.2 Correlative Conjunctions				
either/or	neither/nor	whether/or	both/and	not only/but also

- **Stressing equality:** Correlative conjunctions stress the equality of parts.

  I like both rock and classical music.
  (*Both/and* stresses equal direct objects.)

Practice For the following sentences, circle the best coordinating conjunction in parentheses.

1. I should buy an MP3 player (but, for, or) an iPod.

2. Kelly, Eli, (and, nor, yet) I sometimes share music.

3. We have different tastes, (or, so, yet) we get to hear a variety of genres.

4. Kelly likes hip-hop, (nor, but, for) I like Latin music.

5. Eli likes classic rock, (but, yet, so) he shares '70s bands.

6. Each week, Kelly, Eli, (and, but, or) I meet to talk about music.

7. We want to broaden our tastes, (and, or, yet) we don't like everything we hear.

8. I like rhythm, Kelly likes clever lyrics, (and, nor, so) Eli likes catchy melodies.

9. Ask us for recommendations, (and, for, so) we are committed fans.

10. We'll tell you what we like, (but, nor, for) you have to choose for yourself.

Practice Write sentences of your own, using a coordinating conjunction (*and, but, or, nor, for, so, yet*) as requested.

1. join two words: _____

_____

2. join two phrases: _____

_____

3. create a series: _____

_____

4. join two clauses (place a comma after the first clause, before the conjunction):

_____

Practice Write a sentence that uses a pair of correlative conjunctions.

_____

_____

---

conjunction
a word or word group that joins words, phrases, or clauses

coordinating conjunction
a conjunction that joins grammatically equal parts

correlative conjunction
a conjunction pair that stresses the equality of the parts that are joined

L02 Subordinating Conjunctions

A **subordinating conjunction** is a word or word group that connects two clauses of different importance. A clause is a word group that has a subject and a predicate. **Table 22.3** lists subordinating conjunctions.

Table 22.3 Subordinating Conjunctions				
after	whenever	unless	that	since
as long as	although	where	until	though
if	because	as	whereas	when
so that	in order that	before	as if	while
till	than	provided that	even though	

- **Subordinate clause:** The subordinating conjunction comes at the beginning of the less-important subordinate clause, which does not form a complete thought. The **subordinate clause** can come before or after the more important clause (the **independent clause**).

  > I go out to eat. I like to order Mexican food.
  > (two clauses)

  > Whenever I go out to eat, I like to order Mexican food.
  > (*Whenever* introduces the subordinate clause, which is followed by a comma.)

  > I like to order Mexican food whenever I go out to eat.
  > (If the subordinate clause comes second, a comma usually isn't needed.)

- **Special relationship:** A subordinating conjunction shows a special relationship between ideas. **Table 22.4** shows the types of relationship that subordinating conjunctions indicate.

Table 22.4 Subordinating Conjunctions and Relationship	
Time	after, as, before, since, till, until, when, whenever, while
Cause	as, as long as, because, before, if, in order that, provided that, since, so that, that, till, until, when, whenever
Contrast	although, as if, even though, though, unless, whereas

  > Whenever Mexican food is on the menu, I order it. (time)

  > I order it extra spicy because I dislike bland food. (cause)

  > Even though I ask for it extra spicy, I often add hot sauce. (contrast)

Practice ▷ In each sentence, provide an appropriate subordinating conjunction. Then choose the type of relationship it shows from the options in the parentheses.

1. _____ we washed the car, I got sprayed many times.
   (time, cause, contrast)

2. Car washing is work _____ it feels like play.
   (time, cause, contrast)

3. _____ the hoses go on, a splash fight is inevitable.
   (time, cause, contrast)

4. I usually don't start the fight _____ I'm willing to join in.
   (time, cause, contrast)

5. _____ people can't resist soap-filled buckets, the fight begins.
   (time, cause, contrast)

6. The car may not get clean _____ the people washing the car do.
   (time, cause, contrast)

7. _____ I first get sprayed, I yell in shock.
   (time, cause, contrast)

8. Then I fight back _____ I'm competitive.
   (time, cause, contrast)

9. At that moment _____ we run out of water, we stop fighting.
   (time, cause, contrast)

10. Then we need to dry off _____ we are completely soaked.
    (time, cause, contrast)

Practice ▷ Create three of your own sentences using subordinating conjunctions, one for each type of relationship.

1. time: _____

2. cause: _____

3. contrast: _____

---

subordinating conjunction
a conjunction that connects clauses of different importance

subordinate clause
a word group that begins with a subordinating conjunction, has a subject and a predicate, but does not express a complete thought

independent clause
a group of words with a subject and predicate that expresses a complete thought

L03 Common Prepositions

A **preposition** is a word or word group that creates a relationship between a noun or pronoun and another word. **Table 22.5** shows common prepositions.

Table 22.5 Common Prepositions				
aboard	before	from among	on behalf of	subsequent to
about	behind	from between	onto	through
above	below	from under	on top of	throughout
according to	beneath	in	opposite	'til
across	beside	in addition to	out	to
across from	besides	in behalf of	out of	together with
after	between	in front of	outside	toward
against	beyond	in place of	outside of	under
along	but	in regard to	over	underneath
alongside	by	inside	over to	until
alongside of	by means of	inside of	owing to	unto
along with	concerning	in spite of	past	up
amid	considering	instead of	prior to	upon
among	despite	into	regarding	up to
apart from	down	like	round	with
around	down from	near	save	within
as far as	during	near to	since	without
aside from	except	notwithstanding		
at	except for	of		
away from	excepting	off		
back of	for	on		
because of	from	on account of		

▶ **Prepositional Phrases**

A **prepositional phrase** starts with a preposition and includes an object of the preposition (a noun or pronoun) and any modifiers. A prepositional phrase functions as an adjective or adverb.

The store at the corner advertises in the newspaper.
(*At the corner* modifies *store*, and *in the newspaper* modifies *advertises.*)

Hand me the keys on the rack by the side of the door.
(*On the rack* modifies *keys*; *by the side* modifies *rack*; *of the door* modifies *side.*)

Practice In the following sentences, underline the prepositional phrases and circle the word that each phrase modifies. The first one has been done for you.

1. This morning I (drove) through our subdivision.

2. Another driver behind me leaned on the horn.

3. Suddenly he passed me on the right.

4. Startled, I swerved into the wrong lane.

5. The other driver sped alongside me.

6. Then his car squealed around the corner.

7. I'm glad no one ran into anything.

8. Tomorrow I may walk to school.

Practice Read each sentence that follows. Use each sentence as a model to write your own. Note how the writer uses prepositional phrases to create specific effects.

1. The log went through the rapids, into the air, and over the falls.

_____

2. I don't want to talk at you, nor to you—but with you.

_____

3. After days of arguing and hours of negotiation, the Senate compromised.

_____

4. Go through the back door, up the stairs, past the security guard, and into the party.

_____

preposition
a word or word group that creates a relationship between a noun or pronoun and another word

prepositional phrase
a phrase that starts with a preposition, includes an object of the preposition (noun or pronoun) and any modifiers, and functions as an adjective or adverb

L04 *By, At, On, and In*

Prepositions often show the physical position of things—above, below, beside, around, and so on. Four specific prepositions not only show position but also have other uses in English.

- **By** means "beside" or "up to a certain place or time."

  by the shed, by the road

  by midnight, by April 15

- **At** refers to a specific place or time.

  at the corner, at the station

  at 4:35 p.m., at noon

- **On** refers to a surface, a day or date, or an electronic medium.

  on the desk, on the cover

  on June 9, on Tuesday

  on the smart phone, on TV

- **In** refers to an enclosed space; a geographical location; a certain amount of time, a month, or a year; or a print medium.

  in the drawer, in the room

  in Seattle, in Britain

  in an hour, in May, in 2015

  in the newspaper, in the book

Say It   Team up with a partner. Take turns reading one of the following phrases or words, which the other person must use in a prepositional phrase beginning with *by, at, on,* or *in*. Together, discuss whether the prepositional phrase is correct and makes sense.

1. the living room
2. October 9
3. 11:15 a.m.
4. the cell phone
5. the edge
6. Chicago
7. the table
8. the restaurant
9. sunrise
10. the magazine

Practice For the following sentences, circle the correct preposition in parentheses.

1. Please arrive (by, on, in) 11:55 a.m. because we will leave promptly (at, on, in) noon.

2. Make sure your carry-on fits (by, at, on, in) the overhead compartment or (by, at, on, in) the foot well in front of you.

3. I looked for a science article (by, at, on, in) the journal and found one (by, at, on, in) the Internet.

4. We sat (by, at, on, in) the room, waiting to be called (at, on, in) 3:15 p.m. for our appointment.

5. Four people standing (by, at, in) the corner reported a fire (at, on, in) a nearby garbage can.

6. (By, At, On, In) July 20, 1969, Neil Armstrong stepped (by, at, on, in) the surface of the moon.

7. I will meet you (by, at, on) the restaurant for our dinner reservation (by, at, on, in) 8:00 p.m.

8. Please place your check (by, at, on, in) the envelope, seal it, and write the following address (by, at, on, in) the envelope.

9. A parrot sat (by, at, on, in) the pirate's shoulder and looked me (by, at, on, in) the eye.

10. The song goes, "Under the boardwalk, down (by, at, on, in) the sea, (by, at, on) a blanket with my baby is where I'll be."

Practice Write three sentences. Include the prepositions given in parentheses.

1. (in, at) _____

_____

2. (on, by) _____

_____

3. (at, on, by) _____

_____

Real-World Application

Practice Correct the following email by inserting coordinating or subordinating conjunctions (see **Tables 22.1** and **22.3**) and replacing any incorrect prepositions with correct ones.

To: dkraitsman@delafordandco.com

Subject: Update on Book Revision

Dear Ed:

Thank you for writing about the revision. It is going well. It should be complete on two weeks. I have finished most of the chapters. I have addressed the main points. It is easy to forget to apply a change throughout. I will read the whole book again to double-check those points.

Some of the graphics are still rough. I will need to finalize them. The maps for the inside covers are drawn. They need to be professionally inked.

The permissions requests are also pending. I have gotten permissions for three of the five excerpts. The fee for using the material was reasonable. If the fees for the other two are not, I will replace them in the end of the business day on July 10.

I will wrap up the revision at July 12. You can plan to start editing then.

Thanks,

Maurice Williams

Author

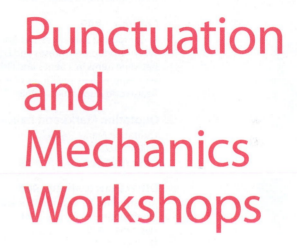

PART 7:

Punctuation and Mechanics Workshops

Part 7: Punctuation and Mechanics Workshops

Doug Lemke, 2014 / Used under license from Shutterstock.com

Chapter

23

"Words, once they are printed, have a
life of their own."

—Carol Burnett

Capitalization

By now you know that good writing
requires correct capitalization. For example, the
first word in a sentence should be capitalized, as
should all proper nouns and proper adjectives.
There are other capitalization rules to keep in
mind as well, and sometimes exceptions occur.
Why, for instance, are some nouns capitalized
in one situation but not in another?

This chapter will guide you in the
conventional use of capital letters in writing.
Throughout the section, examples demonstrate
correct capitalization and serve as a handy
reference during editing and proofreading.

Learning Outcomes

LO1 Basic Capitalization
LO2 Advanced Capitalization
LO3 Other Capitalization Rules

What do you think?

What does a capitalized word reveal to you? What does incorrect capitalization reveal
about a writer?

L01 Basic Capitalization

► First Words

Capitalize the first word in every sentence and the first word in a direct quotation that is a full sentence.

> **T**housands stood in fiercely cold weather to hear John F. Kennedy speak.

> Kennedy said, "**T**hose who look only to the past are certain to miss the future."

► Proper Nouns and Adjectives

Capitalize all proper nouns (names of specific persons, places, things, and ideas) and all proper adjectives (adjectives derived from proper nouns). **Table 23.1** lists examples.

Table 23.1 Proper Nouns and Adjectives

Days of the week	Saturday, Sunday, Tuesday
Months	March, August, December
Holidays, holy days	Christmas, Hanukkah, President's Day
Periods, events in history	the Renaissance, Middle Ages
Special events	Tate Memorial Dedication Ceremony
Political parties, organizations	Republican Party, Habitat for Humanity
Religions, Supreme Beings, holy books	Buddhism, Allah, the Holy Bible
Official documents	Bill of Rights
Trade names	Frisbee disc, Heinz ketchup
Formal epithets	Alexander the Great
Official titles	Vice President Al Gore, Senator Davis
Official state nicknames	the Garden State, the Beaver State
Planets, heavenly bodies	Earth, Mars, the Milky Way
Continents	Asia, Australia, Europe
Countries	France, Brazil, Japan, Pakistan
States, provinces	Montana, Nebraska, Alberta, Ontario
Cities, towns, villages	Portland, Brookfield, Broad Ripple
Streets, roads, highways	Rodeo Drive, Route 66, Interstate 55
Nationalities and ethnic groups	African, Navajo, Serbs
Sections of the U.S. and the world	the West Coast, the Middle East
Languages	Spanish, English, Hindi
Landforms and bodies of water	Appalachian Mountains, Lake Erie
Public areas	Central Park, Yosemite National Park

NOTE: Words that indicate sections of the country are proper nouns and should be capitalized; words that simply indicate directions are not proper nouns.

> I rode **northwest** on my way to the **W**est **C**oast.

Practice In the following sentences, place capitalization marks (≡) under any letters that should be capitalized.

1. Singer jack johnson finds musical inspiration in his hometown of oahu, hawaii.

2. Hawaii is the only state made up entirely of islands and is located in the pacific ocean.

3. Known as the aloha state, it's home to the hawaii volcanoes national park.

4. Another national park, the U.S.S. *arizona* memorial, is dedicated to the navy members who were lost during the attack on pearl harbor.

5. On december, 7, 1941, the United States naval base at pearl harbor, Hawaii, was attacked by japan.

6. The attack triggered the united states' entry into world war II.

7. President franklin D. roosevelt declared December 7 as "a day that will live in infamy."

8. hawaii's beautiful beaches and tropical temperatures attract tourists from all across the continental united states.

Practice In the following paragraph, place capitalization marks (≡) under any letters that should be capitalized in proper nouns, proper adjectives, or first words.

My favorite holiday is thanksgiving. every november, family members from illinois, indiana, and Michigan travel to my parents' house to celebrate the best thursday of the year. While Mom and my aunts work on the dressing and mashed potatoes, my cousins and I watch football on the fox network. it has long been a tradition for the Detroit lions to play a home game every thanksgiving. By the time the game is finished, the food is ready and the feast begins. turkey, gravy, and green-bean casserole— you can't beat thanksgiving.

L02 Advanced Capitalization

▶ Sentences in Parentheses

Capitalize the first word in a sentence that is enclosed in parentheses if that sentence is not combined within another complete sentence.

> My favorite designer is hosting a fashion show for her new collection. (**Now** I just need a ticket.)

NOTE: Do *not* capitalize a sentence that is enclosed in parentheses and is located in the middle of another sentence.

> Rachel's cousin (his name is Carl) can't make the show tonight.

▶ Sentences Following Colons

Capitalize a complete sentence that follows a colon when that sentence is a formal statement, a quotation, or a sentence that you want to emphasize.

> To paraphrase the politician's speech: **The** economy is finally improving.

▶ Words Used as Names

Capitalize words like *father, mother, uncle, senator,* and *professor* only when they are parts of titles that include a personal name or when they are substitutes for proper nouns (especially in direct address).

> Hello, **Senator** Johnson. (*Senator* is part of the name.)
>
> It's good to meet you, **Senator**. (*Senator* is a substitute for the name.)
>
> Our **senator** was born in Minnesota.
>
> Who was your chemistry **professor** last semester?
>
> I had **Professor Willams** for Chemistry 101.
>
> Good morning, **Professor**.

To test whether a word is being substituted for a proper noun, simply read the sentence with a proper noun in place of the word. If the proper noun fits in the sentence, the word being tested should be capitalized. Usually the word is not capitalized if it follows a possessive, such as *my, his, our,* or *your.*

> Did **Dad** (Brad) pack the stereo in the trailer? (*Brad* works in the sentence.)
>
> Did your **dad** (Brad) pack the stereo in the trailer? (*Brad* does not work in the sentence; the word *dad* follows *your.*)

Practice   In the following sentences, place capitalization marks (≡) under any letters that should be capitalized.

1. I can say this about the people in the Midwest: they are known for being nice.

2. Jill spilled her water all over the table. (it's surely not the first time this has happened.)

3. Have you met professor Netzly during office hours?

4. Mark Twain once said this about dealing with adversity: "it's not the size of the dog in the fight; it's the size of the fight in the dog."

5. My sister Abby is starting college today. (my mom finally has the house to herself.)

6. The senator met with representative Casey.

7. Mo'ne Davis (of Little League baseball fame) said this of baseball: "it'll make a huge impact if more girls start playing."

8. When grandma came home from the hospital, I spoiled her with flowers and chocolate. (she deserved it.)

Practice   Read the following paragraph. Place capitalization marks (≡) under any letters that should be capitalized.

    I met mayor Greg Ballard by chance today at the daily brew, a coffee shop. We got to talking about how I had studied art history last year with professor Lawrence, my father. Taking a class from dad (it did feel awkward at first) was actually okay. In class, I called dad professor Lawrence, and he called me Michelle, never Princess. (that's his nickname for me.) The mayor talked a little about his day. He had just attended a speech by congressman Paul Ryan about fiscal responsibility, had contacted commissioner Sheffield for some sort of permit, and was actually looking forward to meeting dad at the golf course by eleven o'clock.

L03 Other Capitalization Rules

► Titles

Capitalize the first word of a title, the last word, and every word in between except articles (*a, an, the*), short prepositions, *to* in an infinitive, and coordinating conjunctions. Follow this rule for titles of books, newspapers, magazines, poems, plays, songs, articles, films, works of art, and stories.

Fast and Furious (movie)   **The Da Vinci Code** (novel)

"**Man in the Mirror**" (song)   "**Cashing in on Kids**" (essay)

► Titles of Courses

Words such as *history* and *science* are proper nouns when they are included in the titles of specific courses; they are common nouns when they name a field of study.

Who teaches **Art History 202**? (title of a specific course)

Professor Bunker loves teaching **history**. (a field of study)

NOTE: Always capitalize *English*, even if it is used as a common noun.

► Organizations

Capitalize the name of an organization or a team and its members.

American Indian Movement   **Democractic Party**

Susan G. Komen for the **Cure**   **Chicago Bulls**

► Abbreviations

Capitalize most abbreviations, including titles and organizations.

MD   **PhD**   **NAACP**   **CE**   **BCE**   **GPA**

► Web Terms

The words *Internet* and *World Wide Web* are capitalized because they are considered proper nouns. When your writing includes a Web address (URL), capitalize any letters that the site's owner does (in print or on the site itself).

When doing research on the **Internet**, be sure to record each site's **Web** address (URL) and each contact's email address. One popular research site is **Bing.com**.

Practice ▸ In the following sentences, place capitalization marks (≡) under any letters that should be capitalized.

1. I'm stopping by the gas station to pick up the Sunday *Chicago tribune*.

2. The Los Angeles lakers play in the staples center.

3. I'm taking american poetry next semester.

4. My favorite author is Malcolm Gladwell, who wrote the best-sellers *blink* and *The tipping point*.

5. How many times have you heard the song "I got a feeling" by the Black-eyed peas?

6. The American cancer society raises money for cancer research.

7. I was happy to improve my gpa from 3.1 to 3.4 last semester.

8. Where did you sign up for introduction to mass communication?

9. She emails her patients when test results are posted on the web site.

10. Who is a good pediatric md in Omaha?

11. Jill was promoted to chief operating officer (ceo) this July.

Practice ▸ In the following paragraph, place capitalization marks (≡) under any letters that should be capitalized.

On our way to the Kansas city royals game, my friend Ted and I were talking about our favorite music. He likes coldplay, while I prefer radiohead. His favorite song is "the scientist." My favorite is "Fake plastic trees." But as we argued about the merits of each band, we completely missed our exit to the stadium. Ted suggested we take a U-turn. Instead, I used my gps to find a new route. Luckily, we made it to the ballpark in time for me to grab a hot dog and sprite before the opening pitch.

🌐 Real-World Application

Practice In the following email, place capitalization marks (≡) under any letters that should be capitalized. Put a lowercase editing mark (/) through any letters that should not be capitalized.

✉ 📎 📇 📝   ● ● ●

To: Ryan Orlovich

Subject: Volunteer Update

Dear superintendent Orlovich:

Last Saturday, the Ball State university volunteer center committee met to discuss new volunteer opportunities for the upcoming semester. We are interested in putting together a service event at big oak park for the incoming Freshmen.

We would like to get in contact with someone from your Department to set up a time and date for the event. we would prefer the event to take place between thursday, August 23, and Sunday, August 26. Also, we hope to design shirts for the Volunteers and are wondering if your office knows of any sponsors who might be interested in funding this expenditure.

When you have time, please contact me by phone at 317-555-3980 or Email at ehenderson@bs23u.edu. (you may also email the office at bsuvolunteerism@bs23u.edu.)

Sincerely,

Liz Henderson

BSU Volunteer President

Pressmaster, 2014 / Used under license from Shutterstock.com

Pressmaster, 2014 / Used under license from Shutterstock.com

Chapter 24

Comma

"I love ham, grilled cheese, and peanut butter and jelly. Comma, comma, and comma, because otherwise it would read grilled cheese and peanut butter and jelly, grouped together, which would make a weird sandwich."

—Jarod Kintz

Commas divide sentences into shorter sections, showing which words belong together and which need to be separated. They signal the reader to pause in order to grasp the various ideas before putting them together into a full sentence. Of all the punctuation marks, commas are used most frequently—and oftentimes, they are used incorrectly.

This chapter discusses the conventional use of commas. Understanding how to correctly use commas is an important step toward becoming a college-level writer.

Learning Outcomes

LO1 In Compound Sentences and After Introductory Clauses

LO2 With Introductory Phrases and Equal Adjectives

LO3 Between Items in a Series and Other Uses

LO4 With Appositives and Other Word Groups

What do you think?

Read the quotation from Jarod Kintz. Why does he think commas are so important? Apart from sandwich ingredients, what else can commas help sort out?

L01 In Compound Sentences and After Introductory Clauses

The following principles will guide the use of commas in your writing.

► In Compound Sentences

Use a comma before the coordinating conjunction (*and, but, or, nor, for, so, yet*) in a compound sentence.

> Phillip had planned to meet a client in New York**, but** he missed his flight connection in Atlanta.

NOTE: Do not confuse a compound verb with a compound sentence. Compound verbs should not be separated by commas.

> The clients learned the news of Phillip's missed flights and postponed the meeting. *(compound verb)*

> Phillip's missed flight connection delayed his arrival**,** but his clients were understanding. *(compound sentence)*

► After Introductory Clauses

Use a comma after most introductory clauses.

> **Because her car needed service,** Harriet rode her bike to school.
> *(adverb dependent clause)*

When the adverb clause follows the independent clause and is not essential to the meaning of the sentence, use a comma. This comma use generally applies to clauses beginning with *even though, although, while,* or some other conjunction expressing a contrast.

> Authors need someone else to check their work for errors**, even though they write professionally.**

NOTE: A comma is not used if the adverb clause following the independent clause is needed for clarity.

> There's no sense making mistakes **if you don't learn from them.**

Practice Read the following sentences. If the clause on each side of the coordinating conjunction could stand alone as a sentence, add a comma. Write "correct" for any sentence that should not contain a comma.

1. I was sick of sitting around on the couch so I walked over to the driving range. _____

2. Her cell phone rang but she decided against answering it. _____

3. Maria downloaded some new music and imported it onto her iPod. _____

4. I wanted to finish my assignment but I couldn't turn away from *The Walking Dead* marathon. _____

5. Should I put a down payment on a new car or should I save my money for a new apartment? _____

6. Kelly is studying frog populations in the rain forest and she hopes to publish her work. _____

7. Ryan wanted to make a new style of chili but he lost the recipe. _____

8. Trisha was looking forward to the baseball game but it got rained out. _____

Practice In the following sentences, add a comma between the clauses if necessary. If no comma is needed, write "correct."

1. While Becca prefers grilled salmon Mia's favorite food is sushi. _____

2. Although the water conditions were perfect I couldn't catch a wave to save my life. _____

3. Perhaps I should rethink my major because I don't enjoy the classes. _____

4. Even though the Cubs haven't won a World Series since 1908 I still cheer for them. _____

5. While *The Voice* is popular in America *Britain's Got Talent* is the craze in England. _____

L02 With Introductory Phrases and Equal Adjectives

► After Introductory Phrases

Use a comma after introductory phrases.

> **At the oddest hours of the night,** I feel motivated to cook and clean.

A comma is usually omitted if the phrase follows an independent clause.

> I feel motivated to cook and clean **at the oddest hours of the night**.

You may omit a comma after a short (four or fewer words) introductory phrase unless the comma is needed to ensure clarity.

> **Before lunch** we will practice our presentation.

► To Separate Adjectives

Use commas to separate adjectives that equally modify the same noun. Notice in the following examples that no comma separates the last adjective from the noun.

> A **harsh, bright** light appeared in the distance.
> Our Web site features **colorful, eye-catching** graphics.

► To Determine Equal Modifiers

To determine whether adjectives modify a noun equally, use these two tests.

1. Reverse the order of the adjectives; if the sentence is clear, the adjectives modify equally. In the following example, *beautiful* and *vibrant* can be switched, but *awful* and *winter* cannot.

> Chicago is a **beautiful, vibrant** city with occasionally **awful winter** weather.

2. Insert *and* between the adjectives; if the sentence reads well, use a comma when *and* is omitted. The word *and* can be inserted between *beautiful* and *vibrant*, but in the sentence, *and* does not make sense between *awful* and *winter*.

Practice ▶ In the following sentences, add commas after the introductory phrases as necessary. If no comma is needed, write "correct."

1. Before receiving your diploma you will need to pay your unpaid parking tickets.   _____

2. At Central Perk the friends sipped coffee and exchanged stories from the weekend.   _____

3. In accordance with state law Hanna decided against sending a text message while driving on the interstate.   _____

4. The game was not canceled despite heavy rain and muddy conditions.   _____

5. After handing in her paper Eva felt a great wave of relief.   _____

6. Eva felt a great wave of relief after handing in her paper.   _____

7. Based on his own primary research Andy came up with a preliminary hypothesis.   _____

8. To save a few dollars Stephanie rode her bike to work.   _____

Practice ▶ In the following sentences, determine whether a comma is needed to separate the boldfaced adjectives. Add a comma if it is needed; write "correct" if a comma is not needed.

1. The **long difficult** exam took a lot out of me.   _____

2. Last night I went to a **fun graduation** party.   _____

3. A good concert includes many **memorable hair-raising** moments.   _____

4. A **thoughtful considerate** friend goes an extra mile to make you smile.   _____

5. I could really use a **relaxing back** massage.   _____

6. When dressing for skiing, consider wearing a **thick well-insulated** jacket.   _____

L03 Between Items in a Series and Other Uses

► Between Items in a Series

Use commas to separate individual words, phrases, or clauses in a series. A series contains at least three items.

> Winston Churchill was known for his **political leadership, military prowess, and fiery personality.**

Do not use commas when all the items are connected with *or, nor,* or *and.*

> Churchill was an accomplished writer and artist and historian.

► To Set Off Transitional Expressions

Use a comma to set off conjunctive adverbs and transitional phrases.

> Churchill**, therefore,** was brash and temperamental; **however,** his candor and decisiveness separated him from average politicians.

If a transitional expression blends smoothly with the rest of the sentence, it does not need to be set off.

> Despite his grumpy reputation, Churchill's nickname was **in fact** Winnie.

► To Set Off Dialogue

Use commas to set off the exact words of the speaker from the rest of the sentence.

> **"Success consists of going from failure to failure without loss of enthusiasm,"** Churchill said.

> **"History will be kind to me,"** Winston joked, **"for I intend to write it."**

Do not use a comma before an indirect quotation.

> Historians say **that Churchill rallied Britain from the brink of defeat.**

► To Enclose Explanatory Words

Use commas to enclose an explanatory phrase that interrupts the flow of the sentence, providing extra information.

> Churchill**, according to many historians,** was one of the greatest world leaders of the 20th century.

Practice Insert commas where needed in the following sentences.

1. I'm looking forward to graduation summer vacation and moving into a new apartment.

2. A new strain of the virus according to biologists could cause future outbreaks of poultry disease.

3. "To confine our attention to terrestrial matters would be to limit the human spirit" said Stephen Hawking.

4. I need you to pick up two jars of peanut butter a half gallon of skim milk and snacks for the party.

5. I enjoy live music; however I don't like big crowds.

6. "With all the advancements in technology" Sara said "you'd think we would have invented a quicker toaster by now."

7. Eighty percent of states as a matter of fact are in financial trouble.

8. We can meet up at either the library the student union or the main hall.

9. The difference between perseverance and obstinacy according to Henry Ward Beecher is that one comes from a strong will and the other from a strong won't.

10. Chicago Detroit and Indianapolis are the most-populated cities in the Midwest.

Practice Insert commas where needed in the following paragraph.

The Erie Canal is a man-made waterway that crosses New York State from Albany on the Hudson River to Buffalo on Lake Erie. It opened in 1825 and according to many historians had a significant impact on the growth of the nation. The canal significantly cut transportation time between the Eastern Seaboard and the Great Lakes opened new markets to farmers spurred the growth of cities along its route and brought settlers to the Midwest. John Moody would later say "The opening of the Erie Canal . . . stimulated . . . cities on the Atlantic Seaboard to put themselves into closer commercial touch with the West." Since the 1990s the canal has seen mainly recreational traffic; however it still transports some cargo.

L04 With Appositives and Other Word Groups

► To Set Off Some Appositives

Use commas to set off a specific kind of explanatory word or phrase called an **appositive**. An appositive identifies or renames a preceding noun or pronoun.

> Albert Einstein**, the famous mathematician and physicist,** developed the theory of relativity.

Do not use commas if the appositive is important to the basic meaning of the sentence.

> The famous physicist **Albert Einstein** developed the theory of relativity.

► With Some Clauses and Phrases

Use commas to enclose phrases or clauses that add information that is not necessary to the basic meaning of the sentence. For example, if the clause or phrase (in **boldface**) were left out of the following two examples, the meaning of the sentences would remain clear. Therefore, commas are used to set off the information.

> The locker rooms in Swain Hall**, which were painted and updated last summer,** give professors a place to shower. *(unnecessary clause)*
>
> Work-study programs**, offered on many campuses,** give students the opportunity to earn tuition money. *(unnecessary phrase)*

Do not use commas to set off necessary clauses and phrases, which add information that the reader needs to understand the sentence.

> Only the professors **who run at noon** use the locker rooms. *(necessary clause)*

► Using "That" or "Which"

Use *that* to introduce necessary clauses; use *which* to introduce unnecessary clauses.

> Campus jobs **that are funded by the university** are awarded to students only. *(necessary clause)*
>
> The cafeteria**, which is run by an independent contractor,** can hire non-students. *(unnecessary clause)*

Practice Indicate where commas are needed in the following sentences. If no commas are needed, write "correct."

1. The U.S.S. *Constitution* is a wooden-hulled three-masted ship that is still commissioned by the U.S. Navy.   _____

2. Gordon Ramsay the fiery chef and television star specializes in French, Italian, and British cuisines.   _____

3. Hall of Fame baseball player Roberto Clemente a notable philanthropist died in a plane crash while en route to Nicaragua to deliver aid to earthquake victims.   _____

4. The concert hall which is on the corner of Meridian Avenue and 1st Street is expected to revitalize the downtown district.   _____

5. Press passes that allow for backstage access are given out to special media members.   _____

6. John Quincy Adams who later became the sixth president of the United States authored the Monroe Doctrine in 1823.   _____

Practice Decide if the clause in bold type is necessary or unnecessary to the meaning of the following sentences. Then circle the correct conjunction in parentheses and supply commas if they are necessary. The first one has been done for you.

1. The flight *(which,* ⟨*that*⟩*)* **our keynote speaker is on** has been delayed.

2. The Modesto Wind Farm *(which, that)* **was built last year** is scheduled to double in size by 2016.

3. Applications for scholarships *(which, that)* **are sponsored by the Kiwanis Club** are due next Tuesday.

4. Scholarship programs *(which, that)* **are funded by several different organizations** help many students pay for college.

5. The museum *(which, that)* **impressed Dad the most** was the Guggenheim.

---

appositive
a noun or noun phrase that renames the noun preceding it

🌐 Real-World Application

Practice Insert commas where they are needed in the following email message.

To: Michael_Green@shieldmarketing.com
Subject: Revised Agenda for Quarterly Update
Attach: Meeting Agenda 04-19-15.doc

Hi, Michael:

I've attached the agenda for the quarterly update with the marketing team. Daniel Gilchrest the senior marketing coordinator will moderate the meeting but I want you to familiarize yourself with the material. Here are some highlights of the new agenda:

1. The advertising allowance for Gillette, Hillsboro Farms and Justice Inc. has increased by 5 percent.

2. The penetrated market which accounts for actual users of products declined in the healthcare sector.

3. We will shift the focus of marketing efforts to meet the digital and social-media demands of today's market.

Please review the agenda by the end of the day.

Thanks,

Tru Sha

Marketing Associate

Camilo Torres, 2014 / Used under license from Shutterstock.com

Camilo Torres, 2014 / Used under license from Shutterstock.com

Chapter 25

"Words can light fires in the minds of men. Words can wring tears from the hardest of hearts."

—Patrick Rothfuss

Quotation Marks and Italics

Your words are significant. They tell others what you think, what you know, what you hope. And the way you punctuate your words is also important.

When you write, you must sometimes use quotation marks and italics to set certain words apart. These punctuation marks can point out a word as a word, call attention to a word's special use, mark someone's exact words, and indicate the titles of books, articles, and more.

Learning Outcomes

LO1 Quotation Marks

LO2 Italics

What do you think?

What do you believe about words? What have you seen words accomplish?

L01 Quotation Marks

► ## To Punctuate Titles of Smaller Works

Use quotation marks to enclose the titles of smaller works, including speeches, short stories, songs, poems, episodes of audio or video programs, chapters or sections of books, unpublished works, and articles from magazines, journals, newspapers, or encyclopedias.

> **Speech:** "The Cause Endures"
>
> **Song:** "Shake It Off"
>
> **Short story:** "Dark They Were, and Golden Eyed"
>
> **Magazine article:** "The Moral Life of Babies"
>
> **Chapter in a book:** "Queen Mab"
>
> **Television episode:** "The Girl Who Was Death"
>
> **Encyclopedia article:** "Cetacean"

► ## Placement of Punctuation

When quoted words end in a period or comma, always place the period or comma inside the quotation marks.

> "If you want to catch the train," Grace said, "you must leave now."

When a quotation is followed by a semicolon or colon, always place the semicolon or colon outside the quotation marks.

> You need to watch the *Breaking Bad* episode "Ozymandias"; you will be thrilled.
>
> I told her, "Don't look away"; she didn't listen.

If an exclamation point or a question mark is part of the quotation, place it inside the quotation marks. Otherwise, place it outside.

> Marcello asked me, "Are you going to the Dodge Poetry Festival?"
>
> What could I reply except, "Yes, indeed"?

▶ For Special Words

Quotation marks can be used (1) to show that a word is being referred to as the word itself; (2) to indicate that it is jargon, slang, or a coined term; (3) to show that it is used in an ironic or sarcastic sense; or for (4) quoting other people's words, such as a definition.

(1) Somehow, the term **"cool"** has survived for decades.

(2) Raymond found an **"Easter egg"** in his new video game.

(3) I made it just in time for a pop quiz—how **"wonderful."**

Practice For the following sentences, insert quotation marks as needed.

1. Kamala loves to listen to the song I Take Time over and over and over.

2. Ray Bradbury's short story A Sound of Thunder has been republished many times.

3. *Fast Company* published an article today called How Google Wave Got Its Groove Back.

4. Angelo told Arlena, I have a guy who can fix that fender.

5. Arlena asked, How much will it cost me?

6. Was she thinking, This car is driving me into bankruptcy?

7. This is the message of the article Tracking the Science of Commitment: Couples who complement one another have an easier time remaining committed.

8. I love the article Tall Tales About Being Short; it challenged my preconceptions about the effect of height on a person's life.

9. How many times is the word aardvark used on this page?

10. We are assigned to read a short story, The Tell-Tale Heart, and define the terms foreshadowing and imagery in our journals.

11. Grant is writing an article called What Meeting? for the school newsletter.

12. If you want to catch the bus, called Mom, you'll have to be ready in five minutes.

13. The phrase head of steam refers to a strong driving force.

14. When Phil asked if I was going to the party, I said, At this hour? No way!

L02   Italics

► To Identify Titles of Larger Works

Use italics to indicate the titles of larger works, including newspapers, magazines, journals, pamphlets, books, plays, films, radio and television programs, movies, ballets, operas, long musical compositions, CDs, DVDs, software programs, and legal cases, as well as the names of ships, trains, aircraft, and spacecraft.

Magazine: *Wired*   **Newspaper:** *Washington Post*

Play: *Night of the Iguana*   **Journal:** *Journal of Control*

Film: *Bladerunner*   **Software program:** *Paint Shop Pro*

Book: *Moby Dick*   **Television program:** *Lost*

► For a Word, Letter, or Number Referred to as Itself

Use italics or quotation marks (either is correct) to show that a word, letter, or number is being referred to as itself. If a definition follows a word used in this way, place that definition in quotation marks.

The word *tornado* comes from the Spanish word *tronar*, which means "to thunder."

I can't read your writing; is this supposed to be a *P* or an *R*?

► For Foreign Words

Use italics to indicate a word that is borrowed from a foreign language.

Bon appétit is a French phrase that many English speakers use to say "Enjoy your meal."

► For Technical Terms

Use italics to introduce a technical term for the first time in a piece of writing. After that, the term may be used without italics.

The heart's *sternocostal* surface—facing toward the joining of sternum and ribs—holds the heart's primary natural pacemaker. If this sternocostal node fails, a lower, secondary node can function in its place.

If a technical term is being used within an organization or a field of study where it is common, it may be used without italics even the first time in a piece of writing.

Practice For the following sentences, write down or underline words that should be in italics.

1. I almost couldn't finish Stephenie Meyer's second book, *New Moon*, because of its deep emotion.

2. What is your favorite part of the movie *Anchorman*?

3. The Spanish say *duende* to describe a transcendent, creative passion.

4. Was the aircraft carrier *Enterprise* named after the vessel from the *Star Trek* series or the other way around?

5. You might use the term *bonhomie* to describe our relationship.

6. One thing I love about the MS Word program is its "Track Changes" feature.

7. In this course, we will use the term *noetics* as an indication of deep-felt self-awareness, beyond mere consciousness.

8. I read a review of the play *Fish in the Dark* in *The New York Times*.

9. Wait, that's not a *7*; it's an *L*.

10. The phrase *mucho gusto* means "Nice to meet you."

Practice Write three sentences, each demonstrating your understanding of a rule for using italics. Underline any words that should be italicized.

1. _____

_____

_____

2. _____

_____

_____

3. _____

_____

_____

🌐 **Real-World** Application

Practice ▷ Insert any missing quotation marks and underline any words that should be italicized in the following email.

Brideshead Publishing

1012 Broadway
New York, New York 10011

May 13, 2015

Laura Kohnen
4004 W. Obleness Parkway
Hollenshead, New Hampshire 03305

Dear Laura Kohnen:

Thank you for your recent novel submission entitled A Time of Dimly Perceived Wonders, which I read with great interest. The setting is richly portrayed, and the main characters are mysterious as well as familiar, conveying a certain je ne sais quois about themselves. For example, although his words are from a different time, I feel deep kinship for Anibal when he cries out, I could've et 'em up right there 'n' then! Similarly, when Kandis softly sings the words of Come One, Come All to the Family Reunion, I feel I'm being called home myself, although I've never actually seen the Appalachians.

While I greatly enjoyed the novel, and it would certainly receive an "A" in my Creative Writing Seminar at Midtown College, I do have a few concerns. For example, the title seems long and vague; I'd recommend Foggy Mountain Memories instead. Also, I think it is unnecessary to print the full text of Abraham Lincoln's Gettysburg Address and Martin Luther King, Jr.,'s I Have a Dream speech in the chapter entitled A Few Words of Hope. Modern readers are familiar with both speeches. It should be enough to include just a few phrases, such as Four score and seven years ago and Let freedom ring from Lookout Mountain of Tennessee.

If you are willing to accept changes like these, I believe we can work together to make your novel a commercial success.

Sincerely,

Christene Kaley

Christene Kaley

Ron and Joe, 2014 / Used under license from Shutterstock.com

> "If the English language made any sense,
> a catastrophe would be an apostrophe with fur."
>
> —Doug Larson

Chapter

26

Other Punctuation

You may be surprised to discover that the words *catastrophe* and *apostrophe* have something in common. Both come from the Greek word for "turn." An apostrophe simply turns away, but a catastrophe overturns.

Even though learning to use apostrophes correctly may be difficult, it doesn't have to be a catastrophe. The explanations and activities in this chapter will help you to keep the apostrophe rules straight. You will also learn how to use semicolons, colons, hyphens, and dashes.

Learning Outcomes

LO1 Apostrophes for Contractions and Possessives

LO2 Semicolons and Colons

LO3 Hyphens

LO4 Dashes

What do you think?

What does Doug Larson's quotation mean?

L01 Apostrophes for Contractions and Possessives

Apostrophes are used primarily to show that a letter or number has been left out or that a noun is possessive.

Contractions

Use an apostrophe to form a **contraction**. A contraction is a word formed by joining two words, leaving out one or more letters and using an apostrophe in their place.

do not—don't	they would—they'd	would have—would've
(*o* is left out)	(*woul* is left out)	(*ha* is left out)

▶ Missing Characters

Use an apostrophe to signal when one or more characters are left out.

class of '72	rock 'n' roll	good evenin'
(*19* is left out)	(*a* and *d* are left out)	(*g* is left out)

Possessives

Form possessives of singular nouns by adding an apostrophe and an *s*. The word before the apostrophe is the owner.

Benson's ball	Custer's last stand	*Hogan's Heroes*

▶ Singular Noun Ending in *s* (One Syllable)

Form the possessive by adding an apostrophe and an *s*.

the boss's office	the class's teacher

> **Insight** Pronoun possessives *do not use* apostrophes: *its, whose, hers, his, ours.*

▶ Singular Noun Ending in *s* (Two or More Syllables)

Form the possessive by adding an apostrophe and an *s*—or by adding just an apostrophe.

Texas's cities	*or*	Texas' cities

▶ Plural Noun Ending in *s*

Form the possessive by adding just an apostrophe. Remember, the word before the apostrophe is the owner.

the bosses' email	the Smiths' van	the boys' game

▶ Plural Noun Not Ending in *s*

Form the possessive by adding an apostrophe and an *s*.

the people's reaction	the men's section

Practice   For the following contractions, write the words that formed the contraction. For the following pairs of words, use an apostrophe to form the contraction.

1. they're _____

2. you've _____

3. Charlie is _____

4. wouldn't _____

5. we have _____

6. have not _____

7. I would _____

8. it's _____

Practice   Rewrite the following sentences, replacing the "of" phrases with possessives using apostrophes.

1. The idea of my friend is a good one.

_____

2. I found the set list of the orchestra.

_____

3. The foundation of the government is democracy.

_____

4. He washed the jerseys of the team.

_____

5. I went to the house of the Kings.

_____

6. The plan of the managers worked well.

_____

7. I like the classic albums of Kiss.

_____

8. I graded the assignment of Ross.

_____

9. The pastries of the chef were delicious.

_____

10. The books of the children covered the floor.

_____

L02 Semicolons and Colons

Semicolon

A **semicolon** (;) can be called a soft period. Use the semicolon to join two sentences that are closely related.

> The job market is improving; it's time to apply again.

► Before a Conjunctive Adverb

Often, the second part of the sentence will begin with a conjunctive adverb (*also, besides, however, instead, meanwhile, therefore*), which signals the relationship between the clauses. Place a semicolon before the conjunctive adverb, and place a comma after it.

> I looked for work for two months; however, the market is better now.

► In a Series

Use a semicolon to separate items in a series if any of the items already include commas.

> The company has offices in Atlanta, Georgia; Austin, Texas; and Portland, Oregon.

Colon

Use a **colon** (:) to introduce an example or a list.

> I've forgotten one other possibility: social networking.
>
> I'll plan to use the following: LinkedIn, Twitter, and Facebook.

► After Salutations

In business documents, use a colon after a **salutation**, the formal greeting.

> Dear Mr. Ortez: To: Lynne Jones

► Times and Ratios

Use a colon to separate hours, minutes, and seconds. Also use a colon between the numbers in a ratio.

> 7:35 p.m.   6:15 a.m.   The student-teacher ratio is 30:1.

Practice In the following sentences, add semicolons and commas as needed.

1. Searching for a job is nerve-wracking however it's also exciting.

2. Don't think about rejections think about possibilities.

3. My friend told me to update my résumé, references list, and LinkedIn profile to network and to do a lot of research.

4. Take time to write a thoughtful cover letter also take time to proofread your application before you submit it.

5. I have an interview next week meanwhile, I'm still applying for other jobs.

6. It doesn't cost much to send out résumés therefore send out many.

7. Job searching can feel lonely and frustrating rely on friends and family to help you through.

8. Ask people if you can use them as references don't provide the list of references until it is requested.

9. Here are a few interviewing tips: Prepare by researching the company you hope to work for wear appropriate clothing arrive a little early and bring a folder with loose leaf paper, a few extra résumés, and a couple of pens or pencils.

Practice In the following sentences, add colons as needed.

1. Use your social resources contacts, references, and organizations.

2. Call for an appointment between 9 00 a.m. and 4 00 p.m.

3. Remember, a response rate of 1 10 is good for job applications.

4. For an interview, remember these three rules Be punctual, be polite, and be professional.

---

semicolon
a punctuation mark (;) that connects sentences and separates items in some series

colon
a punctuation mark (:) that introduces an example or list and has other special uses

salutation
the formal greeting in a letter; the line starting with "Dear"

L03 Hyphens

A **hyphen** (-) joins words and letters to form various kinds of compounds.

▶ Compound Nouns

Use hyphens to create **compound nouns**.

city-state   fail-safe   one-liner   mother-in-law

▶ Compound Adjectives

Use hyphens to create **compound adjectives** that appear before the noun. If the adjective appears after the noun, it usually is not hyphenated.

ready-made solution   a solution that is ready made

Don't hyphenate a compound made from an -ly adverb and an adjective or a compound that ends with a single letter.

quickly prepared meals   grade B plywood

▶ Compound Numbers

Use hyphens in **compound numbers** from twenty-one to ninety-nine and in fractions.

twenty-seven   fifty-fifty   three-quarters   seven thirty-seconds

▶ With Letters

Use a hyphen to join a letter to a word that follows it.

L-bracket   U-shaped   T-shirt   O-ring   G-rated   X-ray

▶ With Common Elements

Use hyphens to show that two or more words share a common element included in only the final term.

We offer low-, middle-, and high-coverage plans.

Practice Rewrite the following sentences, adding hyphens as needed.

1. Two thirds of the students in my class have full time jobs.

2. We had to x ray twenty one people today.

3. The board was three sixteenths of an inch too short.

4. The statistics on low , middle , and high income households are available.

5. A double insulated wire should be used for high voltage applications.

6. The x axis shows months, and the y axis shows dollar amounts.

7. The tax rate table shows I should pay twenty eight cents.

8. My mother in law thinks I am quite a fine son in law.

9. The L bracket measured eleven sixteenths of an inch by twenty seven thirty seconds of an inch.

---

hyphen
a short horizontal line (-) used to form compound words

compound noun
a noun made of two or more words, often hyphenated or spelled closed

compound adjective
an adjective made of two or more words, hyphenated before the noun but not afterward

compound numbers
two-word numbers from twenty-one to ninety-nine

L04   Dashes

Unlike the hyphen, the **dash (—)** does more to separate words than to join them. A dash is indicated by two hyphens with no spacing before or after. Most word-processing programs convert two hyphens into a dash.

► For Emphasis

Use a dash instead of a colon if you want to emphasize a word, phrase, clause, or series.

> Ice cream—it's what life is about.
>
> I love two things about ice cream—making it and eating it.
>
> Ice cream is my favorite dessert—cold, sweet, and flavorful.

► To Set Off a Series

Use a dash to set off a series of items.

> Rocky road, moose tracks, and chocolate-chip cookie dough—these are my favorite flavors.
>
> Neapolitan ice cream—chocolate, strawberry, and vanilla—is my sister's favorite.

► With Nonessential Elements

Use a dash to set off explanations, examples, and definitions, especially when these elements already include commas.

> Ice milk—which, as you might guess, is made of milk instead of cream—provides a light alternative.

► To Show Interrupted Speech

Use a dash to show that a speaker has been interrupted or has started and stopped while speaking.

> "Could you help me crank this—"
>
> "I've got to get more salt before—"
>
> "It'll freeze up if you don't—just give me a hand, please."

Insight In most academic writing, use dashes sparingly. If they are overused, they lose their effect.

Practice ▷ Add dashes where needed in the following sentences.

1. Which dessert would you prefer brownies, apple pie, or ice cream?

2. I love the triple brownie surprise a brownie with vanilla and chocolate ice cream covered in hot fudge.

3. Ice cream it's what's for dinner.

4. "Could I have a taste of " "You want to try some of " "I want to try um could you just choose?"

5. Bananas, ice cream, peanuts, and fudge these are the ingredients of a banana-split sundae.

6. Making ice cream at home takes a long time you'll love it, though!

7. An electric ice-cream maker which replaced arm power with a cranking motor makes the job easier but less fun.

8. Nothing tastes better than the first taste of freshly made ice cream nothing except perhaps the next taste.

9. Anyone who eats ice cream too quickly risks real pain brain-freeze.

10. A danger of ice cream I'll take the chance every time.

Practice ▷ Write your own sentence, correctly using dashes for each of the situations indicated below:

1. For emphasis:

   _____

2. To set off a series:

   _____

3. With nonessential elements:

   _____

dash
long horizontal line that separates words, creating emphasis

🌎 Real-World Application

Practice ▶ The following letter sounds too informal because of the contractions. Cross out any contractions you find and use the words the contractions stand for instead. Also correct any apostrophe errors.

Hanford Building
Supply Company, Inc.

June 1, 2015

Mr. Robert Burnside, Controller
Circuit Electronics Company
4900 Gorham Road
Mountain View, CA 94040-1093

Dear Mr. Burnside:

This letter's a reminder that your account's past due (presently 60 days).

As of today, we haven't yet received your payment of $1,806.00, originally due March 31. I've enclosed the March 1 invoice. It's for the materials that you ordered January 10 and that we shipped January 28.

You've been a valued customer, Mr. Burnside, and we appreciate your business'. We've enclosed a postage-paid envelope for your convenience.

If there's a problem, please call (567-555-1908, ext. 227) or email me (marta@hanford.com). As alway's, we look forward to serving you.

Sincerely,

Marta Ramones

Marta Ramones

Billing Department

Practice ▶ In the following email message, insert semicolons, colons, hyphens, and dashes where necessary.

To: Felton Engineering Staff

Subject: Ideas for Open House Displays

Hello, all:

September 1 that's the big open house when we will celebrate our brand new location. To help visitors understand what Felton Engineering does, I plan to set up these displays heater designs, product applications, and aerospace technology.

Please help me by doing the following look for blueprints, sketches, small models, and prototypes that illustrate what we do identify items that would interest visitors and set them aside as you pack.

Then please respond to this email with this information your name, the name of the product, the product number, and the type of display materials that you have.

Please respond no later than August 22. I will handle the other arrangements picking up your materials, setting up the displays, and returning the materials to you after the open house. Innovation it's what drives Felton Engineering!

Thanks,

Jilliane Seaforth

Practice In the following sentences, insert apostrophes, semicolons, colons, hyphens, and dashes where necessary.

1. Astronomy the study of stars, objects, and matter outside Earths atmosphere fascinated stargazers long ago.

2. Early astronomers learned the movements of the sun, moon, and stars however, they didnt really understand why these things happened.

3. Aristarchus, a Greek astronomer, presented these ideas the earth is round, it rotates on its axis, and it revolves around the sun.

4. Most people did not believe Aristarchus in fact, Ptolemy later described the universe as an earth centered rather than a sun centered system.

5. Ptolemys idea was considered "fact" for nearly 1,400 years then Copernicus came along.

6. Earth rotates on its axis and revolves around the sun this was the controversial "new" theory advanced by Copernicus.

7. The theory still wasnt widely accepted Johannes Kepler, however, believed it.

8. Kepler also discovered three laws of movement that explain the following facts about planets orbit shape, speed, and distance from the sun.

9. Around this same time, Galileo using his newly improved telescope became the first man to see the moons mountains, Saturns rings, and Jupiters moons.

10. Today, the Hale Telescope is one of the worlds largest reflecting telescopes.

11. With its 200 inch reflector, the Hale has helped astronomers discover and explain quasars.

12. Black holes, dark matter, super-Earths, Goldilocks planets these are just a few of stargazers interests today.

PART 8:

Readings
for Writers

Part 8: Readings for Writers

Elena Elisseeva, 2014 / Used under license from Shutterstock.com

"We read to know we're not alone."
— William Nicholson

Chapter

27

Anthology

There are many reasons to read, but author William Nicholson's quote speaks directly to the connection between a reader and writer: "We read to know we're not alone." Reading helps us connect with other people and relate our own struggles and difficulties to those of others.

Through this shared experience, reading can become an instrument for comfort and companionship. It can also unlock new ideas and viewpoints, expanding what we know and what we can achieve.

The readings in this chapter will introduce you to new ideas and ways of thinking. The topics range from technology to politics to dealing with death. It is our hope that you apply the strategies you've learned throughout *Fusion* to the anthology and that those strategies will help you connect to the ideas and people presented in the readings.

Readings

What do you think?

Have you ever read something that made you feel a connection to the author? What was the connection? And how did it make you feel?

This article explains a unique urban planning concept happening in Chicago: a street where pedestrians, bikers, and cars co-exist without traditional boundaries.

About the Author

Jessica Leber is an assistant editor for the "Co.Exist" branch of *Fast Company*, a popular magazine and Web site focusing on innovation, business, and design. Leber has also written for *MIT Technology Review* and ClimateWire. Before her writing career, she worked as a geologist at contaminated waste sites.

Prereading

1. What do the title, first two paragraphs, and first lines of other paragraphs tell you about the essay?
2. What do you think is the purpose of this selection?
3. Who might be the intended audience?

On a New Shared Street in Chicago, There Are No Sidewalks, No Lights, and Almost No Signs

1   Imagine a street with no sidewalks, no crosswalks, no curbs, no lane markings—basically no real distinctions between pedestrians, cyclists, and drivers at all. At first glance, that might seem like an extraordinarily unsafe street. But the city of Chicago is betting on its success as it redesigns a four-block stretch of its uptown.

2   *The New York Times* editorial board recently called the concept of shared streets a "radical experiment" for the city of Chicago, which plans to start construction on its first one on Argyle Street in early 2015. Yet the philosophy behind them—that by removing common street control features, street users will actually act less **recklessly** and negotiate space through eye-contact—is actually

not all that new. Shared streets have been built and shown to be effective in reducing accidents in London already. In the U.S., shared streets exist in Seattle, Washington and Buffalo, New York.

The Chicago project came about as the city was looking to implement   3
a normal street improvement project for Argyle Street, an active block with businesses and restaurants in a diverse neighborhood where many Vietnamese immigrants settled in the 1970s. The street had also shut down for the city's first night market for the last two summers, and Alderman Harry Osterman, whose ward includes the area, says officials wanted to continue spurring the revitalization of the area. The lakefront bicycle path is only two blocks away.

There will be stop signs, so as not to descend too far into chaos.

After researching street designs all around the world, they were taken   4
with the shared streets idea. "It's a very **innovative** concept that we're trying," Osterman says. "We have spent the last two years really trying to build support from the community. . . . One of the best parts of it is that it's been a bottom-up approach to designing a street."

The $3.5 million street renovation will feature a design with no curbs or   5
lanes, and minimal signage, though there will be stop signs, so as not to descend too far into chaos. Different colors and pavers will indicate where the sidewalk would normally end and where the street begins; the speed limit will be 15 miles per hour. Overall, the goal is to change the mood of the street: "Psychologically for drivers, they will know that they can't just shoot from stop sign to stop sign."

Osterman hopes that as a result of the   6
improvement project, more visitors will come to businesses in the area, and that the open space will make it easier to encourage more sidewalk cafes and temporary events. The city is now nudging existing business to spruce up their **facades**.

Once the new Argyle Street is open, the city will be paying close attention to *7* make sure that everyone is behaving safely.

With no real curbs, pedestrians may find it easier to move about. "We're *8* not going to encourage jaywalking, but that may happen," says Osterman. If the project is a success, he expects the city will consider the idea elsewhere in Chicago.

---

recklessly
doing something with a careless disregard for the consequences

innovative
creative; inspired by new ideas

facades
the sides of buildings facing the public

Summarizing

Write a summary of "On a New Shared Street in Chicago, There Are No Sidewalks, No Lights, and Almost No Signs."

Reflecting

- What is the main idea of the essay? Where does it appear in the essay?
- How is the essay organized—chronologically, logically, or spatially?
- What type of voice does the author use—personal or academic? What words, phrases, or ideas in the text lead you to this answer?
- Why does the city of Chicago think this type of street will be successful?
- What questions do you still have about the topic?

Critical Thinking

- What potential problems could occur with the type of street described the in the essay?
- As a driver, how would you navigate such a street? How about as a pedestrian?
- Would you like this type of street to become popular in the city you live in? Why or why not?
- If you were writing the story, what other questions would you ask Harry Osterman, the alderman whose ward includes this new street innovation?

Wallenrock, 2014 / Used under license from Shutterstock.com

In this opinion column from the *San Francisco Chronicle*, columnist Debra J. Saunders defends a thoughtful position on a controversial subject.

Prereading

1. What do the title, first paragraph, and first lines of other paragraphs tell you about the selection?
2. What might be the purpose of this essay?
3. Who might be the intended audience?
4. What are your initial feelings about the topic?

Death on Demand Is Not Death with Dignity

I'd like to think that if I got the bad news that Brittany Maynard received— **terminal** cancer with a prognosis of less than six months left to live—I'd be like her. I'd like to be **stoic** and brave. I'd like to take charge of the rest of my cruelly abbreviated life. If I were facing death at age 29, I would want to find meaning in an end come too soon.

Maynard has done just that. She moved from the East Bay to Oregon, where **assisted suicide** is legal. She has become the face of Compassion & Choices, which wants to legalize assisted suicide in California. "It's crazy to me that other patients suffering with terminal illness don't have the same choice and may not have the same flexibility to pick up and move with their family," she told the *Chronicle*.

I love the spirit, but there is a huge flaw in Maynard's reasoning. She says she wants her story to help change California law so that no one else has to "move to another state to not die horribly." Close to 40,000 Americans kill themselves every year; they make the same choice Maynard is making, although most won't have the media attention that is being lavished on the vibrant and **telegenic** UC Berkeley graduate. Suicide is the 10th leading cause of death in this country.

Perhaps Maynard sees this choice as a way of beating back at death, to not allow the beast to own every turn of an end approaching far too soon. I respect that. But she is wrong to call it, as advocates do, "death with dignity." The very phrase suggests that people who do not choose suicide lack dignity.

"I considered passing away in **hospice** care at my San Francisco Bay Area home," Maynard wrote for CNN. "But even with **palliative** medication, I could develop potentially morphine-resistant pain and suffer personality changes and verbal, **cognitive** and motor loss of virtually any kind." Note she writes things "could" go wrong, which means they could work, too.

Palliative care specialist Dr. B.J. Miller of the Zen Hospice Project told me that he didn't know the particulars of Maynard's case. "Globally speaking, people do develop intolerance to morphine, and **delirium** is very common at the end of life" for patients with brain cancer, he noted, but "it's also true that much of that is treatable." Palliative sedation cannot reverse cancer, but it can provide relief.

Marilyn Golden of the Disability Rights Education & Defense Fund in Berkeley is concerned that Maynard's story **obscures** the larger picture. "For every individual with a happy family who's not at risk for abuse, there are many other individuals who may be **subtly** steered toward assisted suicide by their insurance company or pressured by their family." For every Brittany Maynard, there are others who face serious illnesses—aging, maybe—without Maynard's extraordinary support system. Golden worries lest "profit-driven managed health care" subtly steer the sick in the direction of—what's the word?—dignity.

I love the spirit, but there is a huge flaw in Maynard's reasoning. She says she wants her story to help change California law so that no one else has to "move to another state to not die horribly."

Miller wonders if in the new world of choice, there still will be a place for "people who are sick and beyond their **utilitarian** function."

4

5

6

7

8

Brittany Maynard is a beautiful woman. That's probably why you've seen   9
her so much on CNN. She represents the fantasy of how we all want to be
in the end—wanted, ready and resourceful. But before you sign on to her remedy,
ask yourself what happens to sick people who don't have her youthful spirit.

terminal
incurable

stoic
balanced and unemotional

assisted suicide
process by which terminal, or helplessly ill, patients
take lethal drugs to end their life, usually with the
assistance of a physician

telegenic
the energetic manner of a television personality

palliative
pain and stress management usually through
prescribed drugs

hospice
end-of-life treatment home or facility

cognitive
mental

delirium
sudden mental illness

obscures
distracts from

subtly
indirectly, without notice

utilitarian
normal or regular

Summarizing

Write a summary of "Death on Demand Is Not Death with Dignity."

Reflecting

- What form of writing is displayed in this piece—narrative, expository, or argumentative?
- What is the author's main claim?
- What evidence does the author use to support her claim?
- What counterclaims does she address? How does she address them?
- How would you describe the author's voice? Is it appropriate for the subject?
- Has your feeling about the topic changed after reading the column?

Critical Thinking

- Is Saunders' position on assisted suicide convincing? Why or why not?
- What is your own position on the topic?
- Do you think it was appropriate for Saunders to take a strong stance on assisted suicide?

Gil C, 2014 / Used under license from Shutterstock.com

This selection from *American Government and Politics Today* discusses the effect that social media is having on our political system.

About the Authors

Steffen W. Schmidt is a professor of political science at Iowa State University. He has published 12 books and more than 122 journal articles. He also has a political talk show on WOI Public Radio. **Mack C. Shelley** is a professor of political science at Iowa State University. He has served as co-editor of *Policy Studies Journal* and has written numerous publications on public policy. **Barbara A. Bardes** is a professor *emerita* (retired but retaining her professional title) of political science. **Lynne E. Ford** is a professor of political science and associate provost for curriculum and academic administration at the College of Charleston. She has authored many publications on women and politics.

Prereading questions

1. What it the topic of the selection? (Check the title and first paragraph.)
2. What do you already know about the topic?
3. What do you expect to learn?

YouTube, Jon Stewart, and Stephen Colbert: Changing Politics for the Better?

"Did you watch *Colbert* last night? Have you seen the *KONY 2012* video? My friend just tweeted me the link." If this sounds familiar, you're in good company. "Viral videos" and social networking have become a part of daily life. Politicians and political campaigns are scrambling to figure out how best to take advantage of new social media.

YouTube, a video share site, has been around since 2005. Although many of the videos feature pets, children, and stunts gone wrong, some have tremendous political impact. One such example is *KONY 2012*, posted by the nonprofit group

Invisible Children on March 5, 2012. In five days, the video had 100 million views on YouTube. The film's purpose was to bring global public attention to **indicted** but fugitive Ugandan war criminal Joseph Kony in order to have him arrested by December 2012. Kony and his rebel group Lord's Resistance Army (LRA) are responsible for brutal guerilla warfare in Uganda, the Democratic Republic of the Congo and South Sudan. . . . [Invisible Children continues its efforts today to bring Kony to justice.]

In 2010 Google launched a campaign toolkit designed to help candidates use YouTube and other Google products effectively. Although campaigns work hard to keep candidates from making memorable **gaffes**, viral videos and instant twitter feeds mean missteps live longer, with greater consequences. During the primary campaign in 2008, a remark that Barack Obama made about rural, white gun owners at a private fundraising dinner made it to the Internet within hours. Hillary Clinton used that quote to bolster a win in the Pennsylvania primary. **3**

In 2011, candidate Herman Cain gave a taped interview to the *Milwaukee Journal Sentinel* in which he appeared confused about the U.S. position on Libya, saying, "I've got all this stuff twirling around in my head." Candidate Rick Perry's debate performances provided plenty of material for late-night comedians, including the night he promised to eliminate three cabinet-level agencies but could only name two of the three. It used to be that only a few people heard or saw such mistakes, but today YouTube, Twitter, and Facebook mean that millions share in the moment. **4**

Sometimes comedians use their craft for a more serious political purpose. In 2011, Stephen Colbert and Jon Stewart teamed up to illustrate the **myriad** of **loopholes** in American election laws through performance art. Colbert created "Americans for a Better America Tomorrow, Tomorrow," a **super PAC**, and began raising political money. In the January 2012 filing with the Federal Election Commission, Colbert's PAC had raised more than $1 million. In January 2012, Colbert announced that he was forming "an exploratory committee to lay the groundwork for my possible candidacy for president of the United States of America of South Carolina," requiring him to transfer control of his super PAC. **5**

He did so—to Jon Stewart. Steward promptly renamed the PAC "The definitely not coordinating with Stephen Colbert Super PAC." Colbert was too late to get on the ballot in South Carolina's February Republican primary, so he mounted the "Rock Me Like a Herman Cain" campaign, in which he urged South Carolina voters to cast a vote for Cain as a **proxy** for Colbert and then quickly ended his campaign.

6

Does this political comedy have a purpose? Yes! According to a Rasmussen survey, 30 percent of young people aged 18 to 29 say programs like Stewart's and Colbert's that feature news reports with a comic twist are replacing traditional news outlets. A university researcher found that *The Daily Show* turned the attention of **apolitical** viewers to political issues like the war in Afghanistan and the presidential campaign. The most apolitical viewers were 13 percent more likely to attend to the issue very closely than were similarly inattentive nonviewers. Candidates at all levels will be watching the influence of new media closely in the years to come.

7

From Schmidt/Shelley/Bardes/Ford, *American Government and Politics Today*, 2013-2014 Edition, 16E. © 2014 Cengage Learning.

---

indicted
accused, charged

gaffes
clumsy social errors

myriad
many, a vast number

loopholes
ways to avoid laws

super PAC
a committee allowed to raise unlimited amounts of money

proxy
a person given the power to do something for someone else

apolitical
not interested in politics

Summarizing

Write a summary of "YouTube, Jon Stewart, and Stephen Colbert: Changing Politics for the Better?"

Reflecting

- What is the main idea of the essay?
- What examples support the main idea? (Name two.)
- How are the examples arranged—spatially, chronologically, or logically?
- What is one statistic that supports the main idea?

Critical Thinking

- How does social media make life more challenging for politicians?
- Are you one of the "apolitical viewers" described in the closing? Why or why not?
- Should politics be a subject of comedy?

Don Pablo, 2014 / Used under license from Shutterstock.com

The following selection from an environmental science textbook entitled *Living in the Environment* reports on the negative aspects of drinking bottled water.

About the Authors

G. Tyler Miller, Jr., has a PhD from the University of Virginia and has written 59 textbooks on environmental science. Before devoting his time to writing, he taught for 20 years and created one of the first environmental programs in the United States. **Scott E. Spoolman** is a textbook writer and editor and has worked with Miller since 2003. He holds a master's degree in science journalism from the University of Minnesota and is the author of many articles on science, engineering, business, and politics.

Prereading

1. What is the topic of this selection?
2. What do you already know about the topic?
3. What do you expect to learn?

Is Bottled Water a Good Option?

Despite some problems, experts say the United States has some of the world's cleanest drinking water. Municipal water systems in the United States are required to test their water regularly for a number of pollutants and to make the results available to citizens. *1*

Yet about half of all Americans worry about getting sick from tap water contaminants and many drink high-priced bottled water or install expensive purification systems. Americans are the world's largest consumers of bottled water, followed by Mexico, China, and Brazil. In 2009, Americans spent more than $11 billion to buy billions of plastic bottles filled with water each year, and they drink more bottled water than they do beer, coffee, or milk. That is enough *2* to meet the annual drinking needs of the roughly 1 billion people in the world who routinely lack access to safe and clean drinking water.

Studies by the **NRDC** and water expert Peter Gleick reveal that in the United States, a bottle of water costs between 240 and 10,000 times as much as the same volume of tap water and uses 100 to 2,000 times more energy to produce from start to finish. In 2008, Gleick estimated that more than 40% of the expensive bottled water that Americans drink is really just bottled tap water. And a four-year study by the NRDC found bacteria and synthetic organic chemicals in one-third of the bottles tested.   **3**

Use of bottled water also causes environmental problems, according to a 2007 study by the Worldwatch Institute and a 2008 study by water experts Peter Gleick and Heather Cooley. Every second, about 1,500 plastic water bottles are thrown away. Each year, the number of water bottles thrown away, if lined up end-to-end, would circle the earth's equator eight times. Water bottles are made up of recyclable plastic, but in the United States, only about 14% of these bottles get recycled. The rest end up in landfills or in lakes and in the ocean.   **4**

Manufacturing the bottles and transporting them throughout the world uses huge amounts of energy, primarily from oil and coal. The consumer and environmental group Food & Water Watch estimates that each year, more than 17 million barrels of oil are used to produce the plastic water bottles sold in the United States. This is enough to fuel about 1 million cars a year. Toxic gases and liquids are released during the manufacture of plastic water bottles and greenhouse gases and other air pollutants are **emitted** by the fossil fuels burned to make them and to deliver bottled water to suppliers.   **5**

Because of these harmful environmental impacts and the high cost of bottled water, there is a growing *back-to-tap* movement based on **boycotting** bottled water. Its motto is *"Think globally, drink locally."* From San Francisco to New York to Paris, city governments, restaurants, schools, religious groups, and many consumers are refusing to buy bottled water as this trend picks up steam. Individuals are also refilling   **6** portable bottles with tap water and using simple filters to improve the taste and color of water were necessary.

Health officials suggest that before drinking expensive bottled water or buying costly home water purifiers, consumers have their water tested by local health departments or private labs (but not by companies trying to sell water purification equipment). Independent experts contend that unless tests show otherwise, for most U.S. urban and suburban residents served by large municipal drinking water systems, home water treatment systems are not worth their cost, and drinking expensive and environmentally harmful bottled water is unnecessary.

From Miller, *Living in the Environment*, 17E. © 2012 Cengage Learning.

---

municipal
related to a city or local government

contaminants
unclean parts

NRDC
National Resources Defense Council, works for a safe and clean environment

emitted
sent forth

boycotting
the act of stopping use

Summarizing

Write a summary of "Is Bottled Water a Good Option?"

Reflecting

- What is the main idea of the selection?
- What type of support is used throughout in the selection—*definitions, statistics, reflections*? (Circle one.)
- Do the supporting details seem reliable? Explain.
- What questions, if any, do you still have about the topic?

Critical Thinking

- Which study in the report surprises you the most? Why?
- Why has bottled water become such a big business?
- How has this report supported or changed your thinking about bottled water?

In this expository essay, Katie Moore describes the characteristics of Generation Z—the generational name given to people currently 18 years old and younger.

About the Author

Katie Moore is an editorial intern for the *Utne Reader*, a quarterly publication focusing on up and coming writers.

Prereading

1. What do the title and first few paragraphs tell you about this selection?
2. What might be the intended purpose of this essay?
3. What, if anything, do you already know about this topic?
4. What do you expect to learn in your reading?

The End of the Generational Alphabet

Generation Z possesses **unprecedented attributes**.   *1*

For Generation Z-ers, growing up in a post-9/11 world with social media at   *2* their fingertips has been the norm. And undoubtedly, they will inherit a world **wrought** with challenges, from increasing income inequality to the environment. But the group, defined loosely by those who are 18 and under (making up about a quarter of the population in North America), shows great promise. A study undertaken by Sparks & Honey, an advertising group, found that the lifestyle Generation Z is looking for differs from their predecessors in Generation Y. Not only do more of them want jobs that have a social impact, but they are also more tolerant of diversity and varying gender roles.

However, the digital influence on the so-called "screenagers" or first-   *3* generation "digital natives" is a hotly contested **realm**. **Crowdsourcing** and open-access education have allowed them to create opportunities and be exposed to experiences not otherwise available. A number of teenagers have already made inroads in innovative technology and medicine. Take Ann Makosinki, who invented a flashlight that obtains its power via heat from the human hand, or Angela Zhang, who came up with an MRI scanning protocol that detects tumors more accurately.

But researchers worry about the costs of connectivity. There's been an uptick   *4* in kids with spatial skills problems purportedly due to dependence on digital devices—when Google maps gives directions on a screen, translating that to the real world can become a befuddling experience. Additionally, technology presents a divide between adults and children, which may change the way they communicate (and may cause disagreements between the generations). And while the top two-thirds of young adults may fare better than previous generations in terms of things like education, the bottom third may not be as lucky. Other issues include shrinking attention spans, online bullying, and obesity. However, making generalizations about a generation that's still growing up should be taken with a grain of salt. Robert Barnard, CEO of Decode, a company that collects data on youth, said at times, "You're really looking at the way their parents are operating, not who they are."

Moore, Katie, "The End of the Generational Alphabet." Originally appeared in *Utne Reader* July 31, 2014. Reprinted by permission of the *Utne Reader*. Permission conveyed through the Copyright Clearance Center.

unprecedented	**wrought**	**crowdsourcing**	**protocol**
never before known	shaped by	gaining input from many people	system
attributes	**realm**		**purportedly**
qualities	area		claimed to be

Summarizing
Write a summary of "The End of the Generational Alphabet."

Reflecting
- What is the main idea of the selection?
- Why do you think Generation Z-ers are nicknamed "screenagers"?
- What evidence does the writer use to support her ideas?

Critical Thinking
- Is it fair to make generalizations about whole generations of people? Why or why not?
- What will have a greater influence on Generation Z—technology or parenting?

meirion matthias, 2014 / Used under license from Shutterstock.com

In this essay, which first appeared on National Public Radio's food-themed blog, *The Salt*, Maria Godoy explores the dietary recovery habits of ancient gladiators.

About the Author

Maria Godoy is a blogger, correspondent, and editor for National Public Radio (NPR). She hosts NPR's award-winning food blog, *The Salt*. She also covers news, health, and science topics for NPR.

Prereading

1. What do the title, first paragraph, and first lines of other paragraphs tell you about this selection?
2. What are your first thoughts about the author's purpose and audience?
3. What are your initial feelings about the topic?

Gladiator Gatorade? Ancient Athletes Had a Recovery Drink, Too

So it's A.D. 150, and you've just had a long day at the gym (or *ludus*), thrusting and **parrying** with your fellow Roman gladiators. What do you reach for to **replenish** your sapped strength? A post-workout recovery drink, of course. 1

Modern-day athletes often nurse their muscles with supplement shakes or chocolate milk after a workout. Similarly, gladiators, the sports stars of the Roman Empire, may have guzzled a drink made from the ashes of charred plants—a rich source of calcium, which is essential for building bones, researchers report this month in the journal *PLOS One*.

"Plant ashes were evidently consumed to fortify the body after physical exertion, and to promote better bone healing," Fabian Kanz, a **forensic** 2 anthropologist at the Medical University of Vienna who led the research, said in a statement. "Things were similar then to what we do today."

Evidence for this ancient dietary supplement comes from a second-century cemetery for gladiators in what was once the great Roman city of Ephesus, in modern-day Turkey. Kanz and his colleagues have been studying the remains buried there to unravel how these athletes lived. To figure out what they ate, the researchers examined the remains of 22 gladiators using stable carbon and nitrogen isotope ratio analysis.

3

Carbon can tell us about the plants these people ate, while nitrogen offers hints of their animal protein consumption. The gladiators were eating a pretty varied diet, the analysis showed. Some went heavier on the grains and greens; some ate more meat.

4

When the same tests were run on the remains of 31 regular folks from that era and region, they found the same sorts of variation. In other words, gladiators seemed to be eating the same way as everyone else.

5

But the researchers also decided to look at the trace elements of strontium and calcium in those old bones. And that's where a huge difference jumped out. Compared with the regular Joes, the gladiators had a much larger ratio of strontium to calcium.

6

"This is strong evidence that the gladiators were consuming something high in calcium to replenish their calcium stores that other people weren't and that didn't show up in the isotopes," says Kristina Killgrove, a biological anthropologist at the University of West Florida who studies imperial Rome through ancient bones.

7

> "The researchers wondered: If the gladiators weren't eating more meat than their contemporaries, then where was this calcium boost coming from?"

The researchers wondered: If the gladiators weren't eating more meat than their contemporaries, then where was this calcium boost coming from? A nearly 2,000-year-old encyclopedia offered a tantalizing clue.

8

In his *Naturalis Historia*, published in the first century, Pliny the Elder wrote: "Your hearth should be your medicine chest. Drink lye made from its ashes, and

9

"Ancient texts don't always agree on the finer points of gladiator diets."

you will be cured. One can see how gladiators after a combat are helped by drinking this."

Using ash in food and medicine wasn't limited to the Romans. The **Hopis** used ash from burned plant leaves and pea pods to prepare blue cornmeal foods like *piki* bread and *bivilviki* dumplings. The ash provided essential elements like calcium, manganese, copper and iron.   10

It's a neat bit of detective work, and it ties in nicely with historical accounts, Killgrove says, but the case isn't closed.   11

"It's entirely possible gladiators were drinking ash drink," she says, "but they haven't proven it." The problem? Dairy doesn't show up in isotopes, so the gladiators could have been chowing down on more cheese and yogurt than the rest of the population.   12

One other thing to note: Ancient texts don't always agree on the finer points of gladiator diets. For instance, Pliny credited the warriors' diet—a bean and barley mash was standard fare—for their endurance and toughness in battle. But Galen, a famous second-century physician who also did a stint as a gladiator doc, complained that this diet made the men soft and flabby.   13

The thinking is that gladiators loaded up on carbs to create a layer of fat to protect them from cuts and slashes in the arena, says Barry Strauss, a classics scholar at Cornell University and author of *The Spartacus War*, about the most famous gladiator of them all.   14

"Call it a spare tire, if you will," he says.   15

Hmm, that's a far cry from the rippling muscles Russell Crowe sported in the 2000 film *Gladiator*. So were these ancient warriors more hunky or chunky?   16

"By and large, we are seeing them with their armor on," Strauss says. "They're 17 not showing their abs, so I don't think we know. We do know they were sex symbols—there's a lot written about noble women hanging out with gladiators."

parrying
using a weapon, such as a sword, to avert or fight off

replenish
refuel or make complete

forensic anthropologist
a person who uses scientific techniques to draw conclusions from deceased bodies

isotope ratio analysis
method for discovering the abundance of isotopes (chemical properties) in a given sample

strontium
element whose characteristics strongly resemble calcium

contemporaries
people living at the same time

Hopis
Native American tribe who resided in Arizona

Summarizing

Write a summary of "Gladiator Gatorade? Ancient Athletes Had a Recovery Drink, Too."

Reflecting

- What is the main idea of the essay? What paragraph does it appear in?
- What pattern of organization is employed—chronological, spatial, or logical?
- What types of evidence does the author use to support the main idea?
- How do history, science, and modern technology intersect in this essay?

Critical Thinking

- Based on the evidence outlined in the reading, how does the diet of ancient gladiators compare to the diet of modern-day athletes?
- Writer A. Whitney Brown said this of history: "The past actually happened, but history is only what someone wrote down." How does this idea relate to the reading?
- What value, if any, is there in exploring the habits of ancient people? Explain your answer.
- In paragraph 16, the author asks, "So were these ancient warriors more hunky or chunky?" What leads her to ask this question?

This selection discusses the social and political climate in South Africa before Nelson Mandela made his inaugural speech as president of South Africa. Part of the transcript of this famous speech is also included.

About the Authors

Philip J. Adler taught courses in world history for nearly 30 years. He has published widely in the historical journals of this country and German-speaking Europe. **Randall L. Pouwels** has published widely. His book *Horn and Crescent: Cultural Change and Traditional Islam on the East African Coast, 800-1900* has become a standard work on African history.

Prereading

1. Who or what is the topic of this selection?
2. What do you already know about the topic?
3. What would you like to learn?

Inaugural Address by Nelson Mandela

1   The rise of Nelson Mandela to the presidency of the Republic of South Africa must be one of the more amazing events of recent African history. Imprisoned for 25 years as a **subversive** by the white South African government, Mandela remained the **rallying point** for all those who believed that the day of **apartheid** must finally pass.

2   Raised the son and heir of a thoroughly traditional African chief, Mandela broke with his family and culture to gain a legal education in the city. As a 36-year-old black lawyer, he entered the world of African politics and rapidly rose to **prominence** before his career was cut off by imprisonment.

3   For his mainly black followers in the African National Congress, Mandela's convincing majority in the first **universal balloting** ever permitted in South Africa

was an event of great elation and a satisfying end to an "extraordinary human disaster." But the white and **Coloured** minorities were naturally nervous about what the future might hold. Would Mandela allow his more-passionate black **adherents** to take revenge for their long exclusion from power and from human dignity? Would he remember the humiliation he had suffered both before and during his long imprisonment at the hands of the dominant **Afrikaner** whites? Or would he attempt to calm the waters stirred by a sometimes-bloody electoral campaign and look into the future rather that at the past? His inaugural address of May 10, 1994, was eagerly awaited.

Today, all of us by our presence here . . . **confer** glory and hope to newborn liberty. Out of the experience of an extraordinary human disaster which lasted too long must be born a society of which all humanity will be proud.

Instinia, 2014 / Used under license from Shutterstock.com

4

Our daily deeds as South Africans must **5** produce an actual South African reality that will reinforce humanity's belief in justice, strengthen its confidence in nobility of the human soul, and sustain all our hopes for a glorious life for all.

The time for the healing of the wounds **6** has come. The moment to bridge the **chasms** that divide us has come. The time to build is upon us. . . .

We have triumphed in the effort to implant hope in the breasts of the **7** millions of our people. We enter into a covenant that we shall build the society in which all South Africans, both black and white, will be able to walk tall, without any fear in their hearts, assured of their inalienable right to human dignity—a rainbow nation at peace with itself and the world. . . .

We dedicate this day to all the heroes and heroines in this country and **8** the rest of the world who sacrificed in so many ways and surrendered their lives so that we could be free. Their dreams have become reality. Freedom is their reward. We understand . . . that there is no easy road to freedom.

We know it well that none of us acting alone can achieve success. We must therefore act together as a united people, for national **reconciliation**, for nation building, for the birth of a new world.

Let there be justice for all. Let there be peace for all. Let there be work, bread, water, and salt for all. Let each know that for each the body, the mind, and the soul have been freed to fulfill themselves. . . . *9*

Let freedom **reign**! God bless Africa! *10*

From Adler/Pouwels, *World Civilizations*, 6E. © 2012 Cengage Learning.

---

inaugural
part of a ceremony for a person beginning an important job

subversive
person considered a threat

rallying point
focus

apartheid
a system in which blacks and people from other racial groups did not have the same rights as whites

prominence
a high position

universal balloting
voting by all

Coloured
label for people of mixed ethnic origin

adherents
followers

Afrikaner
South Africans of Dutch descent, once in complete political power

confer
offer

chasms
gaps, differences

covenant
promise

inalienable
something that is ours forever

reconciliation
the process of coming together

reign
rule

Summarizing

Write a summary of "Inaugural Address by Nelson Mandela."

Reflecting

- What do you learn about Nelson Mandela in the first part? (Name two things.)
- Why were the white and Coloured minorities nervous about Mandela's speech?
- What is Mandela's main message in his speech?

Critical Thinking

- Would you have understood Mandela if he had delivered an angry speech? Explain.
- Why do you think he refrained from doing this?
- What does Mandela mean when he refers to South Africa as a "rainbow nation"?

In this problem-solution essay, Marcelo Glesier questions whether our thirst to capture moments on camera is distracting us from experiencing life to its fullest. The essay originally appeared on *13.7: Cosmos & Culture*, a science and culture blog hosted at NPR.org.

About the Author

Marcelo Gleiser is a physicist and astronomer who is currently professor of physics and astronomy at Dartmouth College. He is the author of many books, including *The Island of Knowledge: The Limits of Science and the Search for Meaning*. Along with his research on the physics of the early universe, Gleiser contributes to National Public Radio's *13.7: Cosmos & Culture*, a science and culture blog that he co-founded.

Prereading

1. What do the title and first few paragraphs tell you about this selection?
2. What is your initial position on the question posed in the title?
3. What questions about the topic would you like answered in your reading?

Should We Live Life, or Capture It?

A recent article in *The New York Times* explores the explosive wave of smartphone recordings of events, from the most meaningful to the most **trivial**.

Everyone is, or wants to be, the star of their own life, and the rage is on to capture every moment deemed meaningful. YouTube micro-stars have selfie videos that go viral within hours, like the recent one by journalist Scott Welsh who recorded from inside his JetBlue flight as oxygen masks came down due to a mechanical **malfunction**. If you are facing death, why not share your last moments with those you leave behind?

There is a side of it that makes sense; we all matter, our lives matter, and we want them to be seen, shared, appreciated. But there is another side that leads to a **disengagement** with the moment.

Are people forgetting to be present in the moment, scattering their focus by looking at life through a screen? Should you be living your life or living it for others to see it?

4

It is telling, however, that this all started before the cellphone revolution. Something happened between the private journal we kept locked in our drawer and the portable video camera. For example, in June 2001 I led a group of Dartmouth alumni on a cruise to see a total solar eclipse in Africa. On board were a crowd of "eclipse groupies," people who go around the world chasing eclipses. Once you see one you can understand why. A **total solar eclipse** is a deeply moving experience that awakens a **primal** connection with nature, linking us to something bigger and truly awesome about the world. It needs total commitment and focus of all senses. Yet, as totality approached, the ship's deck was a sea of cameras and tripods, as dozens of people prepared to photograph and videotape the four-minute-long event.

5

Instead of fully engaging with this most spectacular natural phenomenon, people chose to look at it from behind their cameras. I was shocked. There were professional photographers onboard and they were going to sell/give pictures away. But people wanted to take *their* pictures and videos anyway, even if they weren't going to be half as good. I went to two other eclipses, and it's always the same thing. No full personal engagement. The gadget is the eye through which they choose to see reality.

6

What cellphones plus social media have done is to make the **archiving** and the sharing of images amazingly easy and efficient. The reach is much wider and the gratification (how many "likes" a photo or video gets) is **quantitative**. Lives become a shared social event.

7

Now, there is a side of this that is fine, of course. We celebrate meaningful moments and want to share with those we care about. The problem starts when we stop fully participating in the moment because we have this urge to record it. Conan O'Brien, for one, complained that he can't even see people's faces when he performs anymore. "All I see is a sea of iPads," he said. Some celebrities are forbidding personal phones during their weddings. Nick Denton, head of Gawker, said to his guests:

8

"You can tend to your virtual presence—and your Twitter and Instagram followers—the next day."

We can extend this to giving talks using Powerpoint or Keynote, as I can attest from personal experience. As soon as there is an illuminated screen out there, eyes move that way and the speaker becomes a hollow voice. No direct engagement is then possible. That's why I tend to use these technologies only minimally, to show pictures and graphs or put up meaningful quotes.

9

Without trying to sound too nostalgic, there is nothing like eye-to-eye contact or the sharing of an experience through the real act of engaging in a conversation with friends and family. The gadgets are awesome, of course. But they should not define the way we live—only complement it.

10

Glesier, Marcelo. From NPR.org *13.7 Cosmos & Culture,* October 1, 2014. Reprinted by permission of the author.

---

trivial
meaningless

malfunction
failure to work properly

disengagement
to step away from or distract oneself

total solar eclipse
when the moon completely covers the sun's disk, observed as the moon passes between the sun and Earth

primal
basic

archiving
storing and saving

quantitative
able to be counted

nostalgic
wishing for the past

Summarizing

Write a summary of "Should We Live Life, or Capture It?"

Reflecting

- What problem does the author address in this essay?
- Does the author provide a solution? If so, where does he address it in the essay?
- What personal observation does the author offer to explain the problem?
- Does the author prove that disengagement is truly a problem? Why or why not?

Critical Thinking

- Are you ever guilty of the problem the author discusses in this essay? How so?
- How can you "live in the moment"?
- What other solutions to this issue are not addressed in the essay?

Andrew F. Kazmierski, 2014 / Used under license from Shutterstock.com

In this column, which appeared in *USA Today,* Drew Faust argues that the value of a college education extends beyond higher salaries.

About the Author

Drew Faust is the president of Harvard University as well as Lincoln Professor of History. She is the first woman to serve as Harvard's president, as well as being an award-winning author. Both *Time* and *Forbes* named her to their lists of most influential people.

Prereading

1. What do the title and first few paragraphs tell you about this essay?
2. How does Faust's professional background put her in a unique position to talk about the benefits of college?
3. What do you expect to learn from the essay?

College Helps Students Dream of More Than a Salary

From the earliest days of our country, we have seen education as the foundation for democracy and citizenship, for **social mobility** and national prosperity. Higher education opens minds and opens doors. Yet high school students and families are increasingly questioning its value. Is investing in a college or university education still worth it?   1

The short answer is "yes." There is no doubt that college pays off financially. A wide range of statistics shows the economic advantage of a four-year college education. Over a lifetime, students who graduate from college can expect to make about 60% more than those who do not, well over a million dollars more than they would otherwise. Completing college makes an even greater difference to the earning power of young women. A 25–34-year-old female with a bachelor's degree can expect to make 70% more than if she had only completed her high school diploma.   2

College graduates also tend to lead more active lives. They vote more often, volunteer more often and are more likely to own a home. They are healthier and less likely to smoke by a margin of 17 percentage points. They and their children are less likely to be obese, and their children are more likely to go to college. Education encourages people to engage as citizens and live healthier and longer lives—powerful reasons for earning a college degree.   *3*

But what about the benefits of college that are more difficult to measure? They are equally significant and add up to a lot of value over the course of a lifetime.   *4*

College takes students to places they've never been before. College is a passport to different places, different times, and different ways of thinking—from learning new languages to considering the **arc** of human history to diving deep into the building blocks of matter. It gives students a chance to understand themselves differently, seeing how their lives are both like and unlike those who inhabited other eras and other lands. For many of us, it is the best chance we will have to follow our curiosity—to take a course on art or literature or to explore life in another century or another culture.   *5*

> "College takes students places they've never been before."

College introduces students to people they've never met before. This is true both literally and figuratively. One of the most important ways in which students learn, at colleges and universities everywhere, is by interacting with people who are different from themselves both inside and outside of the classroom. I recall one student, an evangelical Christian from Virginia, who was admitted to Harvard but wasn't sure he would fit in at a school in the Northeast. When he attended the recruiting weekend for accepted students, he found himself part of a late-night discussion with other admitted students from around the world, debating the characteristics that define a genuine hero. Not everyone agreed, but the differences were what made the conversation exciting, and he realized how much he could learn at a place full of engaging people with a wide range of viewpoints.   *6*

College teaches students the virtue of slowing down. No one denies the value of speed, connectivity and the virtual world in an economy that thrives on all three. But "thinking" is a word that is too often forgotten, **trammeled** in our rush to communicate faster and left behind as our brains struggle to keep up with our devices. College teaches students to slow down, to convert information to insight and knowing to understanding. It **nurtures** critical engagement, enlightened   *7* skepticism, and an endless desire to self-educate, preparing students for a lifetime of considering information and growing in knowledge and in wisdom.

In these ways and in so many others, college helps students see themselves   8
differently, giving them the room and the license to imagine new possibilities. Yes, it opens opportunities reflected in earning and employment statistics. But, perhaps even more valuable, it opens minds and worlds in ways that defy measurement. I often ask students as they are approaching graduation how they are different from when they arrived at college. They say they know more. Sometimes, they say they found a passion they had never imagined—a field, a profession to which they intend to devote their lives. But what is most important, they often tell me, is that they have a new way of approaching the world, through the power of learning, analyzing, and changing to adapt to what they have come to understand. The value of higher education is embodied by people who dream bigger and achieve more, who create their own futures and shape their own destinies.

---

social mobility
moving up in society financially

nurtures
supports and teaches

embodied
represented, shown

arc
path

skepticism
doubt or unbelief

trammeled
hindered, restricted

defy
challenge, resist

Summarizing

Write a summary of "College Helps Students Dream of More Than a Salary."

Reflecting

- What is Faust's position on a college education?
- Faust identifies three benefits of college that are difficult to measure. What are they?
- In what paragraph does the author share a story or anecdote to prove a point?

Critical Thinking

- How convincing do you find Faust's argument? Explain your answer.
- Why does education "encourage people to engage as citizens and live healthier and longer lives"?
- What counterarguments could someone make to the points made in this essay?
- How does Faust's position as president of Harvard impact her argument? Does the writing seemed biased? Why or why not?

In this personal essay, Rheana Murray narrates an event that helps her grieve and remember her sister who committed suicide.

About the Author

Rheana Murray is a digital reporter for ABC News. Prior to working for ABC, Murray was the online lifestyle editor for the *New York Daily News*.

Prereading

1. What do the title and first few paragraphs tell you about this essay?
2. Turn the title into a question. Search for answers as you read.

Good Scars

The truth was that my little sister was dead. 1

My tattoo artist's name was Aaron, and his voice and eyes were kind, even 2
though skulls were painted on his neck and vines adorned with red roses climbed
up his arms, the ends hiding underneath the **frayed** sleeve of his t-shirt.

"I want 'Janis.' J-A-N-I-S." 3

I watched him copy the information from my driver's license onto a piece of 4
paper and write 'Janice' in the space next to a line that read 'type of tattoo.'

"No. It's J-A-N-I-S. Like Janis Joplin," I told him. I was terrified the memory 5
of my sister would be tarnished by the simple mistake of misspelling her name in
permanent black ink across my skin. He had to spell her name right.

The truth was that my little sister was dead. 6

She killed herself on her boyfriend's twenty-first birthday, after work on 7
a Tuesday night. . . . Maybe she was stressed from work. I can't explain it, but
I try. Branding myself with her name felt like the right thing to do; some sort
of justification that I still can't explain. There are a lot of things I can't explain.

Thankfully, Aaron didn't ask for any explanation.

So here I was, two months later, standing in an unfamiliar tattoo parlor   *8*
in Savannah, Georgia, feeling out of place but strangely comfortable. The
surrounding mirrors and giant black photo albums filled with artwork made me
feel like I was in a fun house. Clowns, Tinkerbelles, skeletons and hearts with
knives stabbed through their middles were everywhere. On the walls, in the
portfolios, on the tiled floor, on the skin of the three men watching me explain
what I wanted as a tattoo. I wasn't prepared.

"I just want a pretty font," I said. "Something kind of Roman, maybe."   *9*

The ends of Aaron's mouth curled upward, and I couldn't tell if his smile was   *10*
condescending or supportive. He passed me a book of fonts, and I saw that there
were millions. The pages didn't seem to end. There were countless ways to write
'Janis.' Was it ignorant, or even just rude, to ask him to decide? I worried that it
was a bad sign that I didn't really care what the letters looked like; just as long as
they were there. . . . He, and then we, decided on a small basic cursive type.

"It's more feminine," he said. Feminine would be fine.   *11*

I sat in a black chair that resembled the one I sit in at the dentist's office, and   *12*
Aaron washed his hands. He wiped my wrist with rubbing alcohol and shaved
invisible hairs with a disposable razor. I looked away while he began to carve into
the softest part of the inside of my wrist. The pain washed away some of my other
pain. These would be good scars, I thought.

Until that moment, I'd still been looking for my little sister, unable to swallow   *13*
her death. There was a funeral, a death certificate, and her cell phone had been
turned off, but I still have pictures, I know there's still a birth certificate, and she's
still number 6 in my speed dial. She wasn't really dead.

On the beach earlier that day, I tried too hard to make eye contact with the   *14*
seagulls that scrambled close to my towel, wondering if each bird was Janis. On
the way to the tattoo parlor, I slowed down when squirrels crossed the road in
front of my car, not wanting to run my sister over, and kill her again. On less sane
days, I looked behind doors and underneath beds, thinking she might be hiding,
and I pretended not to stare into the window of the restaurant she used to work at,
secretly wondering if she was inside, waiting tables.

At the tattoo parlor, though, I found her. Janis was alive again. She even 15 moved. I just had to wiggle my wrist a little, and I could see the letters of her name dancing. The ink on my wrist is more concrete than her ashes. If dust can gather more dust, that's all I imagined those ashes were doing, sitting in an ugly vase in my grandmother's house, two hundred miles away. Her physical remains were too far away from me, and they didn't even look like her. For all I know, they're not even her ashes. The truth is that they probably are, but truths, all of a sudden, were **abstract**.

The truth was that my little sister was dead. People tell me that one's real. 16

I won't wake up from this dream. Every day, I see pretty lines of cursive in 17 undying black ink, spelling my dead sister's name. I use my wrist a lot. I see my tattoo a lot. It once disturbed me when I couldn't find her flesh, see her face and know her body was intact. Now, Janis lives on my wrist. Her name is intact.

The tattoo doesn't hurt anymore. My wrist isn't tender. The scabs have peeled 18 away, and the scar is beautiful. Understanding and experiencing loss still hurts. I carry the pain as weight, inside a heavy heart that seems so hard to lift. It's like straining to pick up a suitcase that someone's stuffed too many bulky sweaters into, making the sides bulge out. But when my heart is the heaviest and the pain is overwhelming, the tattoo makes the suitcase a little lighter. Then, the truth hurts less.

---

frayed
loose and unraveled at the edges

condescending
acting superior

abstract
apart from reality

Summarizing
Write a summary of "Good Scars."

Reflecting
- What is the author's purpose, and who might be her intended audience?
- What descriptive details stand out in the essay? Name two.
- What emotions does the writer display?

Critical Thinking
- Why is the title "Good Scars" as opposed to "Bad Scars"?
- What was the significance of getting a tattoo for the author?
- The author repeats this line: "The truth is my little sister is dead." Why?

The following reading is excerpted from Frederick Douglass's memoir *My Bondage and My Freedom*. The passage recounts a dramatic childhood experience—when Douglass left his grandmother and first home to work at his slave master's plantation.

About the Author

Frederick Douglass is a one of the most influential and respected figures in American history. He was born into slavery and escaped at the age of 20. He would later become an intellectual and abolitionist, fighting against slavery and oppression. He managed an abolitionist newspaper and wrote several famous autobiographical books, including *My Bondage and My Freedom*, the source of this reading selection.

Prereading

1. What do you already know about Frederick Douglass?
2. What information can you learn from the title and the first lines of the first two paragraphs?
3. Who is his intended audience?
4. What questions do you hope to get answered from this reading?

Removed from My First Home

When the time of my departure was decided upon, my grandmother, knowing my fears, and in pity for them, kindly kept me **ignorant** of the dreaded event about to transpire.

Up to the morning (a beautiful summer morning) when we were to start, and, indeed, during the whole journey—a journey which, child as I was, I remember as well as if it were yesterday—she kept the sad fact hidden from me. This reserve was necessary; for, could I have known all, I should have given grandmother some trouble in getting me started. As it was, I was helpless, and she—dear woman!— led me along by the hand, resisting, with the reserve and **solemnity** of a priestess, all my inquiring looks to the last.

The distance from Tuckahoe to Wye river—where my old master lived—was a full twelve miles, and the walk was quite a **severe** test of the endurance of my young legs. The journey would have proved too severe for me, but that my dear old grandmother—blessings on her memory!—afforded occasional relief by "toting" me (as Marylanders have it) on her shoulder. My grandmother, though advanced in years—as was evident from more than one gray hair, which peeped from between the **ample** and graceful folds of her newly-ironed bandana turban—was yet a woman of power and spirit. She was marvelously straight in figure, **elastic**, and muscular. I seemed hardly to be a burden to her. She would have "toted" me farther, but that I felt myself too much of a man to allow it, and insisted on walking. Releasing dear grandmamma from carrying me, did not make me altogether independent of her, when we happened to pass through portions of the **somber** woods which lay between Tuckahoe and Wye river. She often found me increasing the energy of my grip, and holding her clothing, lest something should come out of the woods and eat me up. Several old logs and stumps imposed upon me, and got themselves taken for wild beasts. I could see their legs, eyes, and ears, or I could see something like eyes, legs, and ears, till I got close enough to them to see that the eyes were knots, washed white with rain, and the legs were broken limbs, and the ears, only ears owing to the point from which they were seen. Thus early I learned that the point from which a thing is viewed is of some importance.

I could not help feeling that our being there boded no good to me. Grandmamma looked sad. She was soon to lose another object of affection, as she had lost many before.

As the day advanced the heat increased; and it was not until the afternoon that we reached the much dreaded end of the journey. I found myself in the midst of a group of children of many colors: black, brown, copper colored, and nearly white. I had not seen so many children before. Great houses loomed up in different directions, and a great many men and women were at work in the fields. All this hurry, noise, and singing was very different from the stillness of Tuckahoe. As a new comer, I was an object of special interest; and, after laughing and yelling around me, and playing all sorts of wild tricks, they (the children) asked me to go out and play with them. This I refused to do, preferring to stay with grandmamma. I could not help feeling that our being there boded no good to me.

Grandmamma looked sad. She was soon to lose another object of affection, as she had lost many before. I knew she was unhappy, and the shadow fell from her brow on me, though I knew not the cause. All suspense, however, must have an end; and the end of mine, in this instance, was at hand. Affectionately patting me on the head, and exhorting me to be a good boy, grandmamma told me to go and play with the little children. "They are **kin** to you," said she; "go and play with them." Among a number of cousins were Phil, Tom, Steve, and Jerry, Nance and Betty. Grandmother pointed out my brother PERRY, my sister SARAH, and my sister ELIZA, who stood in the group. I had never seen my brother nor my sisters before; and, though I had sometimes heard of them, and felt a curious interest in them, I really did not understand what they were to me, or I to them. We were brothers and sisters, but what of that? Why should they be attached to me, or I to them? Brothers and sisters we were by blood; but slavery had made us strangers. . . . My poor mother, like many other slave-women, had many children, but NO FAMILY! The domestic **hearth**, with its holy lessons and precious **endearments**, is **abolished** in the case of a slave-mother and her children. "Little children, love one another," are words seldom heard in a slave cabin.

I really wanted to play with my brother and sisters, but they were strangers to me, and I was full of fear that grandmother might leave without taking me with her. **Entreated** to do so, however, and that, too, by my dear grandmother, I went to the back part of the house, to play with them and the other children. Play, however, I did not, but stood with my back against the wall, witnessing the playing of the others. At last, while standing there, one of the children, who had been in the kitchen, ran up to me, in a sort of roguish glee, exclaiming, "Fed, Fed! grandmammy gone! grandmammy gone!" I could not believe it; yet, fearing the worst, I ran into the kitchen, to see for myself, and found it even so. Grandmammy had indeed gone, and was now far away, "clean" out of sight. I need not tell all that happened now. Almost heart-broken at the discovery, I fell upon the ground, and wept a boy's bitter tears, refusing to be comforted. My brother and sisters came

5

around me, and said, "Don't cry," and gave me peaches and pears, but I flung them away, and refused all their kindly advances. I had never been deceived before; and I felt not only grieved at parting—as I supposed forever—with my grandmother, but indignant that a trick had been played upon me in a matter so serious. It was now late in the afternoon. The day had been an exciting and wearisome one, and I knew not how or where, but I suppose I sobbed myself to sleep. There is a healing in the angel wing of sleep, even for the slave-boy; and its balm was never more welcome to any wounded soul than it was to mine, the first night I spent at the **domicile** of old master. The reader may be surprised that I narrate so minutely an incident apparently so trivial, and which must have occurred when I was not more than seven years old; but as I wish to give a faithful history of my experience in slavery, I cannot withhold a circumstance which, at the time, affected me so deeply. Besides, this was, in fact, my first introduction to the realities of slavery.

ignorant uninformed, oblivious	**elastic** flexible	**endearments** affections and love
solemnity seriousness	**somber** dark, gloomy	**abolished** taken away
severe extremely harsh or difficult	**kin** family	**entreated** encouraged
ample many	**hearth** home	**domicile** home, residence

Summarizing

- Write a summary of "Removed from My First Home."

Reflection

- What is the main idea of this selection?
- How is the text organized?
- What do you learn about Douglass's grandmother from the reading?
- What details of the passage particularly stand out to you? How so?

Critical Thinking

- While in the woods with his grandmother, Douglass "learned that the point from which a thing is viewed is of some importance." What does he mean?
- What does this specific experience tell you about slavery in general?
- Separation is a theme in this reading. Who experiences "separation"? Have you read other stories about separation? Have you experienced it yourself?

Appendix A
A Guide to Strong Writing

Figure A.1 serves as a guide to strong writing. Your writing will be clear and effective when it can "pass" each point. This checklist is especially helpful during revising, when you are deciding how to improve your writing.

Figure A.1 A Guide to Strong Writing

Ideas

_____ **1.** Does an interesting and relevant topic serve as a starting point for the writing?

_____ **2.** Is the writing focused, addressing a specific feeling about or a specific part of the topic? (Check the thesis statement.)

_____ **3.** Are there enough specific ideas, details, and examples to support the thesis?

_____ **4.** Overall, is the writing interesting and informative?

Organization

_____ **5.** Does the writing form a meaningful whole—with opening, middle, and closing parts?

_____ **6.** Does the writing follow a logical pattern of organization?

_____ **7.** Do transitions connect ideas and help the writing flow?

Voice

_____ **8.** Does the writer sound informed about and interested in the topic?

_____ **9.** Does the writer sound sincere and genuine?

Word Choice

_____ **10.** Does the word choice clearly fit the purpose and the audience?

_____ **11.** Does the writing include specific nouns and verbs?

Sentence Fluency

_____ **12.** Are the sentences clear, and do they flow smoothly?

_____ **13.** Are the sentences varied in their beginnings and length?

Conventions

_____ **14.** Does your writing follow the rules of the language?

Appendix B

Using an Editing Checklist

Figure B.1 serves as a guide to editing writing. This checklist is helpful for checking your writing for style, grammar, punctuation, and spelling errors.

Figure B.1 Editing Checklist

Words

____ **1.** Have I used specific nouns and verbs?

____ **2.** Have I used more action verbs than "be" verbs?

Sentences

____ **3.** Have I avoided improper shifts in sentences?

____ **4.** Have I avoided fragments, run-ons, and rambling sentences?

Conventions

____ **5.** Do I use correct verb forms (*he saw*, not *he seen*)?

____ **6.** Do my subjects and verbs agree (*she speaks*, not *she speak*)?

____ **7.** Have I used the right words (*their, there, they're*)?

____ **8.** Have I capitalized first words and proper nouns and adjectives?

____ **9.** Have I used commas after long introductory word groups and to separate items in a series?

____ **10.** Have I used commas correctly in compound sentences?

____ **11.** Have I used apostrophes correctly in contractions and to show possession?

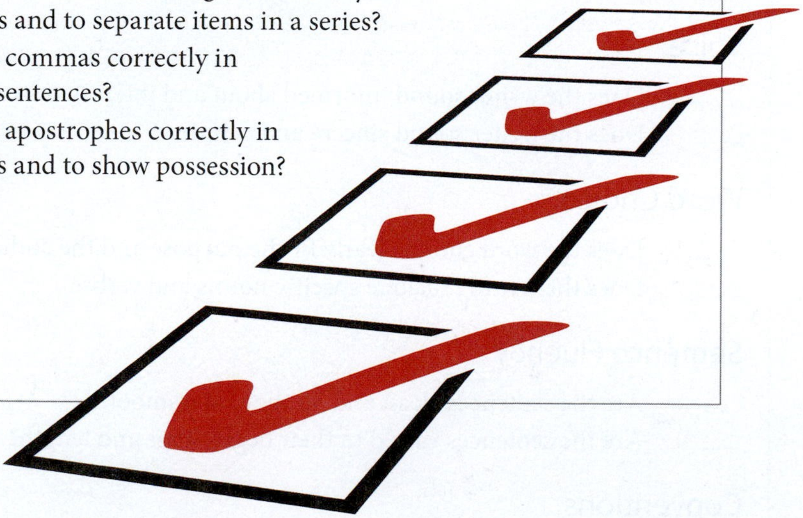

Appendix C

Understanding the Word Parts

The information that follows shows common prefixes, suffixes, and roots. Many of our words are made up of combinations of these word parts.

Prefixes

Prefixes are word parts that come *before* the root words (*pre* = before). Depending upon its meaning, a prefix changes the intent, or sense, of the base word. As a skilled reader, you will want to know the meanings of the most common prefixes, including numerical prefixes (see Table C.1), and then watch for them when you read.

a, an [not, without] amoral (without a sense of moral responsibility), atypical, atom (not cuttable), apathy (without feeling), anesthesia (without sensation)

ab, abs, a [from, away] abnormal, abduct, absent, avert (turn away)

acro [high] acropolis (high city), acrobat, acronym, acrophobia (fear of height)

ambi, amb [both, around] ambidextrous (skilled with both hands), ambiguous, amble

amphi [both] amphibious (living on both land and water), amphitheater

ante [before] antedate, anteroom, antebellum, antecedent (happening before)

anti, ant [against] anticommunist, antidote, anticlimax, antacid

be [on, away] bedeck, belabor, bequest, bestow, beloved

bene, bon [well] benefit, benefactor, benevolent, benediction, bonanza, bonus

bi, bis, bin [both, double, twice] bicycle, biweekly, bilateral, biscuit, binoculars

by [side, close, near] bypass, bystander, by-product, bylaw, byline

cata [down, against] catalog, catapult, catastrophe, cataclysm

cerebro [brain] cerebral, cerebrum, cerebellum

circum, circ [around] circumference, circumnavigate, circumspect, circular

co, con, col, com [together, with] copilot, conspire, collect, compose

coni [dust] coniosis (disease that comes from inhaling dust)

contra, counter [against] controversy, contradict, counterpart

de [from, down] demote, depress, degrade, deject, deprive

deca [ten] decade, decathlon, decapod (0 feet)

di [two, twice] divide, dilemma, dilute, dioxide, dipole, ditto

dia [through, between] diameter, diagonal, diagram, dialogue (speech between people)

dis, dif [apart, away, reverse] dismiss, distort, distinguish, diffuse

dys [badly, ill] dyspepsia (digesting badly), dystrophy, dysentery

em, en [in, into] embrace, enslave

epi [upon] epidermis (upon the skin, outer layer of skin), epitaph, epithet

eu [well] eulogize (speak well of, praise), euphony, euphemism, euphoria

ex, e, ec, ef [out] expel (drive out), ex-mayor, exorcism, eject, eccentric (out of the center position), efflux, effluent

extra, extro [beyond, outside] extraordinary (beyond the ordinary), extrovert, extracurricular

for [away or off] forswear (to renounce an oath)

fore [before in time] forecast, foretell (to tell beforehand), foreshadow

hemi, demi, semi [half] hemisphere, demitasse, semicircle (half of a circle)

hex [six] hexameter, hexagon

homo [man] Homo sapiens, homicide (killing man)

hyper [over, above] hypersensitive (overly sensitive), hyperactive

hypo [under] hypodermic (under the skin), hypothesis

il, ir, in, im [not] illegal, irregular, incorrect, immoral

in, il, im [into] inject, inside, illuminate, illustrate, impose, implant, imprison

infra [beneath] infrared, infrasonic

inter [between] intercollegiate, interfere, intervene, interrupt (break between)

intra [within] intramural, intravenous (within the veins)

intro [into, inward] introduce, introvert (turn inward)

macro [large, excessive] macrodent (having large teeth), macrocosm

mal [badly, poorly] maladjusted, malady, malnutrition, malfunction

meta [beyond, after, with] metaphor, metamorphosis, metaphysical

mis [incorrect, bad] misuse, misprint

miso [hate] misanthrope, misogynist

mono [one] monoplane, monotone, monochrome, monocle

multi [many] multiply, multiform

neo [new] neopaganism, neoclassic, neophyte, neonatal

non [not] nontaxable (not taxed), nontoxic, nonexistent, nonsense

ob, of, op, oc [toward, against] obstruct, offend, oppose, occur

oct [eight] octagon, octameter, octave, octopus

paleo [ancient] paleoanthropology (pertaining to ancient humans), paleontology (study of ancient life-forms)

para [beside, almost] parasite (one who eats beside or at the table of another), paraphrase, paramedic, parallel, paradox

penta [five] pentagon (figure or building having five angles or sides), pentameter, pentathlon

per [throughout, completely] pervert (completely turn wrong, corrupt), perfect, perceive, permanent, persuade

peri [around] perimeter (measurement around an area), periphery, periscope, pericardium, period

poly [many] polygon (figure having many angles or sides), polygamy, polyglot, polychrome

post [after] postpone, postwar, postscript, posterity

pre [before] prewar, preview, precede, prevent, premonition

pro [forward, in favor of] project (throw forward), progress, promote, prohibition

pseudo [false] pseudonym (false or assumed name), pseudopodia

quad [four] quadruple (four times as much), quadriplegic, quadratic, quadrant

quint [five] quintuplet, quintuple, quintet, quintile

re [back, again] reclaim, revive, revoke, rejuvenate, retard, reject, return

retro [backward] retrospective (looking backward), retroactive, retrorocket

se [aside] seduce (lead aside), secede, secrete, segregate

self [by oneself] self-determination, self-employed, self-service, selfish

sesqui [one and a half] sesquicentennial (one and one-half centuries)

sex, sest [six] sexagenarian (sixty years old), sexennial, sextant, sextuplet, sestet

sub [under] submerge (put under), submarine, substitute, subsoil

suf, sug, sup, sus [from under] sufficient, suffer, suggest, support, suspend

super, supr [above, over, more] supervise, superman, supernatural, supreme

syn, sym, sys, syl [with, together] system, synthesis, synchronize (time together), synonym, sympathy, symphony, syllable

trans, tra [across, beyond] transoceanic, transmit (send across), transfusion, tradition

tri [three] tricycle, triangle, tripod, tristate

ultra [beyond, exceedingly] ultramodern, ultraviolet, ultraconservative

un [not, release] unfair, unnatural, unknown

under [beneath] underground, underlying

uni [one] unicycle, uniform, unify, universe, unique (one of a kind)

vice [in place of] vice president, viceroy, vice admiral

Table C.1 Numerical Prefixes

Numerical Prefixes

Prefix	Symbol	Multiples and Submultiples	Equivalent	Prefix	Symbol	Multiples and Submultiples	Equivalent
tera	T	10^{12}	trillionfold	centi	c	10^{-2}	hundredth part
giga	G	10^{9}	billionfold	milli	m	10^{-3}	thousandth part
mega	M	10^{6}	millionfold	micro	u	10^{-6}	millionth part
kilo	k	10^{3}	thousandfold	nano	n	10^{-9}	billionth part
hecto	h	10^{2}	hundredfold	pico	p	10^{-12}	trillionth part
deka	da	10	tenfold	femto	f	10^{-15}	quadrillionth part
deci	d	10^{-1}	tenth part	atto	a	10^{-18}	quintillionth part

Suffixes

Suffixes come at the end of a word. Very often a suffix will tell you what kind of word it is part of (noun, adverb, adjective). For example, words ending in *-ly* are usually adverbs.

able, ible [able, can do] capable, agreeable, edible, visible (can be seen)

ade [result of action] blockade (the result of a blocking action), lemonade

age [act of, state of, collection of] salvage (act of saving), storage, forage

al [relating to] sensual, gradual, manual, natural (relating to nature)

algia [pain] neuralgia (nerve pain)

an, ian [native of, relating to] African, Canadian, Floridian

ance, ancy [action, process, state] assistance, allowance, defiance, truancy

ant [performing, agent] assistant, servant

ary, ery, ory [relating to, quality, place where] dictionary, bravery, dormitory

ate [cause, make] liquidate, segregate (cause a group to be set aside)

cian [having a certain skill or art] musician, beautician, magician, physician

cule, ling [very small] molecule, ridicule, duckling (very small duck), sapling

cy [action, function] hesitancy, prophecy, normalcy (function in a normal way)

dom [quality, realm, office] freedom, kingdom, wisdom (quality of being wise)

ee [one who receives the action] employee, nominee (one who is nominated), refugee

en [made of, make] silken, frozen, oaken (made of oak), wooden, lighten

ence, ency [action, state of, quality] difference, conference, urgency

er, or [one who, that which] baker, miller, teacher, racer, amplifier, doctor

escent [in the process of] adolescent (in the process of becoming an adult), obsolescent, convalescent

ese [a native of, the language of] Japanese, Vietnamese, Portuguese

esis, osis [action, process, condition] genesis, hypnosis, neurosis, osmosis

ess [female] actress, goddess, lioness

et, ette [a small one, group] midget, octet, baronet, majorette

fic [making, causing] scientific, specific

ful [full of] frightful, careful, helpful

fy [make] fortify (make strong), simplify, amplify

hood [order, condition, quality] manhood, womanhood, brotherhood

ic [nature of, like] metallic (of the nature of metal), heroic, poetic, acidic

ice [condition, state, quality] justice, malice

id, ide [a thing connected with or belonging to] fluid, fluoride

ile [relating to, suited for, capable of] missile, juvenile, senile (related to being old)

ine [nature of] feminine, genuine, medicine

ion, sion, tion [act of, state of, result of] contagion, aversion, infection (state of being infected)

ish [origin, nature, resembling] foolish, Irish, clownish (resembling a clown)

ism [system, manner, condition, characteristic] heroism, alcoholism, Communism

ist [one who, that which] artist, dentist

ite [nature of, quality of, mineral product] Israelite, dynamite, graphite, sulfite

ity, ty [state of, quality] captivity, clarity

ive [causing, making] abusive (causing abuse), exhaustive

ize [make] emphasize, publicize, idolize

less [without] baseless, careless (without care), artless, fearless, helpless

ly [like, manner of] carelessly, quickly, forcefully, lovingly

ment [act of, state of, result] contentment, amendment (state of amending)

ness [state of] carelessness, kindness

oid [resembling] asteroid, spheroid, tabloid, anthropoid

ology [study, science, theory] biology, anthropology, geology, neurology

ous [full of, having] gracious, nervous, spacious, vivacious (full of life)

ship [office, state, quality, skill] friendship, authorship, dictatorship

some [like, apt, tending to] lonesome, threesome, gruesome

tude [state of, condition of] gratitude, multitude (condition of being many), aptitude

ure [state of, act, process, rank] culture, literature, rupture (state of being broken)

ward [in the direction of] eastward, forward, backward

y [inclined to, tend to] cheery, crafty, faulty

Roots

A *root* is a base upon which other words are built (see Table C.2). Knowing the root of a difficult word can go a long way toward helping you figure out its meaning. For that reason, learning the following roots will be very valuable in all your classes.

acer, acid, acri [bitter, sour, sharp] acrid, acerbic, acidity (sourness), acrimony

acu [sharp] acute, acupuncture

ag, agi, ig, act [do, move, go] agent (doer), agenda (things to do), agitate, navigate (move by sea), ambiguous (going both ways), action

ali, allo, alter [other] alias (a person's other name), alibi, alien (from another place), alloy, alter (change to another form)

alt [high, deep] altimeter (a device for measuring heights), altitude

am, amor [love, liking] amiable, amorous, enamored

anni, annu, enni [year] anniversary, annually (yearly), centennial (occurring once in 0 years)

anthrop [man] anthropology (study of mankind), philanthropy (love of mankind), misanthrope (hater of mankind)

anti [old] antique, antiquated, antiquity

arch [chief, first, rule] archangel (chief angel), architect (chief worker), archaic (first, very early), monarchy (rule by one person), matriarchy (rule by the mother)

aster, astr [star] aster (star flower), asterisk, asteroid, astronomy (star law), astronaut (star traveler, space traveler)

aud, aus [hear, listen] audible (can be heard), auditorium, audio, audition, auditory, audience, ausculate

aug, auc [increase] augur, augment (add to; increase), auction

auto, aut [self] autograph (self-writing), automobile (self-moving vehicle), author, automatic (self-acting), autobiography

belli [war] rebellion, belligerent (warlike or hostile)

bibl [book] Bible, bibliography (list of books), bibliomania (craze for books), bibliophile (book lover)

bio [life] biology (study of life), biography, biopsy (cut living tissue for examination)

brev [short] abbreviate, brevity, brief

cad, cas [to fall] cadaver, cadence, caducous (falling off), cascade

calor [heat] calorie (a unit of heat), calorify (to make hot), caloric

cap, cip, cept [take] capable, capacity, capture, reciprocate, accept, except, concept

capit, capt [head] decapitate (to remove the head from), capital, captain, caption

carn [flesh] carnivorous (flesh eating), incarnate, reincarnation

caus, caut [burn, heat] caustic, cauterize (to make hot, to burn)

cause, cuse, cus [cause, motive] because, excuse (to attempt to remove the blame or cause), accusation

ced, ceed, cede, cess [move, yield, go, surrender] procedure, secede (move aside from), proceed (move forward), cede (yield), concede, intercede, precede, recede, success

centri [center] concentric, centrifugal, centripetal, eccentric (out of center)

chrom [color] chrome, chromosome (color body in genetics), chromosphere, monochrome (one color), polychrome

chron [time] chronological (in order of time), chronometer (time measured), chronicle (record of events in time), synchronize (make time with, set time together)

cide, cise [cut down, kill] suicide (killing of self), homicide (human killer), pesticide (pest killer), germicide (germ killer), insecticide, precise (cut exactly right), incision, scissors

cit [to call, start] incite, citation, cite

civ [citizen] civic (relating to a citizen), civil, civilian, civilization

clam, claim [cry out] exclamation, clamor, proclamation, reclamation, acclaim

clud, clus, claus [shut] include (to take in), conclude, claustrophobia (abnormal fear of being shut up, confined), recluse (one who shuts himself away from others)

cognosc, gnosi [know] recognize (to know again), incognito (not known), prognosis (forward knowing), diagnosis

cord, cor, cardi [heart] cordial (hearty, heartfelt), concord, discord, courage, encourage (put heart into), discourage (take heart out of), core, coronary, cardiac

corp [body] corporation (a legal body), corpse, corpulent

cosm [universe, world] cosmic, cosmos (the universe), cosmopolitan (world citizen), cosmonaut, microcosm, macrocosm

crat, cracy [rule, strength] democratic, autocracy

crea [create] creature (anything created), recreation, creation, creator

cred [believe] creed (statement of beliefs), credo (a creed), credence (belief), credit (belief, trust), credulous (believing too readily, easily deceived), incredible

cresc, cret, crease, cru [rise, grow] crescendo (growing in loudness or intensity), concrete (grown together, solidified), increase, decrease, accrue (to grow)

crit [separate, choose] critical, criterion (that which is used in choosing), hypocrite

cur, curs [run] concurrent, current (running or flowing), concur (run together, agree), incur (run into), recur, occur, precursor (forerunner), cursive

cura [care] curator, curative, manicure (caring for the hands)

cycl, cyclo [wheel, circular] Cyclops (a mythical giant with one eye in the middle of his forehead), unicycle, bicycle, cyclone (a wind blowing circularly, a tornado)

deca [ten] decade, decalogue, decathlon

dem [people] democracy (people-rule), demography (vital statistics of the people: deaths, births, and so on), epidemic (on or among the people)

dent, dont [tooth] dental (relating to teeth), denture, dentifrice, orthodontist

derm [skin] hypodermic (injected under the skin), dermatology (skin study), epidermis (outer layer of skin), taxidermy (arranging skin; mounting animals)

dict [say, speak] diction (how one speaks, what one says), dictionary, dictate, dictator, dictaphone, dictatorial, edict, predict, verdict, contradict, benediction

doc [teach] indoctrinate, document, doctrine

domin [master] dominate, dominion, predominant, domain

don [give] donate, condone

dorm [sleep] dormant, dormitory

dox [opinion, praise] doxy (belief, creed, or opinion), orthodox (having the correct, commonly accepted opinion), heterodox (differing opinion), paradox (contradictory)

drome [run, step] syndrome (run-together symptoms), hippodrome (a place where horses run)

duc, duct [lead] produce, induce (lead into, persuade), seduce (lead aside), reduce, aqueduct (water leader or channel), viaduct, conduct

dura [hard, lasting] durable, duration, endurance

dynam [power] dynamo (power producer), dynamic, dynamite, hydrodynamics

endo [within] endoral (within the mouth), endocardial (within the heart), endoskeletal

equi [equal] equinox, equilibrium

erg [work] energy, erg (unit of work), allergy, ergophobia (morbid fear of work), ergometer, ergonomic

fac, fact, fic, fect [do, make] factory (place where workers make goods of various kinds), fact (a thing done), manufacture, amplification, confection

fall, fals [deceive] fallacy, falsify

fer [bear, carry] ferry (carry by water), coniferous (bearing cones, as a pine tree), fertile (bearing richly), defer, infer, refer

fid, fide, feder [faith, trust] confidant, Fido, fidelity, confident, infidelity, infidel, federal, confederacy

fila, fili [thread] filament (a single thread or threadlike object), filibuster, filigree

fin [end, ended, finished] final, finite, finish, confine, fine, refine, define, finale

fix [attach] fix, fixation (the state of being attached), fixture, affix, prefix, suffix

flex, flect [bend] flex, reflex (bending back), flexible, flexor (muscle for bending), inflexibility, reflect, deflect

flu, fluc, fluv [flowing] influence (to flow in), fluid, flue, flush, fluently, fluctuate (to wave in an unsteady motion)

form [form, shape] form, uniform, conform, deform, reform, perform, formative, formation, formal, formula

fort, forc [strong] fort, fortress (a strong place), fortify (make strong), forte (one's strong point), fortitude, enforce

fract, frag [break] fracture (a break), infraction, fragile (easy to break), fraction (result of breaking a whole into equal parts), refract (to break or bend)

gam [marriage] bigamy (two marriages), monogamy, polygamy (many spouses or marriages)

gastr(o) [stomach] gastric, gastronomic, gastritis (inflammation of the stomach)

gen [birth, race, produce] genesis (birth, beginning), genetics (study of heredity), eugenics (well born), genealogy (lineage by race, stock), generate, genetic

geo [earth] geometry (earth measurement), geography (earth writing), geocentric (earth centered), geology

germ [vital part] germination (to grow), germ (seed; living substance, as the germ of an idea), germane

gest [carry, bear] congest (bear together, clog), congestive (causing clogging), gestation

gloss, glot [tongue] glossary, polyglot (many tongues), epiglottis

glu, glo [lump, bond, glue] glue, agglutinate (make to hold in a bond), conglomerate (bond together)

grad, gress [step, go] grade (step, degree), gradual (step-by-step), graduate (make all the steps, finish a course), graduated (in steps or degrees), progress

graph, gram [write, written] graph, graphic (written, vivid), autograph (self-writing, signature), graphite (carbon used for writing), photography (light writing), phonograph (sound writing), diagram, bibliography, telegram

grat [pleasing] gratuity (mark of favor, a tip), congratulate (express pleasure over success), grateful, ingrate (not thankful)

grav [heavy, weighty] grave, gravity, aggravate, gravitate

greg [herd, group, crowd] gregarian (belonging to a herd), congregation (a group functioning together), segregate (tending to group aside or apart)

helio [sun] heliograph (an instrument for using the sun's rays to send signals), heliotrope (a plant that turns to the sun)

hema, hemo [blood] hemorrhage (an outpouring or flowing of blood), hemoglobin, hemophilia

here, hes [stick] adhere, cohere, cohesion

hetero [different] heterogeneous (different in birth), heterosexual (with interest in the opposite sex)

homo [same] homogeneous (of same birth or kind), homonym (word with same pronunciation as another), homogenize

hum, human [earth, ground, man] humus, exhume (to take out of the ground), humane (compassion for other humans)

hydr, hydra, hydro [water] dehydrate, hydrant, hydraulic, hydraulics, hydrogen, hydrophobia (fear of water)

hypn [sleep] hypnosis, Hypnos (god of sleep), hypnotherapy (treatment of disease by hypnosis)

ignis [fire] ignite, igneous, ignition

ject [throw] deject, inject, project (throw forward), eject, object

join, junct [join] adjoining, enjoin (to lay an order upon, to command), juncture, conjunction, injunction

juven [young] juvenile, rejuvenate (to make young again)

lau, lav, lot, lut [wash] launder, lavatory, lotion, ablution (a washing away), dilute (to make a liquid thinner and weaker)

leg [law] legal (lawful; according to law), legislate (to enact a law), legislature, legitimize (make legal)

levi [light] alleviate (lighten a load), levitate, levity (light conversation; humor)

liber, liver [free] liberty (freedom), liberal, liberalize (to make more free), deliverance

liter [letters] literary (concerned with books and writing), literature, literal, alliteration, obliterate

loc, loco [place] locality, locale, location, allocate (to assign, to place), relocate (to put back into place), locomotion (act of moving from place to place)

log, logo, ogue, ology [word, study, speech] catalog, prologue, dialogue, logogram (a symbol representing a word), zoology (animal study), psychology (mind study)

loqu, locut [talk, speak] eloquent (speaking well and forcefully), soliloquy, locution, loquacious (talkative), colloquial (talking together; conversational or informal)

luc, lum, lus, lun [light] translucent (letting light come through), lumen (a unit of light), luminary (a heavenly body; someone who shines in his or her profession), luster (sparkle, shine), Luna (the moon goddess)

magn [great] magnify (make great, enlarge), magnificent, magnanimous (great of mind or spirit), magnate, magnitude, magnum

man [hand] manual, manage, manufacture, manacle, manicure, manifest, maneuver, emancipate

mand [command] mandatory (commanded), remand (order back), mandate

mania [madness] mania (insanity, craze), monomania (mania on one idea), kleptomania, pyromania (insane tendency to set fires), maniac

mar, mari, mer [sea, pool] marine (a soldier serving on a ship), marsh (wetland, swamp), maritime (relating to the sea and navigation), mermaid (fabled sea creature: half fish, half woman)

matri [mother] maternal (relating to the mother), matrimony, matriarchate (rulership of women), matron

medi [half, middle, between, halfway] mediate (come between, intervene), medieval (pertaining to the Middle Ages), Mediterranean (lying between lands), mediocre, medium

mega [great, million] megaphone (great sound), megalopolis (great city; an extensive urban area including a number of cities), megacycle (a million cycles), megaton

mem [remember] memo (a reminder), commemoration (the act of remembering by a memorial or ceremony), memento, memoir, memorable

meter [measure] meter (a metric measure), voltameter (instrument to measure volts), barometer, thermometer

micro [small] microscope, microfilm, microcard, microwave, micrometer (device for measuring small distances), omicron, micron (a millionth of a meter), microbe (small living thing)

migra [wander] migrate (to wander), emigrate (one who leaves a country), immigrate (to come into the land)

mit, miss [send] emit (send out, give off), remit (send back, as money due), submit, admit, commit, permit, transmit (send across), omit, intermittent (sending between, at intervals), mission, missile

mob, mot, mov [move] mobile (capable of moving), motionless (without motion), motor, emotional (moved strongly by feelings), motivate, promotion, demote, movement

mon [warn, remind] monument (a reminder or memorial of a person or an event), admonish (warn), monitor, premonition (forewarning)

mor, mort [mortal, death] mortal (causing death or destined for death), immortal (not subject to death), mortality (rate of death), mortician (one who prepares the dead for burial), mortuary (place for the dead, a morgue)

morph [form] amorphous (with no form, shapeless), metamorphosis (a change of form, as a caterpillar into a butterfly), morphology

multi [many, much] multifold (folded many times), multilinguist (one who speaks many languages), multiped (an organism with many feet), multiply

nat, nasc [to be born, to spring forth] innate (inborn), natal, native, nativity, renascence (a rebirth, a revival)

neur [nerve] neuritis (inflammation of a nerve), neurology (study of nervous systems), neurologist (one who practices neurology), neural, neurosis, neurotic

nom [law, order] autonomy (self-law, self-government), astronomy, gastronomy (art or science of good eating), economy

nomen, nomin [name] nomenclature, nominate (name someone for an office)

nov [new] novel (new, strange, not formerly known), renovate (to make like new again), novice, nova, innovate

nox, noc [night] nocturnal, equinox (equal nights), noctilucent (shining by night)

numer [number] numeral (a figure expressing a number), numeration (act of counting), enumerate (count out, one by one), innumerable

omni [all, every] omnipotent (all-powerful), omniscient (all-knowing), omnipresent (present everywhere), omnivorous

onym [name] anonymous (without name), synonym, pseudonym (false name), antonym (name of opposite meaning)

oper [work] operate (to labor, function), cooperate (work together)

ortho [straight, correct] orthodox (of the correct or accepted opinion), orthodontist (tooth straightener), orthopedic (originally pertaining to straightening a child), unorthodox

pac [peace] pacifist (one for peace only; opposed to war), pacify (make peace, quiet), Pacific Ocean (peaceful ocean)

pan [all] panacea (cure-all), pandemonium (place of all the demons, wild disorder), pantheon (place of all the gods in mythology)

pater, patr [father] paternity (fatherhood, responsibility), patriarch (head of the tribe, family), patriot, patron (a wealthy person who supports as would a father)

path, pathy [feeling, suffering] pathos (feeling of pity, sorrow), sympathy, antipathy (feeling against), apathy (without feeling), empathy (feeling or identifying with another), telepathy (far feeling; thought transference)

ped, pod [foot] pedal (lever for a foot), impede (get the feet in a trap, hinder), pedestal (foot or base of a statue), pedestrian (foot traveler), centipede, tripod (three-footed support), podiatry (care of the feet), antipodes (opposite feet)

pedo [child] orthopedic, pedagogue (child leader; teacher), pediatrics (medical care of children)

pel, puls [drive, urge] compel, dispel, expel, repel, propel, pulse, impulse, pulsate, compulsory, expulsion, repulsive

pend, pens, pond [hang, weigh] pendant pendulum, suspend, appendage, pensive (weighing thought), ponderous

phil [love] philosophy (love of wisdom), philanthropy, philharmonic, bibliophile, Philadelphia (city of brotherly love)

phobia [fear] claustrophobia (fear of closed spaces), acrophobia (fear of high places), hydrophobia (fear of water)

phon [sound] phonograph, phonetic (pertaining to sound), symphony (sounds with or together)

photo [light] photograph (light-writing), photoelectric, photogenic (artistically suitable for being photographed), photosynthesis (action of light on chlorophyll to make carbohydrates)

plac [please] placid (calm, peaceful), placebo, placate, complacent

plu, plur, plus [more] plural (more than one), pluralist (a person who holds more than one office), plus (indicating that something more is to be added)

pneuma, pneumon [breath] pneumatic (pertaining to air, wind, or other gases), pneumonia (disease of the lungs)

pod (see ped)

poli [city] metropolis (mother city), police, politics, Indianapolis, Acropolis (high city, upper part of Athens), megalopolis

pon, pos, pound [place, put] postpone (put afterward), component, opponent (one put against), proponent, expose, impose, deposit, posture (how one places oneself), position, expound, impound

pop [people] population, populous (full of people), popular

port [carry] porter (one who carries), portable, transport (carry across), report, export, import, support, transportation

portion [part, share] portion (a part; a share, as a portion of pie), proportion (the relation of one share to others)

prehend [seize] comprehend (seize with the mind), apprehend (seize a criminal), comprehensive (seizing much, extensive)

prim, prime [first] primacy (state of being first in rank), prima donna (the first lady of opera), primitive (from the earliest or first time), primary, primal, primeval

proto [first] prototype (the first model made), protocol, protagonist, protozoan

psych [mind, soul] psyche (soul, mind), psychiatry (healing of the mind), psychology, psychosis (serious mental disorder), psychotherapy (mind treatment), psychic

punct [point, dot] punctual (being exactly on time), punctuation, puncture, acupuncture

reg, recti [straighten] regiment, regular, regulate, rectify (make straight), correct, direction

ri, ridi, risi [laughter] deride (mock, jeer at), ridicule (laughter at the expense of another, mockery), ridiculous, derision

rog, roga [ask] prerogative (privilege; asking before), interrogation (questioning; the act of questioning), derogatory

rupt [break] rupture (break), interrupt (break into), abrupt (broken off), disrupt (break apart), erupt (break out), incorruptible (unable to be broken down)

sacr, sanc, secr [sacred] sacred, sanction, sacrosanct, consecrate, desecrate

salv, salu [safe, healthy] salvation (act of being saved), salvage, salutation

sat, satis [enough] saturate, satisfy (to give as much as is needed)

sci [know] science (knowledge), conscious (knowing, aware), omniscient (knowing everything)

scope [see, watch] telescope, microscope, kaleidoscope (instrument for seeing beautiful forms), periscope, stethoscope

scrib, script [write] scribe (a writer), scribble, manuscript (written by hand), inscribe, describe, subscribe, prescribe

sed, sess, sid [sit] sediment (that which sits or settles out of a liquid), session (a sitting), obsession (an idea that sits stubbornly in the mind), possess, preside (sit before), president, reside, subside

sen [old] senior, senator, senile (old; showing the weakness of old age)

sent, sens [feel] sentiment (feeling), consent, resent, dissent, sentimental (having strong feeling or emotion), sense, sensation, sensitive, sensory, dissension

sequ, secu, sue [follow] sequence (following of one thing after another), sequel, consequence, subsequent, prosecute, consecutive (following in order), second (following "first"), ensue, pursue

serv [save, serve] servant, service, preserve, subservient, servitude, conserve, reservation, deserve, conservation

sign, signi [sign, mark, seal] signal (a gesture or sign to call attention), signature (the mark of a person written in his or her own handwriting), design, insignia (distinguishing marks)

simil, simul [like, resembling] similar (resembling in many respects), assimilate (to make similar to), simile, simulate (pretend; put on an act to make a certain impression)

sist, sta, stit [stand] persist (stand firmly; unyielding; continue), assist (to stand by with help), circumstance, stamina (power to withstand, to endure), status (standing), state, static, stable, stationary, substitute (to stand in for another)

solus [alone] soliloquy, solitaire, solitude, solo

solv, solu [loosen] solvent (a loosener, a dissolver), solve, absolve (loosen from, free from), resolve, soluble, solution, resolution, resolute, dissolute (loosened morally)

somnus [sleep] insomnia (not being able to sleep), somnambulist (a sleepwalker)

soph [wise] sophomore (wise fool), philosophy (love of wisdom), sophisticated

spec, spect, spic [look] specimen (an example to look at, study), specific, aspect, spectator (one who looks), spectacle, speculate, inspect, respect, prospect, retrospective (looking backward), introspective, expect, conspicuous

sphere [ball, sphere] stratosphere (the upper portion of the atmosphere), hemisphere (half of the earth), spheroid

spir [breath] spirit (breath), conspire (breathe together; plot), inspire (breathe into), aspire (breathe toward), expire (breathe out; die), perspire, respiration

string, strict [draw tight] stringent (drawn tight; rigid), strict, restrict, constrict (draw tightly together), boa constrictor (snake that constricts its prey)

stru, struct [build] construe (build in the mind, interpret), structure, construct, instruct, obstruct, destruction, destroy

sume, sump [take, use, waste] consume (to use up), assume (to take; to use), sump pump (a pump that takes up water), presumption (to take or use before knowing all the facts)

tact, tang, tag, tig, ting [touch] contact, tactile, intangible (not able to be touched), intact (untouched, uninjured), tangible, contingency, contagious (able to transmit disease by touching), contiguous

tele [far] telephone (far sound), telegraph (far writing), television (far seeing), telephoto (far photography), telecast

tempo [time] tempo (rate of speed), temporary, extemporaneously, contemporary (those who live at the same time), pro tem (for the time being)

ten, tin, tain [hold] tenacious (holding fast), tenant, tenure, untenable, detention, content, pertinent, continent, obstinate, abstain, pertain, detain

tend, tent, tens [stretch, strain] tendency (a stretching; leaning), extend, intend, contend, pretend, superintend, tender, extent, tension (a stretching, strain), pretense

terra [earth] terrain, terrarium, territory, terrestrial

test [to bear witness] testament (a will; bearing witness to someone's wishes), detest, attest (bear witness to), testimony

the, theo [God, a god] monotheism (belief in one god), polytheism (belief in many gods), atheism, theology

therm [heat] thermometer, therm (heat unit), thermal, thermostat, thermos, hypothermia (subnormal temperature)

thesis, thet [place, put] antithesis (place against), hypothesis (place under), synthesis (put together), epithet

tom [cut] atom (not cuttable; smallest particle of matter), appendectomy (cutting out an appendix), tonsillectomy, dichotomy (cutting in two; a division), anatomy (cutting, dissecting to study structure)

tort, tors [twist] torture (twisting to inflict pain), retort (twist back, reply sharply), extort (twist out), distort (twist out of shape), contort, torsion (act of twisting, as a torsion bar)

tox [poison] toxic (poisonous), intoxicate, antitoxin

tract, tra [draw, pull] tractor, attract, subtract, tractable (can be handled), abstract (to draw away), subtrahend (the number to be drawn away from another)

trib [pay, bestow] tribute (to pay honor to), contribute (to give money to a cause), attribute, retribution, tributary

turbo [disturb] turbulent, disturb, turbid, turmoil

typ [print] type, prototype (first print; model), typical, typography, typewriter, typology (study of types, symbols), typify

ultima [last] ultimate, ultimatum (the final or last offer that can be made)

uni [one] unicorn (a legendary creature with one horn), unify (make into one), university, unanimous, universal

vac [empty] vacate (to make empty), vacuum (a space entirely devoid of matter), evacuate (to remove troops or people), vacation, vacant

vale, vali, valu [strength, worth] valiant, equivalent (of equal worth), validity (truth; legal strength), evaluate (find out the value), value, valor (value; worth)

ven, vent [come] convene (come together, assemble), intervene (come between), venue, convenient, avenue, circumvent (come or go around), invent, prevent

ver, veri [true] very, aver (say to be true, affirm), verdict, verity (truth), verify (show to be true), verisimilitude

vert, vers [turn] avert (turn away), divert (turn aside, amuse), invert (turn over), introvert (turn inward), convertible, reverse (turn back), controversy (a turning against; a dispute), versatile (turning easily from one skill to another)

vic, vicis [change, substitute] vicarious, vicar, vicissitude

vict, vinc [conquer] victor (conqueror, winner), evict (conquer out, expel), convict (prove guilty), convince (conquer mentally, persuade), invincible (not conquerable)

vid, vis [see] video, television, evident, provide, providence, visible, revise, supervise (oversee), vista, visit, vision

viv, vita, vivi [alive, life] revive (make live again), survive (live beyond, outlive), vivid, vivacious (full of life), vitality

voc [call] vocation (a calling), avocation (occupation not one's calling), convocation (a calling together), invocation, vocal

vol [will] malevolent, benevolent (one of goodwill), volunteer, volition

volcan, vulcan [fire] volcano (a mountain erupting fiery lava), volcanize (to undergo volcanic heat), Vulcan (Roman god of fire)

volvo [turn about, roll] revolve, voluminous (winding), voluble (easily turned about or around), convolution (a twisting)

vor [eat greedily] voracious, carnivorous (flesh eating), herbivorous (plant eating), omnivorous (eating everything), devour

zo [animal] zoo (short for zoological garden), zoology (study of animal life), zodiac (circle of animal constellations), zoomorphism (being in the form of an animal), protozoa (one-celled animals)

Table C.2 The Human Body

The Human Body

capit	head	gastro	stomach	osteo	bone
card	heart	glos	tongue	ped	foot
corp	body	hema	blood	pneuma	breathe
dent	tooth	man	hand	psych	mind
derm	skin	neur	nerve	spir	breath